BRANSON

Previous books by the same author

Blind Eye to Murder — the Pledge Betrayed
Klaus Barbie: the Butcher of Lyons
The Paperclip Conspiracy
Maxwell: The Outsider
The Red Web
Tiny Rowland: The Rebel Tycoon
Heroes of World War II
The Perfect English Spy: Sir Dick White
Maxwell: The Final Verdict
Blood Money: The Swiss, the Nazis and the Looted Billions
Fayed: The Unauthorized Biography

BRANSON

Tom Bower

Fourth Estate • London

To Jennifer Bower

First published in Great Britain in 2000 by
Fourth Estate Limited
6 Salem Road
London W2 4BU
www.4thestate.co.uk

Copyright © Tom Bower 2000

1 3 5 7 9 10 8 6 4 2

The right of Tom Bower to be identified as the author of this
work has been asserted by him in accordance with the Copyright,
Designs and Patents Act 1988

A catalogue record for this book is available from
the British Library

ISBN 1-84115-386-9

All rights reserved. No part of this publication may be reproduced,
transmitted, or stored in a retrieval system, in any form or by any
means, without permission in writing from Fourth Estate Limited.

Typeset by Rowland Phototypesetting Ltd,
Bury St Edmunds, Suffolk
Printed in Great Britain by
Clays Ltd, St Ives plc

Contents

Contents

Preface

On 16 December 1998, Sir Richard Branson was preparing to set off from Marrakesh in an attempt to become the first person to circumnavigate the world in a hot-air balloon. Over the previous days I had sought to join his party in Morocco to witness a Branson extravaganza. I was still undecided whether to write a book about Branson but expected that the experience might influence my decision. That morning, my place on Virgin's chartered jet on behalf of a national newspaper was suddenly cancelled.

To my surprise, at lunchtime the same day, I received a brutal, defamatory and untrue letter from Branson, whom I had never met, faxed by his London office. Branson alleged that he had received 'a number of calls over the last six weeks from various friends and relatives who have been upset by your researchers/detectives'. He claimed that on my behalf these hired hands had 'doorstepped' a woman and uttered 'untrue accusations that her son is, in fact, my son'. Not surprisingly, he continued, that behaviour had 'caused a lot of upset to all the people concerned including the real father'. Since those same people were flying to Marrakesh for the launch of the balloon, he felt it would be 'inappropriate' for me to be present. 'To be perfectly honest,' he added, 'none of them would particularly welcome it.' Branson concluded that after the trip was completed we could discuss 'what exactly it is you are after'.

I was flabbergasted by Branson's letter. I had never heard of the people he mentioned. I had not employed any detectives nor had I asked or heard of anyone doorstepping these people. In a faxed reply, I immediately protested.

Three days later, I received a response. In an unexpected call to my mobile phone, an unfamiliar voice announced, 'Tom, I'm sorry about that.'

'Who is that?' I asked, puzzled.

'It's Richard,' he replied.

'Richard who?'

'Richard Branson.'

'But I thought you were in a balloon.'

'I am.'

'Where are you?'

'Dunno,' he replied and could be heard asking about his location. 'Over Algeria,' he continued and then said, 'Look, I'm sorry. When I get back, let's meet and talk things through.'

His bizarre behaviour persuaded me that the real Branson, his methods and his operation remained, despite all the publicity, unknown.

About ten weeks earlier, a tiny announcement in an obscure part of the *Financial Times* about a management resignation from Victory, Branson's new clothing corporation, had alerted my curiosity. The senior director, the newspaper's four-line report recorded, was departing after just five months because 'there was no role for an executive chairman'.

Branson's new company, I knew, was spiralling into debt. The management change could only have been caused by anxiety. Virgin's official denials of problems fuelled my suspicions.

Hence, in January 1999, I began this book. Despite his suggestion that we should meet, I never heard from Branson personally, though I soon became aware of his attitude. Several people I approached for interviews told me that, 'after checking', they would prefer not to meet. I had the distinct impression that Branson or the Virgin press office was discouraging people. From other comments, it appeared that Branson was unwilling to either help or meet me.

On 22 October 1999, having made substantial progress, I neverthe-less wrote to Branson asking 'whether you would reconsider your position and agree to meet?' On 6 December, explaining that my letter had only just arrived, he replied: 'I have been called by a large number of people who you have interviewed about me. Most told the same story, namely that you have a fixed agenda and that no amount of persuasion or argument by them to the contrary appeared to have any influence on you. As it would therefore appear that you have pre-judged me, it would seem that little benefit or pleasure would come from our meeting.'

That was, I believed, impolite and inaccurate. By then, I had interviewed over two hundred people. Many were his sympathisers. I had deliberately sought their opinions to produce an objective book. Certainly, I posed as a devil's advocate in testing his admirers' opinions. The technique is reliable and is even favoured by Sir Richard himself. But there was no justification for concluding that my questions confirmed prejudice. On the contrary, I had striven to understand a man who declined my attempts to meet to hear his opinions.

In his letter of 6 December 1999, Branson did offer to answer any written questions and also requested to read the manuscript of the book. He would later express himself to be 'very disappointed' that I had not allowed him to vet and approve this book prior to publication.

On 11 January 2000, I submitted nine questions. On 18 February, he sent his replies. They contained one serious error, namely about the circumstances and timing of a Japanese investment in Virgin Music in 1989. The significance of Branson's error will become apparent to the reader at the beginning of this book.

By February 2000, however, the relationship between Branson and myself had become complicated. Branson was upset by an article I had written in December 1999 in the *Evening Standard* about his bid for the National Lottery. He believed my comments to be defamatory.

As we exchanged letters about the article and I replied to his threat of commencing legal proceedings if I failed to publish an apology, I was reminded about his letter to the *Spectator* on 28 February 1998 protesting about another journalist, where he recorded, 'I have never sued anyone to suppress criticism of myself or Virgin.' Two years later, on 22 March 2000, that boast became redundant.

In an operation seemingly co-ordinated with *The Times*, a leather-clad motorcyclist served a writ issued by Branson while I was answering questions from a journalist who happened to telephone at the precise moment the writ was served. Branson's action was considered of such importance that *The Times* prominently reported the writ on its front page the following day.

Of the many unusual aspects of Branson's resort to legal action, few were more significant than his decision to sue me exclusively and not, as is customary, also the newspaper which published the article. Branson's decision to deliberately exclude the newspaper was interpreted by my legal advisers as an attempt to undermine the publication of this book. The plan was obvious.

Confronted by the impossibility of matching Branson's self-proclaimed fortune to finance a team of lawyers, I would have been forced to capitulate and apologise, and inevitably discredit my own book. Fortunately, Max Hastings, the *Evening Standard*'s editor, pledged in a prominent article to finance the defence of the piece which his newspaper had published. The trial is scheduled for 2001.

To date, there have been two biographies and one autobiography about Richard Branson. All three benefited from Sir Richard's vetting and approval. I have resisted that blessing. This book is offered as a balanced review of Britain's most visible entrepreneur, an eager recipient of hero worship, trying to influence practically every aspect of British society, who, in his attempt to market a Virgin lifestyle, seeks the widest possible circle of influence.

Introduction

In early June 1988, Ken Berry, a discreet director of the Virgin Group, arrived in Tokyo on a secret assignment. Berry, a deal-maker trusted by Richard Branson, was searching for $150 million.

Although Virgin Music was a publicly owned company, Richard Branson preferred not to reveal Berry's mission to his British shareholders and his two non-executive directors.

Berry had arranged to meet Akira Ijichi, the president of Pony Canyon, a subsidiary of a giant Japanese media company. Their introduction at the Intercontinental Hotel in the Shinjuku district lasted two hours.

'This meeting has got to remain secret,' stipulated Berry. Ijichi nodded his agreement. Berry continued: 'Virgin needs money to expand. We're looking for $150 million.' That was not the complete reason for Berry's search for money.

Three months later, in September, Akira Ijichi arrived in London with his translator Moto Ariizumi, a junior executive in the company. Both stayed at the Halcyon Hotel, in Holland Park, conveniently close to Branson's home. By then, their New York bankers had undertaken an external examination of the Virgin Group's business and finances. Negotiations, the bankers had suggested, should start at $125 million for a 25 per cent stake.

Berry, a natural deal-maker, could sense Ijichi's enthusiasm. The Japanese was flush with cash. During their discussions in Virgin's offices on the Harrow Road, Berry emphasised on several occasions, 'We don't want any publicity. We don't want the shareholders to know.' The secrecy suited the Japanese: they wanted the deal to succeed.

Late, at the end of their second day in London, the two Japanese met Richard Branson for dinner at his home. Their host was charming but firm: 'The company's worth $600 million. Not a dollar less.' Ijichi nodded.

The following morning, the two Japanese were welcomed by Branson on his houseboat in Little Venice. Amid the stripped pine-wood floors, cane furniture and leafy plants Branson shone, in Moto

Ariizumi's opinion, as a 'quite extraordinary but fashionable' representative of the alternative culture.

Before their departure, Akira Ijichi agreed to pay $150 million for a 25 per cent stake although several important details remained unresolved. Branson and Berry were untroubled by the delay. In the meantime, Branson had dramatically announced his decision to privatise the Virgin Group. His unexpected decision to buy back the shares from the public had caused considerable surprise although everyone was grateful that he valued the Virgin Group at £248 million, double the stock market's value. However, when Virgin's shareholders met in November 1988 to formally approve Branson's proposed privatisation, neither the shareholders nor Virgin's two non-executive directors were aware of Berry's continuing negotiations with the Japanese. If the shareholders had known about Pony Canyon's agreement that the Virgin Group was worth $600 million, or £377 million − £129 million more than the sum offered to shareholders − they might have demanded that Branson buy back the shares at the same valuation.

Pony Canyon's investment was formalised in May 1989. The public would remain unaware that the relationship had been initiated before Branson's announcement of the privatisation.

Within two years, Virgin's status would be utterly transformed. Branson was hailed as a genius after selling Virgin Music for £560 million or $1 billion. Since his deal with Akira Ijichi, Branson had doubled his fortune and become one of a rare breed: a legend in his own lifetime, an icon and a billionaire.

Eight years later, on 8 November 1999, Branson was invited as a British hero to deliver a Millennium Lecture at Oxford University. The Examination Room was packed with admirers, students and elderly academics. Mr Cool Britannia, the blameless face of New Britain, was introduced by Lord Butler, the former Cabinet Secretary, as 'a lighthouse for enterprise who owns 150 companies and all of them are profitable'. Branson, dressed casually in his characteristic pullover, smiled. He knew that Butler's praise was inaccurate. With the exception of his airline and rail franchises, all of his major companies in 1999 were trading at a loss.

Branson was rarely asked to face unpleasant contradictions. Voted Britain's favourite boss, the best role model for parents and teenagers, and the most popular tycoon, he was widely admired by most Britons. Branson, the public believed, was at heart a charitable public servant whose companies just happened to earn handsome profits. Idealism was his business.

The opening of Branson's sermon to his young idolaters in Oxford emphasised the irrelevance of education. Only those rejecting university would become millionaires, he preached.

His second theme foretold the future of industry: it was dead. 'Don't go into industry to make money,' he urged. Manufacturers with assets would soon be worthless. 'Focus on customers,' was his gospel. Only brands would be valuable in the future. 'I believe there's no limit to what a brand can do,' he enthused. Expertise was also worthless: 'If you can run one business, you can run any business.' He personally had known little about the music and airline businesses, the sources of his two fortunes, which naturally led to his third article of faith urged on his audience: 'get the right people around you and just incentivise them'. His secrets of success were bold and liberating to an audience unaware of Branson's increasing inability to attract and retain the brightest young brains.

His admirers in the audience sought from Branson an inspiring vision for his personal and Britain's future prosperity. 'What,' one asked, 'is your major ambition in the new millennium?' The hero paused. Bill Gates would have anticipated the next generation of developments of the computer and the internet. Rupert Murdoch, whom Branson once aspired to overtake, would have expounded the future of global communication. But Branson avoided such complicated speculations. The icon's face assumed the countenance of destiny as he intoned his reply: 'To run the national lottery.' Branson gazed thoughtfully across the hundreds of placid faces, unaware of the frisson of disappointment which enveloped his audience.

Aspiring tycoons in the hall, regarding Branson as a model for 'shaking up industries and offering a better product', were fed a simplistic, reductive homily from Britain's greatest entrepreneur. To create real wealth, they were urged by the acceptable face of capitalism, rely on a label. Ignore education, ignore expertise and ignore technology. In a citadel of academic excellence, Branson had preached anti-knowledge. The new generation, he urged, should believe that sustainable businesses could be created without 'a great business plan or strategy. Just instinct.'

Introduction

The generational division among those inside the Examination Hall was blatantly evident. To those dozens of students, eager to shake their hero's hand, proffering scraps of paper for his autograph, Branson's self-generated image of a buccaneer bestriding his own world was laudable. They admired the champion of the underdog who advertised himself as a product. He was the admirable, fun-loving millionaire.

The older, more sceptical members of the audience, as they slipped out of the hall for a glass of sherry in the Master's lodgings, mentioned a fallacy. Unlike Bill Gates, they murmured, Branson's fortune was forged on old ideas that ignored innovation. The result was, they sniffed, self-evident. While Bill Gates's fortune was valued at $100 billion and constantly rising, Richard Branson's wealth was a disputed $3 billion and possibly falling.

Three days later, on 11 November 1999, in Leicester Square, London, Branson was sitting on a bright red sofa in a huge Perspex container fixed on a trailer. Six naked young girls were grouped around the master of self-promotion. His latest extension of the brand was Virgin Mobile, a belated bid to join the New Economy developed and dominated for some years by Vodaphone, Cellnet and others. Branson never paused to contemplate the relevance of six naked girls clutching mobile telephones to herald his entry into the New Age. Nor was he concerned that his latest marketing stunt technically broke the law. Securing free advertising in the following day's tabloid newspapers was his sole ambition. 'Public relations is an important part of running our business,' Branson once explained. 'About 20 to 25 per cent of my time is spent on PR.' No one sold Branson like Branson. His business skills included the publicity skills of a salesman unafraid to yell for attention in a market even if, as he had confided to his Oxford admirers, he lacked any presence or expertise.

Seeing a policeman striding across Leicester Square, Branson abruptly abandoned the naked girls and scurried to a waiting taxi. While the girls were ordered to dress, Branson had time to reflect that it was just another ordinary day, promoting himself and his ambitions.

'We intend to sell 100,000 telephones by Christmas,' he pledged that morning, emphasising Virgin's core values of quality and fun.

'And one million by Christmas next year.' By January 2000, just over 100,000 telephones had indeed been sold, although the figure included 20,000 offered at a discount to Virgin employees and their families, but four weeks later Virgin's telephone network temporarily collapsed. The Virgin brand, promoted by himself as a 'global business', was limping. Anti-knowledge, balanced on the edge of a financial precipice, was an uncertain guarantee for success.

Later on the same day as the launch of the Virgin Mobile, Branson was swigging a bottle of beer at a good humoured promotion party for one thousand young men and women advertised as 'Very Sexy. Very Decadent.' A constant flow of admirers sought a few minutes in his company and the opportunity for a photograph. All were attracted by his courage, his blokeishness and his social conscience. The 'daredevil's' oft repeated ambition to 'make the world a better place' appealed to those attracted by a pleasant, friendly and unthreatening superstar. Calmly, he stood beside his wife, Joan, personifying the Virgin Dream. At 10.15 p.m., his wife signalled their departure. Outside, a car waited to drive the Bransons to their two adjoining houses in Holland Park worth £10 million. One house, after a recent fire, was for sale. A portent, some unkind observers carped, of the fate of a man who, after thirty years within the warm embrace of tabloid headlines, had become unexpectedly imperilled.

Opportunism, luck, energy and genius created Sir Richard Branson, a man of the people, a man of conscience and a courageous adventurer. The same qualities also produced a man of controversy and cunning. Wilfully and repeatedly thrusting himself into the spotlight, the hero seeks public approval but complains about criticism. Proud to be a tycoon of our time, his appetite for profit and power created a conglomerate which he assumed empowered him to write his epitaph in his own lifetime. Instead, his future is jeopardised by his weaknesses. Thirty years of self-glorification have taken a toll of a man seeking everlasting fame while occupying the shadows. The self-promoting blueprint for Britain's economic regeneration offers a tawdry example of mixed blessings and unhelpful lessons. Those prying beyond his veil of secrecy find an entrepreneur unexpectedly contemplating an uncertain future. The impresario of stunts risks unwittingly becoming a casualty of history. The moment of reckoning beckons.

1

The crime

Thirty years earlier, in 1969, money was a singular obsession although mention of the subject was impolite. The floppy haired, nineteen-year-old youth wearing black rimmed glasses held together by a plaster, was hunting for profitable ideas.

'What can we do?' groaned Richard Branson. Three teenagers sat in the smoke-filled basement of a shabby house in Bayswater, London. 'We need some bread.' His audience drew hard on their cigarettes. John Varnom and Tony Mellor regarded the younger man as a friend, host and employer. Living with Branson, a benign sovereign, was an enjoyable self-indulgence.

'What about records?' suggested Varnom desultorily. The twenty-four-year-old-writer and publicist was Branson's Rasputin and jester.

'We could try mail order,' sighed Mellor, a hippie with a passion for music.

Branson jerked excitedly, his imagination racing. Mail order records: the idea would fill a gap in the market, a trader's dream. There was also an angle. 'They've dropped Resale Price Mainten-ance,' he said.

'What's that?' asked Mellor admiringly.

'The record companies can't fix the shops' prices any more,' gurgled Branson. 'Costs nothing to put an ad in a newspaper,' he continued, 'and we could sell them cheaper than the shops.'

The Beatles, the Rolling Stones and the Kinks were just a blur of noise to Branson. Tone deaf and knowing little about music, he rarely listened to records. He was a doer, not a person to wait and listen. But selling cut-price records sounded as exquisite as Cliff Richard singing 'Bachelor Boy', his favourite.

The idea had been sequestrated. A new business shimmered. 'We'll put an ad in *Student*,' he announced. His beloved magazine, tottering

towards extinction, might beget his next enterprise. Readers of
Student would be offered any rock record at 10 or 15 per cent less
than the shop price.

'What shall we call the company?' he asked.

Varnom and Mellor brainstormed. Names tumbled out. 'Slipped
Disc' was suggested and abandoned. Although he was silent,
Branson's demeanour implored his employees to produce more ideas.
Varnom, lustfully contemplating the stream of nubile former public
school girls who regularly passed through Branson's squat, departing
somewhat wiser about the world thanks to his attentions, laughed.
'Virgin,' he chortled. 'Virgin,' he repeated, delighted by his idea.

'That's it,' gushed Branson, loving the combination of sex and
subversion. 'Great.' The new name eventually inherited a new pedigree. 'I thought of the name Virgin,' explained Branson twenty-five
years later, 'while sitting in the crypt of a church surrounded by two
coffins.'

Virgin Records, a mail order supplier of pop, started trading in
April 1970. The advertisement in the last edition of *Student* magazine
produced an encouraging trickle of orders with cash attached. Branson sensed the opportunity. Virgin bought whole-page advertisements in *Melody Maker* and other music newspapers. Dramatically,
the number of orders exploded. Virgin, buzzed the bush telegraph,
was cool. Supplying records at discount prices, breaking the record
manufacturers' rigid price cartel, was heroic; and selling bootleg
records bought from 'Jeff in the East End' for 50 pence to punters for
£3 was profitable. 'I believe in competition,' enthused the wannabe
tycoon, 'and I believe in helping the young.' Branson deftly borrowed
the language of the Swinging Sixties and student revolution to establish his principal sales pitch. His business was to be cheaper and
therefore a service to mankind. Branson was emphatic about his
motives: 'There is nothing phoney about my idealism,' he would
later insist. 'I had a genuine belief that I should be using my skills
and the resources at my disposal to "do good".'

Doing well by doing good was a beguiling explanation except to
the four men isolated in a locked room in St Mary's Hospital, Paddington. From there they scrutinised Virgin's new premises in South
Wharf Road through binoculars. 'Dead as a dormouse,' cursed Mike
Knox, the senior investigator for Customs and Excise.

In February 1971, ten months after Virgin advertised cut-price

records, Mike Knox knew that Richard Branson's expanding enterprise was being financed by a crude fraud. Posing as an unassuming
government tax clerk, Knox had invited himself into Virgin's new
warehouse. The introduction aroused no suspicion. In that era, it
was normal for Her Majesty's Customs and Excise to provide a clerk
every three months to calculate each company's purchase tax, a 33
per cent levy on all sales. Sitting in Branson's congested first floor
office, watching attractive girls flitting around their unsuspecting
tousle-haired employer, Knox glanced through Branson's accounts,
especially those of Caroline Exports trading as an unregistered company. Branson, the director, was too excited by that day's postbag
containing hundreds of cheques, postal orders and cash to care for
the grey man as he sifted through the PT 999s, Caroline's purchase
tax returns. His new business, Branson often chortled, was amazing.
Punters' cash was being banked for records he still did not possess.
Imported American records, bought for pennies, were sold for
pounds. 'Cash flow,' he enthused, 'is great.' But his aspirations were
not financed entirely by conventional means.

The genesis of his fraud, Branson would say, was accidental. Soon
after Virgin Records' birth, Branson himself had driven a van to
Dover with a consignment of records for export. After a Customs
officer had placed the official stamp on a PT 999 confirming that
the records had been exported and were exempt from purchase tax,
Branson had boarded the ferry for Calais. Unexpectedly, the sailing
was cancelled because the French port was closed by a strike. Branson
had driven off the ferry and, unhindered by officials, returned towards
London. During the drive, he realised that the records could now
be sold through his mail order company to British customers without
adding purchase tax. The extra money would belong to him. Two
tax agencies could be deceived. Customs would not receive the 33
per cent purchase tax and the Inland Revenue would be denied the
tax on his additional profits.

On his return to Paddington, Branson had confided his discovery
to his inner cabal of six. 'The Customs office is not near the port,'
he explained, 'so the forms get stamped but they don't have any
barriers or checks to see if you've gone on to the ferry or driven
back to London.' His audience was transfixed.

Branson's conscience was untroubled by the dishonesty. Gambling
against discovery was exciting. A pattern had been established that

he would later describe with evident pride: 'I have always thought rules were there to be broken.' He had cheated in school examinations; he had repeatedly deceived the Church Commissioners, the landlord of his home in Albion Street, by disguising its use as an office; he had defrauded the Post Office by using the telephone without paying; now he was selling bootleg records; and he had just been convicted for poaching game in a magistrates court.

The recent conviction for poaching had been particularly revelatory. Branson had driven in his white Mini with Mundy Ellis, his bubbly, blonde girlfriend, to stay with Caroline and Rob Gold, a music publisher, in a rented cottage in Suffolk.

Branson liked the Golds and the sentiment was reciprocated. The Golds lived on a houseboat in Little Venice and Caroline had become Branson's paid assistant, although she had become wary after Branson had unsuccessfully invited her father, Frank Gold, a shipping forwarder who owned warehouses, to become involved in his purchase tax operation. Nevertheless, the Golds felt sympathy for the young man whose twin laments were, 'I didn't get enough love from my mother' and 'How can I make money?'

Rob Gold had told Branson there was 'some shooting in a public wood' and Branson had brought two shotguns, an inheritance from his grandfather, Sir George Branson. Gold had never shot before but nevertheless took one of the guns as they walked in the countryside with the women trailing behind. Soon after the two started shooting, they heard yells. A gamekeeper was running from one direction and the landowner from another. Branson realised immediately that they were trespassing and ran off with the women. Gold fell and was caught. Both were charged with poaching.

Two months later Branson and Gold returned to Suffolk by train to attend the Sudbury magistrates court. During the entire journey, Branson carefully read *The Financial Times*.

At the hearing, Rob Gold noticed the clerk approach Branson. 'I understand your father's a magistrate?' asked the clerk, confirming information which Branson had earlier supplied. 'Yes,' nodded Branson gravely. Seconds later, the clerk was whispering in the ear of the Suffolk magistrate. Watching with awe, Gold understood the social chasm separating himself from Branson, and the essence of his friend's fearlessness. The fine was only £10 and the confiscation of the guns. Branson smiled. This nonchalance was confusing for those unaware that behind the awkward reticence was an acutely self-confident young man, a master of exerting influence.

'Do you realise who you are dealing with?' Branson challenged a police officer when, shortly after, he was stopped speeding in Glasgow. A growing sense of invulnerability fed his appetite for recklessness, developed as a boy at Stowe, the public school where he was educated. Lacking any signs of self-doubt or fear of retribution, Branson showed remarkable ability to speedily bypass the truth. For him, the plot to defraud Customs and Excise was just another whacky prank.

'It's a great wheeze,' he buzzed. Cheating Customs, he urged his employees, would be effortless. For a child from Surrey's stockbroker belt evading taxes imposed by the confiscatory socialist government was an act of principled defiance. The Establishment's rebels were sure that rules could be ignored, bent or broken. Doubters were swayed by Branson's enthusiasm for the role of Robin Hood. Helping impoverished students hear their music despite the ogreish government's taxation, he urged, would constitute a blow for justice. None of Branson's merry group had ever committed a serious crime but all were mesmerised by Branson's persuasiveness that his interests and theirs were identical, even if the scheme was illegal. Chris Stylianou, the Charterhouse-educated manager of Caroline Exports, was wary until others nodded agreement. Branson's genius was to disguise his impatience for fame and fortune by championing the struggle of down-trodden youth.

The white Transit van was driven regularly to Dover. The documents for the export of records were proffered and, after securing the official stamp on the PT 999 form from the Customs officer, driven unseen back to London. The van rarely transported the records specified on the consignment. Instead, a batch of worthless recordings of the Band of the Irish Guards was loaded. Over a period of months, Virgin's mail-order business attracted gratitude from a growing army of music fans.

By the time Mike Knox reported to his superiors – 'Virgin looks dicey. It's worth an operation' – about twenty young employees, enjoying the permanent party atmosphere encouraged by Branson, were dispatching the 'export' records by post from the warehouse in Paddington. Among the thousands of customers were Mike Knox and Dick Brown, his deputy in the Customs investigation team, ordering records as normal customers from their home addresses.

Their investigation had started after a visit to EMI's head of security in Hayes, west London. Knox had confessed his bewilderment to the record producer's head of security about Branson's ability to sell his records cheaper than the shops. The former policeman employed by EMI admitted his own suspicions that 'Something's fishy'.

'I'll look at his PT 999s,' thought Knox.

Reading through the thick wodge of Customs certificates accumulated by Branson over the previous ten months, Knox noticed the official stamps at Dover testifying to his regular export of records in batches of at least 10,000 to every country in Western Europe and to the United States. Knox was particularly intrigued by two certificates. On both occasions Branson had, according to the certificate, exported 30,000 records in a Land Rover. Amid the clatter of Branson's office, no one heard the staid 'tax clerk' murmur to himself, 'You can't load 30,000 records on to a Land Rover.' Shortly afterwards, a surveillance unit had been established in St Mary's Hospital, overlooking Branson's offices.

Every night at 3 a.m. over the following three weeks, Dick Brown arrived at EMI's headquarters. Neatly stacked in the record producer's loading bay were boxes marked for delivery to Virgin, invariably with a note on the invoice: 'For export'. Regularly, Branson was ordering two hundred copies of 'She's a Lady', Tom Jones's hit, apparently for export to Switzerland. To monitor the fate of those records, Brown marked on each record a letter of the alphabet with an ultra violet pen, invisible to the naked eye. 'A' was given for the first day and consecutive letters were marked on each successive day's consignment. The copy of 'She's a Lady' delivered by post to Brown's home from Virgin bore the ultra violet mark.

At the end of the three weeks' surveillance, Knox gazed down at the building forlornly. No Land Rover had appeared at the warehouse and no large consignment had been loaded on to the white Transit. The report sheets were blank. The only unusual activity was Branson's departure early that morning by taxi and his return by taxi late in the afternoon. 'I'll phone Dover,' groaned Knox. Unknown to Knox, Branson had refined the mechanics of his fraud. To maximise his profits, he had searched for ways to save costs. Since the frequent passage through Dover had not aroused any suspicion, Branson had

6

avoided the expense of sending the Transit to Dover by dispatching someone to the port by train. Knox's telephone call to Dover exposed the refinement. That same morning, Branson had presented in Dover an export certificate for 10,000 records. 'Cheeky chappy,' smiled the Customs investigator. 'He went cheap, on an away-day.'

Knox decided to raid the premises after Branson submitted his next purchase tax returns. After a three months' investigation, his schedule, covering dozens of pages, listed 'hundreds of phoney exports' which had profited Branson the equivalent of £370,000 in the year 2000. 'It's a big case,' he concluded.

An anonymous telephone call the night before the raid sparked frantic activity inside Virgin's warehouse. The caller was a disgruntled Customs officer, jealous of Knox, warning about the plan. Before daybreak, Branson and two co-conspirators had transferred the 'export' records from the warehouse to the new Virgin shop in Oxford Street. Virgin's employees arrived the following morning unaware of any tension. Even John Varnom, a member of the 'family', would remain oblivious about the tip-off and the night-time transfer. Branson felt no compunction to say more than necessary. He already understood the importance of secrecy in creating successful businesses.

Cool nonchalance greeted the team of determined Customs investigators waving a search warrant at 10 o'clock in the morning. The 'gangly, laid-back, long-haired lad' with a mop of fair hair, affecting the nasal tone of Mick Jagger to suffocate his natural upper-class twang, betrayed no hint of concern. He was even, Mike Knox reflected, rather welcoming.

Act One of the performance was perfect. 'It's all legal,' Branson smiled benignly, showing the Customs forms stamped at Dover. 'You won't find any export records here.' The same bluff used successfully at the magistrates court to minimise the prosecution for poaching, he hoped, could disorientate the investigators.

'We personally bought these records from your mail order company,' snapped Dick Brown waving his copy of 'She's a Lady'. 'They were marked for export. Here's the paperwork. And here's your signature on the PT 999. There's no doubt. Now where's the stock?'

'Oh fuck.' Branson was stunned. Public humiliation provoked tears. Discovery was not part of the plot. Tears dripped from his cheek on to his blue jumper. For once, his weakness could not be turned into a virtue. The performance was terminated. 'We hid them in Oxford Street.' A gulp. 'Can I phone my mother?'

'There's a bit of a problem,' choked Branson on the line to Shamley Green, deep in the Surrey Jag and gin belt.

'He's as good as gold,' decided Brown as he listened to Ricky explain his plight on the telephone. Their catch was a vulnerable, public schoolboy, 'not the usual toe-rag but an entrepreneur, and a good bloke'.

'Look upstairs,' ordered Brown over the telephone to the team searching through the stock in Oxford Street. Within the hour, Branson was shown the ultra violet markings on the records brought from the West End. 'If only I'd known,' he spluttered, secretly angry that the records had not been destroyed the previous night.

'You're under arrest,' announced Brown. 'We'd like you to come with us now to Dover.'

'Oh God,' blabbed Branson suddenly aware of his plight. But his good humour soon revived. Searching through his desk, an officer had pulled out a half empty packet of condoms. Glancing at all the pretty young girls in the building, the officer sighed. These were not villains, he realised, but sex-obsessed hippies living on a different planet from Customs officers. His prisoner smiled. The 'scene' – sex, music and friendship – mitigated the gravity of his crime. His charm undermined any remaining barriers.

'I'm starting out in my career,' explained Branson, as the Customs official's car crossed the River Thames heading towards the Channel port. 'I've just opened one shop and I'm building a recording studio in a manor I've bought in Oxfordshire.'

'You should open shops in Bristol and Birmingham,' suggested Brown, warming to the young man. 'Paying your staff such low wages, you'll be a millionaire one day.'

'Do you think so, Dick?' replied Branson, breaking down another barrier. 'My bankers are the problem. We're always short of cash. I need a couple of guys like you in suits to work for me.' The charm was natural.

The joviality continued during an unscheduled lunch stop in a pub. Distracted by Branson's manner, Brown allowed his prisoner to drink alcohol, a breach of regulations. An unusually warm relationship had developed despite the Customs officer's realisation of the fundamental dishonesty of Branson's financial accounts. Not only were the extra profits which Virgin had earned on the 'export' records concealed, but their American imports were deliberately undervalued to diminish import duties.

'I just want to protect my business,' soothed Branson, glossing over the dishonesty. 'I'm just starting. How can I put all this right? We're all human beings.' In that strange British guise, his disarming performance and his social confidence bestowed a veneer of decency.

The officers' procedure could not be changed. Fearful that a hippie would disappear, they had decided upon an arrest rather than a summons. Once in Dover, there was no alternative but to place Branson in jail overnight before his appearance in court the following morning.

At daybreak, the lobbying of Brown and Knox was resumed by Eve, Branson's forty-eight-year-old mother, and the dominant influence in his life. Sitting with Ted, her husband, introduced as a barrister and stipendiary magistrate, Eve Branson glanced at her dishevelled and depressed son. 'Now officers,' cooed the former air hostess, 'how can we sort this out?' Eve's dignity and class confirmed Knox's and Brown's opinion that this was an exceptional case. 'We'd like to arrange bail,' said Eve, 'and settle this amicably. He's only twenty years old. He's been very foolish and it's unnecessary that his life should be ruined by a criminal conviction. He'll repay the taxes and any fine but we'd prefer to keep it out of the court.' The absence of an aggressive solicitor and the impressive honesty of the Branson family persuaded the officers to consider a deal. 'Have you got the money for bail?' asked Brown.

'No,' replied Eve, 'but we'll put up our house, our only home.'

The normally cynical officers were impressed. 'And we'll guarantee the repayment of the taxes and the fine,' continued Eve, 'even if we have to sell our home.' After a suitable pause, she added, alarmed that twenty years of loving ambition were on the verge of disintegration, 'He's very young. He should be given a second chance.'

Knox and Brown agreed. This was a genuine, one-off error. There would be a brief court appearance to set bail at £30,000 secured on the family home. The young Branson would be released without further prosecution. 'No publicity?' urged Eve.

'Absolutely,' promised Knox. Customs were always discreet.

In the following weeks, meeting Branson on the *Duende*, his houseboat just purchased for £200 and moored in Little Venice,

Brown set out the terms of the settlement proposed by his superiors. The investigations had by then revealed the sophisticated nature of Branson's fraud. Contacting the customers across Europe and America listed on Branson's export certificates, the investigators discovered that none of those named had ever bought records from Caroline. 'The scam's enormous,' a Customs official declared.

'You owe us £40,000 in back taxes and we are charging a £20,000 fine,' announced Brown. Just after Branson's twenty-first birthday, he owed the modern equivalent of over £500,000.

'I can't afford that,' said Branson. 'Can I pay by instalments?' After negotiations interrupted by tea, it was agreed that Branson would pay £15,000 immediately and £45,000 in monthly payments of £3,000.

His crime was too well-known to be concealed, so over the years Branson has presented his illegality as an early watershed in life. The sackcloth and ashes version is: 'One night in jail teaches you that sleeping well at night is the only thing that really matters. Every single decision since has been made completely by the book.' That interpretation, however, belied one of his life's principal credos: 'I have always enjoyed breaking the rules.' His prescient headmaster at Stowe had noted that trait, predicting on the eve of the seventeen year old's premature departure from school that Branson would either become a millionaire or go to prison. By twenty-one, he had achieved the latter, albeit briefly. 'He appears modest,' Mike Knox would reflect at the end of his investigation, 'with a disarming personality offering to help everybody. But he's got this ruthless ambition.'

Once Branson had begun to court celebrity as a millionaire tycoon, he progressively introduced distortions to minimise the gravity of the fraud. In 1984, he mentioned that he was 'only eighteen' when the embarrassment occurred rather than nearly twenty-one. The following year he described his 'eighteen-year-old fraud' as occurring 'only three times' before his arrest at the port on the third occasion. In 1986, he told the *Sun* that he escaped imprisonment, 'by convincing the court that he didn't know it was illegal'. Two years later, in 1988, he chose another variation for Mick Brown, his first biographer, recounting that he personally drove four times through the Customs post at Dover before he was caught. His version in 1992 conjured a sophisticated tale about shipping worthless titles and empty boxes to the Continent for 'one month' after discovering himself to be penniless after investing in his mail order business, his shops and the new manor recording studio in Oxfordshire. In truth, the shops and the recording studio were partly financed by the fraud. 'I had a pile of debt and no real money,' he truthfully admitted. By 1994, as the owner of a famous international airline, Branson excused himself from the whole enterprise saying: 'I had not realised the rules.' In his autobiography in 1998, Branson offered another explanation: there were only three trips, he wrote, starting in spring 1971 to cover debts of £35,000 and 'big operators' were far worse. All those variations were a smokescreen. He had simply played the game and, unforgivably, he had lost.

Over Sunday lunch at the manor with his staff after his arrest, Branson expounded his credo. 'We weren't doing any harm,' he said. 'No one was hurt. Customs is only an organisation. If organisations get robbed, it's not a problem because they've got lots of money. Too much money which should be handed around.' Listening to his own espousal of the morality of the righteous underdog, Branson warmed to his theme. Hitting the big boys was justifiable because they were pirates and doing harm to the small people like Virgin. Lying was virtuous if a 'non-profit' group helping society was the beneficiary. His cabal did not disapprove. Deceit, they agreed, was acceptable in business. His forgery of a letter and an invoice from a non-existent American company to suggest that he was an innocent victim in the sale of bootleg records defied contradiction. Surrounded by employees who approved his dishonesty, Branson was classed as a rebel thumbing his nose at the Establishment. Taking money from the government, they agreed with Branson, was a lark and, considering all the rogues in the City, lying was not only acceptable but virtuous for the 'victim' and the 'champion of youth'.

2

The beginning

The first ruse was simple and saved money. 'Operator,' berated the grating upper class voice, 'I've put money into this pay phone and it hasn't worked.'

'Sorry, sir, I'll connect you.'

The second ruse, spoken from the telephone box, was more sophisticated. 'I'm Richard Branson. I'm eighteen and I run a magazine called *Student* that's doing something really useful for young people.' The caller was sixteen and *Student* was no more than an idea.

The third ruse was crude. The impatient bearer of six mediocre 'O' level passes, who had cheated in exams by secreting a crib sheet in the palm of his left hand, proposed that his father should write to Stowe's headmaster explaining that his son wanted to prematurely leave the school to study law at university and enter politics. In fact, unwilling to study either for 'A' levels or a university degree, Richard Branson wanted to launch *Student* magazine. Ted Branson refused to lie but reluctantly agreed his son should leave the school. Thirty years later, journalists would, after interviewing the tycoon, mistakenly believe that the teenager had left Stowe because '*Student* magazine was successful'. The youth's precocious confidence to make his fortune without an education owed much to an unusually dominant mother's extraordinary gestures.

'Find your own way home, Ricky,' ordered Eve Branson as she pushed her four-year-old son from the car into the Surrey countryside. The mother's lovingly reckless bravado was intended to ensure that her only son should not emulate her husband's lacklustre career. Success as a barrister had eluded Ted Branson, despite his father's bequest of Halsbury's *Laws of England*. Eve willed her adored son to surpass Ted's modest achievements. Maintaining the appearance of Establishment gentility was important. Dressing up and placing herself as the centre of attraction at endless social parties, Eve Branson distracted neighbours from the family's dependence on second-hand clothes for her children and her sale of wooden tissue boxes to supplement the family's limited finances. An extrovert and attention-seeker, she taught her son the power of presentation and self-publicity, and gave him the infallibility of fearless independence.

Eve Branson aspired to rekindle the fortunes of her family, the Flindts, one hundred and fifty years earlier. Gustavus Flindt had arrived in Britain from Hamburg to work as a broker on the Baltic Exchange. Julius Flindt, one of his ten children, in turn also became a broker, as did one of Julius's sons and a grandson, until Eve's father broke the tradition after fighting in the First World War against his forefather's kinsmen. In Richard Branson's parents' marriage, the Flindts' trading tradition was blended with the Establishment bias of the Bransons, educated at Bedford Grammar School and in medicine or law at Cambridge. Ted Branson's father, the Right Honourable Sir George Branson, a High Court judge, had been appointed a Privy Councillor in 1940. His grandfather and great-grandfather had been a publisher and a lawyer in India. Eve had every hope that the combination would guarantee upper-middle class Establishment respectability. Her ambitions for her only son were loftier still.

'Ricky's going to be prime minister one day,' she frequently glowed. 'Nothing but the top,' the aspiring parent would assert, 'is good enough.' Neighbours recall her position under a high tree in the centre of Shamley Green which had attracted stern warnings by all the other parents, forbidding their children to climb beyond a low height. 'Right to the top,' urged Eve Branson as her son peril-ously balanced on the highest branches. 'Higher,' shouted the woman famous for hyperactively urging, 'Do something, Ricky.' Eve Branson's emotional exhortations created an obedient son convinced he could do no wrong and that self-doubt was a sin. 'Shyness is very selfish,' the mother regularly admonished. 'It means you are only thinking of yourself.' Her son was not shy but he was awkward and inarticulate. Unable to express himself, he disguised his limitations with nervous gestures and stunts to attract attention, usefully camou-flaging his lust for fame and fortune. Earning money, an unmentioned topic in the polite society of the early sixties, became his dominant preoccupation. He disdained authority and intellectuals. So long as his adoring mother approved of his behaviour, he was impervious to criticism.

'Books, no way,' Branson laughed, reflecting the family's lack of interest in culture and education. 'I don't listen to music either.' Ricky was a doer, not an observer excited by intellectual stimulation. Full of his mother's forceful prediction of his destiny, he naturally dreamed of glory. 'Bringing him up was rather like riding a thorough-bred horse,' chuffed Eve Branson. 'He needed guiding but you were afraid to pull the reins too hard in case you stamped out the adventure and wildness.'

Some of her son's contemporaries at Stowe were intolerant of his exceptional qualities. The most critical lampooned 'Greasy Branson' as a self-centred big-head suffering oily, pimply skin with a smarmy manner towards teachers. But the majority accurately surmised that Branson's diffident charm was exceptional. Since Stowe was a second-rate public school, it was not difficult to shine, especially after the sixteen year old boasted about his introduction to a prostitute by his father. Thirty years later, the former schoolboys could still recall Branson's vivid account of a trip to Soho and the introduction to a woman paid by his father to remove the stigma of virginity. Sex, in every sense, was his obsession.

He suffered only two genuine handicaps: a knee injury which destroyed his enjoyment of sport and slight dyslexia. Despite those impediments and his rejection of books, Branson surprisingly won the school's Gavin Maxwell prize for writing the best English essay. Gavin Young, a well-known newspaper journalist, personally awarded the prize to Branson. Over lunch, Branson listened to Young's description of a journalist's glamorous lifestyle: a good income earned by interviewing celebrities in exotic locations. It was an attractive cocktail which matched his preoccupations: money, sex and fame. Branson was reminded of his discussions with a school friend about *Student*, their proposed magazine for sixth formers, similar to two new magazines, *International Time* and *Oz*. While others only talked about the idea, Branson's energetic self-confidence could make *Student* a reality.

Daily, the schoolboy dispatched dozens of letters appealing for interviews to celebrities culled from *Who's Who*. In the late 1960s, youth was tolerated and even lauded by the famous who were intrigued by the turbulence of their children's generation. Unprotected by a screen of press officers, their replies were surprisingly positive.

To the bewildered admiration of his contemporaries, Branson regularly carried into the classroom stacks of correspondence. He regaled his audience with the words addressed to him by writers, musicians, actors and politicians including Harold Wilson, the Prime Minister, and Ted Heath, the leader of the Conservatives. His success encouraged volunteers to write appeals for advertising and cajoling pleas to the famous for free articles. Richard Branson's gift was his genial enthusiasm which disarmed those whom he approached for help. Even sceptics were seduced to espouse his ambition after listening to his bold account of a return to Soho to interview prostitutes for a sensational article in the new magazine. Soon, for the unusually worldly seventeen year old, Stowe had become insufferably parochial.

In 1967, Branson left the school and settled in the squalid basement of a friend's house in Connaught Square, near Hyde Park, a desirable address in London, where, chanting the fashionable lure of 'doing something really useful for young people' he strove to complete the first edition of *Student*.

In an era when public schoolboys, even from Stowe, were still regarded as members of a rather staid Establishment, Branson was careful to present himself as a benign hybrid: part hippie and part charitable businessman. Controlling his awkward stutter when neces-sary, his telephone manner concealed his age to recruit a respected magazine designer for no fee; to secure paid advertising from major corporations; and to negotiate a printing contract for 50,000 copies of the magazine. In a testament to his style, during his sales patter, he would inaccurately boast of selling 100,000 copies but, if challenged, would switch from talking circulation to readership to conceal his exaggeration. Salesmanship relied upon a quality performance and Branson was a notable actor. The appearance of the slick first edition, a good imitation of many established glossy magazines, more than justified his confident sales pitch.

His unusual success in 1968 enticed other ex-public school teen-agers seeking entertainment to join him. The attraction was his easy lifestyle inhabiting part of a four-storey house at 44 Albion Street in Bayswater which his parents had leased to share with their son. United by the safety net of parental wealth, Branson and his guests enjoyed the liberation of 'Peace and Love' in 'Swinging London'. In a polite reciprocation for his hospitality, they agreed to sell their host's magazine on the streets. The prospect of permanent parties in rent-free accommodation was fun.

Branson's unthreatening self-confidence attracted people older than himself seeking spiritual liberation in an uninhibited atmosphere. Attractive girls, eager to experiment, camped on his floors to escape their parents, and in turn welcomed a stream of ex-public school boys equally willing to produce and sell *Student* magazine. Without questioning their host's authority, they enjoyed music, drugs and sex and ate food collected at the end of the day from the dustbin of a local delicatessen. Their presence reassured Branson of his popularity and guaranteed an escape from solitude. Paying his guests just £12 per week for selling the magazine on the streets, he none the less retained their loyalty by blurring the stigma of their status as employees. Money, he emphasised, was irrelevant; his fun party glued his new 'family' together. In the spirit of the era, they were all contributing towards the good of mankind although no one quite understood how.

'He plucks,' Eve Branson admitted innocently, 'what he wants out of you.' From his office on the top floor, Branson was part of the gang yet avoided immersion in his own party. While the guests played downstairs, he was focused on the fortunes of his magazine. 'He was like a country squire,' recalled Sue Steward, an early employee. 'We were having a party and all living together but it was always on his estate. You always knew he owned it all. He wasn't really a hippie, ever.' Enjoying the sex, ignoring the music, occasionally living in a haze of marijuana, he acknowledged expressions of loyalty and developed the notion that his magazine should become the vehicle for his financial independence.

Profiting from the magazine could have presented a dilemma. After all, he touted *Student* to contributors and advertisers as a philanthropic venture to help poor youth. Among articulate students at the end of the 1960s, the public good rather than personal benefit was the only justification for business. Profits were incompatible with ideals. But Branson was not plagued by the self-doubts infecting so many students of the sixties revolution. He believed in profit and any contradictions were easily brushed aside by fluent self-invention. Sensitive to the mood of the time, Branson convinced himself and others that all his commercial ventures were for society's 'good'. The rebellious public school boy adhered to the credo that his ambitions were for his employees' benefit. Earning money was not a sin, if conducted in the proper manner. But it was preferable to always pronounce, 'I haven't gone into business to make money. I like the challenge.' Combined with his blokeish ordinariness, it was a disarming performance. Connaught Publications, his unregistered company, never published accounts. None of the blissed-out party-goers in Albion Street were sure whether their employer earned profits, let alone how much. Secrecy, Branson learned to appreciate, was preferable to public disclosure and even the existence of that secrecy required concealment. His guests witnessed a performance in which the magazine became the passport to his next incarnation.

Influenced by violent agitation across Europe and America, especially against the war in Vietnam, the baby boomers were trashing traditions in confrontations with university administrators, police and politicians. Students, congregating around the London School of Economics, were immersed in an extraordinary political revolution. Although younger than the undergraduates and not having enrolled as a student, Branson purposefully attached himself to the politicised and articulate agitators as an equal. Among the real activists, the serious-looking youth disguising his comfortable background as the grandson of a judge appeared no different from the thousands of other protestors. Understandably, Branson did not reveal that he was neither left-wing nor understood the political feuds raging among the multitude of student factions in the midst of the Cold War. Branson's natural style implied that he sympathised with the spirit of the times and that he shared the common goal of an egalitarian, classless meritocracy. For Tariq Ali and the other leading Marxists who were preoccupied by endless political arguments and organising perpetual demonstrations, the credentials or motives of any young person hovering silently on the fringe of their turbulence passed unquestioned. But while Ali and others would remain permanently oblivious to Branson, the interloper himself, searching for a niche, exploited his presence at a decisive moment of history.

Unmoved by politics or history, Branson none the less spotted a financial advantage which eluded those participants preoccupied with moral conflicts. Skilfully, by walking with the leaders of London's huge demonstration against the Vietnam War, he positioned himself in 1968 as the editor and owner of *Student* magazine, and as a 'Students' Spokesman'. Newspaper photographs recorded

Branson among the leaders of the march. While most demonstrators ended that day of protest bitter about police violence and frustrated by the state's inhumanity, he had absorbed an invaluable insight into the new fickleness of the era.

Journalists dispatched by middle-aged Fleet Street editors to report and explain the student revolt, searched for a spokesman. Branson was discovered in Albion Street. Stepping over rubbish, unsold copies of *Student* magazine and couples sleeping on the floor, one grateful reporter bestowed credibility on his interviewee by lazily repeating Branson's self-description as a 'student leader' and faithfully quoting his utterances in a London newspaper.

Mention as a 'student leader' in one newspaper brought invitations to appear on television and feature in *Vogue* magazine as a representative of Britain's student rebellion. To enhance his apparent importance for visiting journalists, he arranged for friends to telephone the house from call boxes, creating an illusion of successful activity. Journalists, Branson realised, were unlikely to challenge his exaggerated claims for *Student*'s success or his personal importance. On the contrary, the more outrageous his assertions the better. A single pose alongside Tariq Ali during the demonstration had taught Branson the value of hype.

At eighteen Branson possessed star-quality. His jocular celebrity persuaded the unambitious living in his basement and seeking justification for their fun-seeking lifestyle, to accept his argument for their common goals. Their dependence upon him was gratifying to Branson but also troubling. *Student*'s circulation remained low and static. It was his first taste of a recurring predicament throughout his life: a cash crisis. His solution was to borrow an idea.

To save *Student* he imitated *Private Eye*. Regularly, the satirical magazine promoted its Christmas edition by attaching a record on to its cover. Branson's idea for his magazine's issue in spring 1969 was inspired. In October 1968, he approached Derek Taylor, the Beatles' press officer, requesting an interview and a special song recorded by John Lennon dedicated to Britain's students. Ingratiating himself by focusing polite charm on his targets was Branson's particular skill and Taylor agreed. But by early December, after commissioning an expensive cover design and placing a large printing order, the record had still not materialised. Sitting in Taylor's office, helping him address Christmas cards, Branson pressed for delivery. Taylor,

proud of fulfilling his pledges, had a problem. Lennon had been pros-
ecuted for the possession of cannabis and Yoko Ono, his girlfriend,
had just miscarried. Traumatised, the couple had isolated themselves
in their house outside London. Impulsively, Taylor scribbled on a card,
'Trust me, Derek.' Carefully, Branson pocketed the card.

At the beginning of January 1969, the promised record had not
been delivered. Branson's own despair deprived him of any sympathy
for Lennon. After consulting his father, he issued his first writ: Connaught Publications v. John and Yoko Lennon and Derek Taylor.
The official document, alleging breach of contract, was served on
Taylor in the street outside his office. Listed as proof of an agreement
was Taylor's scribble on the Christmas card. The writ established
that sentiment would never interfere with Branson's urge to earn
money. His verbal awkwardness, his long hair and his broken glasses
might have suggested a hapless, easy-going hippie but they were just
the natural props in a well-marketed performance. At dinner that
night John Varnom asked about the writ. 'My father's a judge,'
replied Branson inaccurately, suggesting that the mighty ranks of the
British Establishment endorsed his behaviour. Varnom withheld any
correction. Branson's grandfather was a judge and, ever since an old
gamekeeper on the family's lost estate had tugged his forelock to the
young boy, Branson had mirrored his mother's determination to
regain his family's lost social status: for the next fifteen years he would
not correct newspaper quotations that 'My father is the sixth in line
in a family of judges.'

In April 1969, Branson, Taylor and their lawyers met in Savile
Row to finally take delivery of a tape provided by Lennon. It was
the heartbeat of Yoko's baby which ended in silence. 'That's when
it died,' announced Taylor. Branson never used the recording and
abandoned his writ. By then, *Student* had flopped. Outsold by his
more original competitors, Branson had exhausted his charitable sales
patter to contributors and suppliers.

Marooned in Albion Street, Richard Branson was a trader in search
of a commodity. Downstairs were the friends and tenants who
enjoyed the loose lifestyle and, while talented, shared none of his
material ambition. Which was precisely why they were partying
untroubled by their low wages. But they had provided ideas and
thanks to John Varnom and Tony Mellor, Branson switched his full
attention to the newly created Virgin Records.

'We're not selling Andy Williams,' suggested Al Clark, a contemplative journalist and Virgin's director of publicity, recruited to Virgin Records after the launch. 'We need an underground feel,' suggested the enthusiast who was more perceptive than most in the company. The records offered by Virgin, Branson meekly agreed, would reflect the lifestyle lexicon of the sixties. Like a sponge, he willingly learned from others, hiring people to perform tasks he could not have undertaken. Those arriving at Albion Street in 1969 included Steve Lewis, a North London schoolboy on the eve of going to university. Lewis enjoyed finding more obscure records, buying them at discounts from record shops and dispatching the packages. Lewis and the other employees never recognised Branson as an aspiring tycoon. Even when he moved the business in 1970 to a warehouse in South Wharf Road in Paddington after the Church Commissioners, the landlords of Albion Street, had exposed his repeated deception that the premises classified for domestic occupation were being used contrary to the lease for business, Lewis and the others never thought of themselves as the underpaid employees of a fame-seeking buccaneer.

The alchemy of his personal relationships had been learned in Surrey and at Stowe. Charm and respectfulness covered an elusive character whose ambitions and class were well disguised. Unlike the majority of entrepreneurs, Branson enjoyed deep roots in English society – he had not had to scramble out of the gutter – but he saw commercial value in shedding that pedigree and veering in the opposite direction. Commercial success was connected, he considered, to classlessness. The informality generated loyalty but his agenda, shrouded behind contrived ambiguity, was quite specific. 'People thought,' he explained, 'that because we were twenty-one or twenty-two and had long hair we were part of some grander ideal. But it was always 99.5 per cent business.' Uncluttered by Sartre or Marx, he could motivate his public school cabal and the working class aspirants by infectious enthusiasm. His dominance was asserted imperceptibly; his genial decisiveness arrived without shouts or threats. Only the astute perceived his insensitivity to the disillusionment bedevilling the sixties generation. While the Class of 1968 unsuccessfully struggled in the early 1970s to disengage from their youthful preoccupations of socialist revolution and free love, Branson suffered none of their emotional turmoil. He had always stood apart

from the soul-searching idealists. Free of their self-destructive agonis-
ing which eventually constrained the revolutionaries' professional
ambitions, Branson breached the moral code of that era and pursued
wealth.

The compartmentalisation began early. One Branson sat behind a
desk in the warehouse playing hardball on the telephones as a tycoon;
while another Branson, doing 'good for society', established the
Student Advisory Centre to help young people solve their problems.
The unemployed, the suicidal and pregnant girls were invited to
telephone for assistance. Although Branson would some years later
say that 'The Advisory Centre was dealing with 3–4,000 people a
week at the time', Jenny Bier, whom he recruited to answer the
single telephone, recalls between 'ten and twenty-five people calling
every week'. Of those, about four sought help for abortions. Among
the callers in spring 1970 was Jennifer Oliver★, a twenty-year-old
undergraduate desperate to terminate a pregnancy. 'Come and see
me,' offered Branson.

The following day, Jennifer Oliver sat on the other side of the
desk in South Wharf Road explaining her predicament, dismayed by
the frequent interruption of telephone calls including one from Ted
Branson speaking from a golfing holiday in the Algarve. Turning to
Oliver, Branson was reassuring. 'Leave it with me,' he said. 'I'll sort
it out for you. I'll ring you within a week.' Two weeks later, Oliver
was in despair. Branson had not called and her pregnancy was
approaching the ten-week deadline allowed under the new Abortion
Act. Oliver's call to Paddington was again answered by Branson. 'Oh
gosh, I forgot. Did I say that? Come and see me immediately.'

Once again in his office, speaking again between telephone calls,
Branson admitted there was a problem. 'It's so close to the deadline
I can't arrange it in the time. It normally takes three weeks.' Oliver
became visibly distressed. 'But I could pull some strings,' offered
Branson, 'if you would do a favour for me.' The businessman's
proposition was simple.

'BBC TV,' he explained, 'are featuring me in a programme called
"Tomorrow's People". They want to feature my Student Advisory
Centre. If you agree to be filmed visiting me, I'll pull strings and fix
up your abortion.'

★ Not her real name.

'But I don't want anyone to know about me,' said Oliver. 'I want secrecy.'

'Well, wear a disguise,' suggested Branson.

'Is there no other way?' she asked.

'There's nothing else I can do. Think about it.'

Four days later, Oliver believed she had no option but to agree. 'Great,' said Branson. 'Come to my office. We'll be filmed and then we'll go straight to Birmingham.' Their destination was the Pregnancy Advisory Centre, a respectable organisation which had agreed to the filming. The documentary, celebrating Branson as a rising personality, was transmitted shortly afterwards. Oliver's disguise, a wig, was ineffective. Branson appeared unaware of her embarrassment. His name, though, was increasingly mentioned among the lists of fashionable youth.

Benefiting from other people's labour and ideas hardly matched the image of the sixties rebel but his style encouraged Branson's trusting tenants and employees to literally plonk ideas on his bed. One morning, as he sat in bed with Mundy Ellis talking simultaneously on two telephones and reaching for papers, Tom Newman entered. Tall, long haired with a hint of cool mystery which attracted women, Newman was the stereotype rock guitarist: an uneducated rake immersed in drugs, sex and rock and roll. Bobbing on the fringes of the music world after graduating from bruising battles with bikers at the Ace Café, he relied upon others to pull his life together after fleeing his home and his father, a drunken Irish salmon poacher. Newman felt socially inferior to the younger Branson described by his girlfriend, an employee of Virgin Records, as 'fascinating but tyrannical'.

'Why don't you build your own recording studio?' asked Newman. 'You could make a lot of money from that. I'll run it.'

'Sounds good,' stuttered Branson as Mundy dropped a grape into his mouth. Quickly Branson warmed to the idea. He encouraged Newman's trust. 'He was the first bloke I ever spoke to who spoke posh,' Newman told a friend. 'But he was approachable, charming and keen.'

'Let's find a studio,' Branson agreed, conjuring visions of a music empire.

Like generals in battle, putative tycoons also rely upon luck. In January 1971, Simon Draper, a twenty-one-year-old second cousin, introduced himself in South Wharf Road. 'I've just arrived from South Africa,' he smiled. Over breakfast, as Branson excitedly unveiled his ambitions to own a record label and a chain of record shops, Draper revealed his encyclopaedic knowledge of modern music. Even better for Branson, his unknown cousin, like Steve Lewis, was more interested in music than money. Branson, who confessed that his favourite tune that week was the theme from *Borsalino*, recognised that Draper's arrival was a godsend. Draper was invited to join the empire and work with Nik Powell, a childhood friend of Branson's and his neighbour in Surrey. In return for leaving university prematurely, Powell had negotiated with Branson a 40 per cent stake in Virgin Music which embraced Virgin Records.★

Powell was a perfect complement to Branson. Quiet, cerebral and unimpulsive, he imposed order on the chaos of Branson's stream of initiatives, restrained his friend's excesses and managed the ramshackle finances of a business not even incorporated within a company. Carefully set apart from other employees, Branson, Draper, Powell and a few other public school friends formed a tight cabal.

Powell's organisation, Branson acknowledged, had saved Virgin's mail-order business from the destruction threatened when the postal workers went on strike. Together, they had rapidly opened a record shop in Oxford Street. 'We'll put an ad in *Melody Maker*,' suggested John Varnom, 'about lying on the floor, listening to music, smoking dope and going home.'

'Great,' laughed Branson. Nothing more was said or expected. Branson often communicated only in monosyllables. Miraculously, dozens of admiring customers regularly queued to enter the first-floor shop. Long-haired hippies slouched on waterbeds listening to music on headphones while others waited outside to enter. A truth had dawned on Branson. Most people were born to be servants and customers. He would be master, provider and richer.

The increasing flow of cash from the record sales and the growing popularity of Virgin among music fans encouraged Branson's dreams of expansion. Profiting from his employees' agreement to earn just £12 per week, Branson was secretly accumulating a fortune. Rifling through Branson's desk, John Varnom had discovered a building

---

★ Throughout the book Virgin Records is not distinguished from the Virgin Music Group.

society cash book showing a £15,000 deposit in the name of Richard Charles Nicholas, Branson's three Christian names. 'Cheeky bastard,' whispered Varnom. Even in 1970 Branson's finances were attracting controversy. *Private Eye* reported that Branson had received £6,000 for advertisements in *Student* but only admitted to £3,000, which Branson vigorously denied. Indeed there was no evidence that he had. Varnom said nothing about the cash book. The amount was too large to envy and the notion of equality, Varnom knew, was bogus. Besides, he knew no better alternative to working and living in Branson's kingdom, especially after the realisation of Tom Newman's idea.

The search for a recording studio had terminated in March 1971 at a seventeenth-century Cotswold manor house in Shipton, twenty miles from Oxford. The price was £30,000. 'How are you going to pay for it?' asked Newman, mystified. Branson smiled enigmatically. 'You're an imperialist,' Newman, a rocker without a bank account and unaware of overdrafts, grunted. He remained puzzled how a twenty-one-year-old hippie could find the present-day equivalent of £275,000 while his employees were earning £12 per week. The unspoken explanation was Branson's unique fearlessness about debt. Money was unthreatening to a man certain of success who assumed that risk would be rewarded.

To buy and convert the manor and outhouses into bedrooms and a recording studio required capital. Branson approached an aunt for a gift. She was advised by her stockbroker to offer only a loan. Branson received £7,500, a sufficient sum for an application to Coutts, the bank shared by the Bransons and the royal family, to advance a mortgage for the remainder. The trusting bankers, reassured by the Branson family's reputation, did not question Virgin's cash flow from the shop and mail-order business, or discover the purchase tax fraud and the sale of bootleg records. Even after his arrest, there was no unpleasantness between the bankers and their client.

As for the £60,000 tax payments and fines, his cabal assumed the same Masonic relationships which had saved Branson from conviction and public humiliation would arrange the money. None could imagine that his imminent collapse could be forestalled only by a bravura performance.

'On my life,' Branson bluffed to his creditors, 'Virgin's finances are fine.' The company, he repeated, was not in financial peril. The flow of cash from fifteen new Virgin record shops opened across the country substantiated the denials of fragility. Branson and Powell precisely timed the opening of each shop in a different town to secure interest-free cash for two months before payments were required. Other sources of income remained undisclosed. Walking a tightrope was intoxicating but the chaos had become perilous. Virgin Records was not incorporated as a company. Branson had forgotten the legalities. His employees paid neither tax nor national insurance. For four years, he had been trading without proper financial accounts. Bereft of cash, Branson was perplexed how to equip Tom Newman's recording studio at the manor. 'Let's play roulette at the Playboy Club in Park Lane,' he suggested to Newman. 'I've got a winning system.' Using £500 taken that night from the till of Virgin's shop in Notting Hill Gate, he and Newman shuttled between two tables as Kristen Tomassi, his blonde American girlfriend, gazed with increasing bewilderment. 'It's the last bet,' Branson gritted at 5 a.m., clutching a few chips. He had risked everything; his system had failed. The flick of the wheel was lucky. 'Great,' he sighed as he stepped into Park Lane with £700. Before the shop opened later that morning, the original money was restored and the profits divided with Newman. Twenty-five years later he could speak from experience that the National Lottery compared to the roulette wheel was 'a licence to print money'.

Tom Newman's enthusiasm, Branson discovered, was not matched by his technical expertise. The guitarist knew little about the technology of recording music. For reassurance, Branson consulted George Martin, the Beatles' producer. Martin laughed. Branson was proposing a four-track studio while Martin was installing sixteen tracks and much more. 'We can't afford all that,' Branson told Newman. 'We'll have to busk it.' They would buy second-hand equipment and Newman would learn on the way. 'I've found some cheap mixers and old speakers,' announced Newman proudly. 'But the acoustics won't be much good.'

'Keep quiet about it,' ordered Branson.

'The best sound you can get,' Branson boasted to musicians and their managers in a frenzy of telephone calls and personal visits to lure the unwary. 'Sell them the image,' suggested John Varnom, the inventor of the Virgin name. 'Act the part of the alternative. No suits and ties like Decca.' Compared to the unfriendly basements hired by the big studios in London, the manor offered a party. Unlimited meals and alcohol served in manorial splendour by four attractive girls, with the promise of huge bedrooms upstairs, created the illusion of a sex hotel with nightly orgies where drugs were served with the cornflakes. In truth, there was less actual sex at the manor than occurred in London nightclubs but Branson calculated that the promise of a party would conceal the inferior quality of the sound and enhance his profits. His intuition proved shrewd.

Branson persuaded Newman and the eager girls to accept low wages. Newman's screaming protests when Branson frequently failed to send any money were brushed aside. 'I'm also not being paid,' lamented Branson, the victim. None of the uninquiring spirits enjoying his company realised that the principal beneficiary of their own low wages was Branson, focused entirely on his own agenda.

Circulating among his staff in the Sun and Splendour, the local pub on Portobello Road, puffing their cigarettes, sipping their beer and groping the girls amid jovial banter eased suspicions about an ambitious businessman. Touchy-feely embraces, pecking at cheeks and spasms of generosity defused the impression of a hierarchy and encouraged the notion of the Virgin family. Employment at Virgin, Branson had persuaded himself and his loyal staff, was benign, generous and equitable.

Occasionally providing a company car, invitations for meals in restaurants and organising holidays for some staff, he was the life and soul of his own party. Acting the fool in front of big audiences, skiing naked down alpine slopes and hosting hilarious mystery away-days terminating in Croydon solidified loyalty and trust in him. For those condemned to dreary office lives, Branson offered the chance to sense magic. Only the cabal, those close to Branson, understood that their garrulous host had created the family as protection from loneliness. Branson required perpetual company to protect himself from boredom. The anti-intellectual was incapable of self-entertainment. But his permanent party could not continue unchecked.

One year after the exposure of his purchase tax fraud, Branson was compelled to abandon the convenience of concealment through chaos. 'You'll have to become directors of proper companies,' Jack Claydon, an accountant, told Branson. In September 1972, Virgin Records was incorporated and over the following months ten other companies were created. Legal compartmentalisation suited Branson's instinct for secrecy and provided the machinery to transfer money from one company's account to another's, giving the appearance of solvency and preventing bankruptcy in one activity infecting the whole business. 'I'm spending a lot of my time,' Jack Claydon told a friend, 'juggling banks and creditors in order to play one off against the other and help Branson to stay solvent.' Claydon, an inconspicuous character, was ideal for many discreet shuffles.

Telephoning early in the morning, Branson summoned the accountant to his houseboat. Unlike a previous call when Branson had even had to ask for advice where to find a hooker for an American contact, Claydon was asked to give respectability to Branson's latest venture. 'I'm going to sign a deal and I need a letter to the bank to borrow more money.' Claydon's task was to bestow credibility on Branson's optimistic financial projections of sales and profits. 'Make it look good,' urged Branson.

'The bank wants to meet us,' Claydon reported later that day.

Lunch with Peter Caston, his bank manager, at Simpsons was Branson's opportunity to shine. Wearing a suit and tie, his enthusiastic projections of wealth were only marred, despite Claydon's warning glances, by excessive talking. The conservative banker was bewildered and became cautious, especially after Branson's cheque for lunch was rejected. The guest from Coutts reluctantly paid. Branson's strength was his robust refusal to accept defeat. 'You're never morose,' said Claydon in grudging admiration of a man whose energy exceeded conventional business talent. 'You'll always find an escape.' Branson laughed. Claydon even urged him to 'stop interfering in the business' to avoid creating chaos. The accountant, whose audit validated the Virgin business, thankfully did not understand that chaos was an essential to Branson's appearance as a classless wealth creator. Parroting the sixties mantra about 'helping to make the world a better place' concealed a more straightforward ambition: that it should be a better place for Richard Branson.

3

Honeymoons and divorces

Seducing Mundy Ellis, Branson's girlfriend, had been an enjoyable challenge for Tom Newman, but stealing away Kristen Tomassi, Branson's bride-to-be, on the eve of their wedding was ecstasy. In the three weeks before the wedding, while working with Newman in the manor, Kristen, a sexually adventurous girl, had focused on the rough diamond.

Artistic, purposeful and coolly sophisticated in a manner still unknown among British girls, the American blonde represented a trophy for Branson. Chasing women was for Branson similar to chasing business, part of the great game in his consuming competitiveness. After bumping into Kristen in a bedroom at his Oxfordshire mansion, Branson decided to pounce immediately. Nothing, he had absorbed from his mother, was unobtainable. Racing in his own car after the woman as she and her boyfriend drove back to London, Branson had lured her to a meeting and soon after moved her on to his houseboat.

Newman judged that Kristen, the daughter of an American business executive, had fallen for Branson's status and wealth rather than eternal love. Branson, Newman believed, was similarly deluded. On the night before the stylish wedding at the manor, Newman and Kristen had a raucous sexual fling. Suitably, one session was across the bonnet of Newman's green Bentley, bought by Branson for £1,000 and parked by The Ship public house. The following morning, 22 July 1972, Kristen smiled serenely to about three hundred guests dressed in hired, ill-fitting morning suits, top hats and flowing dresses. Most had barely recovered from a riotous dinner in a local hotel the previous evening and wilfully indulged at the reception in the frenetic fun of bun fights and pranks.

After the honeymoon in Mexico, Branson moved from the houseboat to a three-storey Victorian house in Denbigh Terrace, Notting

Hill, bought from Peter Cook with the help of an £80,000 mortgage provided by Coutts bank. Branson's ability to meet the mortgage payments bewildered his employees whose salaries in South Wharf Road, after an unpleasant row, had just been increased from £12 to £15 a week. Branson constantly described his salary as 'modest', and Virgin's first registered accounts disclosed Branson's annual income as £1,820. His employees assumed that he benefited from a secret source of money.

Kristen Tomassi's passion for Newman had developed while he mixed and remixed the tracks of over twenty different instruments of an unusual forty minutes of music composed by Mike Oldfield, a diffident guitarist whose handsome looks belied a troubled personality. Newman and Simon Draper's excitement about Oldfield's extraordinary composition washed over Branson. To an unmusical businessman, Oldfield's forty-minute track without a song was difficult to appreciate. Branson's indifference was shared by every established record producer. All of them had rejected Oldfield. 'Why don't we produce Oldfield?' asked Simon Draper. 'We have nothing to lose.' Draper's suggestion that Virgin produce the manor's first record, Branson appreciated, was risk free. Failure would cost nothing. Branson's virtue was his willingness to gamble if the financial risk was minimal.

Taking a standard record company contract, Branson added a refinement. Oldfield was contracted for a decade's work at the low 5 per cent royalty fee and, acting simultaneously as Oldfield's agent and manager, Branson tilted the contract further in his own favour by paying Virgin an additional 20 per cent of Oldfield's income for ten albums. 'We'll put Oldfield on £20 a week,' Branson told a friend, 'like me and all the other Virgin employees.' No one challenged Branson's pretension to earn just £20 per week.

'It's got to have words,' Branson urged Draper and Newman. 'Everyone says that records without a song don't sell.'

'No way,' replied the two men who by spring 1973 had developed what they had named *Tubular Bells* into a polished composition. Branson relented. From his new offices in Vernon Yard, Notting Hill, he was hectically marketing Virgin's first record. To increase his profits, he had retained all the rights. *Tubular Bells* had developed into his personal challenge to the established record corporations. Brashly, he invited the DJs and critics to dinner on his houseboat to

29

preview the new record. The unusual venue gave his sales performance unique style. Among those persuaded was John Peel, who a
few days later devoted his entire programme on Radio One to the
record. His audience was ecstatic. Overnight, thanks to Peel and
others, Branson owned Britain's best-selling album of 1973. The
success was spectacular. Daily, tens of thousands of pounds poured
into Virgin's account. Atlantic Records, after buying the American
rights for $750,000, sold the music to Hollywood as the soundtrack
of the film *The Exorcist*. Branson's personal wealth was assured. Some
would subsequently carp that *Tubular Bells* effortlessly fell into Branson's lap, but that reflected their naivety. Flair and energy had created
the circumstances.

At twenty-three, Branson was a millionaire. Wealth tortured many
in that socialist era but Branson's conscience was untroubled. He
seized the moment to develop a formula for survival and success.
Previously, the mystery about Branson's finances was his fearless
accumulation of debt. The new mystery was the cloak of secrecy he
cast over his business and personal wealth. To disguise his ambitions
from his low-paid employees he plotted a strategy to protect his new
fortune from taxation and future creditors. Although he would boast,
'we still paid ourselves tiny wages', the whole picture was different.

On the advice of his father, and against the background of family
trusts, he sought the help of Robert Maas of Harbottle and Lewis,
his solicitors, to establish his first offshore trust in the Channel Islands.
Hundreds of thousands of pounds of royalties received for both *Tubular Bells* and the use of the Virgin logo, a newly registered trademark,
were being deposited in the offshore trust. Ray Kite, the logo's
designer commissioned by Simon Draper, was paid £250 out of
Virgin's fee of £2,000 and received no further royalty. (Branson's
subsequent account about casually seeing a sketch of the logo drawn
on the back of a serviette while passing through a dining room seems
to be mistaken.) Beyond the view of the Inland Revenue and his
growing Virgin family, Branson, Draper and Powell, the elite, could
discreetly accumulate and manage their millions. Yet despite their
legality, Branson's trusts did arouse suspicions.

Taxes could only be avoided under British law if Branson, as a
British resident, did not influence the management of the trusts. Yet
Branson would speak of his 'family trusts' and enigmatically assure
banks and business partners that the trustees would financially support

his business ventures, appearing to call into question the trustees' independence.

After taking advice as to how he could conceal his fortune from the Inland Revenue, Branson's next step was to reinforce his camouflage from his employees. Austerity was introduced to suggest poverty and to protect his wealth. He expressed a new dislike of expensive cars and clothes. The second-hand Bentleys bought by Virgin for Tom Newman and others were sold. The patriarch, however, discovered that some Virgin employees were becoming jaundiced by the fraying façade of the family's equality.

To capitalise on his success, Branson had become immersed in the millionaire's schedule of international travel and power lunches to negotiate mega-deals with major record companies. He was unaware of his staff's complaints about low wages. 'They want to join a trade union, Richard,' revealed a secretary after a return to London. Horrified by visions of the constant trade union strife ravaging Britain, Branson rushed to his employees' meeting and burst into tears. 'Why are you so interested in money?' he asked, presenting himself as a victim of their demands. The millionaire's question only temporarily silenced his confused audience.

'Do you know how much a pint of milk costs, Richard?' asked Sian Davis, the director of Virgin Records publicity department.

'No,' he replied sheepishly.

'You live on another planet. We need money to live.'

'We've got no money,' pleaded Branson, tears running down his cheeks. His manner reinforced the impression of equality and poverty. Richard, the capo of his family, was giving everyone a chance of their lifetime, so long as they obeyed his rules. The threat dissolved. No one was inclined to contradict the source of so much fun and few appreciated the sharp variation in incomes between the ordinary employees and the inner circle.

Entry into the cabal was biased in favour of former public schoolboys. By accident rather than intention, that selection automatically excluded the racial minorities. Branson's social background and life had not included Jews, blacks or Arabs as intimates. Rather the capo was attracted to like-minded people from a similar mould. The result was reflected in the employees' contractual relationships with Virgin.

For Steve Lewis, a state-educated Jew negotiating publishing rights for music which became the seedcorn of Branson's future fortune, entry to the cabal was barred. Lewis was welcome to dedicate his life to enhance Virgin's fortune by accumulating the ownership of publishing rights in popular music and managing the record company, but he could expect nothing more than appreciation and his salary. Branson appeared to be unaware of the insensitivity of jotting on his notepad under the name Arthur Indursky, a famous New York lawyer, the word 'Jewish'. Branson, Lewis accepted, was not anti-Semitic but merely ignorant of those who lived their lives outside the realm of the Jags and judges inhabiting Surrey and Stowe.

Branson's appreciation of Tom Newman and Simon Draper was expressed by giving each stakes in different Virgin companies. Newman's stake was in the studio at the manor; Draper's in Virgin Records. Both shareholdings were potentially worthless since their value was determined by Virgin's holding company which Branson and Nik Powell controlled. Nothing was needlessly given away. Branson's loyalty was restricted to those aware of his financial secrets, especially to Ken Berry, a skilled accounts clerk promoted to Branson's personal assistant. For the rest, Branson evinced no sense of obligation. In the process of rapid self-education, his canon tolerated nothing else.

Unlike Chris Blackwell, a rival independent who owned Island Records, Branson spent limited time in the studios with artists and appeared less concerned than Blackwell about his artists' lives. His pleasure was the deal: signing artists as fast as possible, even if they were contracted to his competitors. Island Records was a first target. Having pondered whether Bob Marley could be lured, he settled on Peter Tosh. After that deal, Alison Short, his secretary, would say someone punched Branson on the nose in fury, and he faced threats on his houseboat from G. T. Rollins, a musician, over a payment of £2,000. 'You shouldn't go taking other people's acts,' advised Tom Newman. Branson laughed. Poaching was, he replied, acceptable. In the tough rock world, whatever the rights and wrongs, he would fight with the best. Breaking into the big league required risks and he was happy to gamble over his limits, offering huge sums of money which he did not possess. Famous groups – 10cc, The Who, Pink Floyd, the Boomtown Rats and finally the Rolling Stones – were offered fortunes to switch to Virgin but every agent rejected Branson's money. Even his £3.5 million bid for the Stones was spurned. Virgin was too small and failed to inspire confidence. Rejection, however, never embarrassed Branson; it was his incentive to try harder. Outdoing others was the criterion for his life as Jacques Kerner, his French distributor, discovered.

Branson flew to Paris for dinner with Kerner. The impatient tycoon wanted to expand Virgin's distribution in France. At the dinner, Kerner introduced Branson to Patrick Zelnick, his employee with responsibility for Virgin's sales. 'He's just what I need,' thought Branson about Kerner's salesman. One month later, Branson hired Zelnick. 'When you're invited for dinner,' complained his outraged French host, 'you're not meant to walk away with the cutlery.' Branson was chuffed. When people screamed 'foul' he felt pleasure.

By 1976, Branson's hyperactive deal-making, exclusively financed by *Tubular Bells*, had expanded the Virgin empire into more record shops, the creation of Virgin Rags, a putative national clothes chain, Duveens, a restaurant in Notting Hill Gate, a sandwich delivery service, a health-food megastore, Virgin pubs and the sale of hi-fi systems. Juggling many balls, Branson hoped, would produce a major success. His business philosophy was crystallising. 'With many companies we start,' he later explained, 'we don't even do the figures in advance. We just feel that there's room in the market or a need for something and we'll get it going. We try to make the figures work out after the event.' The flaw was his accelerating debt. He had proven dynamism but not business acumen. His shotgun approach exposed an inability to focus on the detailed management of businesses he did not understand and his lack of strategy was perilous.

Virgin's costs were growing and in the developing recession of the mid 1970s its income was dwindling. Branson faced a cash and a commercial crisis. His gambling instinct was to double and redouble his stake to escape from trouble but the trading conditions were dire. Under the Labour government, the British economy was suffering record inflation and high unemployment. To survive, Branson needed to close down the loss-making businesses and dismiss unprofitable artists.

Sitting alternately with Draper, Varnom and others in the cramped offices in Vernon Yard and on the houseboat, he repeatedly groaned as he had eight years earlier, 'What can we do?' Pop and rock music had fallen into the doldrums. Virgin offered nothing to the new teenagers whose latest passion was Punk. His unsuccessful expansive frenzy revealed the unpalatable truth that Virgin was a one-act show relying on the Big One – *Tubular Bells* – and that Branson did not possess a profitable spread of original music.

The distinction between the star players in business and the also-rans is their ability to overcome the challenges of adversity to avoid sinking into oblivion. Branson's gift was to shrug off despair and find an epiphany. While his cabal and employees winced in trepidation, he pondered the outrageous to survive. 'We need the Pistols,' he eventually declared.

In summer 1976, Simon Draper had condemned the Sex Pistols, four violent and drug-addicted hooligans with spiked, dyed hair, dressed in ripped leather, as musically bankrupt. Branson had followed his cousin's advice and walked away from signing an agreement with Malcolm McLaren, the Pistols' thirty-two-year-old manager. McLaren was not disappointed. Renowned for his anarchic artistry and outlandish mastery of pop culture which had created the Pistols' grotesque appearance, he branded Branson a philistine. His suspicions had been fuelled by the story of a meeting on Branson's houseboat with Jake Rivera, an agent representing Elvis Costello and the Attractions. To successfully contract the group, Branson turned on his customary charm: 'I loved your last album.'

'What was your favourite track?' asked Rivera mischievously.

Branson was dumbstruck. His ignorance was exposed. The story of his humiliation raced around London. McLaren's opinion of Branson was so low that he suspected Branson might even consider selling bootleg records of Virgin's own artists.

For their first record, 'Anarchy in the UK', the Pistols contracted instead with EMI. In December 1976, Branson watched television bewitched by the stream of drunken expletives used by the Pistols to prove their notoriety and promote their record. Their violence was headline news. It was just what Branson required. But a hurried agreement the following morning by Leslie Hill, EMI's embarrassed managing director, to transfer the group to Virgin ended abruptly. McLaren had agreed with Branson to 'be in your office this afternoon' to discuss the transfer but he never arrived. However, five months later, in May 1977, McLaren finally arrived in Denbigh Terrace with Steven Fisher, his lawyer.

The Sex Pistols needed a record company and Virgin needed a sensation. McLaren was not surprised by the absence of any records in Branson's house except for one Reader's Digest collection of Mozart, a present from Ted. 'We want someone who's going to run with us,' said McLaren. 'It'll be hair-raising, but it'll be fun.' Branson smiled. 'Sex' in all its guises was richly exploitable. He traded on other people's ideas. 'I'm just piggy-backing,' he would later admit. McLaren's creation offered a chance of financial salvation.

'Those two are loathsome,' Branson told John Varnom after McLaren and Fisher departed. 'They're loathsome,' he repeated with vehemence. 'Loathsome!'

'Richard's utterly over the top,' thought Varnom, who normally shared Branson's prejudices. Branson's loyal acolyte concluded that he had witnessed the clash of two mutually intolerant spin-masters. However loathsome, Virgin and the Pistols were yoked together to ridicule the monarchy.

'We need something,' mumbled Branson. Varnom's sophisticated sense of mischief, he hoped, would contrive an outrageous prank to promote the Pistols new record, 'God Save the Queen'. The record was a vicious curse at the monarch designed to coincide with the nation's extensive Silver Jubilee celebrations. Creating chaos for publicity was commercially vital.

At 4 p.m. on 7 June 1977 Varnom arrived at Westminster pier to hire *The Elizabethan*, a Thames cruiser.

'It's not for those Punks?' asked the boatman.

'No,' replied Varnom, 'it's for a boring German synthesiser band.'

Thirty minutes later, the taxis arrived with the Pistols, their managers and Branson. 'Just sail past the Houses of Parliament,' ordered Branson.

'It's going to be sensational,' laughed Varnom.

'Great,' bubbled Branson. His imagination raced. Pranks were always exciting but this was special. Earning money by insulting the Establishment and basking in celebrity was a blissful combination. As the cruiser neared the Palace of Westminster, the curses of the four drugged and drunken Pistols blared from loudspeakers across the river towards the Houses of Parliament. The result was better than Branson could have imagined. Police boarded the cruiser, ordered that it return to the pier and, amid screams and fights, arrested several people. Branson held back until the mêlée was over and then briefed the newspapers. Chortling at the anticipated publicity, Branson led the Virgin cabal to a Greek restaurant to celebrate. The evening ended with everyone smoking marijuana supplied by the restaurant. Irreverence was certain to restore Virgin's fortunes.

'Fantastic,' screeched Branson reading the universal disgust expressed in the newspaper headlines the following morning. Publicity meant soaring sales and guaranteed profits. He was delighted to attract more headlines by attesting in court later that day to McLaren's good character. Conflict and controversy, he knew, would be even more profitable if he positioned himself as the victim: the helpless innocent fighting for the common good. By stoking the Pistols' notoriety, he would push their second record 'Never Mind the Bollocks' up the charts. 'It was a political statement,' he told the reporters outside the court. 'Those arrested are all victims of the system.'

The only victim was Malcolm McLaren. The agent was the victim of Branson's imposition of an unusually advantageous contract. McLaren had made a fatal error which many mixing with Branson over the years would commit. Coolly devoid of attachment to the music, Branson had viewed the Pistols' contract as a vehicle to earn money. He had planned McLaren's entry into his life, and his exit. In the eagerness to find a record label after EMI terminated the Pistols contract, McLaren had failed to carefully examine the details of the agreements which he had signed. As the Pistols disintegrated amid debauchery, disputes, murder and suicide, McLaren discovered that Branson, to secure his investment, had excluded him from the management of the surviving group. 'He's a dangerous man in court,' was Steven Fisher's brief assessment. Rushing to court in August 1978 to protect his property, McLaren found himself outclassed by his partner. His losses were Branson's profits, financial and tactical. The victor understood the commercial advantage of using the courts. It was part of the formula for survival and success.

During that period, Branson was also 'piggybacking' on the vogue for reggae music and welcomed the chance to distribute Atra records, a black label owned by Brent Clarke, a Caribbean. Reggae records had become profitable in Nigeria and Branson was particularly interested in Keith Hudson, a singer contracted to Clarke. By 1976, Clarke suspected that Branson might try to lift Hudson and feared that Virgin's accounts of Atra sales were inaccurate. A crude check of how many records Virgin had sold suggested discrepancies. 'You owe us money,' Brent Clarke told the Virgin accountants to no response. Branson preferred not to take Clarke's telephone calls. Irritated, Brent and his brother Sebastian called at Branson's home. The businessman was assaulted and fled.

Branson was terrified. In agitated tones, he confessed to Al Clark, his sophisticated publicist, 'I escaped with my life.' To his closest employees, Branson appeared to be shaken and deflated by the rancour. But Branson was not prepared to concede defeat.

After complaining to the police, Branson arranged to meet the brothers at the Back-a-Yard café on the Portobello Road. In what seemed to be a stilted conversation, the brothers explained their case unaware that Branson was carrying a tape recorder provided by the police officers. After thirty minutes, a group of policemen charged into the café and arrested the brothers. Both were accused of demanding money with menaces. 'You're only accepting his word,' shouted Sebastian Clarke, 'because he's white and we're black.' Branson smiled but by the time he arrived at the Old Bailey to testify, he seemed uninterested in the case. His testimony was rejected by the jury and the Clarkes were acquitted. The brothers' euphoria was tempered by their financial plight. By then, Clarke's business was bankrupt.

The ringmaster did not fear any criticism from his cabal. Most were unaware of the entrapment and prosecution of the Clarkes. In the social and economic misery created by the Labour government, Virgin was a sanctuary where music and enjoyment were a lifestyle. Those gathered around Branson were innocent and even unconcerned about his lurches from persecutor to poacher to self-professed victim. Virgin's employees were simply grateful to the catalyst for their licence to play. Branson himself was, it appeared, single-handedly preoccupied to win the battle for financial survival.

Emboldened by his restored finances, Branson was searching for new acquisitions. Established stars were offered huge amounts to switch allegiance. The Marchess group, negotiating with Dave Robinson of Stiff Records, were told by Branson, 'I'll pay you double whatever Robinson is offering.' *Melody Maker* featured his announcement that Devo, an American new wave band contracted to Warner Brothers, had signed with Virgin. The announcement prompted Warner Brothers to issue a writ seeking to restrain Virgin from inducing a breach of contract and infringing Warner's copyright. The articled clerk employed to deliver the writ found Branson in bed with two girls. Five weeks later, Warner Brothers was awarded an injunction. 'I just want you to know,' smiled Branson at the end of the trial, 'that you've hung me on a precedent set by my grandfather.' In 1938, Warner's lawyers discovered, Judge Branson had found against Bette Davis, the actress, in similar circumstances. His calm acceptance of defeat was impressive. Similar to his fearless approach to money and debt, Branson's undaunted use of the law ranked him as a potential big player.

'Injunct them,' he announced in a humourless voice back on the houseboat. Rough Trade, he discovered, a small distributor of records, was selling bootlegs of a Virgin recording. 'I'm going to get them. Put out a press release and call Harbottle's,' he ordered his assistant. The organiser of the Sex Pistols antics had forgotten that Virgin Records owed its existence partly to selling bootlegs. 'Rough Trade will be ruined,' his adviser mentioned. Branson paused. He gazed at his two other shabbily furnished barges moored nearby, *The Arthur* for parties and another houseboat as a private bolt-hole. He enjoyed the barges' discreet testaments to his wealth. 'It's hardly good publicity,' continued his adviser, 'when *The Sunday Times* is preparing its first profile of you.' 'Okay,' agreed Branson reluctantly. The writ was not issued. His attention had switched to *The Sunday Times'* interview. He would, he decided, meet the journalist in jeans and barefoot on the houseboat.

The backdrop of Little Venice for a hippie millionaire was brilliant theatre for impressionable journalists and he agreed to meet only the most susceptible. He encouraged profiles of himself as the genial, happy-go-lucky face of capitalism, a 'man of the future', disguising his workaholic craving for success with the informal backdrop of his humble home. His genius was to disarm any accusations of disingenuity. A handful of sceptics were silenced by his unaffected warmth and the hilarious anecdotes repeated among his loyal employees about Branson's parties and pranks, and about the spectacular antics performed on the unsuspecting on April Fool's Day. Virgin's association with fun won Branson admirers but, like so many clowns performing in the public arena, there were signs of the conductor's deep-rooted unease.

A recent Branson performance – sitting naked on the roof of the manor to attract the attention of a TV cameraman away from XTC playing below to one hundred employees and friends – had aroused embarrassment but he had been oblivious to his guests' sentiment. Frequently, he thrust his nudity and sexuality into the public arena. All his staff, he was certain, were enthralled by his regular bulletins to anyone passing through the office about his painful circumcision conducted after a misdiagnosed illness; and he delighted in the playground humour of secretaries leaving pornography on his desk or flashing their naked breasts. Attracting attention had become a balm to fill the vacuum of a failing marriage evident by the relationships which both he and Kristen were enjoying with others.

The marriage reached its crisis on his houseboat at the end of a drunken meal cooked by Kristen. Their guests, Kevin Ayers, an older, sophisticated rock musician, and Cyrille, his wife, had met Branson at a party, 'a rich middle-class affair with all the usual drink, drugs and rock and roll', recalled Ayers. After the meal, Ayers offered the Bransons cocaine. Taking drugs was not unusual for Branson: he had used marijuana and LSD, and cocaine might have been a predictable progression, although twenty years later Branson would deny taking the drug. Soon after, Ayers disappeared with Kristen into the bedroom while Branson stayed with Cyrille. Each would claim that the other partners had sex together but deny the same about themselves. Cyrille, however, complained afterwards, 'Branson was so cheap, the bastard wouldn't even pay my taxi fare home'; while Kevin Ayers delighted in stealing Kristen to embark on a long relationship. 'Branson exploded,' chortled Ayers later. 'It's pathological because he can't stand losing. For a year, [Branson] kept up a battery of letters, telephone calls and chases across Europe pleading, "How can you leave me?"' Branson loathed rejection. His unrelenting pressure to encourage his wife's sense of guilt reflected the pain of his humiliation. At a concert in Hyde Park where Ayers was playing, Branson confronted the musician aggressively. 'How could you do this to a friend, stealing my wife?' he exploded, castigating Ayers as an enemy. Branson had forgotten that originally he had lured Kristen from another man.

Branson was lonely. Unsatisfied in his own company, he often telephoned Simon Draper late at night to discuss business or arranged breakfast conferences in Draper's home in Holland Park for ten people. At weekends, he would drive to Draper's country home, knowing that his cousin had a dinner party to which he was not invited, and impose himself. To avoid a moment's solitude, he invited his employees to his mother's house in Majorca. Branson demanded full attention from the Virgin family. He received nothing less. Few rejected their employer's summons.

Solace was found among his employees. One-night stands with secretaries were the topic of constant gossip in his office about the 'passing flavour'. Pretty young women were the common currency in the music world and the young, unmarried millionaire who enjoyed partying was a magnet for those seeking fun. Most remained discreet about their relationships. Branson was kind and won the women's respect. Despite the temptation of money, few were inclined to kiss-and-tell.

But there was talk about Branson's strange sexual antics. Cross-dressing appeared to be a passion, suggesting something unusually important about Branson's single homosexual experience soon after his arrival at Stowe. In adulthood, he happily dropped his trousers at parties to reveal fishnet stockings and lacy suspenders; he dressed in women's clothes and allowed himself to be photographed kissing a man; he performed solo drag acts on the dance floor; and he cavorted naked covered in cranberry sauce. 'He had this thing at parties,' recalled Carol Wilson, a secretary, 'of exposing himself all over the place.' Alison Short, an assistant, was puzzled why he dressed as a woman and was 'always throwing water over my breasts and rubbing me down'. Regardless of whatever clothes he was wearing, he could rarely resist propositioning women, even those attached to other men. Like a caricature on a seaside postcard, he drooled over big breasted women and few were more amazed by his habit than Tom Newman, the rock guitarist, who stood at the bar of the War-wick Castle, a public house in Maida Vale, with Maggie Russell, his attractive friend, amused by Branson's unsuccessful attempt to poach. But in 1978, after two years as a bachelor, his fortunes changed.

In starkly similar circumstances to his introduction to his first wife at the manor, he spotted Joan Templeman. The Roman Catholic daughter of a Glasgow carpenter, Templeman had been married for twelve years to Ronnie Leahy, a musician in Stone the Crows whom she had accompanied to a recording at the manor. Leahy would say that the marriage was solid and his wife displayed no hint of unhappiness. Yet Branson was smitten by the Notting Hill shop assistant. The opportunity so close to his home and office was too good to miss. Although upset by Tom Newman seducing his girlfriend,

Mundy Ellis, and his wife, and distraught that Kevin Ayers had taken Kristen, he was prepared to entice Joan Templeman, a married woman, by siege.

In Branson's mind, Joan Templeman, five years older than himself and whose two brothers were well known in local pubs, was ideal. Besides her good looks, she was socially and intellectually unthreatening, comfortably domestic and yet cool. Whenever Leahy was on tour, Branson sought invitations to dinner parties to meet his quarry. Eventually, his persistence was rewarded. Although in late 1977 Branson promised Leahy that he would leave Joan alone for three months to allow the couple to attempt reconciliation in New York, he reneged and flew over, untroubled by Leahy's distress.

Manhattan was cold and to celebrate their decision to live together, the owner of Virgin headed for the sun in the Virgin Islands. In Branson's version, he whisked his true love around the idyllic islands on a trip financed by an estate agent to discover his paradise called Necker, an isolated lump of barren rock lacking water, people and animals. Branson would tell friends that the estate agent's price was £3 million but that he paid just £180,000 to Lord Cobham, the owner. The peer, however, would deny owning the island – Necker was owned by a trust – or demanding £3 million. Branson's self-esteem was always bolstered by his stories of success. The purchase of Necker imposed a legal commitment to spend a large sum to build a house on the island and provide a water supply. His enthusiasm coincided with his staff, earning by then about £40 per week, voicing fears of unemployment because his company was once again on the verge of bankruptcy.

The following year, 1979, Branson knew that Virgin was 'virtually bust' yet, confident about his private finances in the Channel Islands trusts, he bought during the next two years the Roof Gardens in Kensington and Heaven, a popular gay nightclub under Charing Cross Station, using interest-free loans from brewers. 'Those gays are so neat and tidy,' he mimicked. Owning clubs excited Branson. He could be the host of a perpetual party, they were useful buttresses for the music business, and Virgin would have a permanent cash flow as a smokescreen against his return to debt. The reappearance of that albatross was the climax of a familiar pattern.

The windfall from the Pistols, the latest Big One, had financed expansion into films, video-editing suites, property, the Venue nightclub, Reggae singers in Jamaica and a music business in America. All of those ventures had turned Virgin's pre-tax profits of £400,000 in 1977 and £500,000 in 1978 into a projected £1 million loss in 1980. Branson was under pressure from Coutts to repay his debts or declare bankruptcy. Nearly everything, he lamented to his staff, would be offered for sale. To keep up appearances, he sold Denbigh Terrace and moved back on to the *Duende*, his houseboat.

Gossip in the pop world about Virgin's closures and staff dismissals was reported in the *New Musical Express*. Branson was horrified. The truth about Virgin's financial plight, he feared, would deter Coutts from continuing their loans. His friendly and unruffled upper-class manner, he trusted, would disarm the suspicious. With equal effectiveness his approach charmed journalists, bankers and on occasion even the police. Twice he had been stopped for speeding along the M4 with John Varnom. On both occasions, to escape prosecution, Branson encouraged Varnom to persuade the police that he was seriously ill and allow the trusting officers to escort Branson's Volvo to the nearest hospital. Varnom continued his performance until the police had disappeared. On another occasion, Branson produced a driving licence to the police belonging to someone else and successfully escaped conviction. Occasionally, he denied he was driving his white Mini, laughing 'The police couldn't have seen me because the car's got blacked-out windows.' His similarly fanciful tales to his bankers and staff about Virgin's finances, relayed in his casual style, were protected by similar black-outs and compartmentalisation. Although he knew that Virgin had 'no money', he denied that the company was in financial difficulties. In adversity his resilience and methods were remarkable. *New Musical Express* was threatened with a writ if the magazine did not publish a correction, whatever truth there may have been in the original article.

Rebutting Branson's denials had become complicated. Under the guise of encouraging individual entrepreneurship, Virgin's different businesses had been spread in small offices around London, preventing his employees understanding his organisation and blurring his juggling of money between companies. In managing his finances, Branson relied partially upon Chris Craib, a Virgin accountant, to follow his directions on both the administration of his funds and the valuation of his assets to secure ever higher loans from the banks. 'We've spent so much on these things,' he lambasted the accountant, referring to all the new business he had accumulated by 1981. 'Surely you can get higher valuations. They're worth a lot more.' 'Nothing more we can do,' replied Craib, unable to produce the values required to persuade the banks to provide extra loans. To escape that squeeze, Branson's helpline was his fortune secretly accumulating since 1973 in offshore trusts. Although by law, tax-free trusts could not be used under Branson's direction, he had little problem persuading the trustees to provide guarantees for a £1 million loan to Virgin from the Bank of Nova Scotia. Virgin was again saved but the lifeline fractured Virgin's benevolent character. 'The men in suits have arrived,' Chris Stylianou muttered as staff and artists were dismissed, property was sold and costs were cut during that year.

Among the minor casualties was Nicholas James of Saccone and Speed, a wine supplier and friend from Stowe who could not recover thousands of pounds from Duveens, Branson's failed restaurant. 'I could always get through to Richard until I asked him for my money,' James would complain. 'Then he disappeared forever.'

Branson easily lost his sentiment for those no longer deemed valuable to his fortunes. Tom Newman, the whisky-loving recording manager, was deemed dispensable and his stormy departure, abandoning his share options in the manor, passed unmourned.

The major casualty in 1981 was Branson's relationship with Nik Powell. Branson's childhood friend urged prudence by terminating the contracts with Virgin's 'marginal' groups, the Human League and Phil Collins. 'Over my dead body,' snapped Simon Draper.

'You just spend all the money I save in the shops,' countered Powell as the temperature rose. Powell was too cautious, Branson concluded. He had lost his way. The triangular relationship was irreparably fractured.

In Branson's new world, accountability to anyone was an intolerable shackle. The 'mumbling pullover' as he had become known to Varnom, enjoyed working in a team only if he was captain. Since Powell, despite their friendship and partnership, refused to compliantly follow, he was unacceptable. The partnership, they agreed, should be dissolved. 'He's on his way,' Branson told Draper, a phrase frequently used to describe excluded members of the family. 'Nik had no particular skills to contribute to the company as it was at that stage,' was Branson's less than affectionate summary. But he was correct. His savvy outclassed his friend's.

The unresolved issue was the value of Powell's 40 per cent share of what Branson called a 'busted company'. In the final act of severance, even with his oldest friend, Branson wanted to feel that he was the winner.

Under Branson's and Powell's direction to reduce taxes, the accountants had minimised Virgin's profits and had accumulated huge losses which were, for outsiders, as unquantifiable as the group's assets. Not included under the rules of accountancy was the value of Virgin's music catalogue and the rights to the music and records owned by Virgin. Those rights, Branson realised, were worth unquantified millions. Additionally, there was the secret accumulation of money in their offshore trusts which remained unmentioned in Virgin's accounts. Under Branson's guidance, it was finally agreed that Powell would receive £1 million in cash and some assets. Branson's problem was producing £1 million in a way which his accountants would find acceptable.

Until 1973, Branson had been officially earning just £20 per week. Thereafter, his annual salary had been about £2,000. Producing £1 million from his own resources as declared to the Inland Revenue was impossible. So instead he borrowed money guaranteed by the trusts for a transaction which was senseless without Branson's private knowledge of Virgin's true value.

The divorce was finalised on the *Duende*. The two school friends sat across a round table. Between them was Heimi Lehrer, a solicitor employed by Virgin since 1973 as their property specialist. Barely a word was spoken as the signatures were scribbled. For Branson it was an unemotional moment. The division of the business, he believed, was a limited risk. His demeanour was a disorienting blend of innocence and cunning. Branson did not appear sad about the divorce from his childhood friend. Powell would be airbrushed into oblivion. The gap-toothed grin, suggesting a heart of gold, was replaced by a hard-fixed stare. 'We'll trade out of trouble,' the thirty-one year old quipped. Embracing his gambler's gospel, every crisis was an opportunity and Powell's departure left Branson with total ownership.

One of the few relationships he worked hard to protect was with Mike Oldfield. That was endangered by Tom Newman's incitement for separation. 'You've got a lousy contract,' the disgruntled producer of *Tubular Bells* advised Oldfield. 'You should break from Virgin.'

Oldfield's ultimatum terrified Branson. The musician was once again Virgin's major source of income. 'We'll give you a better deal,' pleaded Branson with the graceless recluse, 'even though we're nearly bust.' Eventually, Oldfield succumbed. The continuing income from *Tubular Bells* was Branson's lifeline.

Just one year later, in 1981, Branson's risk paid off. Thanks to Simon Draper and Steve Lewis, Virgin Music produced nine hits to repay all the company's debts. In a decade of honeymoons, divorces and crisis, he could reflect, the Big Ones had provided singular lifelines until the good times returned. Fortunately, his friendly manner had disguised his rough tactics. Browbeating the *New Musical Express* about his financial crisis, he smiled, was justified by his survival.

4

Frustrations

'I can't find the bathroom,' explained Richard Branson. 'Could you come to my bedroom and help me find it?' At about 2 a.m. in early February 1982 in the Hotel Esmeralda in Paris, Branson had just telephoned the nearby bedroom occupied by Suzie McKenzie. The married journalist was puzzled. After all, Branson had occupied the same room for two nights and over dinner at Juliens, a fish restaurant, he had boasted, while noisily slurping a bowl of mussels, 'I've never lost a night's sleep in my life.' She paused. Branson's breathing was suggestive. He had not been as much fun as she had imagined. Certainly he was exceptional – levering each mussel out of its shell with a soup spoon was bizarre – but he remained enigmatic rather than engaging. 'I'll be right over,' she said.

'Here it is,' she announced. 'It's behind this door.' McKenzie smiled. Branson, she decided, was certainly not her type. She walked out. Branson was irked. Poaching McKenzie, he had thought, would be no different from the capture of Kristen and Joan. But attracting intelligent women, he regretted, was difficult. Sophisticated women like McKenzie castigated him as unimpressive and sexually unenticing. 'A vacuum,' she later declared. Branson found McKenzie's disdain inexplicable since admiring secretaries and rock groupies swooned about 'Richard's genius', and more journalists than ever were calling for interviews.

Branson had spotted McKenzie at a party which he hosted in early 1981 at his parents' new house in Surrey. His guests were the staff of *Event*, a new London listings magazine which he had launched to compete with *Time Out*. Ignoring Joan's reprimands about eating with his fingers, drinking other people's wine and pulling cigarettes from guests for a puff, he tried especially hard to ingratiate himself with his new employees. Dressed elegantly, McKenzie had been standing near the pool. Branson manoeuvred himself nearby. Her splash was loud and his laughter was electrifying. Pulling her out-stretched hand, he helped his victim on to the side. Fiercely, he rubbed the woman dry. Some would even swear that he screamed, 'Oh you are saucy!' as he joyfully rubbed her breasts and thighs.

Ignoring her embarrassment, Branson had invited the journalist to co-host business lunches on the houseboat. As she served lumpy minced meat and warm Hock, Branson encouraged his visitors dressed in suits to believe that McKenzie was his girlfriend, if only to deflect attention from their demands for money and their com-plaints about his business ethics. Branson had received writs from Mike Oldfield and Sting, and was embroiled in an acrimonious dis-pute with Carol Wilson, Virgin's successful talent scout, who accused Branson of not signing an agreed employment contract. 'I don't like this Sting litigation,' Branson confessed to McKenzie. 'I feel bad about it.' He was baffled, he continued, why Dire Straits, the Boom Town Rats and Bob Geldorf had all rejected Virgin's contracts. Surely, he asked rhetorically, they should have been susceptible because he was the amiable alternative to the dull suits. But if Bran-son's admissions of failure were designed to inspire McKenzie's sym-pathy he was to be disappointed. McKenzie felt she was the target of Branson's manipulation. But she had misjudged the man. Despite the setbacks, Branson could still conjure success.

Branson's rejection of Nik Powell's arguments one year earlier had proved justified. Virgin's profits in 1981, after selling over two million albums of Phil Collins and the Human League, were £1.5 million compared to the previous year's £900,000 loss. His reviving fortunes encouraged the very self-confidence which alienated many of the journalists whom he had hired for *Event*.

'You're all bluster, and you don't listen,' Pearce Marchbank accused Branson. The anger of *Event*'s editor caused the *Duende* to pitch on the motionless canal. 'You're a rock and roll egomaniac who doesn't understand that magazines take time.' Six weeks after the launch of the new London listings magazine, *Event*'s circulation was declining. Branson's reductions of the budget had reduced the magazine's size and consequently advertisers were deserting. Branson was unwilling to concede defeat. 'You're bringing Virgin down,' Branson griped to Marchbank. 'Fire forty staff. Now.' His second attempt to publish a magazine as a prelude to becoming a media tycoon was souring.

Like so many publicity-seeking businessmen, Branson had hoped that *Event* would bestow glamour, status and influence. Money, he believed, could buy power. A vicious strike in 1981 at *Time Out*, a unique London listings magazine owned and edited by Tony Elliott, a former friend, had prompted Branson to launch *Event* to both improve his fortune and social status.

Tony Elliott's staff, anti–Establishment journalists resentful of the proprietor's right to manage, had for weeks in early 1981 successfully prevented *Time Out*'s publication. Branson, still irritated by the failure of *Student* magazine, welcomed Elliott's predicament as his good fortune. Elliott had been invited to lunch at Mill End, Branson's new country home near the manor in Oxfordshire. As the lunch drifted into the afternoon and then into the evening, Branson tried to lull his target into a false sense of security. His clumsy social performance, scruffy clothes and appalling table manners, he hoped, would lure Elliott to underestimate his intentions. 'Let me buy 50 per cent of *Time Out*,' Branson offered. Elliott smiled weakly. The predator, he sighed, did not understand. *Time Out*'s staff would dislike Branson even more than him. Branson was suburban. He was no rebel. His pride was to be the anti–intellectual, a trader in the market and a hero for the aspiring working class. He would make matters worse. 'No thanks,' replied Elliott later that night. 'Bollocks,' muttered Branson, unable to conceal the hurt. In his mind, business was like the game of Monopoly he played as a child where he customarily placed, against the rules, two hotels on both Mayfair and Park Lane. Any opponent landing on his property was compelled to surrender immediately. Similarly, the pleasure of Elliott's pain was desired immediately.

'If he won't join me, I'll beat him,' Branson decided. Copying Elliott's idea was effortless and enticing *Time Out*'s staff was the most obvious way to crash fast into the market. There was no hesitation. Pearce Marchbank, *Time Out*'s designer, was his first recruit. 'I want to be editor,' stipulated Marchbank. Since Marchbank could hasten the recruitment of other *Time Out* staff, Branson agreed. 'I want *Event* ready to go in twelve weeks,' Marchbank was ordered. The only hint of interference during those weeks, Marchbank acknowledged, was the prudent delivery of cocaine to keep the staff awake, albeit without Branson's knowledge.

Ten weeks later, on 18 September 1981, Branson was puzzled.

Elliott's fox had outsmarted Branson's lumbering hounds. After locking out the strikers, *Time Out* was relaunched with Mel Brooks on the cover, identical to *Event*'s planned first edition due to appear a few days later. 'He's stolen our idea,' moaned the advocate of competition, before rallying to tell John Varnom, 'Fuck. We're going to win.'

Without warning, on publication day, two weeks later, Branson arrived in *Event*'s editorial offices in Portobello Road with television crews and his growing entourage. *Event* was not simply another magazine to earn money for a businessman but Branson's celebrity launch pad. 'Here's my editor,' he beamed. 'My magazine will be Number One this week,' he purred holding up the slick, hundred-page colour magazine. Repeating his predictions on countless radio and TV programmes during the day, he believed, would guarantee fulfilment of his desires. After all, *Event* looked better than *Time Out* and the media had, thanks to his ceaseless encouragement, warmed to its birth. In the mindset created by his mother, Ricky always got what Ricky wanted.

Every launch, every anniversary in Branson's world, required a party. *Event*'s birth was celebrated at Heaven, his nightclub. 'It'll send the wrong signals,' Marchbank complained. Branson was dismissive. Using Heaven saved money and marketing was his speciality. 'We'll be Number One,' he repeated. 'I know.' Having persuaded ITV to broadcast the launch party live, the fun-loving millionaire – selling to his generation – had conceived an appropriate stunt.

Pranks were often Branson's cure to fill the embarrassing vacuum left by his lack of substantial conversation, especially when he felt under pressure. Branson fulfilled his mother's stricture – 'Ricky do something' – by often vulgar, sometimes hilarious contrivances. Dressing up or undressing completely, screaming from the top of a tent or standing naked in a street covered with raspberry jam, Ricky begged to be the life and soul of his party. To attract attention at *Event*'s launch celebration he contrived a 'drama'. Unsuspecting, Marchbank obeyed Branson's summons to come nearer the television camera. Handsome, witty and sophisticated, the editor possessed qualities which Branson envied. With a huge laugh, the proprietor pushed a cream cake into Marchbank's face. 'Live on TV,' Branson laughed, convinced of the audience's appreciation. Marchbank's reaction was irrelevant.

'Sales are not much good,' Branson complained three weeks later. Marchbank urged patience. 'Magazines aren't records,' he replied. 'You've got to haemorrhage money to make it work.'

Haemorrhaging money, however, was unacceptable. Branson was irritated. In the rock world, a big hit guaranteed an immediate avalanche of profits. The mathematics of profits in publishing required careful calculation and an attention to detail which bored Branson. Keeping budgets tight, 'protecting the downside', was his philosophy. Innovation was anathema because he eschewed unquantifiable risks. His formula was to pick someone else's idea and muscle noisily into the market with a fixed sum of money. His gambles, he believed, were carefully controlled. In the launch of *Event*, his plan had been to replace *Time Out*, not to compete. Gradual development was not an option. He wanted, even expected, immediate success. He had grown to dislike journalists. They were a breed who enjoyed high living at their proprietor's expense.

Branson's solution was shock. Publishing embarrassing exposés about the famous, he hoped, would attract readers. After recruiting staff from *Private Eye*, whose regular ridicules of himself as 'The Boy Genius' he condemned as 'spiteful' and 'slurs', he ordered Al Clark to publish an account about two senior Fleet Street journalists found copulating in public behind a bush. 'But they're the parents of a friend,' protested Clark. Branson was impervious. Most journalists, he assumed, were pliable. 'It's part of life,' he smiled. Intrusion would sell. Clark resigned rather than become involved in unnecessary vilification.

Stepping into the gutter did not rescue sales. Nor did the dispatch of Vanessa, his sister, with her husband Robert Devereux on a horse-drawn coach through London throwing copies of *Event* to passers-by attract any attention. To succeed, *Event* required clarity of purpose and originality. Branson offered neither. 'The budget's cut,' he announced after six weeks, pleased that his crude solution stunned Pearce Marchbank. The following week the editor was fired. A man cleverer than him had been decisively humiliated. The blame for any mistakes was heaped on to others. Accepting his personal responsibility for errors was strenuously avoided by Branson. A succession of editors and declining numbers of staff became the pattern at *Event*. After eight months Branson pondered surrender. As a final throw, he telephoned Elliott late in the evening. 'I'll keep pouring money in until you're finished,' he threatened. 'Will you sell *Time Out?*'

'You don't understand,' replied a slightly drunk Elliott. 'If you bought *Time Out*, the staff wouldn't respect you. It would signal us going down market.'

Soon after, in September 1982, *Event* was abandoned. Branson's ambition had cost nearly £1 million.

The legacy was worse than wounded pride and a pile of debts. Disloyalty, he cursed, had caused the failure. Those deemed by Branson to be culpable were classified as traitors to be punished socially and financially. When they next met at a party, Branson ignored Suzie McKenzie. John Varnom, a loyal founder of the family, was similarly dismissed. 'We'll have to find a new home for you,' Varnom was unceremoniously told as the two men drove together through London. 'Bugger you,' scoffed 'Rasputin' and jumped from Branson's moving car to be practically forgotten by the indifferent driver. Martin Tomkinson, recruited from *Private Eye*, recovered part of his wages only after arriving unexpectedly on Branson's houseboat and refusing to depart unpaid. Pearce Marchbank issued a writ for £7,000 for unpaid wages. Refusing to compromise, Branson arrived in court with an army of lawyers. By the end of the first day's hearing, Marchbank surrendered in the face of unaffordable costs. 'Virgin's hierarchy is a laughably primitive tribe,' moaned Jonathan Meades, another disillusioned ex-recruit, into the wilderness. Branson had purged his organisation but at some cost. After fifteen years of business, he had for the first time created a group of intelligent critics. 'He's always harassing folk to win the best deal,' that scattered group complained. But the army of still-loyal admirers agreed with Branson's self-assessment: 'he doesn't cheat his friends and is generous with employees'. Branson the star, most agreed, was only protecting his reputation. Virgin Music's fortunes continued to soar.

On the insistence of Steve Lewis, Virgin Music's deputy managing director, the company had signed Boy George and Culture Club, the world's latest superstars. As a result, the projection of Virgin's profits for 1983 was £11.4 million on turnover heading towards £94 million. Emboldened by the rash of new Virgin offices across the world and his growing fame, Branson's braggadocio emboldened him to crush any challenge to his veracity.

Over one year earlier, he had become embroiled in an argument with Dave Robinson, a rival producer owning Stiff Records. Like

Pearce Marchbank, Branson had expected Robinson to capitulate. The Irishman's refusal had been galling and Branson hoped to settle the dispute over a round of golf near his country house. Robinson, reputedly, was a poor player.

Their dispute centred on a three-year agreement that Virgin's salesmen would represent Stiff Records for an annual payment of £120,000. Branson had contracted not to represent any other record label without Robinson's agreement. But in 1980, unknown to Robinson, Branson had signed an agreement to also sell Island Records. 'I'm not surprised about Richard,' sighed Robinson after unexpectedly discovering the secret. 'He's a greedy bastard.' Weeks later, on 2 February 1981, during his negotiations with Robinson's two managers to renew the contract, Branson formally revealed his agreement with Island Records. 'You can pay less if you sign a new contract for another two years,' Branson offered. Robinson's managers said nothing.

Branson was annoyed. Normally, even the most stubborn were persuaded to understand the virtues of his proposals but Robinson refused to sign the new agreement. Branson pondered an alternative plan: he would simply act as if Robinson had agreed to his offer. The attitudes, the morals and the methods of the bazaar had become part of his nature.

After an inconsequential exchange of letters disagreeing with Branson's conduct, Robinson terminated his agreement with Virgin and established Stiff's own sales force. 'That's a breach of contract,' declared Branson, nettled that his lucrative new plan was endangered. 'I'll sue you,' he threatened. Normally his threats induced surrender but Robinson was stubborn. 'You're threatening because you've been stupid and lost face,' retorted Robinson. 'My managers never agreed to your offer and my letters prove that.' To try to settle the argument in his favour, Branson had invited the Irishman for a game of golf and lunch.

Branson fully intended to win the game. Early on the Saturday morning, he covered the course with the club professional and was still practising when Robinson arrived. 'Bad luck,' smiled Robinson on the first tee. Branson's ball had disappeared into the undergrowth. By the fourteenth hole, Branson was trailing and his ball was lost again. Both men searched through the long grass. 'Found it,' shouted Branson smirking in a sandy bunker. Branson swung and clubbed the ball against a tree. Robinson smiled and drove his best shot of the game. At the end of the game, Branson blurted, 'We've never settled our dispute.' Robinson, victorious on and off the course had been classified as an enemy.

Two weeks later, Branson's writ arrived. 'I should have let him win the game,' Robinson lamented. Fighting Branson would risk £600,000. But the quietly spoken Irishman, puzzled by Branson's attitude, resolved not to avoid the legal challenge.

Breezily, in late 1983, Branson arrived at the High Court in the Strand, in a white, open-necked shirt, bronzed from a holiday on Necker Island. Proudly he stood in the witness box, the only man in the room without a tie. 'I own sixty companies,' he boasted to emphasise his substance and reliability, 'and spend most of my time on the telephone.' Although he would claim, 'I never took anyone to court in seventeen years of business', he did not conceal how much he enjoyed trampling on obstacles.

In the relaxed manner of a man accustomed to court proceedings, Branson testified that his case relied on a conversation, an exchange of letters and his hand-written notes scribbled in a large book. To prove his contention that a new agreement had been concluded on his houseboat on 2 February 1981, Branson quoted from his notebook the 'very favourable' reaction to his offer. 'There was never any question of Stiff being unhappy . . . There was a clear agreement.' Branson's contemporaneous, hand-written notes and his interpretation of the letters and conversations appeared to have sealed the dispute. His performance did not encourage any doubts about his accuracy. To his surprise, Robinson was undeterred.

Branson froze as the lawyer's accusation resounded across the wood panelled courtroom. 'You are fabricating!' Robinson's lawyer alleged that Branson was inventing conversations which had not occurred in order to strengthen his case. Earlier, Branson had insisted, 'I have no motive to fabricate' but Robinson's lawyers contended that Branson was 'fabricating' evidence. This was not the first occasion that Branson's veracity while under oath had been challenged. At the Old Bailey, his oral evidence had not been accepted. But this challenge attacked the heart of Branson's credibility. Robinson's lawyers were suggesting that Branson fabricated notes after the event to sustain his complaint, an allegation which Branson strongly denied.

As his recollection about the conversations was subjected to intense scrutiny, Branson began to contradict himself and deny the credibility of several letters. Suddenly, he paused, searching for answers. 'I can't remember,' he blustered and began to cry. On the knife-edge, the gambler was terrified about the possibility of defeat. At lunchtime, grabbing a pencil, he scribbled a message on a piece of scrap brown cardboard to Robinson: 'David, you're a horse-betting man. Spare us the afternoon. Pay up now and we'll agree to pay our lawyers' costs. Regards Richard.' As the court resumed, the cardboard was passed to Robinson. The Irishman shook his head. Branson was incorrigible. He was the same man who would later drool, 'I was just brought up to behave in a decent way to people. So if someone waves at you, you smile back; if someone says hello, you have a chat. You don't have to be a complete shit to be a success.'

On the second day of the trial, Branson arrived looking sombre, dressed in a suit and tie. As Robinson's lawyer pressed to embarrass Branson further, he was halted by Sir Douglas Franks, the judge: 'I think you've made your point.' The judgement was damning. Branson's notes, decided the judge, were unreliable. His case was rejected. Robinson was awarded costs. As the appeal court agreed, 'At business meetings [Branson] does most of the talking and usually gets what he wants.' But said the judge, even if Branson thought he had achieved what he wanted, 'I am . . . certain he was wrong.' Branson left the court visibly shaking.

'Something terrible is going to happen,' Branson confessed shortly afterwards. 'I just feel it's all going to blow up.' Among those witnessing Branson's unease was Al Clark, unusually welcomed back to the Virgin family. During the eleven years the two had worked together, Clark had watched Branson develop from a stammering youth into an orchestrator of events and people. The Australian, developing Virgin's investment in feature films, was not the only employee to notice Branson's jitters. The unreported humiliation in the courtroom could not explain Branson's nervousness, yet the millionaire repeated, 'I just don't see where I'm going.' Contrary to the image he cultivated of never contemplating failure or fearing the consequences – and contrary to his mother's self-assuring boast, 'He's addicted to danger, of pitting himself against the unknown' – Branson appeared unexpectedly terrified by life's fragility. Everything could collapse if he stumbled or missed the next step. The void had to be filled. Constant activity, he hoped, would eventually generate an idea. Thanks to tenacity, skill and opportunism his activity had over fourteen years transformed a failed student magazine into a successful record business. But no magic or new formula had emerged, other than the shameless vulgarity deployed by a trader to outwit conventional competitors. Branson had tried many other businesses during those fourteen years and had often failed. Now, momentarily, he felt blind. The entourage that had produced new ideas was depleted by so many rancorous departures that no one remained to brainstorm for ideas. But, out of the blue, the void was filled by an excitable, fat American lawyer, Randolph Fields.

5

Dream thief

Richard Branson prided himself on judging within one minute whether he liked or disliked a stranger. Fat Americans were unlikely to pass his aesthetic test but Branson's cultivated ambiguity and awkward hesitations disguised his prejudices, especially if an interesting offer was on the table.

The thirty-one-year-old American Jew was proposing joint ownership of an all-business-class airline flying between Britain and the United States. In the wake of Laker Airways' collapse in 1982 and the popularity of People Express, a discount airline, Fields was following the instincts of many regular air travellers entranced by the glamour of public applause and profits.

Gut instinct rather than careful research persuaded Branson in 'thirty seconds' after reading Fields's business plan that he was 'excited'. Despite having risked and lost money in pubs, film production and shops, Branson was undaunted by possibly risking £3 million on an airline. The son of a former air hostess calculated that an airline would be 'fun'. With all the tickets bought in advance, there would be huge cash deposits in his bank account. If the staff received low wages like other Virgin employees, and costs were controlled, there might be profits. He could easily persuade Fields to abandon the notion of an all-business-class airline. Over weekends and holidays, businessmen would not be flying. There was, he loved to enunciate, 'a thin line' between an entrepreneur and an adventurer. The buccaneer was back in business.

'You're mad,' scowled Simon Draper who, supported by Ken Berry, was appalled by the idea. Branson grinned. His cousin could not grasp the joy for a restless gambler to shift gear. Majestic resolution shone from his face. 'You're a megalomaniac, Richard,' continued Draper. 'What I'm telling you is that you go ahead with this over my dead body.' Branson had never welcomed criticism. He was accountable to no one, even to the architect of his musical fortunes. His relationship with Draper was suddenly and permanently fractured. After fifteen years of fluctuating business experience with only one major success, Branson was certain that he could overturn the old adage that the best way to become a millionaire was to be a billionaire and start an airline.

A mere four months later, on 29 February 1984, Branson and Fields posed in public to launch their airline. Dressed in First World War flying gear – a leather helmet and goggles – to encourage the newspaper editors to publish a picture, Branson, the new people's champion, listed the benefits Virgin would provide for thousands of Britons to fly cheaply to New York. No journalist, Branson knew, would question his sincerity. Glossing over weak finances was concomitant with exaggerations about the cheapest fares and minimising Virgin Atlantic's provision of the same cramped seats and unreliable service as People Express.

The photographs showed Fields, the airline's joint owner, smiling. Disguised was Fields's frustration that Branson had still not signed a contract or released his promised £3 million to finance the airline. Branson's concealment of the disagreement in front of the journalists gave him as much pleasure as dressing up. Disguises of all kinds appealed to him.

In the helter-skelter activity to create an airline within four months, Branson had nonchalantly forgotten what he owed to Fields. It was not only the idea of the airline: before their introduction, the American had started negotiations with Boeing to lease a second-hand 747 on condition that it could be returned at no cost after one year; Fields had identified the prematurely retired British Airways and British Caledonian flying crews prepared to work at low salaries; and Fields had recruited the former Laker executives who would hire and train the cabin, ticketing and service staff. Inevitably, the new airline was a clone, an inheritance from all the existing carriers.

Taking over the negotiations, Branson assumed the credit for Fields's achievements and added two new ideas. 'I know what I don't like about flying,' he said. 'The boredom and not enough leg room.' The new airline should offer something different. Business class passengers would be given extra space and also individual hand-held video screens with the choice of dozens of films.

'Let's announce a £30 million advertising campaign,' he suggested.

'But we haven't got £30 million,' stuttered the new marketing manager.

'Course not,' replied Branson, 'but we'll announce it, get the newspaper coverage and won't do anything more.'

'Richard's embellishments', were introduced to men previously accustomed to routine corporate life. One observed: 'It seems that he likes multiplying everything by ten.'

Amid the furore and hype, only Randolph Fields stood isolated from the euphoria. The American suspected that Branson was a dream thief. Even after their press conference announcing the creation of the airline, Branson delayed signing an agreement binding the two men as partners.

Branson's delay was deliberate. The partnership with Fields was of little interest unless concluded on Branson's terms. Contrary to their original agreement of equality, Branson wanted a majority share and control of the airline. Since Virgin Atlantic could only be launched with his £3 million, Branson began squeezing Fields to surrender. Branson's favoured method was to procrastinate until the plum fell for as little money as possible. If Fields lacked the cool courage and bargaining strength to outface his demands, that was the American's misfortune. If Fields departed, Branson would feel no loss.

Branson was, however, vulnerable. Unprofitable film investments had suddenly plunged Virgin into another cash crisis. The company's overdraft was bumping close to £3 million. He had concealed the crisis from Fields by flaunting the profits Virgin had earned from the success of Boy George's song, 'Do You Really Want to Hurt Me?', and more importantly from the Civil Aviation Authority. 'I decided not to mention [to the CAA],' he would confess about Virgin's application for the original licence, 'that we were having to pay out large sums of money to continue making *1984*', a disastrous feature film. Unfortunately for Branson, Fields held a trump card. Without an agreement and Virgin's deposit of £3 million, the CAA would not issue a licence for the airline to fly. Branson lacked any flexibility to manoeuvre. He signed the contract, deposited the money and invited Fields to the houseboat to celebrate with a glass of cheap, warm white wine.

In Branson's world, signed contracts were only valid if they could be enforced. Whenever necessary and legally possible, he would doggedly renegotiate the contractual terms to tilt the balance in his favour. On the eve of the airline's launch, he knew that Fields was powerless to enforce the contract they had just signed. Many of the airline's staff had refused to work with the excitable lawyer and by then Virgin Atlantic Airways was wholly associated with Branson. His threat to Fields was pure theatre: 'My bankers won't let me do it. Unless we control the company, we'll have to walk away from this deal.' Blaming bankers, like blaming lawyers, was a familiar ploy. 'I'm having none of this,' fumed Fields and he stormed off the boat.

Branson contacted the CAA. If he quickly reapplied for a new licence without Fields, he inquired, could it be approved? The reply was discouraging. A new application, he was told, would require months to be processed. His stratagem failed. Within the hour, Branson had telephoned Fields and withdrawn his threat.

The next morning Branson started again. His aggression was as persistent as his pursuit of publicity. The agreed terms, Branson told Fields, made him 'feel very uncomfortable'. He wanted revisions.

Branson's style was difficult to deflect. The even-tempered upper-class voice was full of imploring reasonableness. The pullover and houseboat shrieked modesty. Gradually, even the irascible Fields was disarmed. After four days of haggling, Fields's wariness had become weariness. Finally, he surrendered to attrition. Exhausted, he persuaded himself that Branson was the sort of man he could trust. Under the new deal, Branson would own 75 per cent and Fields 25 per cent of their company. Fields consoled himself that his interests remained firmly protected in the small print. Branson also congratulated himself on winning control thanks to the contract's same small print. 'He's on his way,' he gurgled about his partner.

On 22 June 1984, 34,000 feet above the Atlantic Richard Branson had every reason to congratulate himself. To the sound of Madonna's hit, 'Like a Virgin', he was wearing a steward's hat and pouring eight hundred bottles of champagne into the glasses of four hundred guests celebrating the launch of Virgin Atlantic Airlines. The party was more than memorable, it was unique. The sight of the famous dancing in the aisles and the pouting, red-suited Virgin hostesses offering food prepared by Maxims was a triumph of Branson's presentational skills. His tenacity had transformed a rejected proposal by a young American lawyer into a major media event. When his boisterous guests returned to London after another party at Newark Airport, the capital buzzed that flying Branson was fun. No one could recall the austere Scottish gals of British Caledonian or the prim matrons of British Airways running out of champagne during a riotous party over the Atlantic. Virgin, a name until then only known to record buyers, had become a recognisable brand basking in goodwill.

In August that year the houseboat was the obvious venue to receive the representative of the *Wall Street Journal* who sought an interview. Stripped to the waist, wearing baggy trousers, no shoes and with a hole in his socks, the informal tycoon welcomed his guest to spread the new gospel: 'We're becoming a global entertainment company and we're going into the United States big.' Virgin Records successes, he rattled off, included Genesis, Phil Collins, Human League, UB40 and Mike Oldfield. The Sex Pistols had sold one million albums and Boy George had just scored a major hit in America. Virgin Films had been promised $45 million from investors following the 'success' of *Electric Dreams* due to be released in one thousand four hundred American cinemas, and *1984* was next. Virgin was also launching a music cable channel, a book publishing company, a video game division and a record label in America. 'That's how we maximize profit,' he repeated, mouthing 'synergy', the latest cliché of the *Bonfire of the Vanities* era.

At the end of his monologue Branson was satisfied that his guest was suitably awed. No discomforting question required him to reconcile his new global ambitions with his other script, 'We want to stay small because small is profitable.' The contradictions had passed unnoticed and no doubts were raised about Virgin's finances. Branson's performance had chameleon-like qualities, adjusting itself to please its audience and to distract from any contradictions within.

'I'm not on a crusade with this thing,' Branson had modestly told his American interviewer about his new airline. 'If we had to pack it all in, the whole venture wouldn't cost but two months' profit of the Virgin Group.' 'Packing it in' was far from Branson's mind. The excitement of owning an airline bit deep. His only concern was managing the chaos of operating even one aeroplane. *Maiden Voyager*, Virgin's single Boeing 747, was occasionally flying either empty across the Atlantic or airport staff were cowering in fear of lynching from crowds of irate passengers complaining about gross overbooking. Administration and technical troubles were causing delays. Occasionally, flights were cancelled when the plane's load was genuinely too low to earn profits and passengers were placated by talk of 'technical problems'. To make a virtue of those problems, Branson regularly telephoned or travelled to Gatwick to apologise to passengers about his 'teething troubles'.

His early flights on Virgin Atlantic's single 747 to New York convinced him that only ruthless care over his finances would guarantee the airline's prosperity. The 747's bubble for business class was often empty during the summer. In winter, he knew, when the major airlines reduced their fares, it would be even harder to fill his jumbo. Copying the blueprint of Laker and People Express had been wrong. 'I knew we had to start working very hard to make sure that within a few years half the plane would be full of business class passengers,' he said. The model to emulate, he realised, was British Caledonian. Their extras had established a uniqueness. Copying British Caledonian, Virgin would also offer business class flyers better seats, two-for-one fares, a special lounge at the airport and a free limousine service. Presenting the old as the new was Branson's genius but one frustration was unassuaged. After the first burst of publicity, Virgin Atlantic had become unmentioned in the media. The indifference was intolerable. 'We need to make waves,' he told his marketing executives.

Stunts and gimmicks were Branson's only tool to find thousands of new customers, especially in America. When a couple were bounced from an overbooked Virgin flight to New York and complained that they would miss seeing their deceased son in his coffin before the funeral, an anonymous marketing executive had, on his own initiative, bought tickets for their flight on Concorde. Within minutes of their flight leaving Heathrow, Virgin's publicity machine fed to the media how Branson's personal intervention had rescued the heartbroken parents. The cause of their 'heartbreak', Virgin's chaos, was brushed aside. Branson understood how to turn every negative into a positive story.

'BA has just fired a girl and she's protesting,' laughed an aide.

'Hire her,' ordered Branson.

'What?'

'Hire her straightaway and get the publicists to tell all the media how Virgin saved the poor girl.'

But the small news items could not compete with the big budget campaigns orchestrated by British Airways and the American airlines. 'They're so greedy,' Branson repeatedly moaned, frustrated by BA's invincibility. 'They're so big.' Influenced by Freddie Laker, he feared BA's misuse of their huge advantages and goodwill against a newcomer. As a customer, too, Branson had every reason to dislike BA. Despite the appointment of Lord King in 1981 to revolutionise the state-owned airline for future privatisation, the corporate culture still reeked of imperious military officers managing an engineering corporation. BA's administrators resembled Whitehall civil servants rather than entrepreneurs and most of the cabin staff patronised the 'punters', as they unlovingly called their passengers.

Branson had good reason to welcome those deficiencies. British Airways' weaknesses were his opportunity to earn profits, although Virgin's single Boeing 747 operating on a peripheral route (Gatwick to Newark) against BA's two hundred and fifty aircraft did not even register on the giant's horizon. Branson, however, wanted to be noticed, especially to attract passengers. His tactic was to play the 'victim' card. His weapons were pranks. 'We're the cheeky airline having fun at the expense of a dinosaur,' he proclaimed.

In establishing Virgin Atlantic, Branson had frequently consulted Freddie Laker, the founder of Skytrain which had collapsed in 1982. At their meetings, Laker had inculcated Branson with his complaint that British Airways and the other major transatlantic airlines had conspired to destroy his airline by undercutting Skytrain's fares. That depiction appealed to Branson. He preferred not to inquire about another cause of Laker's collapse: that the flamboyant businessman had imprudently purchased three DC-10 aircraft financed by an unprotected £350 million loan just as fares were tumbling and before he received permission to fly the planes between London and New York. Laker also preferred to ignore his own imprudence, describing Skytrain as the 'victim' of BA's cartel.

If any British airline had cause to scream 'victim', it was British Caledonian, then British Airways' national competitor, which operated twenty-seven planes. But the managers of British Caledonian usually desisted. Flying was a cut-throat business and every entrant knew that survival depended upon attrition.

Ruthless competition was as natural to Branson as commercial warfare. In seventeen years, he had lied about his finances, he had lured managers, dealt harshly in litigation, denounced friends and had perpetrated a fraud against Customs and Excise. There was an instinctive progression from manipulating individuals in business deals to manipulating public opinion in his favour. Competition, to Branson, implied attacking British Airways. Freddie Laker had attempted the same but Branson subtly concealed his motives – his lust for money and power – by emphasising his altruism. Within days, the people's champion was conceived and born. His first attack coincided with the traditional autumn slump in ticket sales.

In October 1984, British Airways and the American airlines announced their usual price cuts. BA's was a reduction of £19 to New York, from £278 to £259, just £1 above Virgin's fare. Virgin had not featured in BA's calculations. The four-month-old airline operating between Gatwick and Newark, was invisible. Branson's remedy, in a deliberate echo of Laker's campaign, was to bombard the government with complaints that BA's new price was 'predatory' and calculated to destroy Virgin.

The complaint was ignored and Virgin's fares were cut, but in later years sympathetic journalists would accept Branson's version: the cut in the 1984 price constituted British Airways' first attempt to destroy Virgin Atlantic. His assertion was nonsense. The real victim in autumn 1984 was Randolph Fields, a casualty of Branson's ambition to be crowned an airline tycoon.

Partners irritated Branson, especially those who criticised his decisions. Field's latest challenge, Branson decided, was intolerable. 'Your staff at Virgin are making contracts on behalf of Virgin Atlantic without consulting me,' complained Fields. 'I'm a director.' Additionally, complained Fields, Virgin Atlantic's avalanche of cash from advance ticket sales was being used by Virgin Records as if there were a common pot. Branson scoffed denial and outrage. Shuffling money around was normal. Intolerant of criticism, he would not be accountable to anyone. Fields had miscalculated: he was about to discover that he had married a vulture. Branson's tactics were merciless. Formally, Virgin Atlantic announced the appointment of a new director to outvote Fields at board meetings. To stop Branson, Fields appealed to the court for an injunction. He won and departed with the judge's condemnation of Branson's behaviour as having 'left a bad taste in my mouth'. But the American's legal victory was pyrrhic. Branson ordered that the locks on Fields's office should be changed. Pleading, begging and screaming with Branson for reason, Fields was reduced to tears by a man whom he damned to his friends as 'The Devil'. Finally, he accepted defeat and surrendered.

In the settlement on 1 May 1985, Branson paid £1 million for the American's shares and promised a lifetime of free flights across the Atlantic on Virgin planes for Fields and his family. Branson was content. Knowing that Fields had lost was satisfying. But for Branson, minded to count every penny, the free flights rapidly became irksome. Fields's frequent use of the concession, he estimated, cost $500,000 in the first year. Branson disputed the agreement and was again summoned by Fields to court. Branson had no chance of winning. The contract unambiguously gave Fields the right to unlimited flights. Branson was nevertheless determined to make Fields fight for his rights, gambling that a judge might be persuaded against Fields. He was unlucky. The judgment was clear and merciless. Fields's victory found little sympathy in London. The general goodwill towards Branson neutralised Fields just as it silenced Branson's other victims.

His performance was perfect. While Fields complained to friends about Branson's ruthless negotiations, that image was unknown to most of Branson's employees and the public. To the vast majority, he was a charming, fun-loving and blessed entrepreneur, readily embraced by the people.

6

The people's champion

Scattered in eighteen houses across London, Virgin's employees were thrilled by the informality and their proximity to Branson's new fame. Virgin Atlantic and Virgin Music had transformed the company's foot soldiers into icons of glamour. Young, aspiring working-class secretaries and scrawny clerks relished the opportunity to escape their anonymity and win recognition in the pubs and clubs by announcing, 'I work for Richard Branson.' Wherever they held court, regaling envious strangers about the Virgin family, Branson's army boasted something more important than share options and money. They shone status, a quality of life and a unique qualification for the next job. Employment by Branson was an adventure. The people's tycoon satisfied their need for moral purpose. 'And did you see Richard Branson?' they were asked. 'See him! I talked and danced with him,' they sighed about an icon they gladly worshipped. 'He's wonderful. And so generous.' Their audience's interest and envy compensated for low wages.

Annual bonding sessions encouraged staff loyalty. The mystery day trips to Croydon and the Isle of Wight had evolved into wild week-ends in foreign hotels. Under Branson's supervision, the daytime was filled with sport, golf, rounders, cricket and endless pranks and the nights with parties, alcohol, drugs and endless sex. The climax was glorious mayhem. Television sets were thrown out of windows, fire extinguishers were squirted around bedrooms and buildings were trashed. In the spirit of fun, at the centre, was Branson kissing and groping every girl in sight and constantly disappearing into the shadows or passing through bedroom doors.

The party habit had been perfected with the establishment of Virgin Atlantic. Since most of the airline's hostesses matched his stipulation – tall, blonde with big breasts – he knew that if he joined the crew at their Newark hotel, he could probably find one who was willing. Names were never mentioned. Although he was often seen disappearing with a woman, and often with two if he was partying with David Tait in America, or Rod Vickery in the music world, an omerta descended about the night's carousing. One of the exceptions was Pier Walker, a Virgin Atlantic hostess, who described her weekend's affair with Branson in New York. Branson's denial on the grounds of his 'absolute and binding rule' never to go near anyone employed by Virgin was a topic of mirth among the dozens of his former employees recalling his enthusiastic chases after female employees. 'First girl to get them out and shake maracas between them,' he had laughed at a Virgin party, 'wins two first class tickets to the States.' A blonde with big bosoms obliged. Everyone roared their approval and admiration for Branson's generosity, forgetting that the tickets would only be given for empty seats on his own airline, a cost-free gesture. The following day, everyone was certain that Branson had helped the girl to her home that night but Branson was emphatic: 'I'm a great believer in sticking with one relationship. Of course, one will get tempted but I have generally resisted temptation.'

In pubs across London in the aftermath of his company bonding sessions, Branson's disciples spread stories about those riotous weekends. 'Virgin is so different,' John Webster, Virgin's marketing director would say. 'We're part of one big, happy family with a strong, capitalist money-making ethic.' Branson's vulgarity appealed to those flattered to be given opportunities.

Not only had he paid for the weekends but also for lovely gestures at the wedding receptions of favoured employees using Virgin's club in the Kensington Roof Gardens. As the newly weds shook hands with the owner, the King more than once loudly proclaimed, 'It's all on me.' How Branson savoured the cheers, the devotion of his people, but the afterglow was occasionally brief. Some grooms discovered that the largesse was limited and others discovered that Branson's spontaneous generosity did not protect them from subsequent dismissal.

Inside Virgin, the image of 'generous, fun-loving Richard' was fiercely protected. No one wanted to contemplate that the millions and the celebrity of an empire spanning music to an airline had changed their hero. For them, he was still the relaxed hippie who would arrive as the guest speaker at the Institute of Directors full of bravado in a jumper, hand-knitted by an aunt, scornful that the expected dress was dark suits.

Only the old guard noticed how Branson's mood and appearance had modified. The hair was slightly landscaped. The beard was cropped. The shirts were ironed. The sweaters appeared to be fitted. The expensive shoes favoured by City magnates now encased his feet. Occasionally he even wore a jacket. The swagger had perceptively matured. His personality had hardened. The joyously rebellious youth had been replaced by a rebel tycoon on a mission. The eyewitnesses to his reinvention remained loyally silent, noticing Branson's particular sensitivity to the subject of Nik Powell's departure with comparatively little money despite Virgin's exploding fortunes. 'It's the end of the era of innocence,' announced Al Clark, the resident philosopher. Branson, they finally began to understand, was no different from any other hard businessman. Among the new casualties was Jumbo van Renen, a black South African, who had worked for eleven years with Simon Draper. Van Renen's contribution to Virgin Records was considerable but Branson spurned his approach for a pay increase. 'I'm afraid I can't pay you more,' smiled Branson in a superior manner, 'because it's only right that we invest all our profits in the company as a long-term strategy. It's for the good of the family. We're all one big family.' Van Renen nodded apologetically but on reflection he began to query Branson's loyalty to the 'family'.

Branson's real family, receiving big salaries with valuable share options, were Simon Draper and Robert Devereux – Branson's new brother-in-law who had been hired in 1983 to manage Virgin's publishing business – and Ken Berry, the former accounts clerk who owned a 15 per cent stake in the company. Those three, exclusively privy to some financial secrets, and Branson, were the real beneficiaries of Virgin's policy of low wages. All established offshore trusts and occupied houses bought and maintained by Virgin. No one else shared in this 'family's' fortune.

Van Renen had felt betrayed by the stammering performance of Branson as the innocent amateur. 'I'm leaving,' he told Branson. 'Fine,' he was told. Branson's eyes showed no compassion. No one was compelled to work for Virgin. His executives and employees could read their contracts. Some might call it self-centred or selfish. He called it commercial. Everything was dedicated to Virgin's shareholders. In 1982, they had received £1.4 million in dividends from

Virgin. In 1984, the dividend income increased to £4.5 million. The shareholders were the private trusts associated with Draper, Berry, Devereux and, principally, Branson. His share was being reinvested in the airline, struggling to establish itself.

'What are we going to do?' Branson asked his publicists. 'We need something to get us into the media.' His 747 was carrying backpackers on cheap tickets and businessmen were still avoiding his unreliable service. The solution, Branson reasoned, was to promote himself. The method was suggested by Simon Draper.

Ted Toleman, a friend from the motor racing fraternity, was seeking sponsors to promote his catamaran's race across the Atlantic. The prize was the Blue Riband cup which had been awarded since 1935 for the fastest crossing. Toleman's crew included Chay Blyth, the round-the-world yachtsman, and a BBC television reporter. In return for sponsorship, Branson could join as a passenger on the especially named *Virgin Atlantic Challenger*. Branson knew that the challenge was suspect. The Blue Riband was a competition for passenger liners not speed boats refuelling at sea. But unable to pay New York advertising rates, and planning to defray the costs by finding other sponsors, the opportunity of attracting free attention to himself was too important to miss. The moment of metamorphosis had arrived. The actor's performance, until then restricted to a handful of spectators, was to be offered to a worldwide audience. Insiders did not spot any hesitation or reflection. After trading for eighteen years, Branson understood all the aspects of his gamble to become a star. The downside made it risk free.

'We'll use the 747,' Branson told Hugh Band, the airline's marketing director. One hundred journalists were flown on 7 February 1985 above the Scilly Isles to witness, while eating and drinking at Virgin's hospitality, the finishing line for the crossing. Later, limping into a press conference dressed as a pirate, with a black eye patch and a stuffed parrot on his shoulder, Branson wallowed in the attention of his guests. His easygoing manner and availability encouraged newspapers to repeat his self-description as a 'daredevil' for whom 'a race across the Atlantic is all in a day's fun for Her Majesty's wackiest tycoon'. Although the misdescription as 'the son of a judge and a ballet dancer [who] doesn't drink much and doesn't smoke at all' was mystifying, Virgin's active press office, primed to demand swift corrections, was grateful that Branson's occasional collapse into drunkenness at parties and his smoking passed unmentioned. The only casualty was Ted Toleman who was discovering the undeclared price for Branson's co-operation as he was cast into the shadows.

By 10 August 1985, as the catamaran bobbed in the sunlight by a Manhattan quay on the eve of departure, Branson, despite his technical and navigational ignorance, was fêted in the media as the expedition's captain. Four days later, after a trip refreshed by refuelling stops, the first 'race' ended in disaster. The boat hit some flotsam and sank just two hours from the finishing line. It was an ignominious end to what Chay Blyth described as 'An easy trip. Not life threatening.'

Stepping from the sinking catamaran into a life vessel, Branson was inspiring his publicity machine by radio to twist his flop into success: 'Branson – the hero who bravely escaped from the clutches of death.' Conveniently, Branson's son Sam had been born during the first day of the journey and a publicist had arranged for Joan to tastefully pose for photographs which were published by newspapers on the front page reporting how the 'daredevil' father toasted his new born. He was lionised for his bravery. The thirty-five-year-old Branson could chortle about millions of pounds of free advertising. Even disasters could be presented as a success. Many Britons were entranced. Reservations for Virgin Atlantic increased. 'Virgin is worth over £150 million,' he preened to a television audience, notwithstanding that it still owned just one plane flying one route.

His greater bravado was to complete his cosseted transatlantic crossing while disguising his latest financial crisis, during which Coutts had threatened to dishonour Virgin's next cheque. Branson's business, employing 1,100 people, was again on the brink of chaos. Financial crisis had become a normal part of life, but the stakes on each occasion were higher. His knee-jerk entry into new ventures – first the airline, then computer games, television and holidays – had sucked cash from the record business. Buying rock groups had become more expensive, costing millions before any profits were earned. Without organisation or accountability, Virgin's casually managed finances had obscured the losses caused by bad management. Although the company's pre-tax losses in 1981 of £1.3 million had improved to profits of £12 million in 1985, and turnover had risen in the same period from £30 million to £152 million, the company had pressing debts of £7.6 million, tax debts of £7 million and owed in total £22 million, mostly on the aircraft's lease. Branson's optimism about Virgin Communications, managed by Robert Devereux, seemed misplaced despite his annual report's reference to an 'excellent year with turnover more than doubled, with pre-tax profits rising five fold'. As a recent founder of British Satellite Broadcasting, Virgin would be, he proclaimed, 'in the leading position in the television market in the nineties' despite offering European viewers old English language television programmes. To fulfil his ambition to own Britain's biggest international entertainment group, Branson and Devereux required money, creative talent and the respect of the industry regulators. They failed on all the requirements.

His salvation appeared to be Roger Seelig, a confident, talented and aggressive merchant banker at Morgan Grenfell. 'You're lucky that you can take advantage of lax accounting standards,' the banker told Branson, surveying a company on the verge of disaster. The best solution, advised Seelig, was to borrow money in the City by floating the company on the stock exchange. The first step was to appoint professional managers. Branson's instinctive reaction was negative. Outside scrutiny and participation in his secret business was loathsome. But necessity dictated his agreement. At least a flotation would provide money for expansion, settle unpaid taxes and debts, and provide another opportunity to transfer his wealth to offshore trusts to avoid future taxation.

Terry Baughan, Virgin's finance director, was the first casualty. 'He's no good,' Branson was told. On Seelig's recommendation, in August 1984, Don Cruickshank, a forty-three-year-old accountant formerly employed by Thomson Newspapers and Pearson, was appointed Virgin's managing director. In April 1985, Cruickshank recruited Trevor Abbott, a thirty-five-year-old accountant employed at MAM, a diversified entertainment company, as finance director. Both were attracted by the glamour of Branson and Virgin. Branson offered something special, even unique, to some professional businessmen. His 'can-do' enthusiasm attracted those stultified by business's traditional hierarchies. 'He's a man,' Abbott soon after remarked, 'who can turn stone into money.' At the end of that year, twenty-five City institutions loaned Virgin £20 million.

Suddenly free of immediate financial pressure, Branson focused again on his self-promotional campaign. Only a successful speedboat crossing of the Atlantic satisfied his requirement. The publicity for the failure had been substantial. Success would be a bigger prize. He marvelled at its simplicity. Thanks to the media uncritically reproducing his own comparison of himself with Scott of the Antarctic, the public believed the venture was dangerous. But the crossing on a new boat, refuelled by Esso tankers as his crew were fed hot Irish stew, with the promised support of the Royal Air Force and other rescue organisations, would be safer than a drive along the M4 motorway.

Branson's priority was a better boat, not one built by Ted Toleman. Delivering the message was painful – for Toleman. In Branson's customary manner, the bad news was drip fed. Not only did Toleman lose the contract for building the new craft, but Chay Blyth was hired by Branson and three of Toleman's best staff were poached by Virgin, although Branson would suggest that each had asked for the job. Toleman was 'on his way'.

'How can we describe Richard?' Chris Moss, the marketing expert snared by Branson, asked Blyth, the captain of the crossing.

'Call him skipper,' replied Blyth, understanding Branson's vanity. 'After all, he's paying the bills. Just call me Number One.'

On 12 August 1986, Virgin's publicity machine corralled dozens of journalists and TV cameras into New York harbour. Since the single purpose of the trip was to publicise Virgin Atlantic, Branson spoke ceaselessly. 'We are like Scott of the Antarctic,' he repeated. 'We're proud to follow in his footsteps'. Branson's generosity towards the media silenced the cynics who had noted the absurdity of the comparison.

Linked by radio to Virgin's control centre in Britain, Branson set off not on a nautical but a journalistic marathon. During the four days, he ceaselessly gave interviews, endlessly repeating the same thoughts of bravery and derring-do. To enliven an unexpectedly dull voyage, the man who was determined not to be forgotten even invented a passing whale to suggest danger. 'It was just as safe as the first trip,' Blyth grunted, contradicting Branson's on-the-verge-of-death accounts.

With just two hours to spare, the boat crossed the finishing line. Branson's luck was extraordinary. Millions were watching the half-time summary of the World Cup in Mexico on television. His success was flashed on the TV screens followed by live pictures of Virgin's hero. 'More millions of free publicity,' crowed Branson.

'Mrs Thatcher says she wants to see the boat,' Branson told his publicists. His coup – calling in favours – was remarkable. No one understood how Branson's personal telephone call to Margaret Thatcher lured the prime minister on 3 July 1986 to the River Thames to promote Virgin. Standing beside Thatcher, Branson sped at 30 knots, unlawfully fast, under Tower Bridge raised in salute to a British hero. Branson never considered the irony that nine years earlier he had deliberately broken the law on the same river to promote the Sex Pistols, thereby financing his pose next to the Prime Minister. All that mattered was the intoxicating glamour and the media attention. 'He's done it,' screamed the *Daily Mail*'s headline. 'Richard the Lionheart,' worshipped the *Daily Express*. 'Pride of the Atlantic', 'King of the Waves', 'Salute to *Challenger*', 'Towering Triumph', blared other newspapers.

In a round-Britain tour, *Challenger II* docked in harbours to promote Virgin, with Branson making guest appearances. His presence was hailed by ordinary people as historic. Virgin shops reported record sales. Cheered as a national hero, Branson swelled with the adulation. Virgin, he mused, had become more than merely a player. The company had entered the nation's folklore and he had been anointed an icon. Reality chose that inappropriate moment to bite back.

'The fans are puking about you and Thatcher,' Jeremy Lascelles, Virgin Music's A&R manager, told Branson with an unexpected grimace hours after his return to his office. 'It's all very unhelpful with the bands too. They loathe Thatcher.' Branson was shocked. Thatcherism – the encouragement of entrepreneurship, the privatisation of state industries and the moral legitimacy of wealth – enabled his success and he had occasionally accepted invitations to Downing Street. The 'hippie tycoon' and classless toff whose popular appeal straddled social barriers, had never revealed his sympathy for Margaret Thatcher. 'Most young people in Britain are like me,' he scoffed. 'We are more popular than you think.' Momentarily, Lascelles was puzzled. 'We,' Lascelles mused. 'What does he mean "We"?' Moments later, Lascelles, a charming musician, believed he understood. Branson was apparently speaking royally. 'We can do no wrong,' Branson repeated. 'You see,' he told Lascelles, 'the press are treating us favourably.' Reality and illusion merged in the hero's mind, often incoherently. After again posing for newspaper photographers with his children, he pontificated, 'I would never involve my family with the press.' Overwhelmed by the celebrity, he could not imagine that an assistant was struggling to persuade musicians to appear in an edition of *This Is Your Life* to celebrate Branson. 'People don't want to know,' Sian Davis, a publicist, moaned. 'Even the Human League's manager said "No".'

The television programme possibly contributed another subtle change of the chameleon's colour. The new image was modesty. He eschewed expensive cars, preached that he flew economy class – 'the extra comfort is not worth the extra cost,' scoffed the owner of an airline seeking business class passengers – and espoused a carefully refined casual style. With echoes of his sixties credo, Branson chose to speak again as the champion of the people. His natural nonchalance was commercially advantageous. The star had become a valuable commodity. Major corporations were seeking Branson's endorsement in advertisements. In the new yuppie era, socialism was discredited and wealth was no longer sinful. Branson as the classless, benevolent rags to riches tycoon compared well with the suffocating grandeur of his competitors. But the reality was a lifestyle of extraordinary opulence in a life divided between a large house in Notting Hill, Mill End, his country house in Oxfordshire, and Necker, expensively developed by the company.

Hosting parties at the weekend, organising endless sports competitions, ample food and wine and free foreign holidays satisfied Branson's need for entertainment. Jeremy Lascelles, Chris Moss, Simon Draper and many others loved Branson. He guaranteed fun. Few of the chosen jesters could recall what their host actually said but the safety of numbers protected everyone from boredom. Even a growing habit towards exaggeration – 'How I signed the Sex Pistols' – was tolerated. The prankster, placing himself at the centre of attention, conjured scenarios exalting his courage: 'As I bobbed up and down in the Atlantic in a life raft,' he prattled, 'I had this vision of Virgin as the largest entertainment group in the world outside the United States.'

Deluded by his own propaganda and the popular hero-worship, he convinced himself that his business and his methods were sufficiently robust to withstand the scrutiny of outsiders. Fatefully, he decided to ask the public not only for their adoration but also for their money.

7

Confusion and salvation

The national mood in 1986 matched Richard Branson's ambitions. He wanted to lease another Boeing 747 for a new service to Miami and to launch a myriad of other schemes. The only obstacle was his lack of money. Roger Seelig, his merchant banker and a star in the City, offered the solution.

Margaret Thatcher's privatisation of state monopolies had encouraged the public to buy shares. Branson was promised by Roger Seelig that the City would provide the millions he desired. 'You've only got to persuade them to trust you and make them understand that Virgin will produce a fortune,' soothed Seelig. Selling himself and Virgin to the suits in the City, Branson smiled, was not a problem. He was, after all, a man enjoying effortless access to every minister in Whitehall and was fêted by discreet invitations to Downing Street and Chequers. He preferred to ignore the humiliation that year as the failed 'Minister for Rubbish' after the launch of UK 2000, a government initiative to encourage the young unemployed. In the war of whispers after the *Sun* had photographed him holding a broom, even the charitable said, 'He didn't enjoy or understand the complexity, pace and politics of charity work.' The more critical charity workers complained, 'He was frustrated because there was no immediate return.' Although still bruised by the ridicule heaped upon him for failing to perform as promised, his credibility as a businessman was so pristine that barbs from a handful of critics ridiculing Thatcher's favourite with a history of fraud, drugs and rock sleaze were easily ignored.

The critics did not include the bankers and lawyers whom Seelig had invited to Branson's home. Averting their eyes from discarded food and dishes lying around the living room, the suited professionals were startled by his young son waddling into the room and asking, 'Daddy where's my potty?' Branson's guests smiled unctuously.

The raw statistics presented by Seelig were encouraging. Virgin's sales had risen in the twelve months to July 1986 from £119 million to £189 million; its pre-tax profits had risen from £15 million to £19 million; and the company, including the airline, was employing nearly four thousand people. Anyone querying the enhanced profits for 1985 might have noticed that the accounting period had been changed but that was an acceptable legal technique to improve Virgin's image as Branson was introduced by Seelig to an unusual tribe from the City.

Branson presented himself as the head of a worldwide media empire embracing not only rock music, but also books, films and satellite television. 'Virgin operates in seventeen countries,' beamed the thirty-six year old, 'two-thirds of our income is earned overseas and we're growing very rapidly. Because of my gut feeling, I've set up fifty-five companies and closed down only one.' Branson knew that his boast was not quite accurate. Many of his small enterprises had collapsed but they were obliterated from the record.

His personal bankers at Samuel Montagu in the City remained enamoured. 'The sweater's arrived,' announced the banker as their client, wearing jeans, sat down with a warm grin. The telephone call for Branson interrupting their meeting was a reminder of their client's fame. 'Has it got air conditioning?' Branson asked. 'And how many hours has it flown?' Their client, they realised, was being offered a Boeing 747 by Lord King, the chairman of British Airways. At the end of the meeting, his unconventional farewell was amusing. 'Bugger, I've got no change. Can anyone lend me a pound for the Tube back to Holland Park?' Four hands dived into their pockets and proffered handfuls of coins. His performance was immaculate. Bankers, like his employees, would resist demanding high fees if they witnessed his personal frugality. None contemplated an alternative scenario: that while Branson was congenitally tight with money, he also enjoyed cultivating anecdotes for insiders to gossip around London. Meticulously, he was creating his own legend.

The result of those meetings was an unusual package to be offered to the City and the public. To retain absolute control, Branson would sell only 34 per cent of Virgin Music and the other directors would keep 11 per cent. He personally retained 55 per cent of the music company. He would not float Virgin Atlantic or the nightclubs. In an internal transaction, Branson would buy Virgin Atlantic from the new, publicly-owned Virgin holding company for £6 million. The division of the empire, suggesting inevitable conflicts when Branson's energies were focused on building the airline, was spontaneously highlighted by the occupants of the bland City boardrooms which he visited during his choreographed journey to recite the identical story to win the trust of investment managers in the fickle entertainment industry. 'Not much of a problem,' he replied unconvincingly.

Seelig hoped that Branson's disdain for proper financial accountability and his management by whim would remain as unknown as his unhelpful delight at showing a video of himself free-falling on an unopened parachute towards possible death. Although Branson acknowledged that 'there was little chance of me coming to grief because of the back-up chute', his urge to publicise his gamble with death, reckoned Seelig, would hardly inspire fund managers to risk the public's money in Virgin, even if they saw two instructors clasping Branson as he slid from the plane. Branson's bravado nevertheless impressed Seelig. The banker was unaware that minutes after landing, Branson had shakily confessed his terror during an interview with Garfield Kennedy, a television documentary producer. On reflection, Kennedy had decided that the evidence of Branson's emotional collapse was untransmittable, but the producer remained confused. Was Branson's terror genuine or did he record a performance after Branson had persuaded himself of the danger? A similar uncertainty about Branson struck those seeking clarity about his business.

Branson offered no reassuring concessions. Dressed in a pullover and jeans, on his houseboat with four telephones ringing, he explained to an American journalist, 'I was never interested in becoming a businessman. I'm good at spotting gaps in the market and filling them.' A man with a goatee beard writing messages on the back of his hand who exclaimed, 'I want to build the biggest media company in the world', while admitting confusion about the technicalities of the accounts of his allegedly $200 million company, was struggling to inspire universal confidence.

Those concerned about any independent scrutiny of the maverick and his compliance with City rules should have been reassured by the appointment as non-executive directors of Sir Philip Harris, a carpet retailer, and Cob Stenham, the former finance director of Unilever who had just been appointed head of Bankers Trust. 'I am excited at the prospect of working with such an enthusiastic team,' said Harris who had pledged to spend £250,000 of his own money to invest in Virgin shares. 'It's an exciting venture,' agreed Stenham. 'I admire what the company has achieved.' Although both men were renowned as astute, independent operators, gossip in the City suggested other flaws in Branson's business.

Insiders described a board meeting of Top Nosh, Branson's sandwich company, where a director with green hair lay prostrate on the floor recovering from the previous night's excesses, while another director stared blearily into space silently opening and closing his mouth like a fish. Similar injurious reports mentioned Virgin's abandonment of film production after an expensive failure with *1984*; the loss of money from satellite television and Virgin publishing; and the permanent debts from Virgin's shops despite copying HMV's successful Megastore in Oxford Street. Only Virgin Music was profitable but any plans for expansion were vague. 'Does Virgin ever have proper board meetings?' Branson was asked during his City tour.

Branson was irked. The performance required for the flotation was infuriating. The questions targeted at himself or Simon Draper revealed suspicion about the long-term value of owning the copyright to music and records. He did not care for the 'clever dick' who reminded him about the City's requirement for 'transparency if you are going to win trust and confidence'. Of course, he withheld some information. His business could only flourish in secrecy. He would not reveal his ambition to buy EMI Music. He would make no concessions to win their trust. Nor would he tolerate the long, technical discussions about taxes and the minutiae of the offer document. Frequently he walked out of meetings with the excuse, 'I've got to make a phone call.' Draper and Berry could cope. But on one issue he was adamant. 'I want more money,' he demanded, gazing at the accounts prepared by Terrence Webber, the auditor. 'The company's worth more. I want more money for the shares.'

'I can't help you,' replied Webber. 'The rules on valuation don't allow it.' Their arguments were endless.

The slick presentation before flotation day, 13 November 1986, concealed Branson's impatience and the City's bewilderment about Virgin's real value. 'After the Big Bang,' raved the advertisements, 'how about a little pop?' A pin-striped stockbroker disco-danced around his office with the caption, 'From the rock market to the stock market'. Virgin's publicists had persuaded the *Sunday Telegraph* to praise the new shares as potentially 'a great success . . . a pioneering company which looks like carving out a major role in world markets'. In *The Observer*, Virgin was extolled as 'one of the most glamorous flotations this year and should be oversubscribed'. Eighty-four thousand people, Virgin's customers who idolised Branson, had applied to buy shares. Mobbed by his admirers on the City pavement demanding his autograph, Branson acknowledged the defining moment. 'I'm humbled by the interest,' he told the invited media through a permanent smile. The flotation had placed him precisely where he most desired: at the centre of attention. He was a star, who would share equal attention at a concert later that week with Peter Gabriel.

The reality, Branson had been told by Seelig, was gloomy. 'We're floating at 140 pence per share,' the deflated banker announced, 'less than we anticipated.' Branson was distressed. Too many City investment managers were unimpressed by Branson's performance and had shied away. Branson had only sold 34 per cent of the company to the public, keeping 55 per cent for himself. Although Virgin was valued at £240 million, and Branson would personally receive £21.1 million to invest in the airline, there was only £32.1 million for the Virgin Group, much less than expected. Branson spouted a smokescreen. 'We're pitching the offer low,' he told interviewers through his fixed smile, 'to attract a healthy after-market.' Hours after the first public trading, the share price fell. Instead of the big hit with an avalanche of cash, he was saddled with financial stagnation, City suits, regulations and scrutiny. His cure was to escape. Draper and Berry would manage the music business while he focused upon his airline.

'What's the plan?' he had asked Hugh Band and Chris Moss, the airline's marketing directors. The two were godsends for Branson, tumbling over with ideas to promote the airline. Their latest idea was amazing. If successful, Virgin would be guaranteed enormous free publicity in Britain and America. 'Why not try to be the first man to fly across the Atlantic in a hot-air balloon?' asked Moss.

'Fucking hell. We've got to do it,' swooned Branson.

The two explained that Per Lindstrand, a thirty-eight-year-old Swedish balloon manufacturer and pilot, was looking for a sponsor for the epic flight. 'It's an amazing way to promote the airline,' said Moss.

A conversation with Lindstrand confirmed the dangers. 'You're going to risk your life,' warned the Swede.

On reflection, Branson realised that he had reached another milestone. The cosy speedboat dash across the Atlantic had reaped a windfall of publicity which in turn had earned millions of pounds for Virgin's businesses. A record-breaking balloon flight across the Atlantic would elevate him into a unique league. The exposure, he calculated, would produce £25 million in conventional advertising. There were, he told Lindstrand, some conditions before he accepted.

Naturally, there would be no commercial risk, stipulated Branson. Lindstrand would provide the balloon at cost and would not be paid for piloting it across the Atlantic. Branson wanted guarantees that only his bravado and never his terror should be broadcast. Branson would be presented as the captain of the balloon and only he would speak to the media. Lindstrand, the designer, navigator and pilot of the *Virgin Atlantic Flyer*, was not to talk about the crossing without Branson's agreement and that would never be offered. The list continued but the Swede was unconcerned. Branson provided the opportunity to satisfy his dream.

Although Branson would take a course in balloon flying, undergo some instruction in using a parachute and be shown how to operate a radio, both accepted that the paymaster was a passenger. His talent was masterminding a showcase performance at Sugarloaf Mountain near Boston.

Few newspapers and television stations resisted Branson's personal invitation to witness the preparations and take-off, planned for May 1987. His provision of a satellite transmitter to feed pictures and interviews supplied by Virgin's own television crew encouraged even those hesitant about pleasing a self-publicist to journey to Sugarloaf and report the possibility of a tycoon's dramatic death.

The countdown began but bad weather delayed the lift-off. Around the clock, Branson, the brave adventurer risking his life for a mention in the *Guinness Book of Records*, made himself available to journalists and TV crews for endless interviews, even escorting journalists on boating trips to stave off the boredom.

For four weeks Branson waited, managing his business in Britain by telephone until in mid-June an urgent message from London interrupted his frustrating routine. A newspaper had discovered that Virgin was to launch a condom. Despite the denials – 'Your report is extremely inaccurate and misleading,' brazenly asserted a Virgin publicist – the story could not be suppressed. With one balloon marooned by the weather, Branson dashed back to London to launch another variety.

On the transatlantic flight from Boston, Branson explained his latest preoccupation with sex and uttered a doom-laden scare about Aids: 'Potentially, it's a catastrophic problem to the younger generation. If nothing is done, we could be talking about hundreds of thousands of people being stricken with the virus over the next fifteen years.' He proposed a publicity campaign to frighten the British to change their habits. 'He's putting something back into society,' explained his publicists in London summoning a press conference. Branson was associated with a good deed, alleviating the embarrassments of the 'Minister for Rubbish' and UK 2000. In mid-Atlantic his alarmism was uncontrolled. 'Half of America's population,' he continued, 'could die of Aids by 2010. Aids has taken a firm grip on heterosexuals.' Someone more thoughtful might have been more cautious but Branson was prone to exaggeration: 'By 2010, one third of the population could be infected with the Aids virus in one form or another.' Cynics would ascribe Branson's alarm to his permanent obsession with sex. 'My principal weakness is women,' he admitted. 'I inherited it from my dad.' Visitors to his office in Holland Park, like the journalist Cherry Hughes, were repeatedly amazed by the 'over-sexed atmosphere, like a permanent orgy'. The cure was condoms. The brand name, he proposed, was 'Virgin Jumpers' to match the colloquialism, 'Slip a jumper on!' or 'Have a jump!'

Durex, the supplier of 98 per cent of Britain's condoms, had refused to supply Virgin. Instead, Branson had signed a deal with Ansell, one of America's biggest manufacturers. Ansell had been delighted. Repeatedly, the company had failed to break into the British market and Branson had agreed to underwrite a £5 million launch. Fortunately for the American manufacturer, neither Branson nor John Jackson, his representative, appeared to have properly investigated Ansell's misfortunes in Britain.

Before Branson landed at Heathrow, outrage had erupted in the centre of London.

'You won't guess what's happening,' Lawrence Post, Virgin's company secretary, told Cob Stenham, Virgin's non-executive director. 'Richard's going to give a press conference at Heathrow. To announce Virgin condoms.'

'What? When?' asked Stenham.

'When he lands from America,' replied Post. 'Later today.'

'He can't do that,' spluttered Stenham. 'It hasn't been agreed by the board. It hasn't even been considered by the directors.'

Stenham telephoned Philip Harris, Virgin's second non-executive director. Branson, they agreed, should be intercepted and brought to London before he spoke. Both had become irritated by Branson's behaviour. Ever since the flotation, he was breezily announcing deals – 'I've bought Storm, the model agency' – without consulting the other directors, and he rarely attended board meetings.

Only four weeks earlier Lawrence Post had announced, 'The board meeting is cancelled.'

'Why? Where's Richard?' asked Stenham.

'He's gone to America to fly on a balloon,' replied Post.

'He's always buggering off when it matters or calling board meetings at ten o'clock at night,' complained Stenham.

Branson refused to be pinned down. Complaints that he was an erratic manager, careless with documents and unaccountable with the company's money, passed over his head. Despite his responsibility for the public's money, Roger Seelig's warning that 'The City doesn't like your action-man antics', had been ignored. If his critics complained about a nightmare, he was unconcerned. The publicity at the flotation had been marvellous but he had moved on to the next idea. Unlike Ted Turner or Rupert Murdoch whom he had vowed that year to overtake, he disliked constant involvement in the detailed development and management of his business. He prided himself on being a deal-maker, 'good at getting things going', delegating the management and the chaos to Don Cruickshank, the Virgin Group's managing director. 'A publicity-seeking deal-junkie,' was one director's seething assessment.

Cruickshank, a critical ingredient for the flotation and Virgin's first employee to wear a tie, was reminding a maverick marketeer that he could not use the public company's money for private purposes. But Branson had set his annual salary at £60,000 to justify his staff's low wages, to minimise his taxes, and to claim expenses from the company. Too often, complained Cruickshank, Branson had issued a company cheque to charge costs incurred on Necker, his private island. 'But I entertained for Virgin,' protested Branson, apparently unaware that a public company requires accountability. Cruickshank, he realised, would not accept the legality that Necker was 'not my personal island but a commercial venture and a successful part of our hotel division'. Sensing that his explanation was rejected, he retreated, 'It was a mistake. Someone must have used the wrong account.' No one dared to question how he could afford his lifestyle unless he received money as a beneficiary from the offshore trusts.

Branson's dislike of 'the onerous demands' from the City was undisguised. He rarely visited the company's headquarters in Ladbroke Grove – to the irritation of rock groups playing in the street outside in the hope of a contract – and he sat sullenly at meetings held in Harris's home because Virgin did not possess a boardroom. Paying dividends to the new shareholders was hateful. Shareholders' money, Branson appeared to believe, should be his to use at no cost while he pledged his own shares as collateral to raise loans. But he did keenly understand that Stenham and Harris could prevent Virgin's name on condoms. 'Why should a music company go into condoms?' asked Harris. 'Are you doing it for money, charity or publicity?' The answer was incomprehensible. Hours later Branson acted contrite. 'Course they won't be called Virgin condoms,' he promised. Whenever a warning sounded, his performance was honed to perfection. His remorse defused the row.

The tensions at Virgin were unknown in London during his launch of the renamed 'Mates'. No one questioned the background of the deal which John Jackson, an accountant, had negotiated with Ansell, to buy the condoms for 4 pence to be resold by chemists and other retailers for 12 pence, undercutting Durex by 60 per cent. Branson was unconcerned by the detail of marketing condoms. His pitch was that by cutting prices he would capture half of Britain's market within the first year – seventy million units – and treble Britain's use of condoms.

Branson emphasised, in his press conference, his new charity, the Healthcare Foundation, as the fulfilment of a life's mission. 'Aids,' he announced, 'is fast becoming a heterosexual disease.' Mates, sold by shops at no profit, would halt 'a problem which constitutes a crisis of monumental proportions. If it fails, I stand personally to lose many millions of pounds. But it's a loss I'm prepared to accept because I care for the people who represent our future health, wealth and prosperity.' No one challenged his sincerity.

As he rushed back to Boston, Branson was content that the public had accepted Virgin as a company crusading for humanity to prevent a plague. The new charity had won invaluable attention for himself. If the *Virgin Atlantic Flyer* successfully crossed the ocean, the publicity whirlwind was limitless.

The balloon's take-off on 2 July 1987 was exhilarating. As he sat in the tiny capsule watching Per Lindstrand navigate and pilot a balloon larger than the Albert Hall along its unprecedented thirty-hour journey, Branson had every reason to celebrate his own courage and foresight. The radio reports confirmed that the take-off had been quite spectacular and that the sudden loss of two fuel tanks which risked exploding into a gigantic conflagration had added to the excitement. The bid to establish a record gave his life additional meaning and distinction. 'How's the media coverage?' he asked ground control. 'Fantastic,' was the reply. Branson's eyes tightened, gleaming with satisfaction. Everything was going to plan. His relationship with Lindstrand, a sombre hired hand, was polite and professional. There was limited warmth between them, which was Branson's preference. Even in this perilous voyage, he could only tolerate a relationship of master and servant, although he took care to conceal that tension from the video camera fitted in the cramped capsule. Regularly, both he and Lindstrand activated the video to record their activities for a television documentary.

One particular touch before the departure appealed to Branson. Ostentatiously he had sat in the hotel cafeteria with two lawyers who had flown up from New York. 'He's making his last will,' whispered Virgin's publicists. Highlighting the possibility of death was drama. His public gamble against failure would certainly endear him to his many admirers, although in future he would remember, when asked whether he had written a will, to fidget, blush and hesitatingly reply, 'I really do prefer to keep these things private.'

After twenty-nine hours in the air, the balloon hovered to land in Donegal, the first landfall on the west coast of Ireland. A succession of exposed video tapes had been individually placed in sealed plastic bags inside a red Virgin flight bag lying on the floor. A new cassette was recording as Lindstrand prepared the unprecedented manoeuvre required to jettison the fuel tanks and land the biggest balloon ever flown. Branson sat passively, not expecting the sudden gust of wind which flung the balloon to the ground, pulled it across a field before thrusting it up into the atmosphere. This was the beginning of genuine danger. The balloon's cables were twisted, its fuel tanks were lost and Lindstrand was battling to bring his cavorting, twisting craft under control. As the Swede coolly drew on every ounce of strength and years of accumulated expertise, Branson exploded in terror. 'We're going to die,' he screamed. 'We're going to fucking die.' Pulling cables, firing the propane burner and trying to navigate, Lindstrand shouted back, 'Control yourself! We will die if you don't stop.' But Branson had lost his self-control. At the critical moment, the daredevil was terrified. Frenzied, tears rolled down a face contorted by anxiety. Lindstrand's choice was stark. Either he could hold on to the controls and allow Branson to rant, or he could take his hands off the levers and knock Branson unconscious. But the craft suddenly stabilised and Branson calmed. Lindstrand smiled. 'That'll look good,' he nodded. Branson followed Lindstrand's eye. His outburst had been recorded on the video. Branson's face froze. His tantrum could be witnessed by the whole world. With ferocious energy, he ripped the cassette from the machine. Oblivious to the continuing peril, he stamped frenziedly on the plastic box, pulling out the tape to destroy the evidence.

Glancing up from the mangled tape on the floor, Branson saw Lindstrand. During those moments, the Swede had battled to steer the balloon downwards towards a beach. At the last moment, the craft hit the sea and skimmed across the choppy surface, violently tumbling its two passengers. 'Get out,' shouted Lindstrand. The pilot heaved himself through the hatch and plunged into the waves. Branson hesitated and drew back, paralysed by fear. Seconds later the balloon soared upwards. The chance of escape had disappeared. His only reassurance was the sight of seventeen helicopters clinging behind him, led by Garfield Kennedy, the television documentary producer. But once the balloon passed through the clouds, he could only hope that the flotilla would remain somewhere near. Heading north across the Irish Sea, Branson's options had deteriorated. He could either hope to land in Scotland or parachute into the watery wilderness. For a trainee prevented by Lindstrand from touching the controls during the flight, the predicament was horrendous, especially after he mistakenly assumed that none of the seven radios or the emergency locator transmitter was working. He believed he was almost certainly doomed and scribbled a farewell note to Joan and his children. Leaving the note in the capsule, he planned to parachute into the sea, and opened the door. Quickly, he abandoned the idea and for nearly thirty minutes struggled to close the door. Exhausted, he peered out and saw a Royal Navy helicopter and a destroyer, alerted while on an exercise. Manoeuvring the balloon downwards, he hauled himself up through the small hatch at the top of the capsule and plunged into the sea. He was soon rescued. One hour later, Lindstrand, suffering from hypothermia, was also pulled to safety.

During the helicopter ride to Kilmarnock in Scotland, Branson's sense of priorities was restored. He had successfully won the world record. The publicity prize was secure. Quickly, he persuaded a member of the crew to lend him an alluring red jump suit. As he stepped from the plane on to the tarmac, a waiting crowd rushed to hail the hero. Behind, huddled and shivering in a grey blanket, hobbled Lindstrand.

The headlines surpassed Branson's dreams. A wave of accolades verging on worship overwhelmed Lindstrand's courageous passenger. In countless British and American newspapers and television interviews, Branson spoke through his smiles with seeming modesty mentioning, 'How I flew the Atlantic.' The pilot was forbidden by their contract to interrupt. 'The publicity would have cost £45 million,' Branson later laughed. 'Even the cover of *Newsweek*!' The epic trip had crowned a superstar. Those allowed close were, in an almost religious manner, awed.

Abandoned on the capsule was the evidence on the videos of his terror. Strangely, when the capsule was recovered later that day, none of the video cassettes was found. 'Where are they?' asked Lindstrand. 'I left them on the capsule,' replied Branson. 'The cassettes were the only items missing,' replied Lindstrand suspecting that Branson had jettisoned the tapes into the sea to destroy the evidence of his terror. After all, even his farewell letter to his wife was found. Two years later the letter was auctioned by a charity for £2,500. Even his most private emotions were available for publicity.

The hero wanted to rejoice. At his parents' house in Shamley Green, Branson hosted a party to thank all those who had worked for more than one year preparing the balloon crossing. Standing near the swimming pool, Branson talked animatedly with his father Ted, glancing regularly at the garden door. Suddenly, to a burst of music, it was thrown open. Eve Branson, his sixty-three-year-old mother shrieked her arrival. Dressed as Michael Jackson, the singer, his mother's face was painted black, she wore a black suit and white gloves, and stood with her arms outstretched beckoning applause. Instead there was an awkward titter. 'Oh my God,' murmured the crowd.

The moment passed and Branson prepared himself for his speech and the presentations. Four golden medallions hanging from gold necklaces had been specially manufactured for four women who had worked exhaustively throughout the year. Among the four who had been told in advance they would receive the necklaces was Ali Yates, Branson's personal assistant. She had not taken one day's holiday for eighteen months. Her unselfish loyalty, working eighteen hours a day without any extra pay, had damaged her health. Despite her devotion, she had recently sensed Branson's inexplicable hostility. One week earlier, at another party, he had ordered her to hand over a special Virgin Atlantic jacket made only for the balloon team to Joan Thirkettle, the ITN journalist. In Sugarloaf Mountain, Thirkettle, an attractive, serious woman, had edged unusually close to Branson, especially after preparing his obituary in case the balloon expedition failed. At their hotel, Yates had one evening watched Thirkettle walk naked out of Branson's bedroom, clutching her clothes. 'I've just had a sauna,' Thirkettle unconvincingly explained. A special relationship, Yates assumed, existed between Branson and Thirkettle. That evening at the party, Yates looked uneasily at the woman journalist. She resented losing her jacket and wondered why Branson did not fulfil his promise to find a replacement. Her thoughts were interrupted by Branson's opening remarks and then his words of appreciation to 'the four women without whom our success would not have been possible. We've had special presents made for them. Step forward, Laurie, Lisa, Fiona . . .' Yates knew she was the fourth but was thunderstruck. Branson did not say, 'Ali' but instead gushed, 'Joan Thirkettle'. Yates stood paralysed. 'I feel gutted,' she whispered to her neighbour. 'That was meant for me. He's betrayed me.'

Branson ignored Yates as she left the party close to tears. Later, revealing that exhaustion from work had brought her close to a breakdown, she received a telephone call from Branson's office. 'Richard's paid for a two-week holiday for you in Greece,' said a secretary speaking on behalf of Britain's ninth wealthiest man. Yates was grateful until she arrived in the Mediterranean. The accommodation was uncomfortably cheap and her ticket, she discovered on her return home, was a standby. Barred entry to her flight, she slept overnight on an airport chair.

Branson knew Ali Yates would never complain. He credited her silence to loyalty and gratitude. His caprice was never questioned by the beneficiaries of his generous hospitality. Celebrity and success had hardened his attitudes, especially towards a handful of disenchanted admirers. There appeared no reason for him to doubt the public's adulation. His tiny airline, thanks to the boat race and the spectacular balloon flight, was also acclaimed. Wherever he travelled, he was greeted as a hero. Only a negligible minority carped that Branson, like his balloon, was an overblown container of hot air. To Branson's misfortune, the dissidents included some powerful voices in the City.

8

Returning to the shadows

The newspapers' adulation cushioned Branson from the City's scepticism.

'No one's buying your stock because you're not wooing them,' a banker told Branson. The price of Virgin's shares had barely risen above their offer price. 'They think Virgin is a shambles.'

'It's the City,' Branson grumbled. 'They don't understand.' Since he had failed to get what he wanted, the City, he concluded, was unfairly prejudiced, treating him as a hick. Blame was always attached to someone other than himself. He was blind to his own failure to explain his business adequately to the City. The victim overlooked his advantage over the past months – which he owed to the City – of enjoying an interest-free £200 million loan.

'They're only thinking short term,' complained Branson, forgetting his own impatience with the failure of *Event* to produce rapid profits. Virgin, he insisted, was undervalued. The company's profits, according to Virgin's accountants, were rising dramatically yet the analysts were casting doubts. Branson, they sniffed, had failed to fulfil his promise to produce good profits in America. City analysts, Branson cursed, were a dislikeable breed, ignorant about his business. His irritation in turn aggravated the more conservative financiers.

Those same bankers, who months earlier had chuckled about their endearing client driving in a Renault 5 to meetings in the City with packets of Mates spread across the back seat, were also fathers of young children. They disliked Branson's later collaboration with Michael Grade, the director of programmes of BBC Television, to foist crude sexual descriptions and exaggerated alarm about Aids into young children's television programmes. Branson nonchalantly rebuffed their comments. Describing sexual acts on children's television was quite appropriate. Branson was proud of his unconventional values.

City practitioners also mentioned rumours about 'conflicts of interest'. Trevor Abbott was managing the finances in both the private and public companies, suggesting that Branson was managing the music and airline businesses as a single entity. Branson, they murmured, appeared to enjoy the dark. 'You're very secretive,' pronounced one banker.

Branson grinned. His youthful manner normally defused tension and disputes. In London's clubland, Branson's decision to sell Virgin's shares in British Satellite Broadcasting (BSB), the satellite television station, to Alan Bond, the Australian tycoon, aroused mirth. BSB had, despite Branson's bravado, disastrously failed against Rupert Murdoch's competition. Incompetent management, profligate waste, rivalry among the founders and bad programmes had caused losses of £60 million. He had hastened the sale after hearing from Per Lindstrand that Bond was on the verge of bankruptcy. The sale of Virgin's 12.5 per cent stake in BSB earned a £2 million profit. With hindsight, if he had waited until 1994 when Murdoch floated BSkyB, the joint company, his stake would have been worth £300 million. But Branson's ambition to create a worldwide media empire was flawed by his short-term attitude and his lack of creative ability. Robert Devereux's management of Virgin's 45 per cent stake in Super Channel and the Music Box was similarly mediocre. Neither Branson nor his brother-in-law were inspiring managers of media businesses.

'People suspect that you're not telling us the whole truth,' continued the banker uneasy about new whispers that Branson was secretly buying shares in EMI, the major record producer. On this occasion the banker's irritation could not be placated by Branson's equivocation. Branson, his 'waters told him', was holding back. His instinct was accurate.

Without retaining bankers as advisers, Branson and Abbott had decided that Virgin should launch a takeover bid for EMI, a company they believed was greatly undervalued. Both were undaunted that EMI was ten times bigger than Virgin and would cost about £2.6 billion, far in excess of what Branson could raise. The birth of his secret scheme was shambles.

Abbott's genius was to negotiate a £100 million loan from the Bank of Nova Scotia, allowing the two to begin spending £30 million on secret purchases of EMI shares. Occasionally, Stenham and Harris, the two non-executive directors, were not told which was a clear breach of the company's rules. Their unusual trade provoked questions around the City whether Branson would bid for EMI. 'These rumours,' he replied, 'have no basis in fact . . . we have no plans.' By then, he had accumulated a large percentage of EMI shares in anticipation of the bid.

On Monday, 19 October 1987, the world's stock markets crashed. The value of EMI's shares fell by 20 per cent and Virgin's share price collapsed from 160 pence to 83 pence. Undeterred, Branson wanted to launch his bid to buy EMI cheap but, he complained, Harris and Stenham vetoed his plan. Instead, they insisted that Branson should personally reimburse Virgin for its losses. His glacial stare at the directors signalled the beginning of their divorce.

That week, Branson travelled with a Virgin executive by taxi to a meeting of Parents Against Tobacco, a group which he sponsored to campaign against the promotion of smoking. The revelation of his secret purchases and his new debts had aroused anger among the bankers at Samuel Montagu. Their reluctance to defend Branson, caught in the public spotlight, intensified suspicions. 'Give us a fag,' he sighed to his companion. 'I'm knackered.'

The City's distrust could not be dispelled, even after Virgin announced a rise in profits from £14 million to £32 million. In the aftermath of the crash, most share prices remained low, and Virgin's was stuck at around 80 pence, nearly half their original value. Abbott was alarmed. With Branson's encouragement, he had borrowed over £100,000 to buy Virgin shares at the flotation. He had lost half his money and could not repay the banks. His secret proposal to Branson was radical. 'Why don't we privatise the company? Buy the shares back from the public?' The flotation, he told Branson, had become an albatross. 'You can't borrow money using Virgin shares as collateral,' he explained. 'Nor can the music business use the cash generated by the airline.' Branson listened. His second attempt to establish a music business in America was failing to produce profits. Abbott was proving his value, repeatedly pulling levers and shuffling money to keep the group afloat. Thanks to Abbott's financial engineering, the recent losses of Virgin Retail had been obliterated by transferring Virgin Music's profits to the loss-making company. Branson regarded his finance director as a Best Brain, a reliable acolyte. Privatising Virgin was a good idea and Abbott, who could retrieve all the

necessary financial information from Robert Ford, the group trea-
surer, was the ideal mastermind of a horrendously complicated strategy. 'Tell people I'm losing faith in the City,' Branson ordered Will
Whitehorn, his new spokesman. 'We're spending too much time
explaining and justifying what we're doing and we get no benefits.'
Neither Stenham nor Harris would for the moment be informed
about their idea. Nor would Simon Draper. Having spent so much
on cars, art and property, Branson's cousin would surely oppose the
buy-back as a threat to the value of his shares. 'He's lost the plot,'
Branson had sniped.

The sombre mood could not interfere with Branson's 1987 Christmas party. Eighty business associates had been invited to the Roof
Gardens in Kensington for a buffet dinner. Unfortunately, he was
late, stationary on the A4 driving into London. 'Richard is inching
his way to the Hammersmith flyover,' announced a Virgin minion
over the tannoy. 'He'll be here soon.' Among the guests, Don
Cruickshank and Trevor Abbott kept their distance. Cruickshank's
early enthusiasm after recruiting Abbott had soured. Both had been
attracted to Branson's glamour and his heady ability to turn stones
into money but gradually their different appreciation of Branson
caused conflicts. While Cruickshank, the careful manager and at heart
a regulator, had gradually despaired of the maverick's addiction to a
deal-a-day, Abbott had become mesmerised. Virgin, Abbott appreciated, offered the chance to become personally rich. In Virgin's headquarters on the Harrow Road, the two men argued about Branson's
erratic lurches and his tiring lust for publicity. Initially, both deferred
to a man blessed with exceptional instinct but Cruickshank favoured
consistent management rather than impulses. Branson had not concealed his preference for Abbott.

At the end of a recent dinner, Cruickshank had asked, 'Who was
that sitting next to my wife?'

'Phil Collins,' replied another Virgin employee.

'Who's he?' asked Cruickshank.

Branson's eyes shot up. He sympathised with Robert Devereux,
his brother-in-law, who, during an argument in Spain, had pushed
Cruickshank into the swimming pool.

But Trevor Abbott, Branson believed, was different. The man,
unaffectionately known to the twenty accountants rehoused in
Holland Park as 'Black Adder', knew Phil Collins and loved music.

After eighteen months, Abbott had mastered some of the intricacies of Branson's financial web and had made himself appear indispensable. Working ceaselessly, he spirited the transfers of cash through dozens of different Virgin bank accounts to stave off the perennial crisis. Among the advantages of privatisation, Abbott reasoned, would be the welcome departure of Cruickshank. 'I want him out,' Branson had agreed.

'Richard is now on the flyover. The traffic's awful,' intoned the camp voice on the Roof Gardens tannoy. Among one group of bankers, the conversation had focused on the plight of Roger Seelig, the banker, under investigation for participating in a criminal conspiracy to support the price of Guinness shares. 'Richard has cut him dead,' revealed one. 'Bit ungrateful,' commented another. 'Considering everything, you'd think he'd stand by him.' Branson, it slipped out, had become fascinated by Seelig's pitch of 'playing with shares'. The banker's eyes rose. 'Murky,' he mumbled. 'Murky.'

'You'll be pleased to hear that Richard has now come off the Hammersmith flyover,' gurgled the desiccated voice into a microphone, 'and hopes to be here in five minutes. The traffic's awful. He says he hopes everyone is enjoying themselves and says sorry.'

In a corner, Abbott was talking intimately with a solicitor from Freshfields. Their cryptic discussion concerned the secret decision that Virgin should be privatised. Abbott echoed Branson's complaint that Virgin was grinding to a halt. Across the terrace was Ken Berry who would fly secretly in June 1988 to Tokyo to find an investor to finance the privatisation.

'I'm delighted to tell you that Richard has just got out of his car and he's in the hall about to get into the lift. He'll be with us any moment now.' Muted cheers and shaking of heads greeted the news. Branson's narcissism was truly exceptional. No party, he believed, could really begin without him.

His entry was modest yet the atmosphere changed. Even dressed casually in a pullover he was imposing. Smiling and greeting his guests, he had no apparent concerns about the latest financial wrangle. Juggling the debts had become a normal daily chore. Bankers, he believed, existed to be used and not feared. He disliked their scrutiny. He disliked the independent directors even more. He would spend Christmas in Necker and reveal his plans to privatise Virgin in the new year.

The welcome diversion was Mates condoms. In early January 1988, Branson flew to Russia to establish a Virgin music company in Moscow and consider organising Virgin holidays to the Crimea, a deal offered by the Kremlin over the years to Harry Bloom, Robert Maxwell and other controversial British tycoons. To his carefully selected entourage of journalists, Branson extolled his offer of giving Mates condoms to the Russians. 'When I travel,' he giggled, 'I always pack my Mates condoms.' Saucy, sexy Richard appeared to be living up to his pledge 'to put something back into society'. But his performance concealed growing doubts about Mates. Branson had mistakenly assumed that selling sex was no different from selling records.

Although thirty-five million condoms had been sold in the first six months, a spectacular success towards capturing one third of the NHS market, the sales of Mates began suddenly to crumble. His publicity campaign evaporated. Branson's trading loss was over £1 million and rising. Not only had shops refused to sell Mates for no profit, but the senior directors of local health authorities, the major purchasers of condoms, were rejecting Mates despite the low price. Doctors resented Branson's gimmicks, especially his giant advertisements on hoardings. Those visiting family planning clinics were rejecting Mates and choosing Durex.

Their preference, to Branson's irritation, was not based on familiarity. In early 1988, Colin Parker at the Family Planning Association, received complaints about Mates' shape and quality, substantiating the instinctive suspicions by doctors and their patients that the cheaper product was inferior. Men were alleging that Mates condoms 'split' and 'burst'. A damaging report in the *Guardian* had fortunately been retracted with apologies after threats from Virgin, but the newspaper's appraisal had been accurate. John Jackson, Branson's appointed condom supremo, had discovered that the American manufacturer, to save money, had failed to conduct air inflation tests on the condoms. In the rush to finalise the deal, Branson and Jackson were unaware that Ansell's factory in Alabama had also suffered production problems. Subsequent scientific research would confirm that Mates gave 'a sub-standard response to the airburst test'. Edward Shaw, Mates' marketing manager, reported that Branson's challenge to Durex was provoking customers to castigate him for 'obviously just sticking his finger in the pie because it was another big market to make lots of money'.

'We're getting out,' was the message. The complaints and scepticism about his altruism were harming Branson's image. After one year, with estimated losses of £4 million, Branson sold Mates back to Ansell (Pacific Dunlop) in return for a £1 million payment to the Healthcare Foundation. The Americans were delighted. Their association with Branson had been profitable. Thanks to his publicity campaign, especially on BBC Television, Ansell's share of the market, after improving the condoms' quality, would increase to 16 per cent and, after increasing prices to equal Durex's, the company would earn a healthy profit. Branson's declared mission to encourage a significant increase in the use of condoms had failed; and, contrary to his dire predictions, in 1999 four hundred and not tens of thousands of people died in Britain of Aids. It was a saga, like other failures, he gradually washed from his biography.

Unpleasantness was best forgotten or delegated to others. Branson, the chameleon, soon forgot condoms and focused on the privatisation of Virgin. The revelation of his plan to Draper, Harris and Stenham was assigned in February 1988 to Abbott.

'We're going to explore the possibility of going private,' Abbott announced. Harris and Stenham stared silently, evidently displeased. This latest shock would be expensive and Branson did not have any cash. How, they wondered silently, could he afford to service the huge loans to buy back the shares, and repay Virgin's existing debts of £109 million? A meeting was arranged. 'Have you got another buyer?' Branson was asked by Stenham, a non-executive director. 'No,' he was told. Branson's hesitant style, the inscrutable trademark of the benign English amateur, placed him above suspicion, even if the doubts remained whether he was knowingly breaking the City's rules or was unaware that the rules even existed. Anthony Salz, the solicitor at Freshfields, some Virgin executives suspected, would at some stage be consulted, but he only answered to Branson. Yet Branson's vaunted declaration that ever since his Customs fraud, 'Every single decision since has been made completely by the book' was hard to dislodge.

Neither director would be informed about Ken Berry's approach four months later to Akira Ijichi in Tokyo. Berry, looking for $150 million for a 25 per cent stake in Virgin Music, insisted that their meetings had to remain secret. The Japanese accepted Berry's explanation: 'We want the money for expansion. To sign new artists.'

Ijichi did not realise that Branson needed the money to repay his debts after privatisation. The president of Pony Canyon, a subsidiary of Fujisankei, the giant Japanese media company, agreed that he would come to London after making preliminary inquiries. He was delighted to be bound by Berry's request for secrecy.

The privatisation of Virgin was the most delicate operation Branson had ever faced. He needed to conceal any negotiations with the new investors and plan how to minimise the inevitable antagonism in Britain.

Four weeks later, in early July, Frank Kane, a financial journalist employed by the *Sunday Telegraph*, telephoned Will Whitehorn, Branson's new spokesman. 'I hear that Richard is intending to take Virgin private,' said Kane, relying on a tip from a merchant banker.

'I've talked to Richard about this and there's nothing in it,' replied Whitehorn convincingly. 'Even if there was, we couldn't say because of Stock Exchange rules.' With that careful justification, Whitehorn smudged over the truth.

'It's the worst deal I've ever done in my life,' Ken Berry was cursing to anyone within earshot in Virgin's offices about the planned privatisation of the company. 'All just to bail Richard out of his filthy, stupid deals.'

Sitting on the *Duende* on Regent's Canal with a group of bankers from Samuel Montagu and Abbott a few days later, Branson, dressed in jeans and barefoot, was staring at a hole in the window. 'Someone tried to shoot me,' he laughed. The bankers were unsure whether Branson was telling the truth or seeking to impress them. They harboured mixed feelings. Some were enthusiastic about the flippant schoolboy. Others had become disillusioned but, in the interests of earning their fees and future business, concealed their emotions. All agreed that Branson's swift withdrawal from the stock market would terminate any chance of Virgin's acceptance as a substantial, orthodox corporation. Ken Berry's anger, everyone rightly assumed, referred to the huge loans which Virgin required to buy back its shares. No banker was aware about his journey to Tokyo.

The public announcement of the intended privatisation that morning, 8 July 1988, was a sensitive moment for Branson. The *Sunday Telegraph*'s Frank Kane joined the small group who thereafter distrusted Branson and his spokesman.

A disgruntled journalist usually concerned Branson, but Will

Whitehorn dismissed Kane as irrelevant and Branson was, as the bankers on his houseboat recognised, relying increasingly on Whitehorn. Branson had admired the twenty-nine year old's sureness when he handled the publicity for Chrysalis at Lombard, a financial public relations company. Physically, Whitehorn's Ralph Lauren looks also appealed to Branson. Whitehorn's clothes − a blue shirt over a white T-shirt − gave the former steward on British Airways flights to North Sea platforms the appearance of a Hollywood extra flitting around a studio's film lot. Many of those invited to close proximity to Branson bore that noticeably Waspish appearance. Their physical similarities extended to their mannerisms and posture.

Since Whitehorn was first employed by Branson in 1987, the mouthpiece and his employer shared a propensity for exaggerations in their relationships with journalists. Since his original self-promotion during the sixties, Branson's exploitation of the media had become promiscuous. To the bankers' surprise, that morning Whitehorn had, in the midst of a testing question during a television interview with Branson about Virgin's privatisation, waved his arms and coolly stopped the recording after it strayed from his stipulation that 'Richard will be allowed to give positive sentiments about wanting to head Europe's biggest entertainment company.' Smoothly, Whitehorn had persuaded the television producer not to transmit anything that might embarrass Branson. Branson understandably had come to appreciate Whitehorn's skills.

The public's perception, Branson recognised, remained vital to Virgin's future success so he listened carefully to the bankers' advice about the price the public should be offered for their shares. 'Seventy pence,' suggested John Evangelidies of Samuel Montagu. 'It's the market price. There's no need to pay any more.' Others disagreed. 'Your reputation will be permanently tarnished by any shareholder losses,' he was told. 'You never know when you want to come back to the market. You'd better offer a deal which leaves a good taste.' Abbott, mindful of his self-interest to recover his own investment, agreed. The total cost of buying back the shares at the original price of 140p each would be £90.5 million.

Tirelessly, Abbott was trawling through the boardrooms of London's foreign-owned banks pitching for a loan of £182 million. Since the Midland Bank, the owner of Samuel Montagu his merchant bankers, had refused Branson's request for a loan, his task was harder.

At the Crédit Agricole, the president of the French bank, sitting at the end of a long polished boardroom table, listened with dismissive coldness to Abbott's detailed, technical explanations. Abbott had practically raised the white flag and announced his withdrawal when the door opened and Branson entered.

'Sorry I'm late,' the tieless one laughed as he sat down. 'Erm. I just wanted to tell you that Virgin is, erm, a great business. Erm. We've got lots of plans, erm, for the future. Ahm, and we think it's a great thing.' Abbott's head sank practically beneath the table in an effort to conceal his embarrassment at Branson's bumbling effort. But the French banker's response to Branson's presence was a delightful surprise.

'We will help you monsieur. Pas de problème.'

'Well, thanks very much,' replied Branson, conscious of the spell he cast. 'I'll have to go now. I've got to have lunch at Number Ten.'

The excitement was palpable as Branson was ushered through the door with assurances of support. Amid the new positive atmosphere, Abbott resumed his explanations. Four minutes into his new speech, the door opened and Branson re-entered. 'Awfully, sorry,' he apologised. 'Could anyone lend me £10 for a taxi?' In the uproar of everyone reaching for their wallets, the French banker rushed forward and pushed forty pounds into Branson's hand. The gauche schoolboy, in apparent need of protection, had secured another convert.

Although Trevor Abbott worked hectically in Branson's interests, his employer's gratitude was conditional. 'Trevor wants 1½ per cent for his effort,' Branson told his bankers, referring to Abbott's request for a shareholding in the private company. 'But I can find another finance director for ½ per cent . . .' Abbott, he seemed to imply, was dispensable. 'Richard's ruthless and selfish,' one banker concluded. Branson always resisted paying top rate for the right man. But in Abbott's presence on the houseboat, Branson gave no hint of his doubts. The master performer required the loyalty of the entire cabal. 'Offer the original selling price for the shares,' said Branson, deferring to Abbott's advice.

The new debt, Branson acknowledged, would place his finances 'on a knife edge'. Just as interest rates were heading towards a crippling 15 per cent, Abbott's frenzied activity had by October 1988 produced a syndicate of foreign banks willing to lend £182.5 million, half to buy back the shares and the remainder to restructure old debts. Virgin would owe over £300 million although the company's assets were valued at just £224 million.

To an outsider, Branson's finances were inexplicable, which was precisely his intention. While registering record profits for the airline and music business, Virgin Group's losses were enormous. The airline was, Branson acknowledged, 'struggling to make money' and there was insufficient cash to generate investments or repay Virgin's huge debts. Every pound, admitted Branson, was committed to 'frantic juggling to keep one step ahead of the bankers'. The losses included £12 million in bad property speculation and millions of pounds of accumulated losses from Virgin's shops which had never earned real profits since 1971. Branson's remedy was to sell and cut back. Sixty-seven Our Price shops would be sold to W. H. Smith for £23 million. Other ventures were halted. Outsiders, however, would only note Branson's resilience and good humour. They were unaware of the arrival in September 1988 of Akira Ijichi, the president of Pony Canyon.

'We don't want the shareholders to know about our negotiations until they're concluded,' Berry reiterated to Moto Ariizumi, the Japanese executive accompanying Akira Ijichi. Ariiizumi agreed to the secrecy. 'We want the privatisation to succeed,' he conceded, 'so we can invest in Virgin.' Ariizumi did not realise that Pony Canyon's investment was required to repay Virgin's debts. Nor did he appreciate that Virgin's shareholders would be interested that his deal with Virgin would value the company at £129 million more than Branson would eventually pay the shareholders. The single concern shared by Ijichi and Ariizumi was that Berry and Branson continue to favour Pony Canyon until the agreement was signed. To hasten that process, on the Japanese behalf, Bruce Buck, a senior partner at Skadden Arps, an American law firm, had been drafting since July the formal agreement with Virgin while, in similar secrecy, Antonio Lorenzotti, a banker at I. B. J. Schroder's in New York, had been establishing, with the help of Price Waterhouse, an accurate valuation of Virgin Music. Both professionals guarded the secret, just as Ken Berry had originally requested. At the end of their two-day visit, Branson bid Ijichi farewell convinced that eventually a deal could be concluded.

Eight months later, in May 1989, Branson and Ijichi met again in Tokyo. The Japanese was surprised by the length of the negotiations but finally a contract would be signed for a long-term relationship. In that cause, Fujisankei, the controlling company, had forsaken agreements with any other record company, a major sacrifice, limiting Pony's development. Entrusting their future entirely to Virgin was a serious risk. To reassure the Japanese, Branson had mentioned several times 'my discussions with Mrs Thatcher'. Ken Berry had shown his goodwill by inviting Ijichi and Ariizumi to his country house for a weekend. Ijichi was reassured. This was a permanent partnership, he told his superiors. After all, Branson had agreed that Pony Canyon employees could work in Virgin's offices in London. After the signing ceremony, they celebrated their marriage in a Chinese restaurant. Branson returned to Britain extolling the virtues of the Japanese who 'operate on long-term objectives'. A few weeks later, the Japanese request to work, as agreed, in Virgin's offices was flatly refused.

The successful buy-back from the stock market was celebrated with a party and firework display at the Roof Gardens. As Abbott made a short speech of thanks, a contingent of Japanese hovered self-confidently in the centre. Among them were the representatives of Seibu-Saison, a Japanese travel conglomerate, who had invested £6 million with the promise of an additional £30 million loan for a 10 per cent stake of Virgin Atlantic. Trevor Abbott had again attracted Japanese money to cover Virgin's debts.

Branson sat quietly in the corner with a sympathetic banker. 'I've paid all you City people millions of pounds,' he griped, 'and none of you has ever made me any money. I'll never be tempted to go public again.' His resentment of the professionals' fees spilled out a few weeks later as Abbott, glowing that his round-the-clock endeavours had proved successful, unveiled the final package. 'The legal fees are too high,' snapped Branson unappreciatively. Unspoken was his resentment that Abbott, the watchman over too many of his secrets, had apportioned to himself through offshore trusts, a redeemable stake in Virgin which some would value at over £50 million. But even that endowment and his ingratiation, did not qualify Abbott to join the cabal. That was strictly reserved, to Abbott's anger, by Branson for Draper, Berry and Devereux, his brother-in-law. Devereux, in Abbott's opinion, had undeservedly been offered fifty-six million Virgin shares.

Although Robert Devereux was proving a mixed blessing, the

music business thanks to Simon Draper and Ken Berry, alias the 'Ice Man', was prospering unlike Virgin's other businesses which were unspectacular or failing. Even the airline was barely profitable. Branson, voted Britain's most favourite boss, was perturbed. He mentioned a mid-life crisis. Approaching forty, he expressed dissatisfaction. That Christmas 1989, he planned to marry Joan in Necker, a relationship of which his parents disapproved, with his two children as witnesses. He also bought a substantial house in Holland Park for £3.5 million, equipped with a swimming pool, a large garden and other accessories. To some he appeared on the verge of becoming another stagnant middle-aged tycoon seeking comfort in his palace. The impression was deceptive.

9

Finding enemies

'Give them a good knocking,' Branson laughed. 'You've got to fight for Virgin and knock BA.' Virgin Atlantic's newly appointed public relations executive blinked. The directive in 1989 was not merely to develop a business but to damage the opposition. 'They're trying to destroy us,' spat Will Whitehorn, sitting upright in Branson's Holland Park drawing room. Branson nodded. Virgin Atlantic was, he suggested, the victim of a conspiracy. 'We're going to get those arrogant bastards,' he added, emphasising that he and Whitehorn spoke and thought alike. Virgin Atlantic, an airline with just four planes, was simply being ignored by British Airways. Insignificance was intolerable. The brief was explicit: create attention-seeking opportunities to defeat the competitor. As usual, that policy relied upon public relations. 'BA never, ever, has the final word,' Branson concluded. Virgin was to yell loudly from the sidelines.

Branson's brazen confidence stemmed from an unexpected mishap. Two years earlier, in 1987, British Caledonian had collapsed. Cursed by bad management, British Airways' rival transatlantic carrier based in Gatwick had tottered into bankruptcy. The misery for British Caledonian's employees was Branson's ecstasy. 'It's fantastic. Fantastic,' he sang to Chris Moss, the marketing director. 'Hugh says it's amazing luck,' crowed Branson, referring to Hugh Welburn, a former director of economic policy at the Civil Aviation Authority (CAA), who had joined Branson after a further twenty years' employment at British Airways. Welburn was a quiet master of the regulations and finances governing the airline industry. Virgin Atlantic, he told Branson, would inherit British Caledonian's status as Britain's second long-haul airline. Under the restrictive Bermuda II agreement regulating flights between Britain and America, only two national airlines were entitled to fly between the major airports. Virgin, advised Welburn, should claim its inheritance and expand as Britain's

second airline to use British Caledonian's slots between London and
New York and four flights to Tokyo.

Branson concealed his euphoria from the public. Popular heroes,
he knew, were best advised not to dance on graves even if British
Caledonian's demise had been self-inflicted. On the contrary, he
would maintain his stance as the people's champion against British
Airways. With the help of Will Whitehorn, he dispatched a protest
to Lord Young, the Secretary of State for Trade, alleging that British
Caledonian, like Laker, was 'another victim of BA'. The letter had
hardly reached the minister's desk before it was leaked to the media.
In the same protest, Branson had also complained that SAS, the
Scandinavian airline, was bidding for British Caledonian. 'Why
should a foreign carrier be allowed to take control of some of the
United Kingdom's best routes when there are plenty of British carriers eager and willing to fly them?' he asked. Young ignored the
flamboyant protest. Branson, he noted, was not bidding for British
Caledonian and SAS's interest evaporated. The minister was grateful
that BA, the only bidder, had been prepared to pay £250 million
for the debris.

Branson drew a lesson from the hiatus. Two years after its privatisation, British Airways still rigidly ignored his nimble barbs. But if he
posed as the main competitor he could ratchet the pressure. No
doubt it was a gamble, but the downside was minimal – the people's
champion never suffered bad publicity – and the potential rewards
were enormous.

In truth, Branson had every reason to fear competition. Other
than as a record label and music publisher, all his businesses had been
defeated by competition. His magazines had folded, his restaurants,
pub, sandwich service, central heating installation company and
clothes shops had all crashed; his music shops lost money, his purchase
of W.H. Allen, the publisher, had proved disastrous and Mates condoms had misfired. Despite his boast, 'I am no stranger to healthy
competition', he remained an imitator of other people's ideas until
bad management and losses forced his retreat. The airline, thanks to
Randolph Fields's recruitment of good managers, was the exception.

Although in 1989 Virgin Atlantic offered an unreliable and
cramped service for economy passengers seeking cheap fares; the
airline was attracting admirers of the bouncing tycoon, and executives
who preferred a more indulgent and free-spirited alternative to British

Airways' stiff service. In public, his self-promotion and ambitions were reasonable: 'Airlines should be kept small and personal. They should be run like personal clubs. We try to manage ours from the bottom up. We want no more than ten major routes and a dozen 747 planes. If I ever get bigger, hold my head under cold water. I hope I have learnt from Freddie Laker's mistakes. We want to offer a superior product at competitive prices.' Among his weaknesses were organisation and marketing. Branson's dislike of organisational structures, meetings and inquests perpetuated uncertainty. 'Opportunities are like London buses,' he often replied, reiterating that his business was motivated by gut instinct and chance. 'If you miss one and think about it, you'll probably miss the next one.' The cure to chaos and mismanagement was the arrival in 1989 of Syd Pennington from Marks and Spencer.

Pennington discovered that the senior managers, housed in Crawley, bickered among themselves, ignoring the important details which earned profits. Roy Gardner, an engineer, was the managing director of the airline but did not understand the costing of food and drink on planes, or the sales of duty free. Others were unsure of their responsibilities. 'It's a shambles,' Pennington told Branson about the absence of management controls. 'You won't have an airline in eighteen months unless there are changes.' Pennington's introduction of modern systems improved the finances but Branson knew that expansion depended upon recruiting more expertise. His search was satisfied when Mike Batt, an accomplished marketing executive at British Airways, accepted his offer to join Virgin.

Branson was in Japan, unsuccessfully struggling to launch a balloon trip across the Pacific, when Batt arrived at the headquarters of Virgin Atlantic in Crawley. Virgin Atlantic's new joint manager was greeted with sour looks and then ignored, particularly by Roy Gardner, his intended partner. The dislike was mutual and, after discovering that no suitable office had been allocated and that two other Virgin executives claimed to be doing his job, Batt returned forty-eight hours later to British Airways with stories of chaos and misery in Virgin's headquarters.

In Japan, Branson walked smiling across the field towards Chris Moss. 'Maybe you were right,' he laughed to his marketing director. 'Batt was a BA plant.' Rebuffs hurt Branson. On his return to Britain, in January 1990, rather than accept the truth, that Batt had walked away from the chaos that greeted his arrival, Branson was persuaded to believe a tale of 'mystery' and about a conspiracy mastered by British Airways. Batt, he believed, had been inserted and withdrawn to spread spurious stories. There appears to have been no conclusive evidence for that defamation but Branson's enthusiasm to spread speculation among his senior executives that BA was trying to destroy Virgin Atlantic was to become part of Virgin's strategy.

Sitting in his large, newly decorated drawing room in Holland Park, with Will Whitehorn, Chris Moss, Hugh Welburn and other airline executives, Branson spoke about the huge crowds which had gathered in Japan to watch the ill-fated balloon voyage, but he avoided mentioning one detail from the tense hours before the intended launch. As holes had appeared in the balloon's fabric and bad weather was forecast, he had suggested to Per Lindstrand that they nevertheless embark on their trip. 'We'll die for certain,' Lindstrand had replied, shocked that Branson's anxiety about negative publicity could so override his common sense. Close to tears, Branson had watched the slow disintegration of the anchored balloon. 'We'll be the laughing stock in England,' he had seethed to Lindstrand. 'This is embarrassing. The amount of people we have messed up around the world . . .' His voice faded, distressed by the spectators' inevitable disappointment but mollified by the crowd's good-natured cheers. By his return to London, their hero worship had soothed his nerves and encouraged his strategy to enmesh the 'fun and frills' of Virgin Atlantic with a political challenge against the 'monopolies' obstructing his ambitions for more routes to Europe and America.

During their discussion, Welburn succinctly summarised his strategy: 'We need to cherry-pick more of BA's best routes across the Atlantic. That's where they earn more than 60 per cent of their profits.' Virgin Atlantic would be promoted not as a pickpocket but as the slayer of British Airways' monopoly. The people's champion, it was agreed, would use gimmicks, pranks and brutal criticism to undermine the national airline. 'We need to get noticed,' said Branson with unusual intensity. 'I can't stand it that TV programmes show planes with BA on the tail and not Virgin. No one knows about us.'

His advertisements were intended to provoke. 'BA is for short, thin people,' one campaign started. His letters to newspapers clamoured for attention. British Airways, he wrote to *The Times*, ignored 'the current climate [which] welcomes competition'. Virgin inspired newspaper headlines by announcing the lease of a Concorde from France to compete with British Airways. As Syd Pennington admitted to a newspaper, it was untrue but, 'Richard asked me to do it.' Film actresses, bikini-clad models and journalists, flying first class among four hundred guests for a two-day party at Branson's expense on inaugural services to Boston and Los Angeles, were encouraged to disparage British Airways. Businessmen were promised their fares would be returned if the massage, manicure, one hundred in-flight movies and limousine provided by Upper Class did not outclass BA's service. 'The airline business is all about entertainment,' Branson gushed, directing the press office to announce new Virgin Atlantic services which still lacked the formal approval of the CAA and the government. 'Great,' he scribbled on a travel magazine reporting a new Virgin route to Philadelphia, delighted that the press officer had, on his initiative, secured publicity for an aspiration dressed up as a decision. The gullibility of journalists never ceased to amuse him. His credibility was undisputed.

The sceptics were inside his citadel. At three o'clock in the morning he had telephoned Dudley Broster, his deputy operations director. 'I want to put balloons in the plane for the kids,' he ordered.

'You must be mad Richard,' replied the veteran pilot emerging from his sleep. 'It's as bloody crazy as your idea of sand pits on the plane. Have you ever heard of decompression? There'll be sand everywhere and balloons bursting.'

Later that morning, Broster walked into Branson's office. 'I want you to order the pilots to stop smoking,' said Branson.

'It won't work,' replied Broster, a no-nonsense chain-smoker.

Branson became agitated. His diktat should have been obeyed. The exchanges became acrimonious. 'Oh fuck,' sighed Branson. 'Give us a fag. I need one.'

Broster's sympathy was limited. Ever since he had won a furious row in 1987, refusing to order a plane full of passengers at Gatwick bound for New York to disembark, he felt immune to Branson's spleen. The saga still embarrassed Branson. Virgin Atlantic had beaten British Airways for the government's contract to fly British soldiers to the Falklands but one of its two planes had broken down in Ascension Island. The second jumbo, filled with passengers, was about to take off from Gatwick. Fearful of paying a huge penalty payment and losing the contract, Broster had been ordered to disembark the passengers with a phoney excuse and fly south to transport the soldiers. The passengers had disembarked but Broster continued to protest: 'No way, I'm not flying there.' He won and the bewildered passengers returned to the plane. Branson knew that he could rely on Broster's discretion and loyalty not to reveal the embarrassment.

The pilots' admiration did not completely cloud their understanding especially concerning Branson's public indignation about excessive air fares. Repeatedly, Branson damned British Airways' high prices and praised his own championship of low fares. The performance, the pilots understood, was Branson's propaganda war to destabilise his target. 'Virgin's £56 single fare to NY,' was printed everywhere as proof of Branson's championship of the common man but the opportunity expired in a flash. 'We'll slash fares to Jo'burg by 20 per cent,' Branson promised but few benefited. 'Virgin will sell £35 tickets to Europe's capitals,' roared the self-appointed exterminator of monopolies, but the promise evaporated before a ticket was sold.

'There's an Exocet on its way,' Roy Gardner warned amid Branson's frenzy of activity. The war of words against British Airways had intensified. Branson announced in August 1990 Virgin's intention to dispatch *Virgin Saviour*, a Boeing 747, to Iraq to rescue British civilians trapped by the outbreak of war with Kuwait. Since Branson knew that the flight could only proceed after the Iraqi government had approved its safe passage, there was little danger and limited disruption to Virgin Atlantic's regular schedule after the lease of two more 747s. The publicity for Virgin's 'mercy flight' was ceaseless. Will Whitehorn's most incendiary driblet was the suggested anger of Lord King. 'He's fucking furious,' whispered Whitehorn to chosen journalists. 'Virgin, not BA have been asked by the government to fly for Britain.' The Union Jack, implied Whitehorn, was wrapped around Virgin rather than British Airways. Branson and Whitehorn knew that the immediate reaction of journalists would be a telephone call to the corporation to test their outrage.

The director of British Airways publicity was David Burnside, a thirty-nine-year-old Ulsterman, alias 'The Irish kneecapper', whose thick brogue and aggressive championship of the Protestants' cause, even advocating the use of militancy, caused some to question Lord King's judgement. But none doubted Burnside's ability and commitment, and his mentor's absolute trust implied that their opinions were interchangeable.

Until 'Virgin's mercy flight', Burnside had not bothered himself with an airline flying four third-hand jumbos. But the journalists' incessant telephone calls demanded a response. Guardedly, he directed inquirers to scrutinise Branson's new patriotism. In 1986, during a near war between an Anglo-American alliance and Libya, Branson had boasted during a party for Amnesty International in the Roof Gardens that ever since Colonel Gaddafi of Libya had threatened reprisals against British civil airliners, Virgin Atlantic was doing better than its competitors. 'We've got 80 per cent bookings right now. It helps a lot not to have the word British anywhere.' Others were reminded by Burnside that the new patriot's company was registered offshore to avoid paying British taxes.

Burnside's mild gripes were music to Branson. After six years, British Airways had finally acknowledged his existence. On the eve of flying to Iraq on 23 October 1990, Branson and Whitehorn offered selected journalists a confidential whisper to confirm Lord King's fury about the power of Virgin. In an explosive outburst during a private conversation between Lord King and William Waldegrave, a junior Foreign Office minister, said Branson, King had protested about the government's co-operation with Virgin: 'Who the hell does Richard Branson think he is? Part of the bloody Foreign Office?' The image conjured by Branson and Whitehorn was of the ultra-patriotic King, a peer of the realm, inflamed by the people's champion. That incident, Branson would say, 'was the start of an entire campaign by British Airways to try to put Virgin Atlantic out of business'. Thereafter he could cast Virgin as the victim of a conspiracy, which left a bad taste in Whitehall where Branson's version was uncorroborated.

Officials in the Foreign Office recorded in their files a somewhat different story without any mention of King's outburst. In the Whitehall files, both British Airways and Branson had offered to rescue the hostages in Iraq. Virgin's first offer was £1 million more expensive than BA's because Branson expected the British government to pay for the aircraft's insurance. After hearing that the Foreign Office had rejected Virgin's offer, Branson dropped the insurance charge and won the selection. No one in the Foreign Office, however, recorded King speaking to Waldegrave, or Waldegrave telling Branson about

King's unspoken jibe. King denied ever speaking to Waldegrave about Branson. Yet, to Branson's good fortune, neither the politicians nor the officials in Whitehall publicised their irritation about the invention. King also remained silent. 'I might have said something like that to a journalist,' said King, 'but I never spoke to Waldegrave.' Any criticism would have appeared churlish after the massive publicity Branson encouraged for his 'mercy dash'. Their silence gave credibility to his propaganda blitz that Virgin had humiliated BA. Branson's only disappointment, admitted Whitehorn, was that Branson was not crowned 'Man of the Year'. After all, explained the spokesman, Branson should be rewarded for 'trying so hard to avoid personal publicity'. The rebuff hurt Whitehorn as much as Branson. Even Sting, the pop star, had commiserated that 'No act of kindness goes unpunished.'

The excitement alleviated Branson's resentment about his new attempt to cross the Pacific in a hot-air balloon with Lindstrand. His third journey to Japan in December 1990 had been reluctantly undertaken. During the previous year he had sought to ignore his public promise to the mayor of Miyakonojo, the site of the 1989 launch, to return and had hoped that the mayor's visit to Britain to remind him of his pledge would be overlooked. He had even agreed to participate in another balloon trip without Lindstrand. But the accusation of bad faith was impossible to disregard, not least because the mayor's special journey to Branson in London had been filmed and included in a documentary by Garfield Kennedy. 'Cut that out,' ordered Branson agitatedly during a viewing of the video in a Hollywood editing suite. 'No,' replied Kennedy firmly. Branson was compelled to relent. At least, he reasoned, the publicity for Virgin in Japan would justify the risk. But to Lindstrand, it seemed that flying balloons for Branson had become as exciting as a visit to the dentist. 'You're going through with this just to be a hero,' said Lindstrand. 'Not for fun or adventure. It's just, "let's get this over with".'

The take off on 15 January 1991 was perfect. 'What was the press coverage like?' was Branson's familiar mantra to ground control. The next forty-six hours as the massive balloon flew a record-breaking 6,761 miles across the Pacific to the Canadian Arctic was hell. After the loss of two fuel tanks, the balloon climbed to perilous altitudes, lost radio contact and caught fire. Branson cursed that he had agreed to undertake the voyage. 'We're going to land in the sea,' he repeated endlessly. Lindstrand's sombre bravery and skill saved their lives only for both men to discover that their survival and success were ignored because the Allies had invaded Iraq. The misfortune of lost publicity grated with Branson especially. Denied the widespread adulation for their genuine courage, he vented his frustration at Lindstrand.

During the eight-hour wait for the rescue helicopter in the Arctic wilderness, Branson reflected on his partner with whom he was clasped to mitigate the frostbite. His dependence on the discretion of the only eyewitness of his vulnerable lapses stung his vanity. As the paymaster, he resented Lindstrand's lack of deference and blamed the designer and pilot for the mishaps during the journey which jeopardised their lives. Even before their evacuation from the landing zone, he had decided that any future balloon adventure would be undertaken with one of Lindstrand's rivals. He condemned Lindstrand as a 'loner' and too 'quick to criticise'. Branson's public assertion, 'I'd been brought up to look for the best in people but Per always seemed to find the worst', was uttered regardless of the hurt which Lindstrand would suffer and was contradicted by his own attitude towards Lord King after his return to Britain.

Branson, the public schoolboy turned trader, had drawn to his cabal those of a similar upper-middle class background while keeping his state-educated employees, other than the technocrats upon whom he relied, at a professional distance. But at the end of the Thatcher era, in common with his generation, he had grown to dislike the irritable affectations of his own class. More particularly, he cursed those born in the lower classes who affected to be members of the aristocracy. The arrogance and insensitivity of John King, a former car dealer who had been elevated to the peerage in 1983, upset the natural pretensions of a self-made, upper-middle class tycoon.

The seventy-four-year-old chairman of British Airways preferred to conceal his humble background as the son of a postman while extolling his success as an engineer, his enjoyment of hunting and his second marriage to the youngest daughter of the eighth Viscount of Galway. By 1991, King was widely praised for transforming BA from a nationalised, loss-making drain on the Exchequer serving its employees' interests into the world's most profitable long-haul airline, earning £10.5 million profit, and still fighting to win new passengers. The chaotic management at Virgin Atlantic and the haphazard dispersal of Branson's businesses across London would have been intolerable in a corporation employing 60,000 people across the world. But the same personality which bullied BA staff to accept a cultural revolution, aggressively protected his business against competitors.

Personalising a competitor as an enemy had become natural to Branson. To secure victory, he searched for ruses to provoke British Airways and its chairman. 'Youth fighting against an old codger,' was the directive to Virgin's publicity department. 'He's an easy target.' Denigrating King's achievement became Branson's battle cry.

The opening shot was Branson's announcement on television, soon after his successful balloon flight across the Pacific, that Virgin would sue British Airways for £4 million for failing to service a Boeing 747 in 1989. Since BA, as the inheritor of British Caledonian's contract, had continued to service Virgin's planes without complaint, it was particularly warlike to elevate a two-year-old technical dispute into a public issue. But it was the prelude to Branson's onslaught. His denigration was plausible. 'BA,' he chanted, 'is a monopoly controlling 92 per cent of UK's international air services.' The reality was different. On all the transatlantic routes, BA had 39 per cent of the market while the two American airlines, both three times BA's size, were selling 30 per cent of the tickets. Virgin had 9 per cent of the market. The remaining airlines flew 22 per cent of the passengers. British Airways was not a monopoly and unlike the bigger European airlines, Lufthansa and Air France, it possessed only one third of slots at Heathrow while its European and American competitors were allocated up to 90 per cent of the slots in their central hub airports. That interpretation was unappealing to Branson. BA, he knew, was vulnerable, and he intended to exploit that weakness by intensifying his public complaints about the airline.

In January 1991, Lord King was nervous. British Airways planes were flying nearly empty. The Gulf War and a savage economic recession had decimated bookings and slashed the airline's income. King's predicament was certain to become worse the following month. American Airlines and United Airlines, flying 1,500 planes worldwide, would replace PanAm and TWA, two decrepit airlines, at Heathrow. King's only consolation was that every airline was suffering. Virgin Atlantic's troubles were even worse.

Despite the few transfers from British Airways in the hope that

Saddam would ignore an airline not covered in the Union Jack, thousands of reservations had been also cancelled on Virgin Atlantic. The competition for the remaining passengers, Branson knew, would intensify. Virgin's bankers, wary of a small airline's precariousness, were permanently examining the company's finances. His predicament was compounded by the collapse of Air Europe, a bigger independent carrier, bankrupted by huge debts, bad management and finally the recession. Virgin's vulnerability could not be kept secret and on 25 January 1991, the dreaded messenger called.

Sidney Shaw, Branson's account manager from Lloyds Bank, announced, 'We can't see how you can possibly keep Virgin Atlantic going.' Virgin's overdraft had hit £50 million. While Branson admitted that the group's combined net debts were at least £242 million, in reality they were over £400 million, partly guaranteed by his offshore trusts. The level of indebtedness was guarded by Abbott's constant transfer of cash from one account to another.

Branson pleaded with Shaw to be reasonable. The accounts of the other Virgin businesses – music, video games, holidays – he told Shaw, showed high sales. But sales, in technical terms the cash flow which had sustained Branson, were not profits. His deliberate policy of minimising his companies' profits to protect himself against demands for taxes, rebounded. His plight was confused by inter-company trading, an accounting technicality attracting criticism at that moment. In stark terms, Branson's empire was tottering, seemingly unable to repay its debts. Shaw, however, allowed Branson time to reorganise his finances.

Branson's best hope for survival was if the government agreed that Virgin Atlantic's flights could be transferred from Gatwick to Heathrow, a more profitable airport, and awarded more slots for Virgin's flights to Tokyo. If that strategy failed, Branson knew, Virgin 'would be out of business'. His tactic was to play on emotions, casting himself as David against Goliath. 'Let's do something on BA,' he mentioned to Chris Moss, his marketing director.

Branson had never given much thought to the content of his hype and taunts. Whatever he blurted to promote rock groups, his media ambitions or his condoms, his precise words had passed unnoticed in the world of politics and finance. Public pronouncements in the airline industry, he knew after many trips to Whitehall and West-minster, were different. Politicians, civil servants, bankers, shareholders and huge swathes of public opinion were sensitive to every nuance of that volatile industry. Any words uttered by a participant who wilfully sought star status would, just as he hoped, be carefully scrutinised. His decision, towards the end of January 1991 after his Pacific balloon flight had failed to promote his airline, was carefully considered. Using his friends in the media, especially those who had enjoyed upgrades on Virgin planes, he escalated his war of words, just when British Airways was vulnerable.

Evoking the mythology that Laker Airways had been destroyed solely by British Airways' membership of a price-cutting cartel, he called selected journalists writing for the serious broadsheet newspapers. All were carefully briefed that BA was 'deliberately undercutting other airlines on transatlantic routes to win market share'. Branson knew, however, that every airline, including Virgin, was cutting fares to seduce the handful of passengers and that Virgin's fares were the lowest. BA's fare reductions were not exceptional. Branson's allegation, everyone understood, became more serious because of his prediction: 'We're out to grab 30 per cent of the transatlantic air passenger market within three years, putting us on level pegging with British Airways.' In launching his attack against Goliath, Branson would melodramatically sigh, 'nobody would think [BA] could ever feel threatened by a tiny airline like Virgin Atlantic', but that was precisely the fear he intended to spark.

In the popular press, especially the *Sun*, whose readers were targeted as Virgin's natural customers, Branson could personalise the dispute. Fortunately, David Yelland, a senior *Sun* journalist and Branson's guest in Florida, playing golf and throwing Virgin aircrew with his host into the swimming pool, was an unquestioning admirer. Responding to Branson's complaints, Yelland's articles praised Branson in his battle against British Airways. Branson was a 'daredevil', 'a man of great character' and ahead of Lord King's wealth and personal qualities because Branson 'loves adventures'. Branson also offered co-operation to television programmes, especially to London's ITV station, to produce a report which publicised his criticisms of BA and reported Lord King's 'personal abuse'.

Branson's carping was ignored by Lord King until the CAA, the airlines' regulatory agency, released a terse announcement. The CAA recommended to the government that Virgin should be allowed access to Heathrow and be given four of BA's slots to Tokyo. For

Branson, the news was a lifeline, the reward for endless lobbying. To King, it was an inexplicable theft.

Branson feigned surprise that Lord King was 'furious'. That understated Lord King's outrage about the lunacy of bureaucrats. Undoubtedly, King reasoned, they would be overruled by a Conservative minister. Nevertheless, British Airways' policy of deliberately ignoring Virgin Atlantic was no longer sustainable.

British Airways' public response acknowledged that reality. 'Branson,' said a spokesman minimising the criticism as a tease, 'is hiding behind a slick and picturesque PR image . . . His interests are not in the customers' interests.' That harmless response prompted Branson to feign grievous hurt. King, he complained, behaved as if 'I didn't even exist'.

'I was particularly upset by the fact,' Branson cried, 'that the press release attacked me personally. BA seemed to be suggesting that there was something sinister and unpleasant lurking behind my own image.' To rub salt in the wound, Branson even wrote to King, 'I resent the level of personal abuse your people at British Airways have resorted to.' Soon after, Branson decided he wanted it both ways.

Levelling abuse at Lord King and his company intoxicated Branson as he approached Malcolm Rifkind, the Secretary of State for Transport, for support apparently unwary of his entry into uncharted territory. Lord King, he told Rifkind, was privately 'bad-mouthing Virgin Atlantic' about its debts. Although Rifkind could never recollect a conversation with King about Branson's debts, Branson raged that King had told the minister about Virgin Atlantic's 'insolvency'. The failure of either participant to recollect that version of their conversation was irrelevant to Branson. The urgency was Branson's panic that Virgin's true financial plight might emerge.

Ever since 1988, Branson had realised that Virgin's 'mountain of debt' was potentially fatal. The airline was, he admitted, 'struggling to make money'. The breakdown of just one 747 for a few days would have plunged the business into bankruptcy. Although Virgin Atlantic's turnover had soared in 1990 to £180 million, its profits had fallen, not least because Branson was occasionally indifferent to detail. The 1990 accounts only looked respectable thanks to deft cosmetics. Virgin Atlantic's end of year accounting date had been changed from July to October and the profits of two summers and one winter had been consolidated. Virgin Atlantic also sold a Boeing 747 and leased it back, entering the profit of £1.6 million into its accounts. It was legal and consistent with Branson's customary brinkmanship. In 1991, Branson hoped that Virgin Music's unprecedented $25 million contract with Janet Jackson for one album would stifle the rumours about Virgin's debts because 'we were indeed suffering a cash crisis'. Virgin Atlantic was heading towards losses of £21 million.

Laying smokescreens to conceal his plight was a temporary remedy while he searched for money. Either the airline or the music business, he knew, would have to be sold. The previous year, Island Records had been sold and recently Geffen Records, an independent American label, had been bought by MCA for $710 million. Huge sums, beyond the market's valuation, were being paid. Virgin Music, the last of the big independent labels, could be worth a fortune. Sentiment could not be allowed to interfere with business. 'Too many entrepreneurs,' he acknowledged, 'have gone down because they were not prepared to cash in their chips at the right time.'

His merchant bankers were told that Virgin Music would be sold. While a buyer was sought by Goldman Sachs, Branson pondered which other of his companies to sell for cash and how to confuse inquiring creditors and financial journalists with mirages. 'Tell them,' Whitehorn instructed his staff delegated to answer journalists' inquiries, '"you're not comparing like with like". If they press, tell them that the financial years have changed.' Energetically in the background, Branson elevated his bid for survival from simple business competition to a political battle.

Discreetly, Branson invited Malcolm Rifkind for lunch in Holland Park. He wanted to remind the transport minister that Conservative policy was to encourage competition and hence he should support the CAA's recommendations despite the harm to British Airways. 'Our future depended upon it,' he explained.

Rifkind, curious about the idolised music king, accepted the invitation. Deftly, after a flash of his engaging smile, Branson made no apparent effort to impress the minister. Dressed in jeans and an open-necked shirt, he was always indifferent that his visitors would feel overdressed but on this occasion the informality disarmed the politician's natural suspicions. Eating plain chicken in the atrium overlooking Branson's substantial garden, Rifkind was 'pleasantly surprised' by his host's modesty despite his achievements. His manner lent authority to his arguments.

Playing the populist card, the people's hero knew that politicians, like journalists, rarely probed his version of the truth if the sentiments sounded attractive. His script to Rifkind portrayed Virgin as a big, successful, cash-rich enterprise, created thanks to Thatcherism, which required protection from the bullying of a public enemy. Knowing that his application for access to Heathrow and four more slots to Tokyo was opposed by British Airways because it would erode its marginal profits, he meekly suggested that such small concessions, while 'vital' to Virgin, could not possibly influence or significantly weaken BA's finances.

The minister's personal experiences on his frequent journeys to his Edinburgh constituency had bred some dislike of British Airways. British Midland's new shuttle between London and Edinburgh had sharply improved BA's service undermining King's protests against competition. 'We don't favour private monopolies,' the minister assured Branson. 'We're pro-competition to sharpen everyone up.' Branson nodded, innocently observing that 'BA seems remarkably reluctant to face up to competition.' The routine was on the verge of success. 'We're entitled to the route,' Branson told the minister. He forgot Freddie Laker's concession that Heathrow's triumph owed everything to the success of British Airways.

In March 1991, Rifkind ratified the CAA recommendation that Virgin Atlantic should be allowed access to Heathrow. 'Thank you for putting us on a slightly more level playing field,' cooed Branson, anticipating Lord King's sour reaction. 'BA,' chortled Branson, 'will just have to cut back on lobbying and entertaining MPs and put the savings towards passenger services if it wants to compete.' Branson's assertion that Rifkind and others were 'brave' to 'stick their necks out to help me' was calculated to inflame.

Forty-eight hours later, his foe was served a more serious reason to squeal. With Rifkind's blessing, four of British Airways' slots to Tokyo were transferred to Virgin. Branson did not understate his victory. He later revealed his true agenda: 'We were now a serious threat to [BA's] long-term future.' The skirmishes were intended to lead towards war.

10

War and deception

Journalists, Richard Branson knew, were preoccupied by superficialities, especially the appealing image of a bitter battle between himself and Lord King. They responded well to his personal telephone calls pleading with the zealot's sincerity, 'I'm fighting for the consumer. BA's arguments are bollocks. Justice is on my side.' His sincerity was so persuasive that no one dared to suggest that it might disguise his self-interest. After all, the people's hero was boisterously offering £99 fares to New York, vastly undercutting BA's £225 economy fare. Those who closely examined the offer discovered that it was limited to buying and flying within the following twenty-four hours. But his gimmicks attracted customers and his insults, as intended, infuriated King.

On hearing Rifkind's decision, King was livid. 'He probably believes his own crap,' moaned David Burnside, tempering his employer's ballistic anger to compose a reasoned response. Rifkind's assertion, King protested, that the public interest was served by handing over British Airways' investment and profits without compensation to a non-British rival company specialising in avoiding British taxes, contradicted the government's prominent assurance in BA's privatisation prospectus to avoid compulsory route transfers. Rifkind's decision, he continued, also undermined the government's promise to shareholders that 'there would be no forced reduction in British Airways' size relative to the rest of the industry'.

In normal circumstances, King's judicious complaint would have ended the public exchanges. But Branson was rarely satisfied with mere victory. The pirate camouflaged by an easy smile and casual dress desired his foe's utter humiliation. Welcoming a telephone call from yet another journalist he sniped, 'Lord King has managed to con successive governments into believing that big is beautiful in the airline business.' Ribbing his defeated foe as 'a very tired giant', he continued, 'Lord King used to be able to phone up Downing Street and get Department of Transport decisions overridden. Now the best he can do is a photo of himself with John Major.' The insult was premeditated and, to his satisfaction, there was no public criticism of his insolence. Yet even Branson could not have imagined the consequences of pressing King's 'nuclear' button.

Despite the advertiser's slogan of 'World's Favourite Airline' and Lord King's entrepreneurial skills, the staff of British Airways had still not overcome the culture shock nor the requirements of privatisation. Branson's raw competition – his 'fun' airline – offended many loyal BA employees and baffled the corporation's executives. Few in BA's headquarters could identify a quick cure to the airline's ungenerous service and their cabin staff's coolness towards passengers. Any response was confused by divided loyalties towards Lord King and Colin Marshall, the airline's talented chief executive. While King was BA's public face, Marshall toiled beyond the limelight on the unspectacular but critical detail. Gossip about the tension between the charismatic chairman and the cool technocrat was fuelled by Marshall's reported complaint, 'I do all the work and he gets all the credit.' The gossip was inflamed by the presence of Michael Levine, an unusual American adviser retained by Marshall to consider the airline's strategy. Levine's principal concern was BA's response to the imminent arrival at Heathrow of American Airlines and United Airlines. 'The Visigoths will destroy you,' warned Levine. BA, he explained, would need to fight to protect its market against all its rivals. Just one passenger transferring from each BA flight to a competitor amounted to millions of pounds of lost revenue. That was the dilemma which King's executives faced. The prospects that year were dire and from the sidelines a cheeky, low-cost interloper, flying eight planes with the Conservative government's help, was publicly threatening more damage to their most profitable routes.

Lord King vented his fury to David Burnside, his director of publicity. For months Burnside had obeyed his own edict, 'don't give him ammunition'. His reaction to Branson's publicity-seeking provocations had been restricted to silence or terse scorn. But aspects of the media's uncritical acceptance of Branson's self-publicity irritated the Ulsterman. Burnside felt that Branson's claim to have secured a Concorde had been untrue; his attack against British Airways for using Concorde to lure passengers was hypocritical because

Virgin offered upgrades; and his self-promotion as a serious investor in a huge hotel development at County Hall, opposite Westminster, had been contrived. The interloper's stunts, in Burnside's opinion, detracted from BA's own life and death struggle. 'Don't be fooled by Branson's petulance that "I haven't got this and I'm entitled to this",' he urged inquirers. But the wave of questions inspired by Branson and Whitehorn never ceased. Burnside's irritation grew. Branson's inflammable performance, his scruffy appearance and his casual lifestyle offended Burnside's fundamental values. Gradually Burnside's caution was eroded, he misjudged his adversary and he followed King's choleric instincts. King wanted Branson torpedoed. The two men haphazardly played into his hands.

Without considering the consequences, in early June 1991, King announced that British Airways was withdrawing its donations to the Conservative party. Rifkind's favourable decision for Virgin had undoubtedly harmed BA but King's admission that he expected political favours from the government for money was a spectacular misjudgement. Branson delighted in exploiting King's petulance.

On board a Virgin jumbo full of journalists flying free to Boston, good humouredly anticipating the usual party in return for favourable press coverage to announce a new route, Branson glowed. Passing down the aisle, he poured champagne, exchanged jokes, revelling in the contrast of his popularity and King's tactlessness. His hospitality and the promise of future invitations extinguished every nuance of criticism from his guests. Over the previous twenty-four years, Branson had perfected his relationships with journalists, editors and newspaper proprietors to publish favourable reports. The reward for his efforts appeared in the *Sun*, written by his loyal admirer, David Yelland. 'This guy's airline is a serious threat,' Yelland quoted an American. 'People are starting to say: "Hey, you must fly with Virgin, they're so good."' Branson was on a roll. Journalists, especially women, confessed their attraction to the 'gentle, uncomplicated soul whose boyish aura remains intact'. Another female journalist wrote, 'He's got this very calculating mind that plays things out, but his instinct is brilliant.' How he loved being loved. Lord King was never cast as a romantic or a poet warrior. On the contrary, he was an unappealing, floundering whale.

Embarrassing British Airways was no different from parading the Sex Pistols on a Thames cruiser outside the Palace of Westminster.

In his media onslaught to promote Virgin as the victim and himself as the consumer's champion, Branson repeated on countless television programmes and in newspapers that BA had failed to warmly welcome him in Heathrow and was not helping Virgin Atlantic to obtain the ideal slots to fly from Heathrow to America at the best times. 'Completely hopeless,' he complained about BA's 'sinister' reluctance to inflict damage on its own business. To Branson it appeared completely rational that Virgin Atlantic should receive as many valuable slots as it required, immediately and for nothing.

'King's always calling you a pirate,' Chris Moss said to Branson. 'I've got an idea to show we've arrived at Heathrow.' The occasion was Virgin's big party and fun fair at the airport on 1 July 1991 to celebrate the airline's transfer from Gatwick. The striking model of Concorde at the airport's entrance symbolised British Airways. The prank was simple. Dressed as a pirate, Branson would stand in front of BA's hoarding with a Virgin logo draped over the tail. Like in all stunts, there would be a victim: Lord King.

Towards the end of the Virgin party, a group of photographers and reporters were shuttled to the site in a minibus. Branson arrived in costume. 'I'm claiming this as Virgin territory,' he laughed. Moss's mobile telephone rang. The airport's chief constable was irate. 'He'll go ape,' Branson roared as he drove from the site thinking about King's exploding red face. Annoying 'Pompous King' was a pleasure and a written complaint from Bob Ayling, BA's senior lawyer, confirmed the hurt. More of the same, was Branson's instruction to Moss.

Over the summer of 1991, Branson's high profile, posing as the 'doting father' for photographers with his children, preaching that 'small is beautiful', was winning passengers to his flights from Heathrow. 'This year, while other airlines' profits slumped, ours soared,' he boasted. 'Our planes have been three-quarters full. Because we care about small details, care for our staff and care for people, we've hardly lost any customers.'

Branson's claims turned out not to be accurate. Although Virgin Atlantic was attracting enormous publicity and plaudits for excellent service, his airline was suffering from the same recession as British Airways. Arriving at Ashdown House, the airline's headquarters in Crawley, he slumped into a chair. Groping in his brown leather shoulder bag, he pulled out his notebook, faxes and telephone messages before he produced a set of accounts. 'Fuck,' he sighed, dropping his head into his hands. 'We've got to get this sorted.'

In a letter to all Virgin Atlantic's staff in September 1991 Branson admitted, 'our yields have slipped quite considerably. The initial forecast for the next twelve months has given us cause for concern.' The extra passengers were not earning any additional profits. Virgin, he warned, would need to 'take measures' to protect itself.

One unsuccessful measure was his hunt for a loan. Branson had already raised an additional £30 million loan from Seibu-Saison, the Japanese company, but required more money. Lord Young, the former minister and a director of Salomons, the merchant bank, had been trying on Branson's behalf since March to raise £20 million but was encountering difficulties which were compounded by Virgin Atlantic's unusual accounts.

Regularly, Virgin's accountants were altering the company's accounting periods, changing the financial years, making comparisons difficult and his offshore accounts unverifiable. Branson was not legally obliged to reveal many details of his offshore private company accounts, an advantage he exploited. In Britain, he was obliged to register accounts but he requested his auditors to minimise by legal means any appearance of his indebtedness. Accordingly, his predictions of healthy finances aroused little scepticism among the public.

The partial truth was prepared by Virgin's accountants in a preliminary draft of the 1991 results. Virgin Atlantic losses, they calculated, were £2.9 million and the administrative charges of Voyager Travel, the airline's holding company, had increased from £18.9 million in 1989 to £36.1 million. To Branson's embarrassment, the draft was leaked. 'It is laughable,' protested Branson, 'to suggest that we will lose a lot of money over the winter. The airline will make a profit over the next 12 months.' The draft accounts, insisted Branson, were 'obsolete'. Emboldened by his reputation for honesty, Branson was certain that his assertion would remain uncontradicted. Yet the final published accounts would disclose that the airline lost £3 million in one year and the airline's net debt had increased to £39 million. Seven years later, Branson admitted that the real debts had been even higher, at £45 million. The only certainty was the unachievable optimism of his predictions. In 1992, he would forecast that his group would earn £4 million pre-tax profits rising to £29 million in 1993. That did not materialise. But Branson assumed that, shielded by his web of private trusts, his financial predicament would remain concealed. The few bankers aware that Virgin could not even fund the first $11 million payment to Janet Jackson, certainly remained discreet.

In autumn 1991, the mood changed. The City became cautious about any tycoon's unprovable boasts. The optimistic outflow from the Virgin publicity machine began to prompt a few unwelcome questions. From the houseboat, Branson had approved a fusillade of predictions to enhance his importance and wealth. He pledged to build a worldwide media corporation; he predicted that 'within a couple of years' the number of Megastores would be tripled from twelve to thirty-five; and he forecast that the Virgin record company would 'double in size over the next five years'. Constant Virgin press releases announced Virgin investments in television, radio, hotels, clubs, airships and property.

In 1991, the financial state of Virgin Retail was poor. Although the group had recovered since losing £2.5 million in 1988, its European shops were still burdened with accumulated debts of £51 million. Virgin Music's profits were just £13 million but there were debts of £72 million. Virgin Group's accumulated debts were approaching £437 million and the group owed the banks £310 million. To temporarily navigate the crisis, Abbott negotiated in September 1991 the sale of 50 per cent of the Megastores to W. H. Smith, exchanging shares for £12 million. Even that deal was bedevilled. Juggling was Abbott's normal chore since privatisation, but rarely were the obstacles so complicated and the odds so high.

The Megastores shares had been mortgaged for £20 million by Abbott to Lloyds Bank. To recover those shares, Abbott negotiated to mortgage the shares of Virgin Retail for £25 million, and use that money to buy back the Megastores shares from Lloyds, in order to transfer them to W. H. Smith. The complicated deal gave the huge retailer a majority share in Virgin's shops.

The juggling was successful but the contradictions between Branson's publicity and the City gossip spawned bewilderment. He could not be certain whether the mood had influenced the Independent Television Commission (ITC) to reject his three bids in October for ITV franchises. To overturn the ITC's decision, Branson threatened to seek a judicial review. But he was powerless. Grasping for a motive for yet another defeat in his bid to become a media mogul,

Branson suspected that George Russell, the chairman of the ITC, disliked him. 'He thinks he can't trust me,' Branson told his lawyer, 'because I'm anti-Establishment. I just don't understand why he's turned us down.' Apparently, Branson was blind to the impression he created.

His survival required silence about his plight while Goldman Sachs, his merchant bankers, still secretly sought a buyer for Virgin Music. 'I feared that Lloyds was going to foreclose on us,' he admitted, 'and that I had no alternative. Without the cash from the sale [of Virgin Music] I would be powerless to stop the bank moving in. Once I let the banks take control, Virgin Atlantic would be finished.' Abbott spread a thicker smokescreen. 'The position of the group,' said Abbott, 'is healthier than appearances . . . The glory of being private is that we can choose accounting policies to suit us and the taxman. We don't have to say sorry about what the City will think.'

The unexpected appearance on 2 October 1991 of an article in the *Guardian* under the headline 'Will Richard Branson's bubble burst?' was too close for comfort. Roger Cowe, a journalist unmoved by Branson's flattery and freebies, had pierced the smokescreen. Branson's 'grasshopper mind', wrote Cowe, had delivered Virgin into a swamp of debt. The truth, Branson feared, threatened to bring 'the Virgin Group crashing down'. Despite his repeated public denials, he later admitted, 'the only trouble was that we were indeed suffering a cash crisis'.

Through charm and threats of a writ against the newspaper, Branson negotiated the publication of a nit-picking reply, inaccurately blaming Cowe for failing to contact Virgin – he had spoken to Trevor Abbott – and identifying insignificant errors. With relief, he chortled that no City banker read the *Guardian*. But he nevertheless thought it worthwhile to minimise the cash crisis that Cowe had identified. After deducting the debts, Branson boasted, Virgin was worth a clear £1 billion. Proof of his financial acumen were one-off windfalls like £33 million in cash for the sale of a licence for Sega, a computer game, and his demand of £500 million for Virgin Music. 'Overall,' wrote Branson, 'the business is readily able to fund itself from internal resources and outside funding.' Net debt, he wrote in the *Guardian*, was £242 million, not £296 million as Cowe claimed. In fact, the combined gross debts were £468 million and the pre-tax losses in 1991 were £34 million. Contrary to Branson's claim, 'I don't mind a bad press as long as it is accurate,' he was terrified by the truth. The prospect of raising more loans seemed forlorn. Even Lloyds Bank was undecided whether to extend the £50 million overdraft. The palliative and smokescreen to the crisis, the actor reasoned, was a prank.

On 16 October 1991, Branson attended a dinner hosted by *Executive Travel* magazine in London. Virgin's cabin crew always encouraged passengers to complete the forms printed in their flight magazine and vote Virgin the best airline. The result, Branson knew, reinforcing the quarterly International Air Transport Association (IATA) reports which placed Virgin Atlantic as the business traveller's favourite airline, would be another humiliation for British Airways. Especially as Lord King had flown the American celebrity, Ivana Trump, from Los Angeles for the party.

In London, it would be no different. Once again he wanted King to be humbled. Standing on the stage with Ivana Trump, who was presenting the award, Branson suddenly lurched, lifted King's guest into the air, and twisted the bewildered woman upside down. As her skirt fell over her head, Branson stuck out his tongue at King. For Branson it was a show of one-upmanship, a public schoolboy's snub to the lower classes. King's fury was thrilling. Only a few days earlier, at another award ceremony in Geneva which recognised Virgin as the best long-haul airline, Branson had facetiously presented to King a beautifully wrapped Alka Seltzer. King visibly grimaced. Suddenly the cameras flashed. Branson was balancing his latest prize on King's head. As King looked round, Branson was smiling. Publicly branding the loser was a good picture, just as Branson intended. His latest prank in London would entertain even more people.

In flippant self-congratulation, Branson advertised Trump's indignity in national newspapers accompanied by a caption, 'Virgin turns up Trumps again'. Her embarrassment was of no interest to Branson: her written complaint was ignored. None of his entourage dared speculate how incandescent Branson would have been if Joan, his wife, had been publicly humiliated in a similar fashion by Lord King.

Occasionally Branson went too far. At a party organised by Virgin Publishing, he was struck by a beautiful dark-haired girl dressed in a white costume. Belinda Harley, a well-known book publicist, had arrived without any fear of being noticed. The cleavage of her ample breasts was unconcealed which was the reason that Branson had dived into her presence. 'Come to a restaurant with me,' he suggested, 'and then let me do unmentionable things to you.'

'Certainly not,' replied Harley indignantly. 'I'm a respectable girl.'

'Oh, come on,' persisted Branson. 'Come with me and we'll do unmentionable things.'

'No, no,' teased Harley, pouting her lips and thrusting her cleavage closer to Branson.

The moment was interrupted.

'Richard,' called a scruffy voice. 'You're needed by the photographers.'

The vulgarity contradicted the profile Branson conjured of himself as a polite, even deferential man who rarely lost his temper: 'I guess it goes back to my upbringing. I was just brought up to behave in a decent way to people. So if someone waves at you, you smile back; if someone says hello, you have a chat. You don't have to be a complete shit to be a success.' His homilies, 'I try not to flaunt my wealth. It's unfair to my staff to see the chairman turn up in a Rolls-Royce and . . . also I suspect it's not good for business' also inflamed King. But nothing angered the peer so much as the adoration Branson received from Britons for his cheek and the increasing numbers who, keen to be associated with Richard, flew Virgin Atlantic.

Branson could count among his new fans Sir James Goldsmith, the maverick international trader, who sympathised with Branson's campaign against the British Establishment. Branson, his wife and two children were invited to Goldsmith's vast estate in Mexico to join three hundred celebrities to discuss the future of the world. Branson had welcomed the opportunity to mix with the mega-tycoons of the era. But the magnet offered in London soured after arriving in Mexico. Branson's limited attention span and sparse intellectual curiosity rapidly exhausted his enthusiasm. Alongside Goldsmith, Branson felt uncomfortable: the visitor was not the centre of attention and there were no games or entertainment. The maverick's maverick eschewed belonging to any clubs, especially this tycoon's club.

Utterly bored, he spotted Goldsmith walking by the swimming pool and pushed the self-appointed guru of international capitalism into the water. Roaring with glee, he followed making a huge splash. Nothing was said and Branson assumed that his usual prank had been tolerated. But shortly after, returning to his villa, he found all his family's clothes neatly packed in their suitcases, positioned by the door.

'You're mistaken,' Branson said to one of the estate's managers. 'We're staying for another two days.'

'I'm afraid, you're mistaken,' replied Goldsmith's employee. 'I've been instructed to make your travel plans. Your reservations are confirmed on the next plane.'

Branson flew to Miami and then to Necker. Long before he arrived on the island, his embarrassment was the gossip on telephone lines across the world. Branson was oblivious to Goldsmith's pique. He was the sovereign of his own club, the insider playing the outsider surrounded by his own tribe obeying his rules. In such a jungle, he fought with unusual weapons, as Lord King was about to discover.

The re-entry into Branson's life of Chris Hutchins, an undistinguished journalist, transformed Branson's campaign against Lord King from an uncivilised exchange of insults into unprecedented warfare.

Branson knew Hutchins as the author of a mistaken report published two years earlier in the *Today* newspaper alleging that the tycoon was to receive a knighthood. The headline, 'Arise Sir Richard', sparking similar stories across the world, had embarrassed Branson, but no more than Branson's own untrue story which he had fed to *Music Week* in April 1981 about the introduction of cable music. The purpose of the joke had been to embarrass that magazine's editor. Deceiving newspapers was, in Branson's calculation, not sinful. The sin for the tycoon, whose promiscuity with the media had achieved nymphomaniac proportions, was if any journalist failed his total loyalty test. Hutchins was suspect until he could prove himself useful.

Hutchins had telephoned to check a story offered by Eileen Basham, a friend and journalist who in the past had devoted considerable energy helping Hutchins overcome his indulgent lifestyle, once even accompanying an ailing Hutchins into hospital for the cure of a serious illness. That debt was nearly forgotten as Hutchins told Branson how Eileen had offered him a story about Virgin. 'I've got the story from Brian,' she explained, referring to her husband, Brian Basham, famous in London as an aggressive financial publicist.

Among Brian Basham's clients was British Airways. The relationship had been fostered by David Burnside. The sight of the two aggressive publicists sliding through BA's headquarters had evoked the label, 'The Gunslingers'.

Brian Basham had been associated with British Airways since 1984, on the first occasion to promote the airline's privatisation. In early 1991, he had been re-hired on Lord King's initiative to report whether Branson's threat to capture 30 per cent of BA's passengers was realistic. But Burnside had asked Basham to go further than an ordinary inquiry into Virgin's finances. Lord King wanted dirt. Evidence of degeneracy at Heaven, Branson's gay nightclub, suggested Burnside, would satisfy King's request. There were reports that illegal drugs had been sold inside the club and that needles infected with Aids had been discarded in a passageway outside the premises in Charing Cross. King wanted proof that the man who had received the government's blessing to challenge BA was a dubious character.

Basham's investigations had not substantiated the worst of King's suspicions but if a scenario of drugs, seedy sex and a squalid atmosphere was published, the Gunslingers believed, the people's hero would be discredited. Heaven was an ideal story for the tabloids and Eileen Basham suggested that Hutchins would gratefully oblige. Her husband agreed. Over the telephone, Basham told Hutchins that Virgin's income from Heaven, an unorthodox source of cash for the owner of an airline, was a potential threat to Branson's reputation. In turn, Hutchins telephoned Branson for a response.

For good reasons, Branson was nervous before Hutchins's call. Virgin's debts were escalating, Goldman Sachs had still failed to find a buyer for Virgin Music, Virgin Atlantic was losing money, and bankers had refused Salomons invitation to fund a £20 million loan. But Hutchins's suggestion that a publicist hired by British Airways was promoting unflattering stories about Branson was not only frightening but also extraordinary. How did Lord King or Basham imagine that their activities would remain a secret?

Listening to Hutchins, the intended victim began plotting to twist BA's assault into an unexpected opportunity. 'Why don't you come over here?' suggested Branson to Hutchins. 'Let's talk.'

Sitting in Branson's comfortable living room in Holland Park, the journalist repeated Basham's notion that the owner of Virgin Atlantic, relying on the cash flow of a seedy club for homosexuals, was regularly courting British ministers and government officials to undermine British Airways.

'What else did he say?' asked Branson.

'He talked about your finances,' replied Hutchins.

'What about them?' snapped Branson alarmed.

'He said, "I'm taking a really good look at his cash position. It's a dangerous way to operate."' Hutchins explained that while Basham had explicitly declared himself not hired to 'put Branson out of business', he speculated that publicity about a police raid at Heaven might jeopardise Salomons search for investors.

'Who hired him?' asked Branson.

'BA,' replied Hutchins.

Long before Hutchins sat in his house, Branson had schemed how he might exploit the journalist. Without any qualms, he hoped to dispatch Hutchins as an agent against British Airways. Hutchins would be used to establish that BA was employing Brian Basham to conduct a campaign against Virgin.

Although Branson would declare, 'we have never, ever . . . bugged anyone', bugging had by then become acceptable. Twenty years earlier, he had bugged his conversation with an irate neighbour in Oxfordshire; he had bugged Sebastian Clarke in the Portobello Road restaurant; he would later conceal a bug in his trousers during a conversation with an informant; and Frank Dobson, a private investigator, suspected that he had been bugged during a conversation with Virgin employees. If Branson had been the target of secret bugging, he would have screamed 'dirty tricks' but bugging Brian Basham, he reasoned, was justified.

The suggestion that Hutchins should betray his friends succeeded. The journalist agreed to hide a tape recorder bought by Whitehorn in his clothes before travelling to Basham's home in Primrose Hill, in London. Welcomed by Basham, Hutchins was presented with a copy of 'Operation Barbara', Basham's report analysing Virgin. Without inhibition, Basham proceeded to criticise Branson.

The following day, Branson was glancing through Basham's report while listening to the taped conversation. 'His finances are just dicky,' Basham was saying through a poor recording. 'Very risky.'

To overcome the obstacles deliberately created by Branson's secret trusts, Basham had scoured newspaper cuttings and company reports to put Virgin through his self-styled 'daylight test'. His conclusion, delivered seven months earlier in March 1991 to David Burnside, described Virgin's finances as less healthy than Branson boasted.

Emphasising Branson's 'hypocrisy', especially because of his tax avoidance, and his 'sensitivity to criticism', Basham highlighted Branson's 'cash weakness'. Through the poor tape recording, Branson heard Basham's frighteningly accurate analysis: 'What Branson does, he runs his cash flow close to the wire all the time and just before he runs out of cash he refinances.' The publicist was obviously unaware that Lloyds Bank was prevaricating about granting an additional loan.

As the secret tape recording continued, Branson heard Basham echo British Airways' anger that Virgin had been given the Tokyo routes; and Basham quoting Mike Batt, the BA executive who had resigned from Virgin Atlantic after two days, that the airline was '"appallingly run [and] dangerous" . . . He said, "One day, without doubt, an aircraft is going to fall out of the sky 'cause aircraft always fall out of the sky . . . And when an inquiry takes place, somebody is going to swing because the procedures and the way the business is run are appalling . . . It's just the sloppy way everything is done."'

Branson had good reason to fear Batt's testimony. The executive had been recruited by Branson to improve Virgin Atlantic's poor management and, eighteen months later, to resolve the problem, Branson would dismiss three senior executives.

Basham's imagery, however, was unorthodox. His parting shot to Hutchins, endorsed he said by Lord King, was suicidal: 'If you blow Branson out, it doesn't bother me, as long as neither BA nor I are associated with it . . .' Branson had good reason to feel concern. The tape was irrefutable evidence of an aggressive lobbyist. 'I had naively thought,' said Branson, 'that PR men were supposed to promote their own company and its products, not smear the opposition.'

Although Branson would speak about his 'fear', provoked by the tape, that if unchecked, British Airways' activities could destroy his small airline, not all in his cabal recalled that sentiment. On the contrary, those aware of the tape agreed that Basham's folly was a blessed opportunity merely to push BA further on to the defensive.

In the mind of the self-righteous, any threat evoked paranoia. Over the previous twenty years, many had experienced Branson's ruthlessness. He had poached women, rock stars and executives; he had sought to undermine *Time Out*; he had excluded Ted Toleman from the Blue Riband boat race and Randolph Fields from the airline; he had threatened Dave Robinson, Malcolm McLaren and others in the record business with financial ruin; he had initiated the unsuccessful criminal prosecution of Sebastian Clarke at the Old Bailey; and he had humiliated Lord King. While Branson 'the operator' was a master of retribution and retaliation, Branson 'the victim' screamed injury if anyone dared to challenge his saintliness. The tape recording of Brian Basham's denigration was categorised as an unforgivable injury.

'I realised that I was a clearly defined target,' Branson would say, echoing Freddie Laker. 'It was a frightening sensation.' The corollary, that Lord King and British Airways had been Branson's 'defined target', was ignored. In Branson's opinion, there was a moral chasm between his lampoons, gleefully predicting that Virgin would slaughter BA's profits, and his target paying Basham to respond to his challenge. 'There are certain things that are fair in business,' Branson complained, 'but to let it degenerate into a personal attack is wrong.' His public insult that King could do no better than get 'a photo of himself with John Major' was forgotten as he silently recalled all the hitherto inexplicable incidents which might now be explained as part of a giant conspiracy.

There had been an anonymous letter received from a former British Airways employee warning that BA had targeted Virgin Atlantic and that BA's documents referring to Virgin were being shredded; a female passenger had reported an unexpected approach inviting her to switch from Virgin Atlantic to BA; a former executive of Air Europe had described how BA had deliberately inspired whispers about the defunct airline's finances to undermine confidence; and there were rumours that ambitious executives in BA's marketing department had in 1990 secretly scrutinised Virgin's operations at Gatwick. Altogether, Branson knew, those activities represented no more than normal commercial behaviour in the airline industry. Quite properly, he had also received information about his rivals.

In 1987, Branson had been delighted to use a confidential report written by British Airways executives addressed to Colin Marshall after their anonymous flight on Virgin Atlantic. They had been critical of their own airline. He was more pleased by the regular information about the general discussions among senior BA executives supplied by Hugh Welburn and others who had been employed by BA. Regularly, after conversations with old friends, the former employees of BA employed by Virgin provided an invaluable insight into BA's activities. 'We have the following information from BA,' announced one former BA executive reporting that, like Branson's own imitation of British Caledonian's inducements, BA's marketing department was aggressively monitoring all the opposition during a recession. Similarly, to avoid Virgin Atlantic becoming just another cheap fare across the pond, Branson sensibly sought to understand his competitors and, not surprisingly, Welburn or the others were never ordered to cease collecting information. But Branson placed Brian Basham's activities in a different category. Basham's focus on Virgin's finances threatened his very survival. Too many journalists were asking critical questions about his finances, thought Branson. They were inspired, he concluded, by Basham. In particular, Branson recalled a recent *Sunday Telegraph* article written by Frank Kane describing Virgin's competition with BA under the headline, 'Virgin heads for Heathrow dogfight'. Kane, like Roger Cowe of the *Guardian*, had queried Virgin's finances, shrouded in the offshore trusts.

Branson was hypersensitive about the publication of any denigratory information. All the critical articles, he suspected, had been inspired by Basham on behalf of British Airways. 'I'm annoyed,' he later said, 'at having to undergo . . . ill-informed public scrutiny.' But Kane, like Cowe, was raising legitimate questions about what Wall Street called a debt-junkie. Branson was an operator unable to resist the temptation of borrowing; and as with all junkies, the truth could be what suited him at that moment. The fact that Basham, as Branson would eventually concede, was accurate about Virgin's finances did not deter his suggestion of a gigantic conspiracy. In Branson's mind, Frank Kane and Trevor Grove, the editor of the *Sunday Telegraph*, were plotting his downfall, which was untrue. Even Ivana Trump's complaint about his behaviour, he suggested, was instigated by Lord King as part of BA's conspiracy to destroy his reputation. All those incidents, he carefully briefed Bob Graham, a senior journalist employed by the *Today* newspaper who had heard the secret recording of Brian Basham, were evidence of BA's conspiracy to destroy Virgin.

'A passenger on Virgin Atlantic,' he told Bob Graham, 'said that she switched from BA to try Virgin and she got a call from BA offering to rebook her on BA if she changed her mind.' Graham hesitated. Aggressive marketing from British Airways to a long-term customer was hardly evidence of a conspiracy. Branson continued, 'Virgin's engineers say that BA's engineers aren't polite any more.' Graham remained reluctant to recognise this as a conspiracy. Considering that Branson was publicly complaining about BA's engineers and publicising his High Court writ for their alleged failures, their coolness was hardly unexpected. Moreover, Branson seemed quite content for BA to continue servicing Virgin's planes and for Virgin pilots to train on BA's flight simulators. Had BA withdrawn their co-operation, Virgin Atlantic would have been severely handicapped. Graham's objectivity offended Branson's total loyalty test. His solution was abrupt. 'If you don't run the Basham story soon,' he told Martin Dunn, the editor of *Today*, 'I'll give it to *The Sunday Times*.' Since the stakes were so high, he did not wait for a reply. Indirectly, he encouraged Nick Rufford and *The Sunday Times* 'Insight Team' to investigate BA's dirty tricks. Rufford had been in contact with a BA employee, 'a mole', who was giving him confidential information, but until then there was insufficient information to allege a conspiracy.

To Branson's relief, *The Sunday Times*' attitude changed after hearing about delivery of Hutchins's tape to *Today*. Both newspapers were owned by Rupert Murdoch and a leak by an executive alerted *The Sunday Times* that *Today* was planning a similar story. Branson accelerated the race to expose Basham's activities. Repeatedly telephoning Basham, Nick Rufford of *The Sunday Times* begged for an urgent meeting. On Friday night, 1 November 1991, before going to dinner, Basham was lured into personally handing to Rufford published documents which had embarrassed Virgin. The following day, Saturday, to entrap Basham, Rufford tape-recorded evidence of the publicist's recklessness.

'There's a rumour,' said Basham, 'that Virgin is having to pay up front for fuel.' He emphasised that Rufford would have to verify his tip that Shell was demanding cash rather than allowing Virgin normal credit. However, even casting the suggestion of the company's possible insolvency into the public arena posed a mortal danger for the airline. By Sunday morning, Basham realised that his conversation had backfired. Rufford turned the suggestion against Basham, as the rumour was baseless.

On Sunday, 3 November 1991, *The Sunday Times* headline, 'Branson accuses BA of Dirty Tricks', thrilled Branson. At his request, the newspaper had not mentioned the Shell fable but did embarrass

Basham. Quickly, Branson telephoned Martin Dunn, the editor of *Today*. 'Are you going to run the Hutchins tape?' he asked. The reaction was frosty. Dunn and Graham, his senior journalist who had researched Branson's allegations, were irritated by Branson's concealment of his simultaneous discussions with *The Sunday Times*. It smelt of manipulation. Hutchins's story was dropped.

Branson's glee evaporated. On Monday, the media's reaction to *The Sunday Times* story was imperceptible if not negative and *Today* had not published. 'Fuck, fuck, fuck,' Branson moaned as he puffed vigorously on a cigarette. All his fury, faxes and telephone calls had failed to orchestrate public outrage against a conspiracy which he believed was destroying his company. 'We had our backs to the wall,' he would blast. 'We were living so much from hand to mouth.' There was only one explanation, he reasoned: Martin Dunn was a coward, 'bowing to the pressure from BA'. Later, Branson wrote that he had even received 'a faxed copy of the front-page splash that [*Today*] were going to publish the next day', but Dunn said that it existed only in Branson's imagination.

Branson was nervous and not sleeping. Virgin had failed to win sympathy as a victim of 'dirty tricks', which remained unproven, and Virgin's finances were deteriorating. 'Got to get it sorted,' he fretted. Thankfully, the *Daily Express* was persuaded to publish Branson's allegation that British Airways was financing a criminal conspiracy. 'Cars, homes and offices owned by Virgin staff,' Branson's spokesman said, 'are broken into. Confidential papers are stolen and our telephones are bugged.' Branson himself, indiscriminate about the culpability, voiced similar accusations. 'In the past few weeks,' he asserted, 'the managing director's car has been broken into three times within ten days, Will Whitehorn's car has been broken into twice in three weeks and a private eye has followed me for three months.' In Branson's version, his suspicions and hyperbole were rolled together. The confusion suited his purpose.

Some of Branson's 'evidence' had been provided by Joe Flynn, a famous hoaxer, who, posing as Kroll, the investigation agency, received £500 from Virgin for whispering that British Airways had planted bugs in Branson's home. Other 'evidence' that BA had hired Kroll to target Branson was apparently provided by Frank Dobson, a private investigator, and turned out to be without foundation. Much of the rest was, as Branson eventually admitted, supposition.

Frustrated, and under increasing financial pressure, Branson searched for new ruses. Since the worst that could be said against Basham was that his behaviour was unethical but certainly not criminal, Branson decided to confront British Airways directly.

On 11 December 1991, Branson dispatched a letter, drafted by his lawyers, to Colin Marshall and to British Airways' non-executive directors questioning Basham's employment, his fear that BA was intending to destroy Virgin Atlantic in a similar manner to Laker Airways and, in an eight-page appendix, he listed the alleged dirty tricks perpetrated by the airline's employees. No copy was sent to Lord King but Britain's national newspapers each received one. Dirty tricks, Branson hoped, would become a widely publicised scandal.

The response was again disappointing. His complaints were once again disregarded by the newspapers and by Colin Marshall. Branson's suggestion, mocked Marshall, that 'many' of Virgin's complaints 'first came to our attention from reports in *The Sunday Times* and the *Guardian*' was fanciful. Those newspaper reports, suggested Marshall, had been inspired by Branson himself. Instead of evidence, Marshall continued, Branson had offered innuendoes. The dip in his credibility coincided by a stroke of ill fortune with the simultaneous disintegration in November 1991 of Maxwell Communications, Polly Peck and Brent Walker, all from frauds. Banks were re-examining the finances of all tycoons, however honest. Branson was inevitably subject to scrutiny. Lloyds Bank again refused to increase Branson's overdraft and Salomons abandoned its search for lenders to the airline. 'They don't like your war with British Airways,' Branson was told. Unless Virgin Music was sold, Branson faced a cash meltdown.

Fire-fighting and spreading a smokescreen, Branson had hoped, would conceal his predicament. Stories of losing £5 million a month at Heathrow, he scoffed to *The Financial Times*, are 'just farcical. The airline has been profitable since the year it started. It has been profitable through the worst year in aviation history.' As usual, despite his inaccuracy, the newspaper published his comments uncritically with his final quip, 'People think that you need a lot of money to run an airline but it isn't true.' In truth, as Branson subsequently admitted, Virgin Atlantic was 'losing money'.

During Christmas, as Branson realised how 'the numbers looked much worse', he pondered his disappointment that his allegations about dirty tricks had been dismissed as 'mainly nonsense'. His boast that dirty tricks were British Airways' vengeance for losing £150 million every year to Virgin's competition was ridiculed as exaggerated. After all, he had not discussed the alleged conspiracy with Sir Nicholas Pearson, the director representing Seibu-Saison, owners of 10 per cent of the airline. No one took seriously his scoff, 'BA has spent the last two years trying to push us into the abyss. Now it's time for them to accept there'll be two British airlines for the next fifty years.' He appeared to ignore British Midland and other independent airlines, some bigger than Virgin, who never moaned about the fiction of BA's 'monopoly control' at Heathrow. Instead, his campaign had aroused suspicions.

'No one's taking dirty tricks seriously,' Branson complained.

'That's because no one's noticed them,' replied Chris Moss, the airline's respected marketing director.

'We've got to keep dirty tricks in the public mind,' Branson had said. Publicising the 'dirty tricks' had become an essential weapon to avoid bankruptcy.

Branson's good fortune was that on 8 January 1992, Martyn Gregory, an award-winning television journalist, offered to produce a documentary about dirty tricks for *This Week*, a weekly programme on ITV.

'Basham has been planting hostile stories in many newspapers,' Branson told Gregory. 'Loads of journalists have called us with critical questions, all fed by Basham and BA's poison machine run by Burnside.' Gregory accepted Branson's allegations that Virgin was the victim of a dirty tricks operation, although close examination would have revealed that, in contrast to the many anti-British Airways stories which Branson had placed in the newspapers, only a handful of reports, particularly one in the *Sunday Telegraph*, could be directly attributed to Basham.

With Branson's help, Gregory compiled a severe indictment that British Airways' anti-Virgin unit, deploying officials from a secret room at Gatwick, protected by a coded lock, had attempted to transfer Virgin passengers to BA; had spread rumours that Virgin was going bust; had 'swamped' Virgin flights by rescheduling BA flights to fly at the same time as Virgin's; and had flooded bucket shops with BA tickets to undercut Virgin. With the Basham tape and the disclosures of a former British Airways employee who had contacted Branson, the evidence of dirty tricks against a robust competitor appeared overwhelming. To confirm Branson's allegations, *This Week* retained Professor Richard Taffler of the City University to examine Virgin Atlantic's accounts. The professor agreed that Virgin 'doesn't need £50 million for survival'. Since Branson would subsequently admit to a 'mountain of debt' and that the stricken airline was 'losing money' and searching for loans, the professor's analysis was just one of several flaws in the programme.

Enthusiastically, Branson had invited Gregory to fly with him to New York. With the promise of a prime-time slot, the actor was prepared to devote substantial time to his star role. In New York, he arranged to be filmed with Ron Thomas, a limousine driver exclusively retained by Virgin. Thomas told Branson in the film how British Airways employees at Kennedy airport were 'approaching Virgin passengers at the kerbside, in BA uniforms', when his limousine parked at Virgin's terminal. 'They were trying to divert them to BA flights.' Virgin said it possessed letters from complaining passengers to support Thomas's story although the people did not appear in the programme.

Mike Batt, the current director of British Airways' operations in the United States, told everyone, 'it was physically impossible and did not happen'. That denial did not appear in the documentary's indictment of BA which ended with Branson, standing in the Arizona desert, mournfully asserting, 'I've never sued anyone in court for anything.' The millions of Britons watching would be unaware of his writs against John Lennon, Stiff Records, the ITC and even British Airways over his engineering dispute. 'No small airline,' continued Branson in a romantic vein, 'has ever survived before.' He preferred to forget British Midland, Monarch Airways, Air 2000 and Britannia Airways. Each of those airlines flew many more passengers than Virgin.

Violating Virgin was transmitted on 27 February 1992. The damning indictment portrayed British Airways' executives as guilty men avoiding questions about their conspiracy to destroy Virgin Atlantic. For Branson a major hurdle had been overcome. BA was irrevocably on the defensive.

At that defining moment, after the documentary's transmission, Virgin's publicists told Martyn Gregory, 'thirty-six thousand callers were registered by [our] switchboard expressing sympathy, support and outrage'. Four years later, Branson would revise the figure to four hundred calls. The inconsistencies were irrelevant. Branson was ecstatic. After twenty years in the jungle, he could sense the swing of the public's mood in his favour. Even better, although the documentary failed to establish a legal case against British Airways, the corporation's lawyers had committed a fatal mistake. Branson, the businessman preoccupied with exploiting loopholes, spotted his reward for persistence.

Before the television programme, Mervyn Walker, British Airways' legal director, had refused Martyn Gregory's invitation to appear. In his letter, Walker wrote that Branson's allegations were 'motivated by a desire to secure publicity for himself and his airline' and were 'unfounded and scurrilous'. After the programme's transmission, British Airways did not sue ITV for defamation but Burnside published a counter-attack in *BA News* accusing Branson of lying, an allegation BA were to prove unable to substantiate. Burnside and Walker had fallen into a trap of their own making. 'Richard says he's got them,' buzzed the gossip around Virgin Atlantic's headquarters.

The simplicity of the tactic delighted Branson. He had made an allegation and British Airways had denied it was true. BA, Branson claimed, had accused him of lying. Proving libel was much easier than substantiating his allegations of financial damage. 'I had to clear my name,' he announced solemnly.

Branson's demand for an apology was delivered in the midst of an obsession gripping Lord King, Colin Marshall and Bob Ayling. The three senior British Airways executives had become convinced that Branson had launched a secret operation against them.

In a confidential briefing to Marshall and Ayling, Lord King spun an astonishing fantasy. Branson, he suggested, had organised the tapping of their telephones and had suborned senior British Airways staff to provide sensitive information. Both asked for the source of that staggering 'discovery'. The origin, replied King, was private detectives whom he had hired. 'They came highly recommended,' both were assured. King's evidence was worse than worthless. His investigators, operating under the codename 'Covent Garden', had reported a 'conspiracy' but failed to provide the evidence.

In the cauldron of accusations and emotions, neither Bob Ayling, a neat former civil servant and solicitor, nor Colin Marshall, a precise technocrat, could quite understand the undertones of Branson's and King's swashbuckling, jungle warfare. Loyally, both castigated Branson's management of the media, his repeated denigration of British Airways in Whitehall and Brussels, and his entrapment of Basham as a greater sin than Basham's follies and BA's own aggressive marketing. Comfortingly, both were assured by lawyers that while BA's activities were regrettable, the airline was not legally vulnerable. However, their emotions and reason had become confused by the web of intrigue spun by their chairman, which in turn also influenced Branson.

Lord King's suspicions prompted journalists unexpectedly to ask Branson: 'Has Virgin mounted a covert operation against BA?' Branson was surprised but, on 12 March 1992, he innocently substantiated the 'conspiracy' himself.

A Jiffy bag, addressed to Chris Moss, had arrived anonymously at Virgin Atlantic's headquarters. One day after its delivery, an anonymous telephone caller describing himself as an off-duty AA patrolman, prompted Moss to open the bag. Inside was a sound tape. To Moss's astonishment, it was a telephone conversation between Sir Colin Marshall and Robert Ayling discussing Branson and an agreement not to reveal a pertinent fact to Lord King. 'Listen to this Richard,' urged Moss. Branson was mystified. The British Airways executives were welcoming Branson's anticipated writ for defamation. 'It will at least,' said Marshall, 'tie the thing down in some sort of controlled process.' Ayling agreed and recommended that Branson be invited to list all his complaints. The eavesdropper of Marshall's mobile telephone call had provided Branson with proof that British Airways was not plotting Virgin's destruction.

Branson and Moss were perplexed. Moss, an honest and talented man, had been occasionally disturbed by Branson's campaign against British Airways. While he disliked BA's ruthless marketing, he doubted Branson's conspiracy theory. If someone had passed to him a copy of BA's Executive Club list, he told Branson, he would certainly have been tempted to approach all those business class passengers to lure them to Virgin Atlantic. 'They're not trying to push us under,' he told Branson. 'They're just trying to be very smart.'

Branson, however, chose not to interpret the tape benignly. He was irritated that all his staff were not persuaded about a 'dirty tricks' campaign. 'BA planted this tape on us,' he spluttered. 'Someone followed me to a restaurant the other day.' His suggestions were unverifiable but, by March 1992, he could ignore the discordant theories. The ITV documentary had elicited new, damaging information against British Airways from witnesses, both passengers and former BA employees.

British Airways' aggressive sales team, Branson was told, had been systematically reading the details of Virgin's reservations stored on the computer which Virgin Atlantic rented from British Airways. Although the information would be published six months later by the CAA, it was an advantage for British Airways to possess the results earlier. The greater mischief was BA's use of home telephone numbers. These were listed alongside the reservations to help the limousine driver contact the passenger for the free drive to the airport. Those telephone numbers were useful for BA's marketing department. (Virgin's marketing department could have similarly scrutinised BA's passenger reservations on the same computer, but the lists were worthless. The telephone numbers alongside the reservations for BA's business class passengers were usually the travel agents'.)

The consequences of the computer hacking had not been serious. The financial damage was practically invisible. None of Branson's executives had suggested any serious losses caused by British Airways' 'queue combing'. At worst, the total extra revenue BA had earned from all its aggressive marketing in one period was £133,000, of which £47,810 was attributed to Virgin. The potential danger if unchecked, however, was serious.

Poaching passengers was little different from Branson's own attempted poaching of the staff of *Time Out* and musicians and managers for Virgin. But there was no good reason, he decided, to equate the two or disentangle the confusion. With a cast-iron case to support his writ for defamation, he preferred to believe that the tape recording of the conversation between Ayling and Marshall was part of British Airways' campaign to destroy Virgin. 'Someone somewhere,' Branson wrote to Marshall in a letter on 16 March 1992 enclosing the tape, 'is playing mighty dangerous games.'

Branson's letter concluded with an ultimatum. If Lord King had not apologised within two days for the dirty tricks, Virgin would issue a writ for defamation. Branson's sudden willingness to confront King revealed a more confident mood. His new confidence was born ten days earlier when, smilingly, he had said simply to John Thornton of Goldman Sachs, the American merchant bank, 'That's sorted.' Virgin Music had been sold. The financial crisis was over.

11

Sour music

Tears came easily to Richard Branson. On cue, to escape from embarrassment, his face would freeze and he would weep softly.

That trait was useful on the afternoon of 6 March 1992 in the Harrow Road headquarters of Virgin Music. Branson had called a meeting of eighty staff to announce the sale. Standing in front of loyal men and women who had devoted up to nineteen years of their lives to the Virgin family, he knew that most would lose their jobs. That after all was one of the synergies which John Thornton had been promoting to the directors of EMI, the music giant. They had spent the previous night alongside Branson signing countless legal documents transferring the company in exchange for $1 billion or £560 million.

Some of the faces gazing up at him Branson had known all his professional life. All had willingly responded to his exhortations for sacrifices as part of their loyalty to the family, convincing themselves that low wages were compensated by the fun of his parties, away-days and holidays. Many were grateful for his trust, allowing them opportunities to develop as businessmen. But until that afternoon all were blind to the operator who had coldly discarded Nik Powell and Randolph Fields to build his fortune, and who had lied about his finances to defend his empire. To all, he was lovable Richard, the organiser of hilarious pranks, April Fool jokes and outrageously convincing impersonations.

At moments of crisis, Branson could choose between two options: the truth or escape. Usually, he preferred combining the two by dispatching his lieutenants to execute the distasteful chore. The man who sought affection resisted any personal association with bad news. In 1976, he had coldly told his cabal in Denbigh Terrace, 'We need to change gear and fire people.' No one recalled any sign of emotion as Branson delegated someone to deliver the bad news. But they could recall his tears when pleading with the same employees to resist joining a trade union to secure a decent wage and his gratitude when his entreaties were accepted.

In planning his announcement of Virgin Music's sale, Branson chose to emphasise the universal success. 'The music division,' he proclaimed with Simon Draper and Ken Berry standing nearby, 'has been sold but with a guarantee of independence. Ninety per cent of the staff will be kept on. Their future is secure.' A tremor spread through the hall. Gasps of shock spread among the perplexed. 'Anyone dismissed,' he continued, 'will be employed by Virgin Atlantic.'

From the crowd, John Webster, the successful marketing director, burst out emotionally: 'Richard, I've had eighteen fantastic years. I want to thank you.' Three years earlier, Webster had asked Branson for Virgin shares in recognition of his contribution. Branson had replied, 'We're all a big happy family. Don't worry. I'll look after you.' Webster had been satisfied and worked even harder, although other record companies paid considerably more. That morning, Webster was crying out of compassion for his employer who had apparently unwillingly sold his beloved music business.

Branson understood. His employees mistakenly believed he was the victim of a City conspiracy. He glanced at Webster who was obviously on the verge of asking whether Branson, like other owners of independent labels, would share his huge windfall with his employees. After all, Richard Branson enjoyed an image as a charitable soul, a man of the people who offered to help the underprivileged. If that awkward question was asked, Branson would be embarrassed. Branson's tears flowed. Emotion swept through the room. An uninformed observer could have mistakenly concluded that the employees' compassion was kindled by sorrow that Branson had just lost rather than earned $1 billion, the most ever paid to an individual for a single deal in Britain.

The deal had taken nearly one year to negotiate. In private, the trader and salesman had fretted but, in public, he appeared cool. Masterfully, he did not blink. His price for the last of the independent record companies, he told Thornton, was a minimum of £500 million. In 1987, Virgin Music's stock-market valuation was £377 million and the 1991 accounts recorded after-tax earnings of £500,000 and tangible assets of £3 million. Unlike the public, Branson understood the mystery of a sale price one thousand times more than the company's profits. Over the years, Steve Lewis had accumulated valuable copyright and music publishing rights of Virgin's famous artists – Phil Collins, Peter Gabriel, Bryan Ferry, Mike Oldfield and many others. For the right buyer, Branson's price was realistic but alarmingly five major record companies had spurned Thornton's approach, even after Branson had flown in 1990 to Los Angeles to pitch his offer to MCA. The only show in town in 1992 was EMI. The same company which Branson had plotted in 1987 to buy. In a buyer's market, Branson's bluff was cardinal. His patience was enviable.

As Thornton seduced Colin Southgate, EMI's chairman and the son of a fruit merchant, with the potential glory of becoming a world giant with 18 per cent of the market, Branson hid his anxieties behind a coup. On 20 November 1991, he finally signed the Rolling Stones to the Virgin label. To succeed on his third attempt he had borrowed, with great difficulty, £6 million. At the celebratory dinner at Mossiman's, Branson 'tried to forget the bankers closing in on me'. Those who questioned his parlous finances were either silenced by the announcement of the Stones' contract or by the threat of a writ. Travelling on an aeroplane with Per Lindstrand, he had agonised that Lloyds Bank would foreclose. The Stones deal had bought valuable time until Southgate and Thornton, flying together on Concorde, finally agreed that EMI would pay £560 million.

If the money had been paid directly, Branson would have been liable to £92 million in capital gains tax. To avoid taxes which Branson castigated as 'a waste of money', the fate of that cash had been carefully plotted by Trevor Abbott. To exploit a flaw in the 1981 Finance Act, the $1 billion was channelled through Glowtrack, an offshore company representing the six companies owning the Virgin Group, to a complicated web of twenty-eight trusts – Scotia nominees, Abacus trusts and Morgan Grenfell trusts – based in Jersey and Guernsey, the tax havens. The only tax Branson paid was £8 million on a 4.5 per cent stake in shares which he owned personally in Britain. After repaying about £62 million of known debts, Branson was said to receive £229 million. But that was further reduced by the repayment of other debts concealed offshore.

The remaining money was divided between Ken Berry and Simon Draper, who shared about £70 million for their shareholding, also paid into offshore trusts. Fujisankei, the Japanese music company, would receive £120 million for its 25 per cent stake. Akira Ijichi was not wholly pleased by the $85 million profit on the three-year investment. Fujisankei's own music business had been severely limited on Branson's insistence, supposedly in return for a long-term partnership. Ijichi was angry at the abrupt termination of the partnership and that Berry had never fulfilled on his promise to allow Japanese employees to work in Virgin's offices. Branson was unmoved by Ijichi's displeasure. There was nothing personal, it was business. The same sentiment guided his performance in Virgin's headquarters.

Branson's tears during his announcement of the sale and his promises deflected the qualms among his distraught audience. For his part, Branson's thoughts were racing elsewhere. Rather than comfort the people whose lives were disturbed, he fled the room, rushing towards his Holland Park mansion with a tear-filled view of the *Evening Standard*'s hoarding, 'Branson sells for £560 million'. 'I wept when my music business was sold,' he would grieve, 'but I had to save my Virgin empire.' As he sat in Holland Park, gazing at his huge garden, there were no thoughts about the eighty people abandoned in Harrow Road. 'I didn't want to think about all the lost friendships,' he explained. Not once did he telephone to reassure the 'family'. Few heard him bid farewell. The tears were for himself. A crown jewel had gone but with financial security he made one resolution: 'I took a conscious decision that I never wanted to be in a position where I have to sell a company again.'

Left behind in Harrow Road, Simon Draper offered the family little more. 'I'm sad,' he admitted to his staff, 'but I have also become very rich.' Bemused expressions stared back.

'You'll be getting a big cheque,' Jeremy Lascelles was told by a friend. After thirteen years building up Virgin Music's A&R (Artists and Recordings), Lascelles became certain that Branson would copy the other independent record owners who had sold out to the Big Six. In gratitude for their contribution, some former executives of Island Records had received over £500,000 each and one secretary had found £100,000 in an envelope. 'Richard's bound to say thank you for all I've done,' Lascelles reassured himself.

The misgivings emerged as EMI issued the redundancy notices. Branson appeared unconcerned at the fate of his former friends. The employer who had hosted free holidays and fun weekends drew the line at ex-employees. Those with nothing further to offer were not entitled to gratitude. Branson clasped his pot of gold. Liberated from financial hardship, he was not minded to share his new fortune with anyone. Like any deals, his only interest was to win, keep the money and enjoy his opponents' sense of failure. Branson, his former friends discovered, would not be sharing his huge windfall.

'We've been duped,' fumed Steve Lewis, the managing director of the music publishing company. Nineteen years' service which produced substantial long-term value for the group had been ignored by Branson and Draper. 'We thought we were special,' complained Lewis. 'He made us believe that Virgin Music was our business. We should never have believed all his talk of "we" and the "family". He got us like we're the Moonies.' Lewis fumed and fumed. 'We've been betrayed. I've been too trusting. I've been married longer to Virgin than to my wife and he betrays me.'

Lewis's anger was shared by John Webster who invited himself to Holland Park to complain to Richard, his old friend, with whom he had holidayed and shared girlfriends. But even after eighteen years, Branson was not sentimental. 'I gave you a job for all these years,' Branson replied curtly. 'I don't need to give you any more.' Webster left Branson's house dazed by the frosty blow.

Genial Jeremy Lascelles was as angry as Webster and Lewis. In return for all the profits he had helped to create over thirteen years, Lascelles was hoping for a generous gesture. After a persistent request, Branson agreed to meet. He regarded Lascelles, unlike Lewis, as one of his own – a former public schoolboy educated at Westminster. He had not expected the unrestrained ferocity of Lascelles's criticism: 'It's a nightmare. We all feel disgusted and insulted about the way you've gone about selling the company. We feel fucked up that you've just sold us down the river.'

Branson stared at the carpet. Since the truth – that he wanted to keep the money for himself – would be unpalatable and inconsistent with his image, he adopted the familiar pose of a stammering innocent dressed in a pullover to present a curious scenario. 'The music group,' he told Lascelles, 'was losing money and would have gone bust if we hadn't sold.' That Branson knew was ridiculous. After all, he had boasted that Virgin was 'the label of choice for many of the world's biggest bands'. He paused, listed more woes, then looked Lascelles in the eye: 'You might find this hard to believe, but none of this money's coming to me.' Lascelles was flummoxed. Branson seemed to be saying that even with £560 million, he was struggling financially. 'This is so preposterous,' thought Lascelles. 'The conversation's hit a dead end.' In the heat of the moment, Lascelles forgot that Branson had never contradicted the assessment of his wealth by *Forbes* in July 1992 that he was worth $1.2 billion, or *The Sunday Times* estimate of £900 million. Lascelles knew nothing about the offshore trusts which technically separated Branson from his money. He could not reconcile Branson's repeated vaunt, 'I have never been interested in making money as such', with his unexpected avarice. He departed silently, knowing he lacked any legal entitlement to Branson's funds.

Since 1967, Branson had always disguised his interest in money. Encouraging team play, sacrifice and low wages was easier if his employees were unaware of his obsession with wealth. Few realised that he retained accountants, lawyers, bankers and tax advisers not only to maximise but also to conceal his income. Just as he obscured his fortune from the British Inland Revenue, he dissembled his interest in money from his employees. To perpetuate that fiction, Abbott was encouraged to reply to any query about the trusts, 'We've got to do it to prevent Richard getting his hands on the money.' Extraordinarily, his employees were so trusting and so naive about finance that Abbott's myth was never challenged. After all, Branson never paid for restaurant bills or offered cash for a taxi fare. 'Richard has never heard of B&Q,' someone reported. The cashless billionaire performance was perfect. Seven years later, at a libel trial in 1998, Branson would deny under oath that any of the £560 million from the sale had gone 'into [my] pocket'. All the money, he would say, 'went into starting a lot of new companies'. The distinction was artificial and confusing: the companies were privately owned by himself. The compartmentalisation and disguise were effortless, but also profitable.

In denying any personal income from the sale to Lascelles, Branson revealed his parsimony since he later admitted, 'For the first time in my life I had enough money to fulfil my wildest dreams.' But at that moment Branson believed his illusions of poverty excluded any generosity towards his former employees. Any notion that Lascelles or Webster had ever been a friend with whom he had got drunk and chased women was severed. The man who boasted, 'personal relationships in business are vital and people should be directly accountable for their actions', finally blamed Draper for his miserliness: 'I would give you some money, but Simon's against it.'

Soon after leaving Branson's mansion, Lascelles met Draper. 'I'd give you money,' Draper told Lascelles, 'if Richard does, but he doesn't want to.' Reflecting on that excuse, Draper would admit, 'People were naive that they had allowed themselves to be seduced by the informality and no suits. It was always about money.' He, Berry and Branson had no intention of sharing the pot. 'Honestly, these things are less calculated than they appear,' offered Simon Draper. 'People look for some key, but Richard is much more simple than you think. There's no hidden agenda.'

Branson showed no shame about Lascelles's anger. Lascelles's accusatory letter – 'You've pissed people off' – hand-written in sorrow and frustration as well as anger after several months of brooding reflection and sent from Turkey, was ignored. Their accidental meeting two years later was brief. Avoiding Lascelles's eyes Branson stuttered with embarrassment, 'I owe you a reply.' Lascelles, who had philosophically drawn a line under the issue, was confused, unable to tell if Branson was naturally awkward or if the awkwardness was part of his performance; and if his performance was deliberate, was he consciously deceitful? Confronted with the top dog presenting himself as the underdog, Lascelles finally realised that Branson's publicity skills were his business skills. The confusion was deliberate.

Nearly one year after the sale, Steve Lewis was still bewildered by Branson's deafening silence. Why, he wondered, after nineteen years had Branson simply ignored him? Not even 'a goodbye' or 'thank you'. Had he unknowingly done something wrong? Since leaving Virgin, Lewis had been recognised by his peers as Britain's best music publisher and, unsolicited, Chrysalis had offered him a partnership with considerable responsibility at a higher salary. But Lewis was nevertheless disturbed. Like others, he was puzzled why in all his publicity, Branson avoided explaining his motives and uttered instead meaningless thoughts about his lifestyle, feelings, Necker and his family. Certainly, the newspaper descriptions of 'a modest, unassuming man who listens more than talks', and of a millionaire who is 'unafraid of the consequences of failure', were nonsense. As was his laughable idea that 'If I went bust, I would simply pack up the family and take them around South America because it would be fun.' Was his trust of Branson, Lewis agonised, a mistake? He hoped not. After one year, he arranged to meet Branson at Holland Park. From the moment their meeting began, Branson was obviously in no mood to offer any comfort.

On his own luxury turf in Holland Park, Branson extended a neutral, uncomfortable reception to Lewis. In Branson's opinion, Lewis was not a special employee nor a crony for whom he bore any affection. Lewis had not enjoyed the parties nor participated in the sex, sport and away-days. Branson was unapologetic that Lewis had only become aware of his redundancy from a trade newspaper. 'I created jobs,' he told Lewis, expecting gratitude rather than blame for terminating his employment without thanks. There was, Branson expected Lewis to understand, nothing personal about his dismissal. It was simply business. Like Lascelles, Lewis departed deflated by the rebuff. 'He could pass a lie detector test even when he's lying,' he told friends.

Beyond their tight circle, the disillusioned muffled their complaints. Casting doubts on Branson's stainless popularity seemed churlish. Few, Branson prided himself, dared to broadcast their dissatisfaction. Among the exceptions in 1991 was Heimi Lehrer, his property solicitor, whom Abbott had abruptly dismissed after eighteen years' loyal service, 'without a thank-you'. Instead, Lehrer received a writ from Branson accusing him of negligence and worse. Lehrer refused to be cowed and the Court of Appeal's decision justified his resistance. Branson's unsuccessful threat cost Virgin over £500,000 in costs. But Lehrer's victory passed unnoticed. Across Britain, individuals feared tangling with Branson. Their reticence and his huge, traceless war chest, encouraged the megastar to revise his public explanation for the sale of Virgin Music.

The truth, Branson knew, was a serious cash crisis concealed by lies to survive. 'My overriding objective,' he said later, 'was to save Virgin Atlantic from going under and – cruelly – the only reason I was selling Virgin Music was because it was so successful.' But that truth was sometimes forgotten. After wiping away his tears in March 1992, Branson summoned journalists to spread a different version about the debts. 'I've had eighteen months of rumours that Virgin Atlantic is in trouble,' he said. 'These rumours are not true.' In unison, Whitehorn spread the gospel that the sale was 'to pay for expansion and [the debts] are not the result of financial difficulties'.

In their rush, there were some glitches. On the same day, Branson said Virgin's debts were £150 million while Whitehorn quoted £200 million. 'We sold because we were bored with the record business,' Branson explained. 'You've got to cash in a chip'. Flush with cash, his machismo was sated. But in 1993, empowered by his war chest and the absence of any critics, Branson would again alter his explanation of the sale to match his new political and business interests. Paramount was his requirement to place the blame elsewhere. The original explanation was self-defeating. He presented a new story, casting himself as the victim.

In his revised version, Branson would complain that British Airways' dirty tricks had 'forced me to sell Virgin Music'. Dirty tricks was his explanation for the cash crisis. He had chosen to avoid that truth in 1992, he explained, to protect confidence in the airline. Whether he was not telling the truth or had forgotten that his hunt for a buyer for Virgin Music started long before the dirty tricks argument began, was questionable. But his fable enhanced his image as a beleaguered victim. That confusion was an important public evidence of his plight when, on 16 March 1992, he dispatched his ultimatum to BA demanding an apology for their dirty tricks. The alternative, he threatened, was a writ.

Bedlam was corroding the objectivity of British Airways management. Ever since the delivery of Branson's letter enclosing the tape recording of the intercepted telephone call between Ayling and Marshall, the triumvirate – King, Marshall and Ayling – were convinced that Virgin was conducting a secret operation against British Airways Hampered by tensions and personal antagonism among themselves, none of the BA directors was inclined either to investigate soberly Branson's allegations, especially those against Basham and Burnside, or to negotiate peace. Branson's complaints, they concluded, were wild exaggerations. No apology, they decided, would be offered. Branson's writ was issued on 21 March 1992. Shortly afterwards, Lord King authorised a counter writ accusing Branson of defaming BA.

Buoyed by the confidence of 'financial freedom', Branson sought the spotlight and the publicity to tilt the forthcoming trial in his favour and establish Virgin Atlantic's importance despite operating only eight aircraft and carrying one million passengers compared to British Airways' two hundred and twenty-seven jets carrying twenty-five million. A blizzard of activity and announcements sustained his campaign.

There were announcements about a relationship between Virgin Atlantic and Midwest Express, an airline based in Milwaukee; about a daily Virgin service between Gatwick and Johannesburg; about the launch of Vintage Airways to nostalgically ferry holidaymakers in 1940s DC3s around Florida; and he submitted an application for six licences for short-haul flights to Europe. All of those ventures collapsed either in silence or amid recrimination against British Airways. His failure to establish short-haul flights to Europe was especially embarrassing. In self-defence he blamed BA for sabotaging his application for slots, an accusation which Tim Walden of British Midland condemned as 'wholly misleading and inaccurate'. But Branson escaped any criticism.

The free flights, hospitality and fun he continued to shower on journalists were repaid by goodwill. No aviation or travel correspondent was minded to embarrass such a generous hero. All recalled the parties and fun on the inaugural flights to Miami and Tokyo, and the promise of more to come as Virgin Atlantic cherry-picked British Airways' profitable routes to California. There was, however, a price Branson charged for his favours. Habitually, during promotion trips abroad, he scrutinised the newspaper coverage of the trip faxed overnight from London. Those journalists responsible for favourable reports would be rewarded by instant flattery and the promise of future upgrades by the simple inclusion of 'RB' alongside their computer reservation. By contrast, the Ulsterman David Burnside's leaden personality and feudal lunches on BA's behalf with journalists at the Savoy, Branson chortled, bore no comparison to wild nights in exotic clubs hosted by Virgin. The cheeky minnow could always outwit the hippopotamus.

Seducing the editors, especially Kelvin Mackenzie, the editor of the *Sun*, had become unusually important. *Sun* readers remained Virgin's natural customers and fortunately, in Mackenzie's judgement, Branson was a good news story. Mackenzie had fired Ronald Spark, an experienced leader writer, who damned Branson as 'another unscrupulous Laker'. Spark criticised Mackenzie for seeking upgrades on British Airways while simultaneously approving leaders favouring Virgin against BA. This terminated a successful career just as Branson called on his trusted friends at the *Sun* with another story. David

Sour music

Yelland was pleased to report in September 1992 Virgin's bid to save Dan Air, a thirty-nine-year-old airline, on the verge of bankruptcy with debts of over £70 million.

Dan Air's recent history was a saga of incompetent management and forty-four unsuitable aircraft. The airline's managers had hired David James, a renowned corporate rescue specialist, to find a saviour and £26.2 million to guarantee two thousand jobs. Hearing that British Airways had declared itself uninterested, Branson presented himself to David James as the Good Samaritan. The newspaper headlines after Branson's successive late-night meetings with James reflected the source of their reports. 'Branson throws lifeline to Dan Air,' reported *The Times* and 'Virgin is James's only hope,' glowed David Yelland in the *Sun*. 'Branson,' added Yelland, was committed to a 'handshake deal' with a 'weird and wonderful package' which would be 'formalised' in two weeks.

Since British Airways had excluded itself from the bidding, Branson sought to extract the best terms, which meant the minimum cost to Virgin Atlantic, beset by an intensified financial crisis. Contrary to his pronouncements about his airline successfully being 'close to breaking even', the travel group's losses in 1992 were £14 million and the secret forecast for 1993 was for losses of £21 million to £23 million. Millions had been lost by the move from Gatwick to Heathrow, the high maintenance costs of old 747s, the continuing recession and fierce competition.

Branson's offer for Dan Air was £10 million. He was not bidding for the airline's staff and its planes but only the airline's slots at Gatwick to increase his flights to North America. Contrary to the newspaper reports, he was not interested in competing with British Midland against the monopolies in Europe. 'The Good Samaritan only wants to pick the carcass,' scoffed a desperate executive from Dan Air. 'He's even planning to dismiss all of us.'

Branson's proposal was rejected but David James sought his help. 'Could you pretend,' asked James, 'that we are still negotiating so that I can get an offer from BA?' Branson agreed to the ruse: 'I'll say later that I withdrew because Dan Air's losses were higher than I expected.' James was grateful. Soon after, James persuaded British Airways to buy Dan Air for £65 million and some jobs were saved. In appreciation for Branson's help, James remained silent as Branson sought out journalists to present an unflattering portrait of BA's deal.

BA, cursed Branson, had orchestrated Dan Air's collapse: 'BA's a monopoly and shouldn't have been allowed to buy Dan Air because it undermines competition.' The publicity was helpful as the date for his libel trial against BA approached.

'Got to keep dirty tricks in public view,' said Branson, demanding ideas. Within the week, Chris Moss had erected a huge inflatable gorilla outside Lord King's office. Inscribed on a plaque was the slogan, 'Stop the monkey business BA.' King's fury electrified Branson. 'We need more of that,' he laughed.

His enthusiasm for mischief avoided an unfortunate embarrassment. Over the previous six months, Branson had tried simultaneously to position himself as an aspiring owner of the world's biggest entertainment corporation and as an emerging transport giant. The survival of Virgin Atlantic had convinced him that he could revolutionise Britain's railways, a notion encouraged by Conservative politicians. But his initiative had misfired.

Four weeks after the Conservatives had been re-elected on 2 April 1992 for a fourth term, Branson asked to meet John McGregor, the new transport minister. Besides reciting his familiar complaints about British Airways' monopoly, Branson also mentioned rail privatisation, an important pledge in the Conservative election manifesto. Despite Branson's refusal to endorse any political party, the transport minister was enthusiastic for Virgin's participation in the proposed privatisation of the rail network. Branson symbolised the entrepreneurship which the Thatcherites yearned to encourage. Branson was, therefore, not surprised by Conservative encouragement. Winning access to Heathrow for Virgin Atlantic, Branson believed, had been a commercial victory but, more importantly, signified an endorsement by Whitehall, Westminster and the Conservative government of Virgin and its owner as 'one of us'. In their mutual self-interest, Branson emerged from his meeting with McGregor to praise the Conservatives' 'enterprise culture', expecting the politician's support to blazon the Virgin logo across the nation.

Eleven weeks later, Whitehorn arranged for Branson to pose beside a model train, painted with the Virgin motif, to announce his bid to run four luxury trains daily from London to Edinburgh. By cherry-picking the most lucrative of Britain's rail links, he expected to profit from the same formula as used against British Airways. His promised adornments were a familiar menu of hostesses, business lounges, facilities for mothers and young children, airline seats with videos, massages, free limousines, free drinks and three-course meals. 'It will bring a quality of service to rail that's unheard of in Britain,' he promised, adding, 'Virgin's service will not be more expensive than British Rail and possibly less.'

Four months later, on 25 November 1992, Branson made his debut in the public arena as the railways' saviour. An invitation had been arranged for him and Will Whitehorn to address the House of Commons Transport Committee examining the future of the railways.

Both Branson and Whitehorn, Thatcherite buccaneers, entered the panelled committee room certain that the ownership of a small private airline which was immune to public pressure bequeathed expertise to pontificate about the management of a giant one-hundred-and-fifty-year-old monolith subjected to public, political and regulatory scrutiny. Undaunted by the handful of politicians whose cynicism was matched by their expertise, Whitehorn was confident that his self-taught transport economics, enhanced by the experience of travelling on trains in Japan with his employer, would prove persuasive. Branson's flashing smile towards the MPs might have suggested naivety but he genuinely believed that free market principles and competition would cure the railways of habitual neglect. The railways in Sweden and Japan, began Branson, provided the model solutions for Britain. Breaking up British Rail, he continued, to allow dozens of private companies to compete along the same network would encourage competition and improve the railways. 'Japan,' said Branson, 'is the best example where there are seventy private, relatively small operators.' A fragmented track authority which would license slots to several operators on each route, he advocated, was ideal. 'Small is beautiful,' he soothed, because it was safe. Rail privatisation, he confided, would benefit from his management of an airline: 'There are a great many similarities between the two businesses.' In full flow, he forgot his particular audience. One remark, accompanied by a distinctive swagger, was unintentionally crass: 'Our trains will arrive faster because Virgin drivers will be more motivated.' He was impervious to the politicians' incredulity.

Robert Adley, the committee's chairman and an acknowledged rail expert, was particularly unimpressed. The witnesses, he believed, were crassly ignorant. Branson's vision bore no resemblance to Britain's dilapidated trains travelling on inadequate tracks linking inhospitable stations. After discounting Whitehorn's glorification of Swedish railways as 'living in a dream-world', Adley castigated Branson's ignorance about Japanese privatisation as 'a myth'. Branson's brow twitched as the politician explained that 2,000 kms of new track in Japan had been built by the government and the publicly financed train companies. 'The core,' he told Branson, 'is state-owned.' Branson stared in disbelief and began to contest the rebuttal. Suddenly, he found himself open-mouthed, but silent. 'I'm sorry,' he mumbled. 'I have completely lost my track.' Concentrating on details for more than a few minutes under pressure was, he found, irksome. His salvation was to resort to a familiar refrain of having 'energy' and 'getting things done'.

Adley was scathing. Even Branson admitted that there was no train operation in the world similar to the one he had advocated. How, asked the politician, could all the different operators effectively compete on the same railway line to the same destination? If a single locomotive broke down, the whole line would be brought to a halt.

'We are talking about a minute problem,' replied Branson, unaware of the daily chaos caused by breakdowns. 'Not a major problem.'

'I am sorry,' Adley pronounced, 'but I have to bring you back to the real world.' Branson's smile, suggesting complacency, provoked an unexpected censure. 'Your understanding of the railways,' intervened Paul Flynn, a Labour member, 'does seem to be on a protozoan level.' Branson paled, flustered by the politician's unexpected accusation about his 'lack of knowledge'. To his inquisitors, Branson's appearance had been derisory but the man's survival gene, although he abandoned the idea, cocooned him from self-doubt: 'I have not said anything as daft as you seem to indicate.'

The rejection of his wilder notions, even in humbling circumstances, was easily forgotten. The big picture was of a rising star, cash rich and on the verge of reaping a huge windfall from his adept manoeuvre to humiliate British Airways.

12

Double vision

Branson's confidence was bristling. In the weeks before the libel trial, British Airways had been successfully presented as a sinister enemy of cheap travel and he, as the head of the contented Virgin family, was the plucky, admired champion of competition and the people.

Public attention was focused by Branson against 'BA's monopoly', the cause of all the airline industry's ills. Daily, Branson repeated that Dan Air's collapse, like Laker's, British Caledonian's and Air Europe's, was caused by 'BA's monopoly'. 'They all had lower costs than BA and charged lower fares,' he chanted. 'They failed because British competition policy failed them.'

Branson's popularity masked a distortion. British Caledonian, Air Europe, Laker and Dan Air had failed principally because of massive debts and mismanagement. 'BA's monopoly' was a myth. In 1992, British Airways carried 37 per cent of the passengers across the Atlantic, American Airlines 21 per cent, United Airlines 11 per cent and Virgin 7.5 per cent. Branson championed competition by promising to launch Virgin European Airways offering low scheduled fares, but nothing materialised. No more evident was Virgin Atlantic's promise of permanent low fares. The airline's cheap offers were brief and burdened by restrictions. Popular goodwill protected Branson from criticism, especially from those Virgin Atlantic employees who were dismayed about their conditions of work.

A low-wage policy at Virgin Atlantic was essential for Branson's profits and maintaining Virgin's fares below British Airways'. In 1984, the wide pay gap between Virgin Atlantic and BA pilots had been irrelevant. The senior pilots recruited by Randolph Fields had been declared redundant by BA and Cathay Pacific and, aged over fifty years with good pensions, they were grateful for the opportunity to continue flying. An attempt in 1986 by Michael Martin of the Transport and General Workers Union to recruit members had been

153

sabotaged by Branson. 'If you join the union,' Branson had threatened, 'we will wrap up the airline.' No pilots had protested. In 1992, the wage gap remained significant. Virgin's salaries had increased from £16,000 to £40,000 per annum but BA pilots were earning £61,000. (Virgin's senior stewards were paid £6,000 per annum while BA's earned up to £15,000.) Some Virgin pilots were also becoming uneasy about the long hours after one fatigued pilot had been killed driving home from Gatwick. Virgin, rightly denying any legal liability, had refused to pay any benefits to his widow. That decision incited the new, younger pilots to pry further into the conditions of their employment. In the late 1980s, they had been hired with Branson's promise of 'large pay rises in the pipeline' and a highly competitive pension scheme. But the truth, they discovered in 1992, was different. Virgin was contributing only 6 per cent of their salaries to their pensions compared to 18 per cent by Britannia and more by BA, albeit for markedly different schemes.

At meetings during February 1992, Branson and his directors robustly defended their parsimony. 'The airline,' the pilots were told by Branson's emissary on 22 February 1992, 'is unprofitable despite high loads. The airline is performing badly and we don't have enough money.' The pilots who protested were bluntly rebuffed by Nick Potts, the director of personnel: 'Why are you working for Virgin? If you want the same conditions as BA, then go and work for BA.' Potts, the pilots knew, echoed the opinions of Nigel Primrose, the finance director, who had agreed that Saxby Associates should be the agents for the pilots' pension funds. Saxby had appointed Sun Alliance as the fund's manager. The agents and the insurers, the pilots asserted, deducted up to 18.6 per cent in commission compared to the usual 3 per cent. After four years' payments, most pilots' pension funds were worth less than their total contributions.

At the same moment, Branson imposed a tiny pay increase on the pilots. Despite the recession, Branson's imposition was rejected and several pilots and 20 per cent of Virgin Atlantic's first officers resigned. Morale dropped and Branson discovered that Virgin aircrew had stolen, during a brief period, duty free drinks worth more than £300,000 from the planes. To resolve the unrest, Branson agreed to meet the pilots' representatives on 15 July 1992. 'I know you're unhappy,' he explained, 'but in twenty years of business I've never had any industrial problems. I know you're paid less than BA and basically I'd love to improve things but improvements can only be paid from profits and the airline is not doing well enough. We will only pay what we can afford.'

The pilots, Branson could see, were puzzled. Their planes were full and, in public, he was saying that Virgin was profitable, yet he was pleading poverty to the pilots and insisting 'the company is not making a profit and is unlikely to do in the next financial year'. 'Show us the evidence,' he was challenged. 'No,' he sniffed. 'You can't see Virgin Atlantic's accounts. It's a private company.' By 10 November 1992, Branson's position had hardened. Without negotiations, he sharply reduced the number of crews, extracted 9 per cent more productivity and his representatives refused to discuss the inadequacy of the pensions.

To seal the tougher conditions, John Hayward, his operations manager, informed the CAA that the pilots had, in a vote, split evenly in a ballot about the new conditions of work. In fact, the pilots had voted six in favour of the changes and about one hundred and fifty against. To suffocate the dissent, Branson introduced Francis Farrow, his charmless lawyer, to confront those pilot representatives whom he deemed unhelpful. He also instructed his managers to spread a good news message. 'We've got a happy, jolly working atmosphere,' the pilots were told by Syd Pennington. 'Don't ruin it.' Not once did the official minutes of the management's meetings with the pilots record Branson blaming British Airways' dirty tricks for his decisions. Nor could any member of the committee recall their mention. The public, however, was offered a different image.

As the libel trial against BA approached, Branson blamed British Airways for the distress dirty tricks had caused. 'Virgin Atlantic staff,' he would claim, 'had to suffer from the pressure which BA put us under in the form of reduced salaries and cuts in their bonuses.' The assertion, for which there appeared to be no evidence, was bizarre. In public, Branson emphasised that his employees were his priority. 'Staff should come first,' he gushed. 'If it means making £5 million less, then that is the right decision to make. It's like family. But if the going was tough, I would never throw my children out. Everyone shares a bit less. It should be exactly the same with a company.' No one, he believed, would dare to utter a contradiction as he focused on permanently maiming BA's management.

British Airways offered a minimal defence to Branson's writ. Bob
Ayling could prove that 'switch-selling' was lawful and that BA had
been the target of the same tactics by American Airlines and United
Airlines. BA might also expect to discredit Branson's witnesses and
probe his finances to establish the insignificance of the losses caused
by the alleged dirty tricks. They possessed no insight, however, to
prove whether Virgin had benefited from the confidential information obtained by Hugh Welburn and others. However, the disadvantages of arguing that case in open court were overwhelming.

The damaging testimony of former British Airways staff disclosed
BA's pursuit of Virgin's customers, the misuse of the computer reservations system and the shredding of documents referring to Virgin.
Additionally, as the lawyers representing BA learned more about the
activities of Brian Basham and David Burnside, they concluded that
the case could not be defended. The potential cross-examination of
BA directors threatened total corporate destruction. The balance was
firmly in Branson's favour. Surrender was the only solution. Two
weeks before the court hearing, in late December 1992, BA agreed
to pay £610,000 in damages and Branson's costs.

At a council of war at Harbottle and Lewis, Branson's solicitors
in Hanover Square, Branson, Whitehorn and Virgin Atlantic's press
officers discussed how the victory could be presented. The humiliation of British Airways was to be, Branson instructed, choreographed
to vindicate himself as a truthful hero. 'Turn it on King,' agreed
Whitehorn. Regicide, the death of the king, was to be celebrated by
a war dance. Every newspaper and television station was to be alerted.
'Tell Joan,' said Whitehorn, referring to Joan Thirkettle of ITN, still
a Branson favourite, 'we want a big show.'

In the courtroom on 11 January 1993, Branson, wearing a suit
and tie, basked in his victory. With unconcealed joy, he sat behind
the wigged lawyers listening to British Airways' cringing apology
and to Lord King's acknowledgement that some employees had been
engaged in 'regrettable' activities. Unfortunately, he had been compelled to tolerate in the same statement Lord King's denial that he
and his fellow executives had any knowledge of the dirty tricks or had
sanctioned a conspiracy. The complete blame, despite his vigorous
protests, was passed on to Brian Basham.

Surrounded by his family, employees and lawyers, walking through
the towering stone chamber of the High Court towards the exit into

Fleet Street, Branson considered the appropriate words for the waiting media. By the time he emerged, laughing, his hands held high,
he had decided upon magnanimity. 'I won't bear a grudge,' he said
to the cameras. 'We hope that BA's apology heralds a new era for
British aviation.' But moments later, his true sentiments burst out.
The winner deserves to take all, he reasoned. His gamble had come
off. He wanted King and his cronies to suffer. Victories were best
enjoyed by a merciless war dance. The new sentiments came easily.
'The public,' he announced with a deceptive smile, 'should boycott
BA and fly Virgin or any other independent carrier.' His war would
continue. 'This is not the end of Virgin's dispute with BA,' he would
say later. The *Sun*, his loyal mouthpiece, published his sentiments
the following morning. 'He has never forgiven them and is likely to
remain a sworn enemy.' The *Sun*'s headline, 'Virgin screws BA',
enraptured Whitehorn. 'A dream to die for,' Whitehorn's staff
chortled.

Lord King's humiliation and the anger in Westminster and Whitehall about British Airways' conduct were exciting: how, Branson
pondered, could he profit from BA's catastrophe which had caused
David Burnside's removal, Lord King's premature retirement and
the collapse of morale within BA. In the soundbite culture, Branson
was confident that no one would delve into the detail of his allegations. The focus would be his vindication and his generous distribution to his Virgin 'family' of the £500,000 paid by BA in damages.
The individual £160 payments – the 'BA bonus' – given to his
beloved employees, pronounced Branson, were compensation for
their suffering 'so much unfair hassle'. None of his 'family', he
emphasised, had ever suffered redundancy. The memory of the
redundancies in Virgin Music and the pilots' complaints were conveniently forgotten.

Carefully reading every day during breakfast the thick wodge of
newspaper articles echoing the thunder of sympathetic applause,
Branson decided to intensify his vilification of British Airways. 'We're
going to break them at Heathrow,' he told his directors. Without
the profits from Virgin Music to support his trading, his singular
strategy was to expand Virgin Atlantic at BA's expense to produce
the necessary cash. His proclamation was unambiguous: 'We are
going to make Virgin Atlantic a global airline by 1995.' That required
nothing less than the brutal diminution of BA. His campaign to win

the government's further support against BA began hours after his courtroom victory.

Each twist of the saga, Branson estimated, would attract passengers from British Airways and justified the increase of his fleet of aircraft from eight to sixteen planes at a cost of £1 billion. Virgin Atlantic, carrying 1.5 million passengers, would be the same size as British Midland. Although matching BA's two hundred and fifty aircraft would be a long battle, and Virgin Atlantic's annual £347 million turnover was still dwarfed by BA's £6.3 billion, he was committed to ruthlessly pursue the injured giant in the regulatory agencies and courts across the world.

The apparent reluctance one year earlier to issue a writ was replaced by the threat of an orgy of litigation. 'We are at the end of our tether,' he seethed at the opening of Virgin's new Heathrow lounge in February 1993. 'Furious' about the continuing absence of any compensation for the 'incalculable millions' which BA 'stole from Virgin' and the commercial damage allegedly suffered by Virgin, he issued demands for £75 million from British Airways for lost passengers, damages for insults to his reputation which caused the withdrawal of an unnamed investment partner in the airline, and threatened an anti-trust suit in New York if 'many millions are not forthcoming'. In what he called 'crunch week' in late February 1993, Branson demanded settlement by lunchtime the same day of claims ranging between $325 million and $975 million. After talking to Branson, Whitehorn encapsulated his employer's mood: 'If we don't get them, we'll sue the pants off them.'

The vulnerability of British Airways encouraged Branson to cast a fly to justify his demand. 'Virgin,' he told an approved journalist, 'nearly did go bankrupt during the dirty tricks time and that's why I had to sell the record company.' In April 1993, he again presented his unreliable version of history: 'One of Britain's biggest companies had decided systematically to put us out of business. It was like Bosnians against the Serbs.' BA, he later added, 'forced me to sell Virgin Music which had affected a whole group of people who had nothing to do with the airline. It made me furious.' Emotion, he hoped, would tilt the government and the public in Virgin's favour. 'Passengers are flocking to Virgin from BA,' he repeated endlessly without pondering that his success undermined his need for government assistance. Although it was a contradiction for a veteran champion of deregulation to demand state intervention, Branson was never troubled by such inconsistencies.

Securing the support of the Secretary of State for Transport was vital for Branson's fortune. His airline's expansion relied entirely upon that minister's discretion. John McGregor, the incumbent minister, was, like his predecessor, an admirer of Branson. McGregor had enthusiastically 'opened' Virgin's new lounge at Heathrow and awarded Virgin's new route to Boston. Branson hoped that the politician could be persuaded to grant a slew of new demands. He invited McGregor to Holland Park for lunch to 'sort out' Britain's aviation policy and, in particular, approve Virgin Atlantic's expansion.

For years, Branson had preached 'small is beautiful' and challenged people to 'hold my head in a bucket of water for ten minutes if I show any signs of wanting to expand to more than twelve planes'. That homily was discarded. Branson's shopping list from McGregor included forbidding British Airways to use Concorde as a lure to upgrade passengers; terminating all BA's inducements to compete for passengers; and a government order for BA to transfer 3,500 slots to Virgin. In particular, McGregor should order BA to give up one of its twice daily routes to San Francisco.

The lunch was an anticlimax. Although keen to support Virgin, the minister was explicit: 'I'm not doing anything to weaken BA. They've got enough problems against the American airlines.' Branson became curiously quiet. 'Why should Virgin get any advantages over all the other airlines who for years have demanded access to Heathrow?' asked McGregor. 'Surely you realise there would be uproar if I help you against the others?' Branson remained silent. Uneasily, the minister departed.

Branson brushed McGregor's rebuff aside. His bellicose agenda ruled out making peace with British Airways. He searched for a stunt. Colin Marshall was invited to Holland Park for a private conversation ostensibly to begin repairing relations. BA's chief executive arrived on 25 January 1993. The plaques and medals around his host's drawing room, the framed photographs of Branson with celebrities and the mounted letters of gushing praise on the walls were to remind Marshall of the popularity of himself and Virgin Atlantic. 'I'll sue unless you give me compensation,' threatened Branson, savouring his moment. He demanded hundreds of millions of pounds, about 3 per cent of BA's routes from Heathrow and the termination of all hostility. If his shopping list was not met, then the world would engage in a war of attrition. After ninety minutes, Marshall neither rejected nor accepted the ultimatum. Branson's proffered cup of tea left a bad taste. The host was not easily understood.

As Marshall stood by the open door to bid Branson farewell, he was startled. Waiting on the street below were camera crews. Someone at Virgin had leaked news of the meeting. Branson smiled. The image, he hoped, would confirm his status as a powerbroker. Before Marshall had had time to return to his office, Whitehorn, speaking on Branson's behalf, described the visit as an apology from British Airways and expressed Branson's confidence that his demands would be met. Marshall would offer another version. The investigation by British Airways, Marshall explained, revealed that many of Branson's allegations were 'unfounded' and 'the actual tricks used were comparatively minor and not unusual in what is a worldwide cut-throat business.' Throat cutting was precisely Branson's desire – the more blood the better. Beyond the public sparring, it had been agreed that Bob Ayling would discuss with Trevor Abbott a final settlement. That evening, Branson telephoned Ayling in his modest Stockwell home. 'When it's all over, we'll have a drink and a good laugh,' he promised.

Abbott's brief from Branson was to draw blood. 'We want £100 million,' Abbott told Ayling at their first meeting. This was a poker game Branson enjoyed.

'Before we agree to figures,' replied Ayling coolly, 'I want everything listed so we know what we're getting for our money.'

Days later, Abbott returned with a shortlist and a demand for an immediate £30 million. The two were locked in an aggressive stalemate for three weeks until Branson invited Ayling to Holland Park. 'I want £30 million,' reiterated Branson. After further negotiation, Branson agreed to reduce his demand to £12 million. On 1 March, Ayling offered £9 million in final settlement. Included in their agreement, said Ayling, would be a clause stipulating that both sides 'will use their best endeavours to discourage media coverage or comment about their past relationship' and that in reply to media inquiries, both agreed to 'ensure that such coverage is limited [to say that] the disputes are resolved and that both parties are looking to the future'. Ayling wanted to draw a line. Branson disagreed. Dirty tricks had enormous potential. His opinion was encouraged by Bob Beckman, Freddie Laker's American lawyer, who was encouraging Branson to pursue anti-trust litigation in the American courts and even mooted the possibility of a criminal prosecution against British Airways. Criss-crossing the Atlantic during the negotiations, Branson was advised by Beckman that he could win hundreds of millions of dollars.

On the night of 18 March 1993, Branson telephoned Ayling at home. Branson was angry that Ayling had not capitulated and repaid 'the money BA stole from us'. Not getting his own way was intoler-able. 'I'm just asking you to agree,' Ayling responded, 'not to always use these allegations every time we disagree in the future.' That drew further ill-temper from Holland Park. Branson had already fixed his sights on $1 billion compensation from British Airways in an Amer-ican trial. He had constructed a scenario featuring himself as the victim, convinced that the world would accept as indisputable truth that 'BA is a monopoly' plotting to destroy Virgin Atlantic by 'unfair and illegal means'. The publicity alone in an American trial would be priceless. No one dared mention to Branson that since Virgin's Upper Class was cheaper and better than the equivalent in BA, there was thin evidence of a plot. 'My feeling is we could really hit the jackpot,' Branson told his cabal – Abbott, Farrow and Whitehorn – lured by Beckman's mention of $1 billion. Even Abbott, in the room with Branson as he spoke to Ayling, was surprised by the vehemence. 'You fucking . . .' began Branson, cursing and yelling at his foe. 'I expect £12 million without any conditions or else.'

Branson's ultimatum was unambiguous: 'You might think I'm mad but I'm not going to give up my right to free speech for nine million quid.' In Branson's version, British Airways had spurned peace by not accepting his terms. 'The gag is contemptible,' he scorned, furious that Ayling and Marshall would not concede and had not been dismissed from BA. Ayling's letters and telephone calls suggesting further meetings and offers encouraged his aggression. 'It's unreasonable for them to request our silence in the future,' he raged. 'We're at the end of our tether. If there's nothing on the table tomorrow, that's it.' BA, the wounded dinosaur, he was certain would capitulate. His performance was part of the drama. The col-lapse of the negotiations was announced on 19 March 1993.

To deepen the wounds, Branson accused King, Marshall and Ayling of lying by denying any knowledge of the dirty tricks. 'They should resign,' he said, 'unless my proposals for peace are accepted.' To increase the pressure, he agreed to help Martyn Gregory write a book called *Dirty Tricks* and produce a second documentary for ITV. Gregory proved his skill by persuading Brian Basham to appear on television. The publicist, outraged by British Airways' betrayal of himself to take all the blame, was eager to denounce Lord King and Bob Ayling for having approved all his undertakings. 'If they'd been able to put [Branson] out of business,' Basham volunteered, 'they would have been happy to do so.' Branson's bandwagon was moving. With promises that more incriminating evidence would emerge, he speculated, 'There is always the possibility that some British Airways directors could face criminal charges.'

To further discomfort his enemies, Branson demanded that the Monopolies Commission and the Department of Trade and Industry should formally investigate British Airways, he issued another writ alleging BA's infringement of Virgin's copyright by the unauthorised use of Virgin's reservations computer, and he instructed Bob Beckman to issue writs in New York. There was pleasure, and profit, in war.

13

Unfortunate casualties

The telephone call was like thousands of others: Branson testing, pitching and seducing. This time, on 23 September 1993, to a complete stranger. The mention of his name guaranteed that even the most famous and secretive in London responded personally. In less than one minute, Guy Snowden's gruff drawl acknowledged his enticement. Branson was telephoning about his latest passion, the proposed British lottery. Snowden's skills, he knew, would help secure the prize for Virgin, but initially he disguised his excitement.

'I'm bidding for the lottery,' explained Branson casually, 'and I just wanted to see whether we might talk.'

'Sure,' replied Snowden, flattered that the famous Englishman recognised his expertise.

'I'm forming a group to bid for the franchise,' Branson continued.

'Well, I've nearly finished putting together my consortium,' replied the forty-eight-year-old American, 'so I'm not quite sure where we would start.'

Snowden's reply was certainly not the introduction Branson expected or desired. Since 1988 he had been lobbying Conservative ministers to launch a non-profit-making lottery to benefit national charities, although the idea of a lottery had been first suggested to a royal commision in 1979. John Major's announcement on 6 March 1992, he believed, vindicated his campaign. But his raw ignorance about the management of a lottery was indisputably a handicap. To resolve that disadvantage he had, three weeks earlier, dispatched John Jackson, an accountant and an utterly unremarkable businessman, to research and prepare Virgin's bid. Although Jackson had unsuccessfully managed Mates condoms until their sale and would be blamed for poor management of the Sketchley dry cleaning business, he was trusted as a loyal servant. Jackson returned from a three-week whirlwind tour with a list of requirements. At the very top he placed

GTech, Guy Snowden's company. That was not surprising. Since 1982, the American company had accumulated the management of about 70 per cent of the world's lotteries. With an annual turnover in 1995 of £460 million, GTech controlled seventy-seven lotteries in thirty countries, including twenty-six out of thirty-seven American state lotteries.

Guy Snowden, the co-founder of GTech, employed six thousand staff including three hundred engineers and two hundred software designers, to produce unique systems and terminals to supervise ninety million lottery transactions every week. Based in Rhode Island, his staff were available around the clock to repair any fault across the world. For Snowden, who had just won the Texas lottery and was paid about $2.1 million a year, the proposed British lottery was the gold prize: the world's biggest. Months before John Major's announcement, he had moved to London from Florida to assemble a winning consortium. 'Everything I have done in my life,' he would later say, 'has been a dress rehearsal for this.'

Branson's telephone call coincided with Snowden's successful formation of Camelot, his consortium for the bid. During the negotiations, Snowden had rejected a stream of eminent suitors because they failed his test of ranking as the best. Shrewdly, Snowden's final recruitment was Cadbury-Schweppes, the soft drinks and confectionery manufacturer. That corporation possessed unique access to Britain's network of high street shops where GTech's terminals would be ideally located. Some of the famous companies and banks that Snowden had rejected were forming rival consortia although, until the government's prospectus was published, the lottery's rules remained unknown. Branson's telephone call to Snowden was a surprise but hardly different from dozens of others. Except, Branson's pitch had become swaggering, even challenging, although he still had not committed himself to launch a bid.

'I'm doing it for free,' said Branson disingenuously. 'You can forget about your bid. We're going to win.' If Branson's tone had not been quietly polite, Snowden would have adjudged his approach aggressive. With irreproachable candour, Branson had not concealed from intimates that a Branson lottery, enhancing his own reputation and extending his business empire, would be 'a very exciting new brand to build' and a 'great morale booster for all the Virgin staff'. A Branson lottery, he calculated, would generate unlimited free publicity in newspapers and television especially when his organisation regularly presented huge cheques to the lottery winners and charities. In public, however, Branson had pitched his bid exclusively as a charitable scheme to raise money for good causes. This was, he would suggest, his opportunity to 'do good' for ordinary Britons without grubby profiteering.

Branson was not renowned as a major benefactor to Britain's huge charity movement. Other than his unhappy dalliance as 'Minister for Litter', his launch of Mates condoms and his support for a campaign against selling tobacco to children, he was unusual among Britain's billionaires in eschewing large public gifts to the unprivileged, to the arts and to science. There was no public building, university scholarship or rare painting endowed by his generosity although he occasionally appeared as the celebrity at fund-raising parties. But emboldened by his victory against British Airways, Branson beamed honest conviction and wore the garland of popular heroism. Conservative ministers described Branson as their embodiment of the Gospel of competition and privatisation. His merest mention of an interest in any key government initiative guaranteed that ministers – the 'fans of Branson' – would respond enthusiastically to their icon of free enterprise. His entry in 1993's *Current Biography* was flattering. Branson, the authoritative book recorded, 'is not only Britain's most successful entrepreneur since World War II but perhaps the world's most charismatic business person . . . Initially derided as a "hippie businessman" with practically no chance for long-term success, virtually every one of his enterprises has prospered.' Branson assumed his anointment as the indispensable ingredient of every government-inspired venture, including the lottery. Snowden, however, was insensitive to Branson's self-importance.

'I don't care where the money goes,' Snowden told Branson. 'I've got the best systems in the world. We've got all the specialists. I've got a consortium. You've got nothing. You'll never make it in time.'

'You don't understand,' said Branson in no mind to concede, 'I'm doing it for free. That's why we'll win.'

Snowden laughed: 'Look, it's obvious that we each have a position and if you would like to discuss it further, I would.' The conversation was over. As far as Snowden cared, he had won the brief sparring match.

Branson's certainty was unscathed. He made a virtue of his

ignorance and his reliance on others. The lottery was no different. In the aftermath of his victory against British Airways, his popularity, he believed, guaranteed his selection as the people's choice to manage a risk-free monopoly which he deemed to require no special marketing skills. The only important requirement was to place the computer terminals, which were misguidedly called 'sophisticated electronic cash registers' by a Virgin spokesman, around the country. That, he realised, was GTech's expertise. Snowden, he decided, should be persuaded to supply his consortium. Fifteen minutes after their conversation, Branson's secretary telephoned the American with an invitation for lunch the following day, Friday, 24 September 1993.

Snowden arrived at Holland Park in an ebullient mood. During his shooting lesson that morning in west London, he had enthusiastically aimed at the clays as though each represented a rival bidder. The repeated shower of splinters reflected his mettle. Perhaps he was too gung-ho as he stepped into the tastefully decorated living room to await Branson. Crucially, he had ignored the advice of David Rigg, a publicist and Camelot director, that his host was 'a tricky man to deal with' who was 'quick to bring a law suit' and was 'well known for taking people on publicly'. Instead, intrigued by the opportunity to meet a living legend, Snowden pondered whether Branson could be lured to join rather than oppose Camelot. If Branson agreed, there remained the obstacle that the other members would object, but they might be persuaded to embrace such an important player.

In Branson's world, first impressions count. 'I decide within five seconds if I like someone,' he says. The heavy American squinting through dark eyes in his designer house was decidedly distasteful. 'Odious' was the word which later sprang to his mind as the former Surrey public schoolboy gazed at the bulldozer driver's son from New York State.

Mixing gambling and politics in many countries was a sensitive task – a 'tinderbox' Snowden joked – but, despite the inevitable investigations by police and state security agencies in many countries, neither he nor GTech had ever been charged with any crime. But the company had been mentioned in criminal trials involving bribes and corruption in Washington, Kentucky, Maryland, New Jersey and California. A GTech employee was under investigation for defrauding the company itself and a state senator had been imprisoned for receiving funds from a GTech lobbyist to oppose unfavourable legislation. But that had not dented Snowden's personal holding of GTech shares worth $45 million, nor directly impugned his personal reputation.

Branson was unaware of that controversial history as he and John Jackson led their guest to the atrium overlooking the garden. Politely, he concealed his thought that his guest resembled a Mafia hoodlum, but he avoided any small-talk. 'We're going to win because we're doing it for free,' Branson recited several times after they sat down to eat baked salmon and salad. He then made his offer. GTech, suggested Branson, should provide its expertise to Virgin's bid, 'The UK Lottery Foundation', because it was certain to win. 'Join us,' said Branson. 'Supply us.'

Usually, Branson's offers received respectful consideration. But forcefully, probably too forcefully, Snowden ridiculed his host's confidence. Jackson's superficial research, scoffed Snowden, could be barely compared to GTech's worldwide experience. As he recited a stream of relevant statistics and data that would influence the success of the winning bid, Branson was scribbling in his A4 notebook.

'If you read the government's outline prospectus,' preached Snowden, sensing that neither Branson nor Jackson had bothered, 'you'll see that you'll need to prove a lot of requirements to win.' Specifically, Peter Davis, the government's regulator, required certainty that the winner was capable of organising the National Lottery's technology, guaranteeing its security and accurately forecasting the millions which would be raised. 'We've got a track record to show that we can raise more millions than the others.'

Branson stopped taking notes. He did not like the American. 'You don't understand,' he said yet again. 'We're not taking any profits. We're giving everything to charity.'

Snowden appeared to scoff. The government's rules, he knew, would ignore whether the operator gave his profits to charity. In any event, Virgin, he suspected, would take a substantial management fee decided by Branson. That was in Snowden's opinion profit dressed under another name. 'You don't understand lotteries, Richard. You don't understand the British government's rules, and you don't even have a consortium. I've got everything in place. You're plain too late.'

Branson stuttered. To his side, Jackson glanced across subserviently. One thing was certain. Branson did not appreciate people telling him what he did not want to hear. Worse still, a fat American who had arrived in Britain believing that he could snatch his dream of a Branson lottery. He was deaf to Snowden's certainty that his proposal to distribute the profits to charities would be irrelevant under the government's legislation. The conversation was deadlocked. Branson felt insulted. Snowden's rejection of his offer was insufferable and a victorious smile appeared to play across the American's face. Snowden's suggestion that he could easily drop Camelot's profits to 'take Virgin out of the game' followed by a suggestion that Virgin join Camelot was obscene. Under no circumstances did Branson want to be part of someone else's show. The putative partner had become a competitor on Branson's home turf.

After a pause, Snowden spoke. Suspicious of Branson's involvement in a lottery for charity without any commercial angle, he asked, 'You know, what is the real agenda here?' Branson was upset. For twenty-five years, his accumulation of millions had been varnished by the suggestion of charitable idealism. The façade had deflected attention from his secret use of recording tapes, his threatening letters to critical journalists, his tax-free fortune hidden in offshore trusts and his equivocations about his finances. Now the odious American was bluntly questioning the sincerity of his charitable motives. The atmosphere became cold. Snowden noticed Branson stiffening. The possibility of a partnership was doomed. Hamfistedly, Snowden asked, 'What can we do for you?' Branson wrote those six words in his notebook. Jackson looked on quietly. There are two versions of what followed.

In Snowden's version, he asked, 'So Richard what can we do together? Is there something I can do for you?'

Snowden would later say he had in mind co-operating with Virgin in another project, perhaps introducing gambling on Virgin's aeroplanes. But his offer was uttered without an explanation. His words were liable to misinterpretation.

Branson appeared to Snowden to be agitated by his remakrs. 'I'm quite successful,' Snowden heard him say. 'I only need one breakfast, one lunch and one dinner a day.' Branson rose and left the room. Some minutes later he returned. Snowden and Jackson were talking at the table. Branson resumed his seat and dessert was served. The three continued talking until Snowden, unable to eat the chocolate-encased meringue, decided to leave. 'Shall we get you a taxi?' asked Branson politely. 'I've got a car, thanks,' replied Snowden. The American departed, aware of the sour atmosphere.

Branson's version of those last ten minutes was starkly different. Snowden, he said, was sweating profusely. 'If you continue with that approach,' Snowden had said about the non-profit-making lottery, 'you are going to cost us millions . . . we are going to have to change our bid.' Mopping his brow, Snowden continued, 'I do not quite know how to phrase this, Richard. There's always a bottom line. I will get to the point. In what way can we help you, Richard?'

Branson replied, 'What on earth do you mean?'

Snowden either answered, 'Everybody needs something in life', or, 'There is always something in life that everybody needs.'

Believing that he had been offered a bribe, Branson spluttered, 'Thank you. I'm quite successful. I only need one breakfast, one lunch and one dinner a day.'

Branson, in his account, then left the room and rushed downstairs to a lavatory where he scribbled Snowden's key words on a piece of scrap paper taken from his pocket. Holding the paper, he rushed two floors upstairs to his office where he told Julia Madonna, his secretary, 'You will not believe what has just happened. Someone has tried to bribe me.' Why he should write his note in a lavatory would never be explained; nor did anyone ever see the writing on the paper. Minutes later, Branson reappeared downstairs in the atrium. Dessert was not served, said Branson. Rather, Snowden was standing ready to leave.

The minute the American departed, stepping into his waiting car, Branson said to Jackson, 'Am I correct in saying that I have just been offered a bribe?' Branson's conviction permitted no contradiction. Branson was in no doubt that although he had initiated the meeting just twenty-four hours earlier, an American worth peanuts compared to his own one billion pounds had contrived to offer him a bribe in front of a hostile eyewitness. 'It was blatant,' insisted Branson. 'The guy was definitely trying to buy us off . . . He was actually trying to bribe me.'

Three aspects of the bribe story as presented in the trial were undisputed. No sum of money, Branson agreed, was ever mentioned; Snowden did not ask Branson to drop his bid or clarify the purpose of his unquantified bribe; and Snowden had never mentioned the prospect of a bribe to other members of his consortium. Branson was nevertheless convinced about his interpretation.

Over the weekend, Branson told many people about Snowden's

offer. On Monday morning, he telephoned Colin Howes, his solicitor at Harbottle and Lewis, and recounted his story. Howes advised him not to raise the issue with Peter Davis, the lottery regulator, because offering a bribe 'was unimportant' and should be 'played down'. Branson agreed. Being offered a bribe, it seemed, was unexceptional.

By that Monday, Branson had decided to launch his own bid. Snowden's accurate explanation of the government's rules was disregarded. Rules, Branson believed passionately, should be broken. Or in this case, simply be ignored. His campaign, as the businessman working for the public without profits, would raise more money for the lottery because his costs were lower and his profits would be distributed to charities. That stark contrast, Branson was sure, would trump Camelot and especially GTech. The regulator, he was convinced, would discriminate against an American who would profit both by supplying the terminals and from his 22 per cent stake in the Camelot consortium. No American, Branson was convinced, would be allowed to earn such huge profits from a British charitable lottery.

Four days after Snowden's departure, Branson received a telephone call from Tim Bell, the publicist employed by GTech. Bell, whose fame and expertise had been recognised ever since his membership of the inner circle masterminding Margaret Thatcher's 1979 election triumph, had been told by Snowden about the unsuccessful lunch. 'It was cold at the end,' admitted Snowden at their regular mid-week meeting. 'He probably thought I'm a prick because I said "no" to his offer.' Uneasy about his failure to establish a good relationship with the famous Englishman, Snowden was anxious to prevent GTech's exclusion if, against the odds, Branson won the bid. 'I'll try to smooth things out,' offered Bell. Snowden was grateful. 'I know him,' continued Bell. 'You're not British. I'll test the waters.' Bell's telephone call to Branson was unsuccessful. Branson was cool and non-committal. Although he did not mention the offer of a bribe or his anger, his allegation was already circulating in London.

In November 1993, David Rigg, a Camelot director, heard the gossip about Branson's allegations of Snowden's bribe. Rigg knew about the disastrous lunch and had advised Snowden 'not to pick a fight with an 800 pound gorilla'. Rigg and Snowden agreed to remain silent. They agreed that it could only be a joke. Another very good reason to say nothing was Branson's latest major publicity coup.

Soon after the Snowden lunch, Branson had again been searching for a stunt. The first new Airbus was due for delivery to Virgin Atlantic.

'We need an idea,' he grizzled, meaning a story to capture the front pages of the newspapers.

'Why don't you ask Princess Diana to a naming ceremony?' suggested James Murray, Virgin Atlantic's press officer. An epiphany crossed Branson's face as his hand instantly darted towards the telephone. He was in no doubt that a favour was owed. In March 1990, Diana and her family had spent a week on Necker. The publicity and photographs had, to Branson's satisfaction, filled newspapers across the world. Diana's acceptance to launch Virgin Atlantic's first Airbus would promote a more important financial asset than his island. Within a minute the Kensington Palace switchboard had completed the connection.

'She'll do it,' Branson smiled victoriously.

'Get her to dress in red,' suggested Murray, 'and we'll name the Airbus "Lady in Red".' Murray's touch for publicity had exceeded even his master's.

Over two hundred journalists and the world's finest paparazzi were commandeered on 6 December 1993 to Heathrow. Diana's presence, Branson chortled, had infuriated British Airways. Ever since his courtroom victory against BA, she had edged slightly towards the outsider, admired for taking on the Establishment. Occasionally, they had played tennis at the Harbour Club and Vandebilt and she had visited Holland Park to eat with Branson and his wife. Gossips had ridiculously even talked of an indiscreet relationship with Branson on Necker, after which she had sought to minimise their public encounters. But there was no caution before accepting this unexpected request. Branson expected nothing less.

Standing near Diana on a raised platform, overwhelmed by the guaranteed publicity, Branson put his arm around the princess's shoulders. 'I cringed when he did that,' Diana later complained to friends. 'I cringed when I saw him do that,' Murray told his staff. Branson was oblivious to the embarrassment. All that mattered was Virgin Atlantic's major triumph.

Practically slapping his thighs in excitement, Branson joined his airline's executives for dinner. 'Fantastic,' he gushed. 'Amazing.' The publicity had been priceless. 'Worth millions,' agreed everyone. Working for Virgin was special, a unique experience. Virgin's customers felt precisely the same. Virgin offered the promise of fun and the unexpected. Those around the dinner table identified with a man who beamed disinterest in money and telephoned in the middle of the night to say, 'They've found a new tomb in Egypt. We're flying down there in the morning. Why don't you come?' In their excitement, they barely noticed that Branson unprecedentedly had paid the restaurant bill. For a man living a cashless life, it was a phenomenon. On reflection, they recalled he had paid with an American Express card. Recently he had featured in their advertisements. Part of the deal was to let him use the card for free, they agreed.

Branson departed with a glow. Fortunately, no one had mentioned the airline's poor finances or the pilots' latest complaint that 'the jolly fun airline is an illusion'. The increment to the pilots' wages had been suspended, 'due to the financial predicament of the company'; their hours of work had been increased; and the company had only agreed to pay the pension on a previous increment after a threat of legal action. 'Morale is very low,' Syd Pennington was told. 'Hang in there together,' he had urged the staff. Pennington was snubbed. On Branson's instructions, Pennington's response· was robust: 'Take it or leave it.' The pilots' disenchantment was ignored by Branson. Keeping tight control of Virgin's cash was his primary concern.

In Holland Park, Abbott was grappling to keep the empire afloat. 'We haven't got enough money for the payroll,' he told a loyal accountant. The internal projections prepared by accountants had, as usual, been optimistic. The inevitable disappointment created an air of crisis. Trying to find the truth was difficult for Abbott. Since accurate accounts were not legally required for the offshore trusts in the Virgin Islands and Channel Islands, Abbott kept a mental list of bank accounts with cash and assets which could be used as security for loans. Unfortunately, Virgin possessed few assets and only leases on planes and property. One of the few reliable assets was Necker which, as Abbott regularly chortled, could be reliably revalued every two years 'for another million'. Some minor companies showing trading profits were legitimately inserted into loss-making companies to neutralise the liability of corporation tax payments. Abbott prided himself that Virgin rarely paid any corporation tax. Preparing business plans for banks to negotiate loans, however, plunged him into despair.

He disliked releasing genuine information about private companies and preferred to offer optimistic forecasts to banks which, in the case of Virgin's Voyager hotels, eventually proved embarrassing. Like the internal accountants who queried Abbott's calculations, the bankers were stalled by his cursory snub: 'You don't need to know that.'

Not only Virgin employees, but Seibu-Saison, the Japanese investors in the airline, had also discovered Abbott's sharpness with money. Ever since their purchase of a 10 per cent stake in 1989 and the subsequent £30 million loan, the Japanese directors had complained about Virgin's failure to repay the money as agreed. Regularly, Kenzi Hashedate, the company's astute lawyer, commuted to London to seek financial information and returned to Tokyo frustrated. 'They haven't got the money to repay us,' he reported. 'It's a shaky business.' Despite Abbott's repeated promises, 'We'll give you the information you want', it never appeared. Branson's welcome three years earlier of a 'long-term' investment appeared to be a tokenism. The Virgin executives, Hashedate suspected, misjudged the Japanese politeness as unintelligence and weakness.

In 1992, Hashedate had arrived in London to negotiate a divorce. For one year, Abbott energetically procrastinated, sometimes disappearing for three days, repeatedly reneging on agreements. In mid-1993, Hashedate issued a threat: 'I've briefed a QC and we'll issue the writ tomorrow unless you come to the table with sensible proposals.' Derry Irvine QC had advised Hashedate that his claim was 'cast iron'. In October 1993, Abbott offered $65 million, considerably less than Seibu was originally promised. The Japanese felt cheated but relieved to have rescued some money. Abbott was proud of cutting a profitable deal. 'I'm a businessman,' said Abbott bluntly. Sentiments were irrelevant. Branson's only comment was that he still possessed the '£250 million cash mountain' from the sale of Virgin Music to EMI. But to the injured Japanese that seemed doubtful.

Cutting a rough deal with the Japanese left Branson with more debt and quiet gossip around London about Virgin's tactics which did not enhance his reputation. Those incestuous City gripes, however, did not interest the outsider. The Japanese were forgotten as unfortunate casualties. Another day, he could find another player to charm into a deal. All that mattered was the afterglow of Princess Diana's public display of admiration. For three days in succession, she was even photographed wearing a Virgin T-shirt. 'I pulled a muscle in my back,' Branson casually told a director of the airline one morning in his office. 'How?' he was politely asked. 'Playing tennis with Diana,' he replied, exulting in the power of his celebrity and his exceptional affluence. Her magical assent provided, Branson judged, the perfect opportunity to announce his bid to run the lottery.

In the rush to create a team, the 'grinning pullover', as Lord King had damned him, understood that his bid would be enhanced by 'suits' to reassure the government. Among those telephoned from his car was Lord Young, the former Secretary of State for Trade and Industry and Branson's occasional banker. 'Would you like to be the chairman of my group?' asked Branson. Young had been a supporter of Virgin Atlantic and had flown as a minister on Virgin's inaugural flight to Tokyo. He accepted Branson's offer confident that, if successful, neither man would ever have to pay for lunch again. Yet he was concerned that, unlike other bidders, Branson was not assembling a consortium but retaining total ownership of the company. 'He's calling it a "lottery for charity",' Young told friends, 'but I've never seen him as a benefactor of charities.' No enduring philanthropic venture in Britain was associated with Branson. His charity based upon the lottery, like all his ventures, would be financed by others. Young was not as disturbed by Branson's 'protecting the downside' as by his silence about the Snowden lunch. 'It was odd,' Young remarked years later, 'that Richard never mentioned Snowden's offer of a bribe to me.'

Branson's final selection of the other trustees of the charity's fund was the litmus test of his standing in London. Among his nominees were Sir Angus Ogilvy, condemned in 1976 by DTI inspectors for tax evasion and dishonesty; Lord Callaghan, aged eighty-one, the country's worst post-war prime minister, who was tainted by his association with the managing director of a much criticised secondary bank in Wales; and Lord Tonypandy, aged eighty-four, another Welsh MP, who took undisclosed payments from the same controversial bank.

Branson's publicist was Des Wilson, famous for campaigning against poverty and renowned as an effective political lobbyist. During their first taxi ride, Branson had casually mentioned, 'Guy Snowden tried to bribe me.' Wilson took little notice of Branson's anecdote. 'Richard's probably misinterpreted a business offer,' Wilson thought, warming to his employer's honesty and purposefulness.

Branson next visited Peter Davis, the director of Oflot, the lottery regulator, to discuss the ground rules of the bid. The accountant's personality was not reassuring. Timid and leaden, Davis epitomised those bureaucrats disliked by buccaneers. In precise terms, the regulator explained that Branson's proposal to give the profits to charity could not influence his decision. 'The Act is quite explicit,' said Davis. 'And I'm looking for the group that assures me that its computers will work perfectly on the very first day and will maximise its profits.'

'I'm going to do it my way, anyway,' retorted the great salesman. The government's agenda would be subordinated to his.

On 14 December 1993, Branson announced his bid to create the 'People's Lottery'. His application, he persuaded himself, did not require thousands of pages of technical submissions as Camelot was accurately rumoured to be preparing, nor would he spend more than £1 million to prepare his proposal although some of the seven other bidders were spending up to £10 million. Instead of technical detail, he would rely upon publicity. 'What have you got?' he asked Des Wilson. The answer was a succession of photocalls, interviews, colourful stories – like Branson paying £6,500 worth of airline tickets to a reluctant cabby for a taxi ride to Heathrow – and an opinion poll reporting that an overwhelming majority of Britons would play a non-profit-making lottery. Branson also played the victim card. An anonymous letter, revealed Wilson, was circulating attacking Branson's commitment to the lottery. 'They cannot attack our motives,' said Des Wilson about a new 'dirty tricks' war supposedly launched by an unnamed rival, 'so they attack our credentials.' By 14 February 1994, when he delivered his application, Branson was confident of success although he had not properly scrutinised Jackson's proposals or understood how his bid lacked conviction. Branson's concern that his costs would be covered under the heading of the 'retention' fund was satisfied. Any wrinkles, he assumed, could be brushed aside by his oral presentation after his formal bid was presented to the Heritage Department on 14 February 1994. Standing in a deluge of rain in Trafalgar Square alongside Desert Orchid, the famous race horse, Branson was paraded as the 7–2 favourite to win. The isolated commentator noting that Branson was 'not St Francis of Assisi [but] an astute businessman who . . . goes out of his way ruthlessly to promote his own virtues' was easily ignored. While he was not seeking 'beatification', snapped Branson, his motives were charitable rather than commercial. His tactical amnesia about Virgin's realities and failures was hardly surprising. Reaffirming the positive image of the Virgin brand relied on aggressive, selective salesmanship to spread a smokescreen, especially to veil the continuing war against British Airways.

Quietly, in January 1994, Branson accepted £2.6 million in damages from the airline instead of the £6 million he had demanded in 1988 for the failure of British Airways' engineers to maintain his Boeing 747. More embarrassingly, Virgin's £29 million claim against BA for losses caused by the alleged poaching of passengers had, despite his outcry, proved impossible to establish. Reluctantly, he accepted just £265,000 in damages while agreeing to pay £449,000 to BA for their legal costs. Pursuing 'dirty tricks', a spellbinding slogan endlessly recited, had after the libel trial actually cost Virgin Atlantic £184,000 plus Virgin's own legal expenses. The cost to Virgin of 'dirty tricks' had proved to be a considerable exaggeration.

The brief announcement of the settlement irritated Branson. 'They are trying to score a point,' he sighed, unaccustomed to losing. 'It's all very sad and disappointing.' Rapidly, Whitehorn concealed his defeat. Amid a fanfare, the publicist announced Branson's claim of at least $325 million against British Airways in his anti-trust suit in New York. That, Whitehorn reasoned, would smother any suggestion that Virgin was not a victim of BA. 'We've noticed,' declared Branson, 'that BA's old cockiness has returned.'

In Branson's life, resorting to lawyers was the natural impulse of the son and grandson of a lawyer who, from his teens, had shown a fine appreciation of both sides of the law. Issuing writs, like concluding a deal, massaged Branson's sense of achievement. Destabilising weak opponents created unfortunate casualties. That talent was now deployed in the European Commission. Branson travelled to Brussels to file a formal complaint that British Airways managers, behaving like a 'cartel of drug barons', were 'lying and using bullying tactics' towards 'terrified' travel agents by offering discounts on routes Virgin did not fly on condition that agents bought British Airways tickets on routes which Virgin did fly. The practice was common among all European airlines but Branson deployed his lawyers to find legal provisions in Europe's competition laws, a gold mine for

The young tycoon, 1969.

Branson in his Holland
Park office with Penni Pike,
his loyal personal assistant,
1992.

A houseboat and the Sex Pistols: the perfect props for a rebel tycoon.

Ungentlemanly conduct?
Branson pleasing his mother
in 1996, and, left, infuriating
Ivana Trump in 1992.

Stunts to sell Virgin Cola, Megastores and Virgin Cosmetics with Virgin's ever willing Debbie Flett.

An obsession with sex to sell: telephones in 1999, the Virgin flotation in 1996.

Ballooning was a testament to courage amid the self-publicity. Here Branson embraces daughter Holly in 1998 with wife Joan looking on and, below, in 1996 with Rory McCarthy and Per Lindstrand in Marrakesh.

Princess Diana, Virgin's ultimate publicity coup.

Two casualties of Virgin Atlantic: Randolph Fields (*above*) who introduced Branson to the idea of the airline and BA's chairman, Lord King (*left*).

Virgin Trains: Sir George Young (*right*) lured Branson to bid for rail franchises. Virgin Trains would be cursed by some travellers and would tarnish the Virgin brand. In 1998 Branson sold to Brian Souter's Stagecoach, another criticised operator, 49% of Virgin Trains (*below*).

Virgin's ill-fated bid in 1986 to become an orthodox public company ended in rancour. Trevor Abbott (*back, right*) was credited as a financial genius of the Virgin empire, but he eventually committed suicide.

Will Whitehorn (*left*), Virgin's publicity director, is regarded by many as the new Svengali.

With Margaret Thatcher (*above*), with Tony Blair (*below*).

With John McGregor, Secretary of State for Transport (*above*), and Lord Young, politician, banker and co-bidder for the first lottery franchise (*below*). The Conservatives saw Branson as an ideal Tory entrepreneur.

A Labour luvvie: with
Cherie Blair (*left*),
and the Creative
Industries Taskforce
(*below*). The Labour
leadership saw
Branson as an ideal
Labour entrepreneur.

The Victor and the Vanquished. Two High Court libel victories – against British Airways in 1993 (Branson pictured with Joan his wife and Ted his father) and against Guy Snowden in 1998 (*below*) – have established Branson's reputation for honesty and truth.

Sometimes it's hard to be a man. Branson partying and promoting.

'The most important thing in my life' – bidding for the lottery, November 1999.

astute litigants. One irony escaped his attention. While he championed his rights as the underdog in London, Brussels and New York, the complaints of his own airline employees had become bitter.

On Branson's instructions to save money, Syd Pennington terminated the pilots' annual increment, refused to pay the pilots an 8 per cent increase in productivity and unilaterally reinterpreted the calculations for the overtime payments which reduced some pilots' wages by 22.5 per cent. In the uproar, Pennington was reported in the official minutes as rejecting the allegation that Virgin was 'trying to avoid its contractual obligations' and ordering the pilots' representatives at the risk of dismissal, 'not to send any communications' to their members. By early July 1994, the pilots were on the verge of joining BALPA, the pilots' trade union, a horror for Branson. In July, he pleaded with the pilots that membership was 'unnecessary'. His threat was unambiguous: 'I'll fold the airline if they join unions.' A handful ignored the threat.

The mood in Virgin Atlantic had changed. Some would call it a cultural revolution. Others accepted that the original pioneering atmosphere would inevitably disappear after the airline grew from a single third-hand 747 into an internationally acclaimed operation. But the absence of Branson's personal kindnesses hurt old loyalists. They noticed that he no longer sent birthday cards to each of his staff or get well greetings if someone fell ill. There were no funny telephone calls to show he cared about a birth or a wedding. The Christmas hampers supplied by Wendy Keith-Roch with Branson's hand-written greetings on a card were cancelled. Lilly Liu, his personnel director, told the managers of all his companies that the annual parties had to 'break even'. Each subsidiary was invoiced to pay for accepting Branson's hospitality. Virgin Retail refused after its employees were offered McDonald hamburgers because there was insufficient food. The paternalism and the family spirit had withered. Branson's personal warmth, some griped, had never been anything other than shrewd business. Instead, Abbott was assuming control and his dour presence was pervasive.

Styled as the genius in the backroom of the empire, Abbott had become renowned across London as the eighteen-hour-a-day man and the director of over one hundred Virgin companies. His omnipresence was the glue: he buried the secrets, perpetuated the lies, kept the cash running and struggled to keep Branson's ego in check. But the more praise Abbott received, the more he believed in his indispensability, and the more his frustration grew. 'My job is hard enough without Richard interfering,' he often moaned before lapsing into concern about losing his influence and control. His employer, Abbott complained, took the credit for his skill in pummelling down eager partners and extracting miraculous deals while he simultaneously fought off bankruptcy and saved money. The cost, Abbott acknowledged, was fraying relationships among Virgin's executives.

Branson blamed many, including the airline's managers. The launch of Virgin's service to Hong Kong was messy. The inaugural plane had arrived late, baggage had been lost, his invited guests had been forced by surly Chinese officials to queue for hours at the border into China and the famous party to seduce the journalists had been a disappointment. Branson had worked furiously to prevent bad publicity but there had to be consequences.

A whispering campaign blamed Syd Pennington as 'too disciplined' and 'no fun'. Whatever considerable benefits he introduced had been outweighed by his resistance to the Virgin culture. He had even, it was whispered, opposed Branson's order to recruit fifty massage girls for Upper Class passengers.

Days later, on 19 July 1994, Abbott was dispatched to Crawley to clear out those whom Branson deemed to be worthless and dangerous. Syd Pennington, Nick Potts and Dick Plowes were dismissed. 'The reshuffle,' said Branson about the latest casualties, 'will pave the way for further growth.' Curiously, Branson had just told a newspaper interviewer, 'I look for the best in life and it is my experience that if you look for the best you get the best. That's why I always give my staff lots of praise.'

Syd Pennington was shocked by his treatment. He had assumed that Abbott's telephone call was to discuss promotion after nearly five years' outstanding service, not his dismissal. After transforming the airline to win so many awards, he felt abused by Branson's caprice, and not least by his homily that 'my employees' interests are paramount'. Like the former employees at Virgin Music, Pennington cursed his own poor judgement for accepting Branson at face value. Seeking an explanation for Branson's lack of gratitude, he asked Branson's aunt for an explanation. 'Richard never knew if you liked him or not,' she replied.

'I didn't know that was important if I produced the right results,' said Pennington.

'He likes to know he is loved.'

Branson refused to explain his decision to Pennington. Nor would he compensate Pennington for having originally exchanged his valuable Marks & Spencer share options for worthless Virgin shares. Branson's thanks were thin. Even the termination agreement was a deal which he wanted to win. Only Pennington's threat to sue extracted fair compensation.

14

The underdog

On 25 May 1994, Branson invited forty-five staff to his home in Holland Park for a champagne breakfast to await the award of the lottery franchise. The announcement would emerge on a fax machine at 9 a.m. in an office on the first floor. Outside in the leafy road were journalists invited to await Branson's victory words and a smiling photograph. As the deadline neared, Branson edged into another room, unable to bear the tension. On time, the fax emerged. Simon Burridge, one of the organisers, Lord Young and Des Wilson crouched together to read the sparse lines announcing Camelot's victory. Seconds later, Branson burst into tears, tore up the fax and lost his temper. 'I've been robbed,' he raged, fuming that his acolytes' adoration was not shared by the regulator. Branson's guests watched the ugly tantrum with disbelief. The competition, he seemed to be suggesting, had been fixed. The result was an unprecedented public humiliation. Even his unstinting admirers expressed shock about his screams and hysterics. 'You look like a bad loser,' Des Wilson angrily rebuked Branson. The billionaire was deaf to the reprimand. Quite simply, he never lost. Only others suffered defeat. In his mind, he was no longer Goliath, certain to win, but David, the victim right-eously seeking revenge.

'It's a nasty little fax,' he rushed to tell the journalists, gasping for publicity. 'Perhaps the most crass made by any government depart-ment. It's absolutely wrong.' Like a bewildered fox he sought sym-pathy: 'I've lost the chance to do the most important thing in my lifetime. There will be nothing else in my life that could equal this.' The photographers recorded the unexpected emergence of a moody and angry Branson, a man outraged that his propaganda had not been obeyed. As his guests left his house, Branson disappeared to walk alone through the streets, unable to understand rejection.

By lunchtime, his anger had not subsided. Camelot's shareholders, he huffed, had been presented with a licence to print money. 'It's wrong,' he steamed. The decision, he was convinced, could be proven to be flawed. He, the underdog, wanted action. He would visit Peter Davis and threaten to apply to the courts for the regulator's decision to be overturned on the grounds of negligence and mal-administration.

The regulator was well prepared for Branson's visit the following day, 26 May 1994. Accompanied by John Jackson and Gerrard Tyrrell, his solicitor, Branson arrived emboldened by the newspaper headlines reporting Branson's loss rather than Camelot's victory. Fearful that Branson would seek a judicial review and delay the lottery's launch, Davis showed Jackson how his calculations confirmed the success of Camelot's bid.

Although Davis was uninspiring, he was surrounded by civil servants who understood how to construct a selection process which would withstand the sharpest scrutiny for honesty, accuracy and compliance with the law. While Branson waited in another office, Jackson listened to the description of the extraordinary process conducted by the expert evaluators. Each application had been subjected to two thousand, six hundred calculations to judge whether the proposal was financially sound, could provide a system to sustain a £36 billion business and had presented a marketing and game plan guaranteed to generate maximum interest.

Jackson was then shown how the two thousand, six hundred calculations on Branson's proposal had unearthed unfavourable comparisons to the other bidders. Camelot planned four times more retail outlets to sell the tickets than Virgin; Branson's projections of the money to be raised for the good causes ranked only as average among the eight applicants; and the amount Branson anticipated generating for the whole lottery fund was the sixth lowest. On other assessments, Branson's bid ranked bottom. In questioning Branson's managers, the regulator had concluded that the IBM terminal and computer systems proposed by Branson were unreliable. Most significantly, contrary to Branson's repeated protestations that 'our costs were lower', Branson's retention fund including administrative costs and profits was the sixth highest of the eight bidders while Camelot's was the lowest.

To Jackson's dismay, Oflot's calculations showed that Branson proposed to take out more in service charges than Camelot and contribute less to the fund of good causes. His hugely vaunted promise of a non–profit-making lottery was suspect because the 'profits' appeared to be hidden among 'administrative costs'. An independent audit would confirm that Branson's bid ranked fourth out of the eight bidders.

Predictably, Davis's process had ignored Branson's proposal to dispense his company's income from the lottery to selected charities. Not only was Branson's proposed non–profit lottery irrelevant to the contest but Oflot's research showed that, contrary to Branson's private poll, total sales of tickets would barely be influenced by the slogan. Whatever the public told pollsters, they bought tickets to become millionaires, not to help charity. That conclusion undermined Branson's entire bid.

A subsequent independent audit endorsed Davis's decision. Camelot was rightly chosen, the auditors reported, because the consortium's experienced management, proven technical system, sound marketing, game and security plans promised 'all round strength and dependability'. Branson's hype had been rigorously tested and, after an exhausting audit, robustly rejected.

At the end of Davis's explanation, John Jackson was visibly shaken. Branson's propaganda had been rejected as manifestly wrong. The grounds for challenge had disappeared. 'We're not going to court,' Jackson told Davis. 'Good,' replied Davis, relieved. The atmosphere became relaxed. Branson accepted a cup of coffee. 'It seems incredible,' Branson said to Davis in passing, 'that you have given it to an organisation where they effectively offered us a bribe.' Davis interrupted: 'We did our investigations and they came out with a clean bill of health.' The informal exchange went unrecorded by both Davis and Gerrard Tyrrell, Branson's lawyer, who was still unaware of Branson's allegation. As a signal that his anger had subsided, Branson politely complimented Davis as he departed, 'I'm sure you're an honourable man [who has] conducted a fair process.'

All that remained was for Virgin's publicity machine to repair the damage. Branson had been criticised as a 'media tart' for assuming that he would win just because the newspaper headlines inspired by himself promised victory. The man who had dressed up as Long John Silver, Spiderman, Biggles, Peter Pan, City Man, a rabbit, a clown, an air stewardess and in a bikini decided to assert his gravitas. He sought to rewrite history by summoning a sympathetic journalist.

Journalists continued to be vital to Branson's fortunes and he delighted, with Whitehorn's connivance, in elevating each interview into a special event. In February 1994, the *Independent* had published what was billed by the newspaper as the 'first interview with Richard for three years'. There had been at least seven. After the lottery débâcle, there was no pretence about exclusivity. Branson was desperate to expunge the bad image. 'I do not believe I behaved badly on receiving the news,' he explained. 'There were no angry outbursts. No ripping up of faxes. There were also no photographers. An hour later the popular press asked for some staged shots.'

He was satisfied that the public would accept his version. His narcissism excluded any self-doubt. After all, in a recent advertisement for Apple Computers, he was ranked with Albert Einstein and Mahatma Gandhi as an icon of the twentieth century. That idolatry might have obviated any remorse, yet the anger festered. Losing was always painful, but for a man reared to win at any cost, not winning the lottery, his lottery, remained inexplicable and unforgivable. The loss ached as if a tooth had been pulled. 'It's a lottery driven not by fun but by greed,' he would repeat, revealing searing resentment at Camelot's success. Gradually, his anger subsided. During summer 1994 a new ambition and foe gradually preoccupied his passion.

All publicity, Branson knew, attracted more opportunities and proposals. Like moths, those needing money and prestige to launch their own ideas appealed for his partnership. Branson relied on those approaches. Expanding the Virgin brand by jumping on to a bandwagon depended upon the dozens of ideas aspiring entrepreneurs sent to Holland Park hoping for Branson's endorsement. Most of Branson's new products had been inspired by a friend or stranger. *Student* magazine, Virgin Music and the airline were other people's ideas which he had developed. His gamble was offering the public an established, popular product supposedly better and cheaper. No product was better known than Coca-Cola.

One year earlier, in January 1993, Ric Huning, a Welsh businessman, had written to Virgin suggesting the idea of Virgin Cola. The reply from the Holland Park headquarters was dismissive. 'Unfortunately your idea is a little too far removed from those businesses to be of interest to us,' wrote Craig Dixon. Virgin, he concluded, 'was concentrating on other ideas'.

Undeterred, Huning approached Cott, the Canadian producer of cola syrups. After success in North America and Japan, aggressively selling its own cola to supermarket chains as a cheaper alternative to Coke and Pepsi, Simon Lester, Cott's managing director for Europe, was offering six cola recipes for sale to British supermarket chains. Lester's success had been gratifying. The launch of Sainsbury's 'Classic Coke', produced by Cott in a bottle similar to Coke's, had sparked a battle of writs and a spectacular own goal for Coke in the media war. Two other supermarket chains were committed to buy Cott's syrup. Lester was searching for other customers when Huning telephoned. Having registered Virgin Cola as a trade name, Huning sought Lester's collaboration to launch the drink despite the certainty of Branson's aggressive writs. 'Don't worry about Branson,' urged Huning.

Lester was intrigued. Like all good ideas, its simplicity was brilliant. Virgin Cola was a natural product and Branson was an outstanding asset to promote the brand. As Lester replaced the receiver without commitment, he gave little thought to Huning's claim to ownership of the copyright. That was not Cott's concern although the course of the dispute became interesting. When the Welshman eventually threatened Branson with a writ for taking the idea, Virgin's lawyer replied that Craig Dixon's letter was 'written by mistake'. Branson, the lawyer wrote, was already involved in a cola project. However, Huning was eventually offered a substantial settlement. By then, Simon Lester was reeling from his own turbulent experiences with Branson.

Ignoring Huning, Lester had written to Branson proposing a joint venture to produce Virgin Cola. He had never expected more than a brief acknowledgement to his letter. Every multimillionaire businessman, he knew, received countless proposals. Yet the following day, Branson in person was on the telephone. In person. There was no secretary, no power play, just the man saying, 'Liked your letter. Come round.'

The introduction was unexpectedly casual. There was the famous face yet a quiet, shy manner. Eyes permanently staring at the carpet, Branson spoke hesitantly, stuttering diffidently until Lester proffered the can. Miraculously, Lester had produced a can of cola embellished with the Virgin logo. Branson's face erupted. Images excited the man as much as the promise of greater exposure and money. Selling millions of cans every week would explosively spread Virgin's name.

His body noticeably heaved. The potential was exciting. 'Every American,' said Lester, 'drinks three hundred cans of Coke every year. In Britain it's half. Coke is undermarketed here. There's huge potential.'

Lester offered Branson some Cott cola to taste. Two weeks earlier he had sold another formula to the Safeway chain, so the choice for Branson was already limited. 'I like it,' said Branson, sipping the sample like others taste a fine claret.

The idea was glorious. Sugar, syrup and herbs mixed in water was sold in red metal cans for an amazing profit. As he calculated the potential of more wealth, few would have recognised the man who had recently blamed his failure to achieve O-level maths as his curse for not understanding figures. 'Virgin Cola. I love the sound,' he gurgled, proud that raw instinct had spotted a certain winner. Cradling the can Branson spoke about his 'fascination' and how his vision was 'excited'. The opportunism evoked the usual imagery: David challenging another Goliath. Branson's bravery would defeat Coke and Pepsi. 'I'll try it on the kids and let you know.'

The voice on the telephone two days later was enthusiastic. Trevor Abbott was offering Lester a deal. Abbott spoke the gobbledegook so beloved of those seeking acclaim as Masters of the Universe. 'We have a tremendous opportunity to build an international brand of some pre-eminence,' he told Lester. 'In twenty-five years we haven't had a situation that hasn't worked.' Abbott's presentation was seductive. Virgin Cola was projected to be an inevitable success.

Branson's ambition was raw: 'I want Virgin to be as well known around the world as Coca-Cola. I'm going to beat Coke and Pepsi.' Challenging corporate behemoths had become Branson's ensign. His assumption of success depended upon sneering at the opposition, not least as a motivation to win. That year, the mighty Coca-Cola corporation's global sales were $48 billion. Virgin Group's were $2 billion. Five hundred million cans of Coke were sold every day, just part of a vast empire supplying 40 per cent of the world's soft drinks. Yet Branson derided Coke for 'offering an expensive, poor quality product'.

Simon Lester's initial excitement soon waned. The contract proposed by Cott was a standard franchise agreement to run the business and pay a royalty to Virgin. Cott would assume the full responsibility for the ferocious battle of prices, special promotions, distribution contracts and advertising. Branson rejected that deal. 'We want to paddle our own canoe in marketing,' said Abbott, who had fashioned a horrendously complicated proposal for an equal partnership. Branson's requirements never varied: he wanted to retain control and preferred to sign agreements containing clauses which could be disputed as ambiguous. Virgin's executives enjoyed signing contracts which could, if necessary, be renegotiated. Threats about breach of contract were laughingly ignored. The entry might be painful but the exit was certainly torture.

Lester's vision was to sell Virgin Cola in small shops and cash-and-carry stores, not in those supermarkets selling own-brand cola supplied by Cott. Branson's objective was different. He had already told Charles Levison, one of his many lawyers, that he envisaged selling Virgin Cola across the world.

Branson welcomed the intervention of Gerry Pencer, Cott's dynamic, opportunistic chairman. Inviting the American to Necker, Branson spun his charm to obtain his precise requirements. 'We want to sell Virgin Cola to supermarkets. We want to sell worldwide. We want to challenge Coke.' Like others, Pencer succumbed to the temptation of a deal with an idol. 'Doing a deal' fed Pencer's own dream of a worldwide empire. Bedazzled, he failed to realise that his control of the combined business would be sacrificed, which was precisely Branson's intention. Branson, Pencer agreed, could try to open the doors.

Branson proved his genius. Five retail chains – Tesco, Co-Op, Threshers, Cullens and Iceland – agreed to stock Virgin Cola. His optimism was infectious. 'We'll sell one billion cans in the first year,' he told Pencer. That was a respectable 7 per cent of the market. Branson, Pencer swooned, was more than a facilitator, he was a hero. Together they could take on the world. America, however, would be barred to Virgin.

Celebrating the agreement was an anticlimax. Trevor Abbott insisted they sign the complicated contracts in the coffee shop at the Hilton Hotel near Terminal Four at Heathrow. On the tarmac was Pencer's personal Gulfstream jet but he was obliged to conclude a multimillion pound deal in a public canteen with Abbott, dressed in jeans and a casual shirt, exuding the faint boredom of 'another day, another deal'.

Pencer resolved to ignore the mood. Mesmerised by Branson, he even rushed to buy a camera to record the event. Pencer felt privileged by the chance of an adventure with the brilliant billionaire. Naturally, Pencer assumed that Branson's jocular banter and staccato phrases shielded the shrewdest financial mind. Even Branson's admission, 'I've never read a business book', was inspiring. When he had spoken about attacking 'the fat underbelly of a giant organisation like Coke', Pencer like others had been inspired. The courage, the individuality, the energy of the man were awesome. 'There is always room for a small aggressive company with a respected brand name to give them a run for their money,' Branson pontificated about his challenge to Coke. But the motive puzzled Pencer. 'We often do things,' Branson explained, 'and then work out afterwards what the strategy was. Personal experience is the best way of tackling business.'

After reflection, no Cott executive was quite sure he had understood. How could Virgin challenge Coke? The jest by Coke's former president, 'Our only true rival is tap water', was too true to ignore. Coke's annual advertising budget in Britain was £40 million and their distribution network was superb. Although Branson had publicly boasted that his cash mountain of variously £250 million or £300 million could fund Virgin Cola's victory, he had offered to spend only £5 million on advertising and, in the event, he committed in the first year a mere £250,000. Free publicity, which he tirelessly invented and generated, and the 'pull' of Virgin's reputation as an honest, quality, fun and stylish company would, Lester was confidently assured, compensate for the unequal expenditure. Those who questioned Branson's wisdom in extending the Virgin brand were dismissed by Whitehorn. Solemnly he lectured, 'We are being very careful, only choosing products where the brand name works and where we have done a lot of research. Cola is associated with youth and fun and it suits our corporate colours of red and white perfectly.' The publicist, whose renowned silver tongue rarely ceased moving, ignored a golden rule: 'You never learn anything in life if you always talk.' Virgin Cola, he believed, would succeed because the colour scheme matched perfectly.

Branson had undertaken no detailed research about Virgin Cola. As usual, he had relied upon instinct and the hope that many Britons, especially the young, would sympathise with his struggle against another Goliath. Personalising battles was Branson's trademark. Unlike Virgin Atlantic's subtle campaign against British Airways, slowly cherry-picking the best routes and offering something different, this challenge had burst out with a wham-bam to the Big Boy. Wildly optimistic predictions and claims of success were intrinsic to his plot. His hyperbole at the launch of Virgin Cola in summer 1994 was nevertheless excessive. 'Virgin Cola will be as valuable as Virgin Atlantic within four years,' he gushed. 'We'll sell one billion cans by the end of the first year.' The magic vow that Pepsi would be overtaken within a blistering flash and his billion-can promise were echoed endlessly by Virgin publicists. Virgin Cola would be King. The marketing plan, primitive but well-tested, featured stunts by Branson to secure free space in newspapers and television.

In the past, selling cut-price records and cheap airline tickets had won Branson acclaim as the champion of the underdog, or as the buccaneer tilting at sacred cows. Ever since he had stood waving outside the High Court after humiliating British Airways in 1993, the readers of the tabloid newspapers had acclaimed him as their hero. Exceptionally, he was a saintly toff whose outrageous antics or embarrassing disclosures endeared him to the working classes. Virgin Cola, he was certain, would appeal to his followers, especially if clothed with sex appeal.

His launch showed photographs of himself holding a can of Virgin Cola in sunny California (in reality Knightsbridge) with Pamela Anderson, the buxom star of *Baywatch*, and with Debbie Flett, a raunchy British model. The tabloid newspapers granted him instant free publicity. Once sex was exhausted, he proffered an invasion of his privacy to attract more attention to his new drink. At the end of a week in Los Angeles, appearing in a cameo part in *Baywatch*, and flying between Lisbon, Tokyo and Dublin, he invited the *Sunday Mirror* to join him for a day as he opened a Megastore in Liverpool and visited Virgin Cola's bottling plant in Pontefract. Drugs, sex and money, he knew, were ideal ingredients to capture a whole tabloid page. To sell his sugared water, he mentioned his escapades, always described as 'daredevil', his beautiful homes and his love for the houseboat. But sustained tabloid attention, he knew, required a sensational confession, something to guarantee a headline to promote Virgin Cola. The man who had disavowed using his family in publicity to promote his business, decided to confide how he had personally taken drugs and had even encouraged his parents to smoke marijuana. And there was more. His young children, he revealed, slept in his bed. 'A strain on marriage?' asked the journalist. 'Well,' laughed Branson in the provocative manner the tabloids called saucy, 'there are always ways and means – and it's a big bed.' Few other businessmen would risk such vulgarity to promote a drink, but from Branson it seemed remarkably unconceited. Even if his boastful assessment of his wealth at £1.4 billion was exaggerated, he knew that big numbers impressed his bankers and rivals, and his followers applauded his self-made fortune. A deft codicil to the publicity spin deflected one possible criticism. His two children, he added, received no cash from their parents, and he was also seriously thinking of excluding both from his will. Soon after, he quietly changed his mind.

For the best publicity he was grateful to Joan Thirkettle. His friend had managed to persuade ITN's editors to transmit a report of Virgin Cola's launch. Supposedly random members of the public were shown tasting different and unlabelled glasses of cola. 'The majority,' Thirkettle reported, 'prefer Virgin Cola.' Cott's directors swooned about an advertisement worth millions.

ITN's publicity, like all the other glowing newspaper articles, was carefully monitored by Branson. Every positive report enhanced Virgin's brand – across all its products and services. The exposure created in the cola campaign would be beneficial in the underdog's bid to overturn a recent refusal to transfer Virgin Radio from the AM to the FM waveband.

Ever since the launch in April 1993 of Virgin 1215, a national rock music station, he had cursed the 'media turkey'. His £6 million investment had promised to attract ten million listeners. Success would be delivered, he hoped, by poaching the personnel and format of a popular BBC local rock station. But by the end of 1993, Virgin Radio was attracting only three million listeners compared to sixteen million for Radio 1. Advertisers, it was suggested, were demanding repayment. Unlike with his profitable minority stakes during the eighties in three radio stations, Mercury, Piccadilly and Kiss FM, Branson was losing money and his reputation for success. His solution was to fabricate outrage. How, he screamed at the officials surrounding Lord Chalfont, the chairman of the Radio Authority, could anyone be expected to broadcast music on the inferior quality of AM?

Lord Chalfont, a former journalist and a minister in a Labour government, was surprised by Branson's outburst. He had, after all, applied for an AM licence fully aware of the frequency's limitations. But inconsistencies were easily ignored by Branson. In the weeks before the Authority awarded new licences in May 1994, Branson inundated the Authority's officials with protests, challenging Chalfont not to ignore his national popularity and implying unfortunate consequences if Virgin's request for an FM station was not granted. In what appeared as a co-ordinated campaign, he also attacked John Birt, the director-general of the BBC, for refusing to transfer Radio 4 to AM and hand over the BBC's FM slot to Virgin Radio. Talk radio listeners, he insisted, did not require good quality. But his slogan, 'Put Virgin on FM and we'll smash Radio 1', reproduced by the *Sun*, failed to win much sympathy among officials despite his claim to have six hundred thousand letters of support. As a last throw, he threatened to close Virgin Radio unless the station was transferred to FM. His petulant bluff failed.

One month later, the Radio Authority advertised three more FM licences in London. Branson announced his unprecedented intention to renew his bid. By then, he understood the obstacles. Several members of the Radio Authority disliked him intensely. For the same reasons as the new Independent Television Commission rejected his bid for a Channel 3 franchise, some members of the Radio Authority believed he was untrustworthy, louche and juvenile. A second rejection was a foregone conclusion until Lord Chalfont intervened.

Although Chalfont shared the distaste for Branson, he was impressed with his new application. In truth, Branson's staff had compiled the best pitch. To help Branson win over his critics in the Authority, Chalfont invited him as the official guest to speak at the Authority's annual dinner in a hotel near the River Thames. Branson accepted knowing that his hosts would wear dinner jackets for an inevitably stuffy evening. Despite the stakes, Branson offered no compromises.

Dressed in jeans and an open-necked sports shirt, he grabbed the first glass of champagne offered and did not stop drinking until the moment of his speech. He had prepared nothing and, after a few rambling comments, asked for questions. There were none. He sat down and continued drinking champagne until the early hours. 'He's eccentric,' Chalfont told friends, but others were insulted. 'You're the Gerald Ratner of radio,' John Grant, a trade unionist, former Labour MP and member of the Authority, told Branson, referring to the high-street jeweller who had described his merchandise as 'crap'. Branson gazed back icily. Regulators were as contemptible as regulations; both existed to be broken.

The seven members met in late 1994 under Lord Chalfont's chairmanship to award the new licences. In the first ballot, four voted for XFM, a rival bidder, and three for Virgin. Margaret Corrigan, the eighth member was ill but had, in a fax to Chalfont, voted for XFM. Branson, it appeared, had lost. But Chalfont, convinced that Virgin's bid 'is the best', used his position to achieve his wishes. Corrigan's vote, Lord Chalfont declared, was disallowed since she was not present. Chalfont cast his own vote for Branson. Then, since the vote was tied, he cast the deciding vote as chairman. Virgin Radio was awarded a lucrative FM station and a licence to print money.

The good news for Branson was contaminated by the reminder of a defeat. Five months after winning the radio licence, Camelot launched the National Lottery without a hitch. Britain was mesmerised. At prime time every Saturday evening, huge audiences watched the draw on television and newspapers were ferociously competing to identify the gleeful ticket holders transformed into millionaires. Only Branson was displeased. All the excitement of distributing millions in prizes and to the good causes could have been his. Every week his smiling face would have been reprinted in countless newspapers and magazines, and regularly he could have been seen live in a television studio – handing out the cheques to the winners and to the beneficiaries of his private charity. Instead of thousands of Britons expressing their gratitude to his generosity, a group of faceless businessmen and bureaucrats were giving away huge jackpots, earning obscene profits, paying themselves greedy wages and choosing the wrong good causes, especially culture. Nasty spivs, he cursed, were bringing the lottery into disrepute. Camelot, his publicity machine fumed, had 'deliberately underplayed the potential sales and are making huge monopoly profits'. Once again, Branson implied that freewheeling Virgin had been devastated by a villainous monopoly.

In January 1995, there was more disappointing news. Virgin Cola was selling at less than half his initial predictions. Despite his attack on Coke and Pepsi for charging inflated prices – 'a brand tax to finance expensive advertising' he called it – the public was ignoring his cheaper Virgin brand, selling at 69 pence for two litres compared to £1.09 for Coke. Infuriatingly, the Coke and Pepsi corporations were also ignoring him. He could not be the victim struggling against Goliath if he was ignored by the giant. The routine response was to ignore defeat, speak noisily about success and exaggerate for the media. On this occasion, the selected tabloid was the *Daily Mirror* which guaranteed a page entitled, 'Breakfast with the Boss'.

The venue, Simpsons in the Strand, was just one hundred yards from the High Court, a perfect stage for Branson's performance, equating his challenge to Coke with his humiliation of British Airways. 'Taking on Coke is our latest venture,' he bubbled. 'In two months we have sold sixty million cans of Virgin Cola. We would expect to overtake Pepsi within a year and be as big as Coke in three years.' Only five weeks earlier, Branson had predicted that across the whole world 'it'll take five years to catch up Pepsi and in ten years we will be biting the tail of Coca-Cola'. Irrepressibly optimistic, the attention-seeker believed he could deliver the impossible, not least because he had so often achieved the apparently unrealisable: he had sold his music business for $1 billion and he had created an international airline at Heathrow. Thanks to his friends in the media, any unfulfilled prophecies or inaccuracies were conveniently ignored.

'We're earning £1 million profits a week from Virgin Cola,' Branson had said publicly, 'and the business will be worth £500 million within a year or two.' Insiders knew, however, that the sales of Virgin Cola were poor and the business was losing money. Naturally, none in the charmed circle stepped out of line to correct the mistakes. Branson's optimism was etched in their culture: always stress the positive, emphasise the Virgin difference, deny that anything can ever go wrong. Virgin Cola's staff, eager to prove themselves, spread the gospel, even if the truth was stretched. Virgin, they chanted, never failed.

One month later, Virgin Cola's falter was confirmed. Despite Whitehorn's assertion, 'consumers consistently demonstrate, when given a free choice, that they prefer our product', Martin's, a retail chain, jettisoned Virgin Cola because of 'poor sales performance' caused by 'lack of national advertising'. Even raising the price from 69 pence to 85 pence provided no advertising revenue.

Branson's response to the negative news was brash. 'Virgin Cola,' said the chairman, 'controls 10 per cent of the British supermarket sales' which are 'topping £40 million'. In fact, Virgin Cola's share was 4 per cent. Profits in 1995, he confidently predicted, would be

£7 million to £8 million. To fulfil his forecast, he searched for a diversion. 'Where could we succeed?' he asked. 'Japan,' he announced. 'We're well known there. It'll be a winner.' His enthusiasm was reassuring. 'We'll make profits of £5 million in the first year,' he forecast. 'Virgin Cola will sell a quarter of Japan's cola. We're expecting to be the second largest cola seller in Japan after Coca-Cola within five years.' His failure to meet his predictions generated wilder pronouncements. 'My ultimate goal is to become the world's cola king.' To rebut any suggestion of defeat, he prophesied, 'we have plans to launch in one hundred and forty countries over the next two to three years. We will overtake Coca-Cola in most countries outside America.' Global victory against Coke, it seemed, was certain.

Branson's exaggerations and elasticity with the facts troubled some of Cott's managers. Nasty disagreements were fizzing. Branson, they suspected, was more interested in cola to promote the Virgin brand and to create a nuisance which Coke and Pepsi might be tempted to buy off, rather than engaging in the dreary chore of persuading shops to stock the bottles. His butterfly lack of concentration was baffling. 'Where are we going to sell next?' Branson complained during a meal in a Greek restaurant, adding that he had seen so many Coca-Cola advertisements during his recent visit to Spain. 'Why don't we try China?' Could Branson, wondered Simon Lester, really be as uninterested in detail as he appeared? He apparently wanted tomorrow's glory today without the nit-picking toil. The ambivalence struck Lester as unusual in an entrepreneur. By the end of the meal, Branson, casting his spell, dissipated the doubts. 'Working with Richard is great kudos,' Gerry Pencer said as they emerged into the west London street. Lester paid the restaurant bill. Just telling friends about 'dinner with Richard' soothed his irritation that Branson was simply too big for his boots.

Virgin Cola's first birthday party at Stringfellow's momentarily dispelled the anxiety. Parties in Branson's life stimulated his self-confidence. At the centre of attention, swigging a bottle of beer, the King horseplayed with girls, swapped laddish jokes with men and allowed his courtiers to ingratiate themselves as they pitched their latest ideas. Among the cluster was Robert Campbell, recently retained as Virgin's new advertising maestro. 'Guerrilla marketing will get Virgin Cola going,' puffed Campbell about his latest plan.

'We've got to disguise the fact that we've got no money.' Campbell's solution was 'a terrorist campaign designed to undermine the Giant's pompous advertising activity'. Some described his idea as tacky, even vulgar, but that was exactly what appealed to Branson and Whitehorn. 'My frontal attack on "The Real Thing",' gushed Campbell, 'is "Unreal". It undermines all the masturbatory conventions of the cola wars and makes Virgin a new subversive force in the cola market that Coke and Pepsi don't have the armoury to fight. We're like Charlie in Vietnam.' Campbell's petulance was hailed as 'brilliant' by James Kydd, Virgin Cola's lanky thirty-seven-year-old marketing director. In turn, Kydd was praised by Whitehorn as 'totally disorganised, totally scruffy but always comes up with the goods because he's a very, very good marketeer'. Kydd's qualification as Branson's latest Best Brain was his similar lack of respect for the one-hundred-and-seven-year-old Goliath. 'At some point,' scoffed Kydd in his phoney cool manner, 'Coca-Cola will start to grow up and start trying to run their own business instead of constantly trying to discredit ours.' If a rival had scoffed something similar about Virgin, Branson might have considered court action.

Kydd approved Campbell's 'guerrilla campaign' and a budget of £500,000. 'Unmistakable humour,' promised Kydd, was the key to success. 'There'll be no supermodels, no glamorous sets, no multi-million pound productions costs but plenty of "unreal" claims.' Kydd managed to overlook Pamela Anderson's pouting promotion of 'Virgin Energy', a new drink, handed out with Virgin condoms, promising 'to keep you up all night'. The contradiction would have been ignored if 'guerrilla marketing' had not been such a miserable flop.

Nielsen's ratings in June 1995 showed that Virgin Cola's share of the market had fallen from 4.6 per cent to 3.3 per cent. Branson's claim of 10 per cent of the market was wildly inflated. 'It's completely and utterly incomprehensible,' moaned Kydd. His wounds were aggravated by Pepsi's £3 million advertising blitz that month starring Branson's own favourite, Pamela Anderson. The model's disloyalty mocked Branson. Bereft of self-criticism, Branson fumbled to understand a simple truth: cola was cheap to produce but expensive to sell. He had misjudged Coca-Cola and Pepsi. His solution, ignoring his own gospel of competition, was to ban Coke on his planes. Such parochialism separated him from the real tycoons. 'Sort it' was the monosyllabic instruction of a man passionate to become the Goliath.

15

Another day, another deal

Branson needed a deal. He was hunting in summer 1995 for new excitement. The mood, he sensed, was moving in his direction. The City was optimistic as the economy recovered from the recession. Even Virgin Atlantic was finally earning a trading profit of about £35 million, although not enough to repay the huge debts. Branson inhabited a special league, owning an empire with annual revenues of about £2 billion, but, sadly, his daily diet of newspaper cuttings at breakfast was dull. Bad weather had compelled the postponement of a round-the-world balloon trip, curtailing the opportunity for personal publicity. To fill the void, Whitehorn offered exclusive interviews with sympathetic journalists.

Some were lured with the suggestion, 'If you'd like to interview Richard, why don't you join him on a trip to Greece?'; others were invited on a drunken 'ligger's trip' to Brussels; one flew with Branson on a helicopter trip across southern England; another interview was arranged on a Virgin Atlantic flight to New York; while the remainder were invited to 9 Holland Park. Those visitors were disarmed by an enticing performance.

Despite his wealth, Branson wanted his admirers to know that their hero remained the same relaxed, fun-loving, honest friend who, drinking tea from a mug, conveyed credibility and trust through a succession of hesitant stutters and inarticulate gasps. As he sat with his hands wedged between his crossed thighs, back curved, head down, eyes averted, his nervous grin tempered the inevitable impression of the vast, expensively furnished living room in one of the most exclusive safe havens of London. Combining an office and a home, in a room dotted with family photos, personal mementoes and awards to Virgin Atlantic, Branson cast himself as an unpretentious star whose exceptional business life seemed an open book. Whenever there was an unbridgeable silence or a question about detail which he preferred not to answer, he pulled from his larder well-honed anecdotes about 'my luck', 'life is fun', 'I've got, you know, energy' and 'I love, you know, getting things done', to please the interviewer. The syrup offended no one. No one departed without the impression of an emerging Titan. The constant announcement of new deals allowed no other interpretation.

The visitor to 9 Holland Park could not overlook the context. While all Branson's employees entering his room were dressed in jeans, emphasising their informality by mentioning 'Richard', on the four floors of the neighbouring cream stucco house at 11 Holland Park were serious professionals, pulling files from briefcases, conducting high-powered meetings with dark-suited bankers. In a room near to 'Richard' were three personal secretaries, sensitive to their soft-voiced employer's impatience about delay, his irritation if plans were changed and his expectation of unquestioning obedience. Their loyalty was indisputable. One, Emma Donna, was the partner of John Templeman, Branson's brother-in-law. Those arrangements, giving the appearance of uncomplicated familiarity and purpose, deflected the uninquiring from any suspicions of dark secrets beyond. But even the few seeking to peer beneath the layers of gushing testaments about 'enjoying life' found their inquiries barred by a magician cannily elusive about the darker features of his methods and ambitions. Inappropriate disclosure, he understood, could undermine the pristine motives of his onslaughts against his rivals, and Branson thrived on combat.

The unexpected offer of the MGM cinema chain lifted the torpor. For years, the aspiring global entertainment potentate had stalked the company as it was tossed beyond his financial reach among sixteen successive corporations. The latest offer for sale coincided with Branson's new relationship with David Bonderman, the senior partner of the Texas Pacific Group. Based in Fort Worth and San Francisco, Bonderman was an international investor hungry for the excitement offered by a relationship with Virgin. 'We're going to dynamise the cinemas,' enthused Branson. 'Just by putting Virgin's name outside will increase the business every year by 5 per cent.' Bonderman rushed to join in, contributing £45 million to the £195 million purchase price of MGM. 'We've paid top dollar,' Bonderman told Branson, who paid the same, after more than a dozen other suitors had been defeated.

'Don't worry,' replied Branson. 'With Virgin's name, it's going to be fantastic. We're going to open twenty-screen cinema complexes across the States and Japan.' Virgin Entertainment's debts as recorded in the next accounts exceeded £130 million.

Soon after the purchase, Branson walked into a cinema on Shaftesbury Avenue in central London. 'I'd like to look around,' Branson told the manager. 'Absolutely, sir,' replied the man enthusiastically. At the end of the tour, answering Branson's detailed questions, the manager looked puzzled. 'You know, Mr Branson,' he said. 'You think you're in an MGM cinema. But you're not. This is the ABC. Your cinema is further down the road.'

Later that day, Branson retold the story to cronies in Holland Park. Everyone laughed. 'But Richard,' asked one, 'didn't you look at all the cinemas before you bought them?'

'I dunno,' replied Branson.

There was an uncomfortable silence. Virgin, it seemed, had bought one hundred and twenty-two cinemas across Britain without inspecting all the sites. Branson did not realise how many of the buildings were dilapidated.

'Well, who's going to run them?'

'I dunno,' replied Branson. 'Better get it sorted.'

Chaos followed as divisions of Virgin competed to acquire responsibility for the latest acquisition. 'We'll sell 70 per cent of the cinemas,' it was suggested. 'That'll get rid of the rubbish.'

'Fine,' agreed Branson. The grasshopper mind had already darted to another deal, pausing only to impose Virgin Cola as the exclusive drink in the cinemas. Coca-Cola was ousted by the King of Competition from his premises. Snubbing a Goliath was fun. Becoming a Goliath was even better and a new opportunity was presented by admiring Conservative politicians.

Ever since his victory over British Airways, Branson's musings about a Virgin rail network across Britain had been welcomed by those Conservative politicians dazzled by the Virgin brand and Branson's glamour. Branson was not the only businessman interested in the rail business and the promise of huge subsidies, but he was the most famous. Intent on privatising the railways before the next general election, John McGregor, the departing Minister of Transport, identified Branson within the department as the ideal plutocrat to invigorate and manage the rail network.

In 1995, the opportunity arose to recruit Branson to the cause. The government announced the sale of the franchise for Eurostar, the passenger service between London and Paris through the Channel Tunnel. The prize for the successful consortium was not just the unprofitable passenger service, but the £3 billion construction contract for the sixty-eight-mile link between London and the tunnel. Among those assembling a consortium to bid for the franchise was Nick Wakefield, a banker at Warburgs.

Branson knew that the telephone call from Wakefield was partly inspired by Sir George Young, the new transport minister. 'Branson's got the essential marketing expertise,' Young told all those inquiring about the government's thinking. Eurostar was operating at just 40 per cent of its capacity and the minister had suggested that Branson possessed the 'management depth' to attract more passengers and end the huge losses.

Like many Britons, the politician had been influenced by Virgin Atlantic's perceived success. Whitehorn's publicity machine had convinced Young that Virgin's salesmanship could cure the long queues of frustrated passengers at Waterloo Station waiting for tickets by introducing the computerised marketing synonymous with airline travel, and he had encouraged the vision of Virgin's passengers eating free choc ices and watching videos as their pristine trains zoomed punctually across the Channel. Young had not pried into the details to realise sufficiently that Virgin Atlantic had in the previous year carried only 1.7 million passengers, sold a mere 22,000 holidays and, on a turnover of £600 million, was barely profitable. Just as Virgin's propaganda encouraged the minister's assumption that Virgin could rescue Eurostar, Wakefield and his team were comforted by Branson's enthusiasm.

Wakefield had attracted major players to his consortium. Bechtel, London Electric, Arup, Halcrow and National Express, the bus company, had pledged £100 million to finance the initial bid for the '747 on bogies'. For certain success, he needed an airline specialising in marketing and selling tickets. With British Airways ruled out because of 'dirty tricks' and to avoid accusations of a monopoly, Virgin was the best candidate. But Wakefield had been cautioned by a friend at Rowe Pitman, the City stockbrokers. 'Careful about doing business with Branson. Virgin Music's flotation and Branson's buy-back left a sour taste.' For similar reasons, some of his colleagues at Warburgs were cool. During their early work for Virgin's flotation, they had read the technical 'long form report' revealing Virgin's brushes with bankruptcy before 1985 and the juggling by Trevor Abbott. 'Abbott's the murky side of Virgin,' murmured one disenchanted banker. 'He's always floundering in the dark.' Recruiting Branson to market Eurostar's £2 billion business plan seemed, to some, to be foolish. One banker recalled a particularly revealing exchange with the businessman in 1985. 'What's your marketing strategy?' Branson had been asked. 'My personal press,' he replied. But in the end, Wakefield was compelled to ignore those warning of Branson's confusion between salesmanship and marketing and the protest of a minority of the consortium. The chance of Branson joining the rivals, the government's pressure and Branson's enthusiasm could not be discounted, the banker pleaded. In preliminary conversations, Wakefield stipulated that he hoped that Virgin working with National Express could double Eurostar's passengers from 3.5 million every year to 7 million.

Branson did not dampen the optimism. On the contrary, Virgin, he suggested, would perform wonders. Branson wanted the prize as much as Wakefield. Not only would membership of Warburgs' consortium confirm Virgin as a big league player but when the new company, the London and Continental Railways (LCR) group, was floated on the stock market eighteen months after winning the franchise, he would earn huge profits. In February 1995 Branson agreed to buy a 17 per cent stake for £10 million. 'I'll be offering a completely different experience to travellers with all the Virgin flair,' Branson promised when Virgin's membership of LCR was announced. He would work hard to win the franchise.

Offering bottles of Virgin Vodka, his latest wheeze, to Eurostar employees as he made his way through their office in Rathbone Place, he spoke about 'my new low-flying airline' before heading to his first board meeting. His fellow directors, tough engineers and builders, he imagined would be grateful for Virgin's magic. 'Virgin's service will be a revelation to those used to British Rail,' he told everyone. The Virgin formula was familiar: 'We will undercut the airlines on price.' Branson added a crucial reflection of his overriding interest, 'We won't need to put in a lot of our own money.' Ever since the sale of Virgin Music, he favoured increasing his fortune without risking his own money. Contrary to the image, he was not an innovator or by then a full-blooded entrepreneur. He was a piggyback rider, earning on the turn. Unspoken was his financial predicament. Besides the debt-laden airline there was nothing left to sell and he was guarding what remained of his 'cash mountain' in the offshore trusts. Branson was joining Eurostar to extract value for himself using a linguistic smokescreen he had recently heard from Americans: 'leveraging up' – increasing his debts.

The other directors listened enthusiastically to the great salesman's predictions: 'We're sure that "Virgin Eurostar" will triple passengers to ten million in eighteen months.' Branson had been encouraged by Jim Steer, his transport consultant. Steer's computer model had ridiculed Wakefield's original plan of seven million passengers and preferred the Treasury's forecast that the service would eventually attract fifteen million passengers a year. Virgin's expert assured the LCR directors that his safe prediction of ten million passengers 'has been agreed with the government and British Rail'. That was not strictly accurate.

Steer, accompanied by Mark Furlong and Ian Brookes, both Virgin marketing experts attached to Eurostar, had visited Richard Edgeley, the manager of Eurostar for seven years. The sturdy British Rail employee had recently revised his own forecast that by 2000 Eurostar might attract five million passengers. 'We'll do much better than that,' scoffed Brookes. Edgeley, suggested the Virgin experts, was a dinosaur. He had failed to secure a single corporate account, only sold tickets at Waterloo Station and had approved new carriages which restricted passengers to travel with just one suitcase. The Virgin brand would revolutionise Eurostar, said Branson. His partners agreed to expensive redesigns masterminded by Virgin's executives. In return, according to Virgin's agreement with LCR, Branson would earn huge bonuses if his prediction of ten million passengers was fulfilled. None scented Branson's principal objective: to rebrand the train 'Virgin Eurostar'. For the moment, Branson was untroubled by that misunderstanding with his partners. There were disputes within Virgin requiring urgent solutions.

Picking at a salad in the atrium overlooking his garden in Holland Park, Branson was enjoying the spat between Trevor Abbott and Stephen Murphy, the newly appointed deputy of his finance director. Murphy, an ambitious thirty-nine year old who lived in Hampstead, north London, appeared to enjoy riling Abbott. The outburst of tension between the two entertained Branson. Abbott, the lord chancellor, he had realised finally, resented working tirelessly in the shadows to enhance his employer's fame and fortune. Increasingly, Abbott disagreed about Virgin's future strategy, especially Virgin's involvement in railways. By contrast, Murphy was more attuned to Branson's latest ideas. The company's accountant was hungry for power and adored the proximity to Branson, access which he was encouraging. If the outcome led to a fissure in the cabal as his two moneymen lunged at each other, that would not be displeasing. Loyalty to himself was all that mattered.

That lunchtime, in summer 1995, disagreements had resurfaced about Virgin's future. Research had confirmed a decline of Virgin's appeal among teenagers. The new generation, unaware of Virgin's rebellious history, was insufficiently attracted to Branson's personality. Although a NOP poll reported that 92 per cent thought Branson was 'clever' and only 2 per cent resisted Virgin products due to his personality, insiders feared that eventually an old, bearded man wearing a pullover would not excite the young. During successive discussions, Brad Rosser, the bright young Australian recruited to Branson's 'central strategy department' from McKinsey's, the management consultants, and Alan Bond's organisation, had urged that Virgin be 'more relevant to the young'. Virgin, Branson understood, required new ideas to reinvent itself. Youth and irreverence were the qualities needed to enhance the brand. In a business built on trends and copying the ideas of others, Branson had asked Rosser to consider a new product, Virgin Jeans.

The idea had been offered by Rory McCarthy, a thirty-five-year-old Irish-Greek businessman who held the world hang-gliding altitude record at 36,700 feet. By 1995, the proficient skydiver and his brother had personally accumulated about £10 million and their company, McCarthy Corporation, quoted on the Alberta stock exchange, was worth about £35 million. Their first fortune had been earned from a motorcycle dispatch company and their second by prawn farming in Thailand. 'We churn assets,' Rory McCarthy explained. 'We're as good as our last deal but we have a good track record.' The McCarthys were hardworking, talented but surprisingly trusting businessmen.

Branson had plucked Rory McCarthy into the limelight in early

1995 to resolve a crisis. He had flown to Marrakesh in Morocco to try, in a mammoth balloon built by Per Lindstrand, to become the first to circumnavigate the world. Soon after his arrival, Branson had argued with Lindstrand about the additional, uncontracted payment of £1.2 million for the new balloon. Lindstrand, Branson insisted, should pay half. 'That'll ruin me,' protested Lindstrand. 'That's six years' earnings. You're ruthless.'

'A deal's a deal,' Branson replied unmoved.

'You always want something for nothing,' snapped Lindstrand. 'You love seeing people sweat.' He could never forget that Branson had once considered selling cans of air 'captured' on a balloon trip at ten times the price of Virgin Cola; nor could he forget Branson's reaction on seeing the giant cans of Virgin Cola hanging beneath the latest balloon. 'It's going to make me so much money,' he had chirped about the drink.

Money also interested Rory McCarthy, suddenly recruited as the balloon's third crewman. As the days passed in Marrakesh waiting for the weather to improve, over games of tennis McCarthy developed a good relationship with Branson. Unlike his customary grunts and laughs, Branson appeared, during their conversations, to be unburdening himself, explaining his life's philosophy. Nothing memorable was uttered but McCarthy was touched by Branson's indiscretion: 'You know sometimes I wake up and I ask myself, "Who the fuck is this girl in my bed?" They just throw themselves at me.' They got on well. Like so many others, Branson had ensnared McCarthy by his energy and star quality. Eve Branson's description of her son's courage – 'he's addicted to danger, of pitting himself against the unknown' – was so true. One evening, while McCarthy was standing at the bar, Branson asked for a private favour, which reflected the real trust which existed between the two men. After bad weather caused the launch of the balloon to be abandoned and they had returned to Britain, McCarthy resolved to pitch some business proposals to Branson. Virgin Jeans was his first idea.

Ignoring the suspicion and resentment by some in Holland Park, Branson had warmed to McCarthy as a kindred spirit and a soulmate who shared his love for fun and daredevil exploits. By Branson's standards, McCarthy's wealth was minuscule but since partying in Marrakesh, Branson had allowed McCarthy to believe that they were close friends. 'He's got this naughty innocence,' the star-struck Greek-Irishman gossiped. 'He's so talented.'

Branson knew how to dazzle McCarthy by allowing him access to his social life of film premières and dinners with endless introductions to the celebrities and powerbrokers attracted to the famous tycoon. 'I adore Richard on a personal level,' McCarthy sighed after a weekend game of tennis. 'His enthusiasm is so infectious. Just being around him you are sure to be having a good time. He's such fun even when he appears positively stupid.' Unspoken was McCarthy's conviction that any association with Virgin would be hugely profitable.

McCarthy's enthusiasm for Virgin Jeans was shared by Branson. Brad Rosser's criteria for youth appeal were 'first class products at business-class prices' which were 'innovative, challenge authority, good quality and for a growing market'. By chance, Rosser was also considering a proposal to create Virgin cosmetics, an industry whose annual £4 billion sales in Britain were growing.

Branson had been secretly approached by Liz and Mark Warom who were employed by the Body Shop, the cosmetics company owned by Anita Roddick. The Waroms suggested that Branson should support their own venture to launch Virgin cosmetics. With the Branson mystique, the Waroms anticipated a dramatic increase in their personal fortunes. To build the brand, they intended to employ twenty employees from the Body Shop to compete with their old employer. Initially, the Waroms had feared that Branson might feel loyalty towards Anita Roddick, a supporter of several Virgin ventures, but their reservations proved unfounded. The Waroms were encouraged by Branson to transfer their loyalties to Virgin. Another day, another deal.

For Branson, the association of Virgin with jeans and cosmetics was irresistible. Rosser and Abbott endorsed the idea although both had opposed Branson's enthusiasm to finance Virgin Bride offering everything for weddings. 'It'll be a lot of fun,' Branson had insisted. 'Virgin Bride. I like the name.' Abbott and Rosser had disagreed. 'He's got the hots for Ailsa,' sighed Abbott, realising that Ailsa Petchey, the former Virgin Atlantic hostess, had struck when Branson was itchy to announce another deal, especially one promising the certainty of meeting pretty girls. But not even Abbott had anticipated that Branson would dress up as a bride for the launch party. Virgin's management, he moaned, was truly haphazard.

'We must look more serious,' Abbott suggested. 'Why don't you explain how careful research inspires your decisions?'

'Right,' replied Branson.

At a suitable opportunity, Branson articulated a strategy. 'We have targeted about ten industries,' he explained, 'which we think are fairly large and fairly complacent, and maybe overcharge quite a lot, and where we think we can do it differently.' But Branson knew the truth: with pride, he avoided business-school jargon. He admitted his reliance upon instinct. 'If I think it is being done badly by other people, if I feel we could do it better, if we could have fun doing it, then we go ahead.' Indifferent about his ignorance, he credited 'personal experience' as 'the best way of tackling business'. The frenzy of activity tolerated no contradictions. The perpetual noise of announcing deals drowned any cautionary warnings.

The summer of 1995 was the hottest for decades. Sales of soft drinks in Britain soared. Of the 2.2 billion litres of cola consumed, Coca-Cola sold over one billion litres; Virgin sold merely forty-six million litres. Virgin's share of the market according to Nielsen was 3.1 per cent, although other statistics suggested that Virgin Cola held barely 1 per cent. One year earlier, Branson had claimed that Virgin Cola held 10 per cent of the market and was earning £1 million per week, and he had forecast £35 million profits in 1995. Instead Virgin Cola lost £1.5 million. His predictions of controlling 20 per cent of Britain's cola sales by 2000 were proving wildly inaccurate. Potentially, the embarrassment was considerable. But in Branson's world embarrassments were simply deflected or ignored. 'We've got 6 per cent of the market,' said Branson, repeating without query the information provided by Nick Kirkbride, his manager, 'and that's good enough.' Virgin employees were similarly encouraged to disparage negative news. 'Nielsen's figures,' scoffed Whitehorn, 'are nonsense. These figures do not make sense to us . . . Our sales rose by 40 per cent over the summer.' Whitehorn's boast one year earlier that Virgin Cola would sell one billion cans during the first year was now denied. 'We said those were eventual sales,' he explained. 'It's all about bending the rules or breaking the rules,' the publicists encouraged each other. 'We're not breaking the law.' Their cavalier attitude towards the truth was adopted by a Virgin employee to complete a hand-written application for an advertising award. Virgin Cola, he wrote, controlled 8.7 per cent of the market and its success had 'far exceeded expectations. Incredible. Phenomenal. Mind-blowing . . . We have been approached by every region of the world asking for distribution rights.' Turning illusions into reality was proving more troublesome than Branson had imagined.

The self-proclaimed 'master of the brand' had miscalculated the strength of Coke. He was not a revolutionary or an original iconoclast overturning entrenched ideologies. Rather, he was a carpetbagger following trends. Pranks and price-cutting, he had deluded himself, could undermine one of the world's most powerful brands. 'Your problem is, Richard,' Gerry Pencer, the chairman of Cott, wearily told his partner, 'that you don't understand brands or marketing. You took on Coke and offered nothing new. No added value.' Branson's eyes tightened. His expression was hard. He disliked critics. His admitted no mistakes. Unknowingly, he had reached a crossroads. In his mid-forties, transfixed by the cult of brand and image, he had become blind to genuinely new developments.

While the trader was looking for other opportunities to offer the Virgin Dream with sex, stunts and cut-price quality, he could not understand the revolution in California's Silicon Valley. No prospective partner arrived to explain the Internet and invite Branson's participation. Without an eager suitor, he would remain unenlightened until he tried the Internet himself in 1999. His genuflection towards the technology was to endorse Robert Devereux's small investment in Virgin Net, a collaboration with NTL, which would be tortured by repeated management departures. For himself, Branson preferred to rely on old-fashioned ventures – cola, jeans, cosmetics and cinemas – and the most well-trodden, finance.

Virgin Direct, launched in early 1995 to provide financial services – mortgages, pensions, PEPs and share tracker funds – at lower fees than charged by the City, was Branson's idea of revolution. 'I have identified,' he explained, 'a sector that was arrogant, complacent and fleecing the customer. I saw an opportunity to shake it up. So I set up Virgin Direct to offer people straightforward financial products that are easy to understand.' The financial services industry, over-charging customers and failing to invest astutely, he continued, 'specialises in bullshit . . . Its record includes pensions mis-selling, endowments that don't come up to scratch and massive investment underperformance.' His partner was Norwich Union which had just been condemned and fined by the government's regulator for mis-selling pensions. Less than one year later, their joint company was dissolved amid disagreements and he linked up with AMP, an Australian fund manager. Virgin invested £14.5 million for a 50 per cent stake while AMP invested £450 million. Once again, the promises were gargantuan. 'We're enormously successful in Britain and we're going to roll that out into Europe . . . More British companies could do this if they got off their backsides.' His manager was Rowan Gormley, a South African. Compared to that of the super league players in the City, Gormley's track record was undistinguished, but Gormley suited Branson's principal criterion: he would accept a much lower salary than demanded by the stars. Saving money always appealed to Branson.

In the first months, responding to expensive advertisements promoting Branson's 'humanity' and 'trustworthiness' to remedy the 'superdogs'' failure, tens of millions of pounds were deposited in response to Branson's promise of 'no-nonsense value for money' in Virgin Peps. 'We will make a minimal management charge,' he assured everyone. 'We will cut the present level of charges by 40 per cent. It will be the cheapest PEP ever offered in Britain.' In truth, some of those investing £50 every month discovered there was a £2 charge. The 4 per cent commission was attacked in the *Mail on Sunday* for having made Virgin's PEP the third most expensive in Britain. Charging high fees was Branson's best means to fulfil his prediction of earning profits by 2000 but this was obscured by the salesmanship.

Branson, who revealed that his personal fortune was £1.6 billion, had reached a new plateau. Rushing between meetings and continents, he appeared to be building a solid and vast empire. His numinous qualities gave the impression of an exceptional buccaneer who was invulnerable to criticism and able to effortlessly neutralise his few critics. Among those reconverted to his cause was Gerry Pencer.

'We've got a great new idea,' breezed Pencer at a brain-storming meeting in Holland Park in early 1996. 'We'll take Coke on at their own game.' Pencer was bubbling that he could out-stunt Branson. 'We'll sell Virgin Cola in a curvy bottle just like Coke.' Branson caught the idea. Coke's bottle had been shaped on Marilyn Monroe. Virgin's, gushed Branson, would 'carry the signature of a woman famous for her curves – Pamela Anderson'. No one dared to mention that Anderson, with her phoney bosom and stormy relationship with a violent, tattooed drug addict, might not be an ideal figurehead. 'I'll talk to Stuart,' said Branson, silencing any dissent by the certainty of priceless publicity from Stuart Higgins, the amenable editor of the *Sun*.

'It's a profitable relationship for both of us,' Higgins would say about his friendship with Branson. The *Sun* readers liked 'Richard's' raunchy antics and Branson profited from the prominent displays across the editorial pages. 'Baywatch fans can run their fingers over Pamela Anderson's sexy curves thanks to a new Virgin Cola bottle based on her stunning figure,' screamed the tabloid's headlines in a succession of launches and relaunches of the Pammy bottle during early 1996. For all their noisy enthusiasm, the Pammy bottle failed to revive Virgin Cola's sales. Branson's only consolation was that Pepsi's £200 million global relaunch starring Cindy Crawford and Claudia Schieffer had also flopped. But the lessons he drew ignored the irony. 'If Pepsi think that supermodels are going to get their sales back,' the Virgin supremo scoffed, 'good luck to them.' He enjoyed the public combat and if the Americans were impregnable, he was content to re-engage with a tastefully vulnerable British target.

16

Another day, another target

One year after the lottery began, and six years before Camelot's licence was due to expire, Branson was stirring. The influence of his bid, he told everyone, was manifest. Camelot had been forced to reduce its profits from 13 per cent to 10.1 per cent. Millions of extra pounds, he was convinced, were going to charities thanks to him. The glaring fault, he complained, was Camelot's weekly profits of £1.5 million, totalling £78 million in the first year; and the £443,367 salary which Tim Holley, the chief executive, received in the first ten months. Branson charged Camelot with greed.

Camelot's defence, that the lottery had been more successful than predicted by any of the bidders, won little sympathy. Few wanted to praise the lottery's launch without a single technical glitch. Branson joined the chorus of derision. Peter Davis was another target. The regulator, asserted Branson, was to blame for 'swallowing the Camelot hyperbole which laid emphasis on the risks and skills of running the lottery rather than the morality of the process'. The white knight was itching to ride to the rescue. The telephone call to Will Whitehorn in July 1995 from Mark Killick, a respected producer working for *Panorama*, the BBC television current affairs programme, offered an unusual opportunity.

Killick's message differed from other approaches. The producer explained how a *Panorama* researcher in America had uncovered a pattern of bribery perpetuated by GTech to secure lottery contracts. 'There have been three indictments,' said Killick, 'and there's more to come.' Killick wanted to know whether Branson would appear in a *Panorama* documentary. Whitehorn, an acquaintance of Killick's, remained uncommitted.

'I know it sounds crazy,' continued Killick, 'but I've even heard a rumour that Camelot offered Richard a bribe.'

'I can't really comment on that,' replied Whitehorn after a pause.

'That speaks volumes,' thought Killick who persuaded Whitehorn to arrange a brief meeting with Branson.

'There's nothing in it for us,' said Branson, dismissing the idea of an interview. 'I don't want to be the bad loser.'

'GTech is corrupt,' persisted Killick. 'There's a pattern of bribes. They shouldn't be involved in the lottery. I need you in the film.'

'No one will believe me,' insisted Branson. 'I've left it two years.'

The businessman's reluctance appeared consistent with his soured idealism. The fate of the lottery, he complained, was 'the greatest disappointment of his career'. The offer of a bribe, Branson volunteered, would possibly be revealed in his forthcoming autobiography. He added, 'we've never been asked before'. That was incorrect. The previous year, Branson had told Tim Jackson, a biographer, about Snowden's offer. Jackson's publishers, fearing a writ for libel, had decided to delete the allegation from the book. That disappointment encouraged Branson to promise Killick, at the end of their five-minute meeting, he would reconsider his decision once *Panorama* had completed filming in America.

Two months later, on 22 September 1995, Killick returned. As he sat around a large wooden table with Branson and Whitehorn, Killick 'set out his stall' to entice Branson and secure the scoop. *Panorama*'s story would recount, said Killick, how GTech 'sprayed money around' to state legislators and officials in California, New Jersey, Kentucky and Texas to win the lottery contracts. 'A pattern of bribes has been established in America,' continued the producer. 'It's obvious that Snowden would attempt the same in London.' Branson's eyes sparkled. Killick was serious, possessed the evidence and, most importantly, could guarantee a slot on prestigious prime time television. Just as the approach by Martyn Gregory, the television producer, three years earlier about British Airways had inflamed his battle with his competitor, Branson may well have seen his appearance on *Panorama* as a route to engineer a new bid for the lottery before Camelot's licence expired. 'We'd love to bid for it sooner,' he would admit. History would record that he had not lost a fair competition but had been cheated out of a prize he deserved. His appearance, he knew, was a public declaration of war at an opportune moment.

John Major's Conservative government was beset by repeated

evidence of sleaze among its ministers and backbenchers. Branson's allegation against Snowden matched the pattern.

Dressed in a shabby blue pullover, Branson settled back in an armchair in his drawing room and faced the BBC's video camera. Viewers would have seen Branson's shock about being offered a bribe, anxious to purge the lottery of corruption and devoted to cleansing British public life. No one would suggest ulterior motives. Unlike in the idealistic sixties, the vogue of the nineties was to admire millionaires. The public would be persuaded that his appearance was a charitable service. Only cynics would grunt that his risk was inconsequential because his wealth immunised him from the consequences of a writ. Among those cynics only a handful would notice how his faulty memory would eventually lead him to deny on oath his involvement in litigation on more than 'two occasions', an inaccuracy considering that his lawyers' threats of litigation had become a weapon in his or his companies' commercial armoury and had led to at least seven writs.★

Branson's frequent appearance in front of a camera and lights consistently won the public's trust. Smiling at *Panorama*'s interviewer and glancing at Whitehorn nearby, the businessman suffered no passing doubt that publicising a two-year-old allegation might be 'unfair', precisely his own emotional complaint after Liz Heinko, an American employee, embarrassingly publicised her claim of sexual harassment against himself. Guy Snowden, for Branson, was, like Lord King and Randolph Fields, a legitimate target of his unremitting sense of righteousness. Only the malicious could accuse him of seeking a trophy to promote his interests. Branson had long forgotten his exhortation about dirty tricks. 'There are certain things that are fair in business,' he had complained about Lord King, 'but to let it degenerate into a personal attack is wrong.'

Telling his story to a camera was second nature to Branson. In his relaxed manner, he juggled his words as he described how Snowden took the initiative for the lunchtime meeting in order to offer a bribe.

'Normally,' he soothed as he began his story in an Olympian tone, 'if I lose I will bow out and fight other battles elsewhere.' That

---

★ John Lennon, David Robinson, Heimi Lehrer, Randolph Fields, London Rubber and British Airways; and he would soon issue a writ against the Independent Television Commission.

sophism was a foretaste of Branson's potential difficulty that he had issued the invitation to Snowden. If Snowden had been intending to offer a bribe, it would be argued, the American was more likely to have taken the initiative. While Branson had no doubt that a bribe was offered, Snowden's lawyers would fruitlessly assert at the eventual trial that Branson had invented his version in order to [lend] credibility to the bribery allegation.

'They weren't particularly the kind of people we wanted to deal with,' Branson spoke emphatically towards the camera. Snowden, he stuttered and smiled, had 'heard we were planning to make a bid and that we were going to put all the profits to charity in good causes. [He] asked to see us for lunch.' Either Branson, as the defence would claim at the subsequent trial, was suffering from a faulty memory or there was a more sinister explanation.

Mark Killick, the *Panorama* producer, preferred not to rely on Branson's memory. He asked the businessman to produce his 1993 notebook with the contemporaneous hand-written record of his conversations with Snowden. Branson consulted his notebook. On two pages were his actual notes from the conversation on the telephone and at lunch. On another page, were the actual words of the bribe offer which he had copied, forty-five minutes later he would say, from the scrap of paper. His writing on the piece of paper − 'the loo note' − had never been shown to anyone and, Branson explained, the paper had been destroyed.

For the *Panorama* interview, Branson had recopied his notebook entry on to a new sheet of paper. The sheet was clipped into his current notebook.

To establish the context, Branson explained how Snowden had lamented Camelot's losses if Virgin did not withdraw: 'Look, you know the government have made it very easy and open for us. They are going to let a private company make a fortune out of this. But if you go and bid on a charitable basis and offer to put all your money to charity, we are going to have to drop what we offer considerably, which is going to cost us hundreds of millions of pounds.'

That soundbite fitted neatly into Branson's claim that Virgin's bid had forced Camelot to divert extra 'hundreds of millions' of pounds towards the charities. Despite Davis's praise for Virgin's proposals, Branson could not prove that assertion.

The climax of the interview was his dramatic rendition of

Snowden's offer of a bribe. To maximise the drama, Branson repeated his version three times. Each was different. The first attempt rambled. On the second Branson said, 'I can't remember the exact words but the gist of it was . . .' Fifteen minutes later, he corrected himself: 'I've got the record of the exact words.' 'Gist' had become 'exact words'.

Picking up the notebook in the middle of the third attempt, Branson delivered the killer quotation from Snowden's mouth: '"I don't know how to phrase this Richard. There is always a bottom line. I'll get to the point. In what way can we help you Richard?" Then I obviously asked him what he meant and he said, "I am sure everybody needs something in life." I basically told him that I was quite successful and only needed one breakfast, one lunch and one dinner a day . . . I was so flabbergasted that I actually went to the loo and scribbled what he said on a piece of paper. I just couldn't believe that I had heard it. No one's tried to bribe me before in my life.' In one version, Branson said that Snowden had said, 'there must be something personally that you want Richard'. It would transpire that Branson had not written the critical word 'personally' in his notebook, although on the third attempt he implied that he was repeating the 'exact' words in his notebook rather than relying on his memory. Snowden would unsuccessfully accuse Branson in court of inventing the word 'personally', fabricating his notes and lying – which Branson vigorously and successfully denied.

Branson's presentation of each version of the conversation struck none of the coterie in Holland Park as noteworthy. No one ever queried his uncertainty about the value of Snowden's bribe. To *Panorama*, Branson spoke of 'many tens of millions of pounds'. Later, he would escalate the bribe: 'I knew that the offer was worth maybe £100 million, £150 million at the minimum.' Snowden, he admitted, never specifically offered any money. Moreover, although he was certainly wealthy, the American did not possess tens of millions of pounds in cash. Nor had Snowden discussed bribes with other members of his consortium.

Initially, Branson realised that weakness. After thirty years in business, Branson was not a sensitive soul. Snowden's question, 'In what way can we help you Richard?' was, as Branson admitted, not indisputably an offer of a bribe. Snowden's words could be interpreted, Branson knew, as 'a business offer' and he agreed, 'There's 'nothing illegal in it.' Branson also acknowledged that Snowden had not asked in precise words for something in return if the undefined bribe was accepted. But that incongruity did not detract from Branson's veracity. Repeatedly, he emphasised that Snowden had risked offering a bribe in front of John Jackson, a hostile eyewitness sitting at the same table.

While the video camera continued to turn, Branson began to contemplate the consequences of his attack. Dropping his gaze to the floor, he appeared to have second thoughts. 'I'm beginning to feel,' he said intemperately, 'why did I bring this up in the first place?' Three minutes later, he again voiced his doubts: 'Fuck. Why the fuck did I say it in the first place?'

Reassured by Whitehorn and Killick, he returned to the fray. With evident forethought, he included Sir Tim Bell, the publicist employed by Guy Snowden, in the conspiracy. 'Later that day [of the lunch], I had a telephone call from one of his PR agents wishing us well . . . trying, I suspect, to offer us, you know, quite a considerable sum of money to move away from bidding.'

In Branson's considered scenario, Tim Bell had telephoned, less than two hours after Snowden departed, with an incriminating message: 'Guy said something he might regret. Are you going public?' The juxtaposition of Bell's call 'later that day' and his unambiguous message reinforced Branson's story of a rejected bribe. The damning confirmation was repeated from a hand-written note in Branson's book recording Bell's telephone call.

But Branson's version of a panic telephone call from Snowden's emissary was inaccurate. Bell's telephone call was not two hours after Snowden's departure but four days later. Nonetheless, Will Whitehorn provided corroboration for his inaccurate version, telling Killick that Bell had telephoned 'ninety minutes' after Snowden left. Both were mistaken or, as Snowden's lawyer would contend, both had embellished their story. Snowden would argue in court that Whitehorn, like John Jackson, would never contradict his employer.

'It's an interview to die for,' chortled Mark Killick, the *Panorama* producer, as he returned to his office to edit the film. Fortunately, John Jackson, the eyewitness at the lunch, confirmed Branson's memory with one exception. The initiative for the lunch, recalled Jackson, had come from Branson. The detail was potentially serious because on 31 October 1995, during a telephone conversation,

Killick noted Branson's denial of ever speaking to Snowden on the telephone. Puzzled, Killick telephoned Branson, by then in Necker. Branson was disarmingly apologetic: 'I can't remember, Mark. I may be wrong.' The BBC decided that the 'shift' was genuine and not serious. Branson's memory of those conversations was simply faulty.

Killick also telephoned Tim Bell. Branson and Whitehorn had both insisted that Bell knew about Snowden's bribe. 'There's an allegation against Snowden,' said Killick, 'and you know all about it.' Bell professed ignorance. His denial was discounted.

Killick's checks with Snowden produced evasions suggesting bad faith. Snowden's spokesman neither recalled nor denied Branson's account of the conversation but insisted there was no impropriety.

Beyond Branson's gaze, Snowden and his camp were desperate. Fourteen lawyers and advisers had gathered in Snowden's offices for what was called 'a damage limitation exercise'. Snowden had accepted Tim Bell's advice: 'You're a short, fat American who wears dark glasses, so don't be interviewed.' Their decision not to comment to *Panorama* would not be revised. At the last moment, Snowden's spokesman agreed to be interviewed. Then he withdrew. The unreliable conduct contrasted unflatteringly with Branson's veracity.

Panorama's principal target was Peter Davis, the lottery regulator. Faisal Ali, *Panorama*'s researcher, had discovered that in October 1994 Davis had accepted hospitality in America from Snowden and a free flight on GTech's jet. Although the gratuities were accepted after the lottery contract had been awarded, the regulator's independence was compromised. Ali gave the information to a Parliamentary select committee which was due to question the regulator on the same day the *Panorama* programme would be transmitted.

That morning, Monday, 11 December 1995, Branson was visiting Japan while Snowden, in his Mayfair office, nervously awaited the explosion. In Westminster, Davis was facing MPs in a session closed to the public. Unexpectedly, the regulator disclosed to the politicians that *Panorama*'s criticism of GTech that evening had been shared by himself when awarding the contract to Camelot. His 'serious concerns', he admitted, would have prevented GTech receiving the licence if the consortium had not included trustworthy British giants. Davis's admission remained unknown amid the anticipatory excitement of Branson's appearance that night.

Branson was in Tokyo awaiting the reaction. Since the interview, another good reason for provoking Camelot had arisen. Sir George Russell, the chairman of the Independent Television Commission, had rejected Virgin's consortium to operate the Channel 5 franchise. Despite its winning bid of £22,002,000, the ITC declared that Virgin's proposal failed to pass the quality threshold. Branson had been outraged by another failed attempt to own a television station. The ITC, he complained, had acted unfairly, unlawfully and 'irrationally' in selecting a rival. Pertinently, six months earlier, George Russell had been appointed the chairman of Camelot. Although the Divisional Court eventually rejected Virgin's claim for a judicial review as 'impermissible and hopeless', Branson enjoyed the unexpected opportunity to embarrass his nemesis.

The transmission of *Panorama* on 11 December was a disaster for Snowden and a triumph for Branson. 'Go on sue,' challenged Branson in the headlines dominating the following morning's newspapers. 'My lawyers are waiting.' In Tokyo, Branson was enthusiastically responding to inquirers, wondering whether Snowden would walk into his snare. In the middle of the night, he heard the news. The ill-advised American had blurted, 'Mr Branson's allegations are grossly defamatory and untrue.' Just as in the British Airways case, Branson fastened deep into his victim: 'GTech have accused me of being a liar and of having spread an evil smear. Given the nature of the accusations they have levelled against me and their attack on my integrity, I have no other option than to issue a writ.' Restoring his 'good name' was the headline but Branson did not disguise his ambition. Since the lottery and Camelot were destabilised and Peter Davis was under investigation, a prospective Labour government, he urged, should revoke Camelot's licence after the next election. His charity, he offered, was prepared to bear the burden of managing the lottery. For a brief moment, his dream appeared possible.

On 15 December 1995, Branson wrote to Davis reminding him that he had mentioned the bribe attempt when they met on 26 May 1994, the day after Camelot's victory. Branson added that Gerrard Tyrrell, his solicitor, had a 'clear recollection' of the exchange. That appeared not to be accurate. Gerrard Tyrrell could not 'remember the exact words used' and, contrary to Branson's memory, the solicitor and his client had not discussed the exchange which, in any event, Davis denied. The outcome of the libel trial, Branson v. Snowden, did not seem a foregone conclusion. Much depended upon Branson retaining his indisputable credibility over the intervening two years. That depended on the reluctance of the media to publicise unattractive disputes.

17

The cost of terrorism

Dudley Broster, the senior pilot and operations manager of Virgin Atlantic, Branson decided, had become an irritant.

The two men were drinking champagne in the bar of the Double Tree hotel, in Marina del Rey near Los Angeles, in January 1996. Oblivious to the beautiful sunset, Broster was complaining about Virgin's refusal to pay a promised bonus. Virgin, explained Broster, had failed to honour the payments promised under the Profit Share Scheme. 'Abbott came down and told us "it's been a tough year and there's no money",' continued Broster, 'but your profits are good.' Branson stared ahead and said nothing. Throughout 1995 he had been angered that the pilots had voted against his proposed schemes and pay freezes. They had ignored his entreaties that 1994 was 'one of our most difficult years to date' and were unsympathetic that he had been compelled to 'plough many tens of millions of pounds into the airline'. To Broster it seemed odd that while Branson warned his employees how he hoped to 'break even' in 1995, he boasted to the media that the airline was 'throwing off cash'.

Frustrated by the lack of response, Broster launched into a tirade about Virgin's pension scheme. Four years earlier, the management of the fund had been transferred from Sun Alliance to Scottish Equitable, but the improvement was minimal. On Branson's orders, Francis Farrow, his tough lawyer, refused to consider any compensation. 'We've told you that the fund's badly managed and you've done little about it,' said Broster in that uniquely British 'I'm-not-putting-up-with-this-nonsense' cadence. 'It's a rip off,' he continued. That struck home.

'I'll look into it,' Branson began.

'There are pilots who after four years' contributions have less in their pension funds than they paid in. It's a scandal.' Branson nodded. 'I'll look into it,' he repeated, but he appeared uninterested. Across the room, he saw two Virgin hostesses staring at him. His voice trailed off. 'Got to go,' he laughed and veered off towards the women.

Later that week, at Virgin's headquarters in Crawley, Broster recounted his frustrations to a fellow pilot. 'He's all focused on women,' said Broster. 'He's always chasing off after women or puts himself in the middle of the girls at the flight centre.'

'I just flew Richard back from LA,' replied the second pilot. 'He is a bit weird, isn't he? He told me he was going to be one of the biggest train operators in Europe. So I asked him, "Are your trains diesel or electric?" Branson replied, "What? I don't know."' Both pilots shook their heads. 'Bit weird,' they agreed.

On 29 February 1996, John McGregor announced that London and Continental Railways had won the franchise to run Eurostar and build the rail link from London to the Channel tunnel. Branson congratulated himself on the victory. Virgin's membership of the consortium, he was certain, had been the trump card. He would quickly seek to rename the service 'Virgin Eurostar'. Sleek red trains thundering across Europe at 180 m.p.h., emblazoned with the Virgin logo in huge white letters, would spread the brand. The only obstacle, he feared, might be objections by other members of the consortium. To fulfil his plan, he personally called on the chairmen of the Belgian and French railways, the other major shareholders.

David Azema, the high-flying, intelligent and personable representative of French railways, was appalled by Branson's suggestion. 'Eurostar goes to Geneva, Lyons and Bordeaux,' explained Azema. 'No one has heard of Virgin south of Folkestone.' That was precisely the point, thought Branson.

The French veto was ignored. He would brazenly announce the creation of 'Virgin Eurostar'. The normal arrangements were made for a Virgin launch – 'lots of media, free drinks and food and Richard being Richard' – at Ashford International, the Kent station between London and the tunnel. To bounce his unsuspecting partners into his plot, Branson telephoned Adam Mills, the company's newly appointed chief executive. 'Glad to have you on board,' Branson enthused.

Eurostar was, Branson knew, in some turmoil. Mills had replaced the original chief executive who had been cursed as 'a man who just sits there with a vacant smile'. The destabilisation so soon after winning the franchise was, in Branson's opinion, a gift to be exploited.

'I've heard a lot about you. Love you to come to the launch of a new project at Ashford.'

'What new project?' asked Mills innocently.

'Oh, my people have done some work. I'll tell you in due course.'

Mystified, Mills contacted insiders. By the end of the day he had discovered Branson's plan to rebrand the trains as a Virgin product. 'What?' shouted Nick Wakefield, the Warburgs banker, when told. 'He bloody well won't.' For the first time, Branson suffered the consequences of Virgin Music's stock exchange débâcle.

To finance the construction of the rail link from London to Folkestone, LCR intended to seek £5.4 billion on a stock market flotation within two years, by far the biggest appeal for private capital in Europe for a private engineering project. The City, Mills was told, would not trust a multibillion pound flotation with a Virgin name tag. 'Tell him, no way,' Mills was ordered. 'No way.'

On hearing the decision, Branson refused to contemplate that the City was wreaking its revenge for his own display of mistrust. He only observed a truculent executive delivering bad news. Mills was tainted as an enemy. 'If he's going to behave like that, then fuck him,' said Branson in a phrase familiar to his staff as a declaration of war.

'Unless Mills is fired,' Branson told Sir Derek Hornby, the chairman, 'I'm out of this.' The response was silence. Leaks about his anger appeared in newspapers. 'Jesus Christ, he won't even talk to Mills,' sighed an incredulous American engineer after reading reports in *The Times* and *The Daily Telegraph* describing dissension among LCR's directors. Less than two weeks after winning the bid, they had been introduced to Branson's style of business.

Renegotiation was Branson's strategy as he manoeuvred for an advantage. 'I'm leaving unless you agree to Virgin Eurostar,' Branson threatened the company's directors who were assembled at Warburgs for a council of war. More than twelve hired hands, clothed in immaculately tailored suits, were seated according to the ritual of a City bank's boardroom. The exception was Branson, lounging in an oddly patterned pullover, a gift from Aunt Joyce. These were moments the maverick star savoured. His informality was a deliberate display of self-segregation, to remind his partners that their elusive partner enjoyed the independence afforded to those blessed by exceptional personal gifts and the freedom to shun conformism.

Branson had arrived to 'get it sorted', which meant extracting the best deal for himself. 'Course, the service will be called "Virgin Eurostar",' he smiled, placing a lampshade adorned with 'Virgin Eurostar' on the table. 'We'll sell much better with the Virgin brand,' he continued, hoping to convert his audience. He had anticipated curiosity but not the probing, aggressive questions that uncovered a reluctant admission. Eventually, he agreed, Eurostar would be charged a licence fee for using the Virgin brand. 'He must be joking,' muttered one banker. The mood grew hostile. Branson's smile disintegrated. His ill-concealed disappointment turned to anger as the French director spoke. 'If there is a crisis in one Virgin brand,' Branson was told, 'there will be a knock on effect on to the trains. We cannot take the risk.' Branson departed, irritated to read in the board's minutes that the directors had expressed their confidence in Mills. 'I'm thinking of pulling out,' Branson reiterated to Hornby. The flash of shock across Hornby's face was pure pleasure. Dangling threats in front of the suits was thrilling. He loved the brinkmanship. On the telephone later that day, he slapped his thighs with excitement as he repeated his threat.

Two weeks remained before the deadline, Thursday, 4 April 1996, for all the partners to transfer their cash into LCR's £100 million development fund. The executives, he was certain, feared the government's outrage if their marketing genius resigned. As the days passed, Branson remained nonchalantly stubborn. In his world, threatening, renegotiating and introducing new issues at the last moment, if he possessed the power, was an acceptable tactic. His last fax, on Wednesday night, 3 April, reaffirmed that his £10 million would only be deposited in LCR's bank account if Eurostar was renamed. Branson suspected that Hornby and Mills were searching for an alternative to Virgin but was confident they would be unsuccessful. The following day, he flew to Lake Como in Italy for the Easter holiday. With the banks closed on Good Friday, the deadline could not be changed.

Sir Derek Hornby took Branson's telephone call on Thursday morning. Although no replacement had been found, Hornby refused to contemplate his eventual retirement with Branson's mocking success as his epitaph. 'As far as I'm concerned, you can stay out,' Hornby rebutted Branson with an accomplished bluff. 'We're not having Virgin Eurostar.' The silence from Italy was encouraging. 'He'll buckle,' chuckled a supportive banker.

One thousand miles away, Branson loathed his predicament. As much as he hated being browbeaten by an Establishment figure, he feared jeopardising his relationship with the government and the City. His plan to elevate his business from peripheral ventures into the big league, especially the future privatisation of the railways, would be damaged by any suggestion of refusing to play with the team. He was thwarted. Without any announcement, just before the banks closed, £10 million was transferred by Virgin into LCR's account.

'No hard feelings,' said Branson in an unexpected telephone call to Mills soon after. 'Come to my party at the Mill End. Just turn up. There'll be plenty of air hostesses for you.' Mills was both puzzled and pleased by the gesture but the reconciliation crumbled days later. Branson could not tolerate a subordinate role. He wanted Mills shunted to the side. His publicity machine unrelentingly promoted the theme which was echoed in newspapers: 'The Eurostar consortium headed by Richard Branson which has taken over the running of the trip to Paris . . .' That self-glorification intensified Mills's pessimism. 'It's chaotic,' he had confided to his advisers. 'It's all much worse than I imagined.' The inheritance from British Rail had proven to be a poisoned chalice. The state-owned corporation's accounts were inaccurate. The reports from Ian Brookes and Mark Furlong, Virgin's marketing experts, were doomladen.

Despite their lack of any railway experience, neither Virgin executive had believed the despondent forecasts of Richard Edgeley, Eurostar's manager over the previous seven years. In March 1996, to 'validate our numbers', they had been allowed for the first time to examine British Rail's raw data. Both emerged 'astonished and horrified'. The prediction that Eurostar would carry ten million passengers within eighteen months suddenly seemed wildly optimistic. Jim Steer, Virgin's consultant, seemed to have misunderstood London's segmented, social geography which lured many of Eurostar's potential customers to Heathrow rather than Waterloo, and to have mistakenly relied on irrelevant French experience to generate new passengers.

'We'll have to revise our forecasts,' Ian Brookes told LCR's directors. Their anger, Branson knew, was focused on him. Virgin was responsible for sales to match their own forecasts. Steer's over-optimistic calculations threatened LCR's existence. Salvation depended upon sophisticated marketing to create a mass of new travellers. But Branson was a publicist not a marketing expert. He resorted to the single cure he could always rely upon to sell records, books, sandwiches or seats on trains: gimmicks.

'Special offers, stunts, buzz and fun are what we need,' Furlong and Brookes chanted in unison. 'Loads of publicity will get loads of bums on seats.' The Virgin gospel was to 'pack 'em in' at low fares with 'Richard Branson's special offers . . .'. Newspapers were inundated with stories about £50 return tickets to Paris, free first class tickets, special 'booze trains' at £20 per ticket, £49 tickets to Disney, and seat-back TVs for all passengers. 'We intend to be very aggressive in pricing,' Furlong promised. 'Special offers, discounts and all the other techniques learnt on Virgin Atlantic,' he chanted, 'will make LCR profitable.'

To invigorate Eurostar's staff, Branson issued a directive for every employee to report for a pep talk to a theatre in Clapham. Adam Mills, the company's chief executive, was not invited. 'I insist on coming,' he told Branson. 'You're not even a director of the company. You rarely come to board meetings but you want to go over our heads to address the staff. It's not on. We're a team.' Branson relented.

Dancing girls, fire eaters and musicians greeted Eurostar's staff as they awaited their host. These were moments Branson cherished: he was the focus of attention, standing in the spotlight, winning new admirers. The music blared, the lights flashed and Branson appeared on the stage. As he opened his large notebook, the excitement evaporated. He remained an uninspiring public performer. He coughed and began speaking in his monotone voice about 'my company'. Mills fumed. 'It's not his company. If anything, it's my company.' In the following days, Mills's fury grew.

'What were you doing?' asked Mills.

'We thought it would be helpful to get the company going,' replied Branson in his familiar royal syntax.

Virgin sent the invoice for the meeting to Eurostar. Reluctantly, Mills authorised payment but when Virgin later sent a bill for entertaining Eurostar's staff at Branson's summer party at the manor, Mills balked, and he balked again, rejecting another bill for Virgin's advertisements in newspapers appealing for funds to repair the Albert memorial. 'No way,' replied Mills, appalled by Virgin's confusion. 'He knows how to spend our money but not how to earn it,' complained a banker. But Mills had not anticipated Branson's next surprise.

A noticeable hint of impertinence shrouded Branson's arrival at Waterloo in May 1996 to promote a £49 fare to Brussels. With a tape recorder attached to his belt, he posed for photographers and then embarked on the train with the journalists. The revelry began immediately. By his arrival at the Palace Hotel in Brussels, he was boasting that Eurostar might carry twenty-five million passengers within four years. His absurd exaggerations were soberly reported. By the morning of the following day, his drunken bonanza in his hotel had attracted publicity about his hospitality and his limited capacity for alcohol but had generated no profits for the train. 'It's all very good for Virgin,' sniffed Richard Edgeley, the managing director, 'but what about Eurostar?' Branson was unconcerned. His discounts, he boasted, were filling the trains. Unknown to Eurostar's managers, Ian Brookes, Virgin's marketing expert, was contracted to Virgin on a bonus system to provide huge numbers of passengers regardless of their fares. The accounts were only gradually revealing that Virgin's low fares were increasing the losses.

Branson's personal promotions placed in *The Times*, a friendly newspaper, had attracted three hundred thousand passengers but the success was a poison pill. Research would show that one hundred thousand people would have travelled anyway and another one hundred thousand tickets had been given away at cost. Eurostar's income, or yield, for each passenger had fallen from £70 to £39. 'Any damned idiot can sell something for nothing,' complained a banker, astonished by Branson's clumsiness. Eurostar would be more profitable transporting one third of the passengers paying higher fares. 'I can't stand it,' Richard Edgeley complained. 'Brookes is always consulting Branson. The business is disintegrating. It's unpleasant.' Edgeley resigned. But Branson was not listening. The grasshopper tycoon was already groping towards his next deal. He would, he prided himself, shock Mills and Hornby and the rest.

In the same month, May 1996, Branson announced the take-off of Virgin Express, a low-cost European airline offering flights to many destinations, including between London, Brussels and Paris. That week's hype about another Virgin revolution excited Branson but appalled his partners in LCR. 'What about Eurostar?' asked a member of the consortium. 'He's attacking our market. And he didn't even tell us.' There was concern that Virgin might have broken its contractual undertaking with LCR not to compete with Eurostar. Trevor Abbott's response revealed the unexpected perils of agreements with Branson. 'LCR is contracted with Virgin Group in London,' Abbott explained. 'But Virgin Express was established by a Branson family company registered in the Channel Islands.' Branson's use of two separate legal entities was infallible. Abbott did not reveal that with Branson he was a beneficiary of that particular Channel Island trust.

The egoism of Virgin's executives particularly astonished Sir Derek Hornby. In early July 1996, on board a Eurostar train speeding at 270 k.p.h. through France for yet another press launch, Hornby stood in a dark pinstripe, double-breasted suit, white shirt, long cuffs and spotted tie in the buffet car. Beside Hornby sat Branson, perched on a table with his arms wrapped around his knees, wearing an odd jacket, frayed trousers and no tie. Branson was patently discomforted by sharing the salesmanship with Hornby and soon after their arrival in Paris paraded his individuality. For dinner, everyone changed into suits while Branson appeared in jeans and a grey T-shirt, eating chips with his fingers. Branson believed that his irreverent performance would attract hundreds of thousands of new passengers. If only Eurostar could be rebranded as a Virgin product, the losses would be transformed into profits. The trip to Brussels convinced Hornby and LCR's directors to irrevocably reject that proposal. Trevor Abbott and Stephen Murphy, Virgin's representatives, passed an unambiguous message to their employer in Holland Park: Virgin and its representatives are failing to inspire confidence. The message was spurned, with unpleasant consequences.

'You're fired,' Adam Mills told Ian Brookes, Virgin's marketing expert. 'Your ad campaigns are all wrong. We're not getting the passengers Virgin contracted to deliver.'

Blaming a Virgin appointee was certain to outrage Branson, especially if he considered it unjustified. 'You've got it all wrong,' he seethed to Mills less than thirty minutes after Brookes's dismissal. He would not allow himself to be associated with failure, nor with the possible loss of his £10 million investment. 'You'll regret it.'

'You're not a team player,' retorted Mills. That was a compliment to a man proud of breaking the rules to play his own game. The positive story placed in *The Times* by Virgin's publicists was his retort to his supposed partners. Eurostar, the sympathetic newspaper reported, was 'finally up to speed' thanks to Virgin.

Branson was perfectly content to humiliate any opposition. He was short-sighted that the consequence of his boardroom terrorism was whispers around London complaining of distrust. Contemptuous of his besuited critics and emboldened by Virgin Atlantic's success, the restless predator and his loyal cabal singularly lusted for kills. But in their frenetic hunt for deals, profits and the daily gratification of mention in newspapers, the stable consolidation and thoughtful management of the Virgin empire were forsaken. A familiar fracture had reappeared in Branson's operation. Every business, with one exception, was losing money. Virgin's trains, clothes, cola, cosmetics, shops and finance were all dependent upon the airline. The continuing prosperity of the golden goose depended upon debilitating British Airways while simultaneously minimising Virgin's unique privileges to perpetuate the attrition.

'We'll catch BA. We'll get them,' Branson repeated regularly. For over a decade, Branson had won widespread sympathy as the consumer's champion. After his courtroom victory against British Airways, he had fashioned commercial animosity into a political and marketing tool to reach his target of ten million passengers by 2000. The billionaire presented himself as the victim of the marauding giant but Virgin Atlantic's success belied his pleas of weakness.

Virgin's weekly frequencies between Heathrow and the United States had increased over the previous six years (1990–96) by 700 per cent, from fourteen services to one hundred and twelve. Virgin held an equal share with British Airways of the market between Heathrow and New York (32 per cent) and was selling more tickets than BA in Britain on those American routes served by both airlines (45 per cent to 33 per cent). Since Virgin's costs were 25 per cent lower than BA's and its ticket prices were practically identical, Virgin's profits were considerably higher.

Still humiliated and weakened by Branson's courtroom victory, British Airways was vulnerable and oppressed by huge costs. Virgin Atlantic's harsh advertisements – 'BA don't give a shiatsu' – reflected Branson's ambition to weaken or even, in his wildest dreams, take control of the airline. None of his entourage stalked that quarry more ferociously than Will Whitehorn who, since 1995, had predicted that Virgin Atlantic would become a 'global challenger to British

Airways'. Within three years, Whitehorn had confidently asserted, Virgin would have spent $5 billion, own forty jumbo jets, and match BA. 'We've taken the plunge,' said Whitehorn about Virgin's eighteen new routes. His fantasies echoed his master. Exaggerations opened doors and prophecies, however wild, became self-fulfilling. 'We have decided, if possible, to take British Airways on worldwide wherever they fly,' Branson told members of the House of Commons. 'We are going for broke to try to catch BA.' His zeal was dazzling. To those who warned, 'You can't do it', he replied, 'I've heard that one hundred times before. I can and I will.' Those sceptical about his finances were scorned. 'Our airline,' he trilled, 'is throwing off cash.' Millions of pounds, he repeated, real cash not paper shares, were pouring into his coffers.

To enhance his status on the world's stage, Branson projected an image of an international airline tycoon, owning a vast fleet of aeroplanes landing at airports across the globe. In fact, in 1996, Branson owned fifteen jets, amounting to a niche operation. After Vintage Airways in Florida had crashed with substantial losses, he was reminded of his vulnerability. His survival depended on protecting Virgin Atlantic's shared monopoly on the cherry-picked routes, demeaning British Airways and always offering the cheapest fares. But in Branson's game of poker, the consumer's champion seldom took the initiative to cut fares. Almost invariably, he responded to BA's reductions, offering fares £1 lower while claiming to 'slash fares by 50 per cent'. But in November 1995, Virgin Atlantic's ruses were punished. The airline was fined $14,000 by the US Department of Transportation for issuing dishonest advertisements on the internet promoting bargain fares which were unavailable when the public telephoned. Instead of the advertised $499 for a transatlantic journey, the lowest fare was $557. Virgin agreed not to mislead customers in the future. It was a minor illegality but symptomatic of Branson's methods.

In Branson's topsy-turvy logic, he condemned British Airways for plotting to destroy Virgin Atlantic by 'price-fixing', yet BA's fares were higher than Virgin's. Like a piranha, he automatically snapped. But on 21 June 1996 his snap seemed toothless when British Airways announced an intention to form an alliance with American Airlines.

Over that weekend, Branson had celebrated his sister's birthday in Chichester, flown by helicopter on Saturday afternoon to Norwich for a Virgin Direct party, driven back to Chichester and returned on Sunday to Holland Park to prepare for the launch of Virgin's first flight to Washington. As he was chauffeured, dressed as Uncle Sam, to a photo opportunity for newspapers beside the river Thames, he heard Robert Ayling's announcement. 'BA's alliance with American Airlines will provide seamless worldwide travel on a single ticket between 36,000 locations at cheaper prices.' Branson's instinctive reaction was to prevent those two airlines uniting their reservations and ticketing systems.

Richard Branson disliked Bob Ayling. Not only because the former civil servant was, he believed, a co-conspirator in Lord King's 'dirty tricks', but because the quiet, self-made solicitor lacked class. For Branson, Ayling epitomised safe bureaucracy, the antithesis of a buc-caneering tycoon. Ayling, with his innate modesty still inhabiting a small house in Stockwell, south London, surrounded by council estates, was denigrated by Branson as a 'stern schoolmaster' or a 'dunce'. The superiority he exercised over Branson, thanks to British Airways' size, was by appointment rather than brash ingenuity, and that alone was an incentive to wage war. And winning was never enough. Someone had to lose and be seen to lose, and humbling Ayling was a noble prize.

That night, Branson met Ayling at the BBC's television studios in White City. Although he disliked the prospect of a public debate, Branson had agreed to appear on *Newsnight* to discuss BA's proposed alliance.

'How are things?' Ayling asked cheerfully.

'OK, until you cooked up this wheeze,' Branson replied.

The 'wheeze' was nothing less than British Airways' best hope for prosperity. Bob Crandall, the chairman of United Airlines, the world's largest carrier, had hailed 'the alliance system' as the 'corner-stone of the future in commercial aviation'. Global alliances, predicted Crandall, would replace individual airlines. United Airlines had com-bined with Lufthansa, Europe's second biggest airline, to create the Star Alliance. As a piggybacker, Branson echoed Crandall's senti-ments. Code sharing with suitable partners had become, Branson pontificated, critical to every airline's survival.

In 1995, Virgin Atlantic had signed a code sharing agreement with Delta, the American airline. Combining the computer reservations systems of both airlines, travel agents could sell tickets to fly on

Virgin and Delta on all their routes. The agreement guaranteed Virgin Atlantic $150 million of sales every year. But Branson had camouflaged his profit motive from the public. The Delta agreement, he had advertised, was 'a great breakthrough for consumers' by 'increasing competition in the marketplace'. Similar agreements followed with Malaysia Airlines and British Midland. He watched sanguinely as British Airways' major European competitors forged their own alliances with other American airlines.

'I bet he doesn't dare mention our alliance with Delta,' Branson scoffed with a wry laugh to a group of Virgin Atlantic executives. Among the many beneficial legacies of 'dirty tricks' was BA's timidity towards Virgin. It was Roy Gardner who observed, 'ours are just the same as what BA wants', only to be told, unconvincingly, by Branson, 'Bollocks, it's completely different.' 'We're keeping very quiet on our alliances,' Virgin's spokesman was ordered.

The alliances had alarmed Bob Ayling. Lufthansa was not only subsidised by state funds but, with the aggressive help of the German government, controlled over 60 per cent of the slots at Frankfurt airport compared to BA's 38 per cent at Heathrow. The Star Alliance had entrenched Lufthansa's domination, compelling American Airlines to cancel three routes between the United States and Europe, while Delta had abandoned all its flights to Germany. 'By relaxing the anti-trust laws,' commented Ayling, 'Lufthansa has reduced the level of competition.'

Ayling was unashamed about his change of policy. British Airways could not stand aside from the trend dictated by its bigger competitors. Becoming a global airline with combined ticketing, the merging of facilities of two airlines at airports and a joint frequent flyer programme offering 'free miles', had become an essential ingredient in the precarious economics of the airline industry. Although the new alliance would not be allowed to retain all 62 per cent of its merged transatlantic market, BA's extra profits could, he estimated, still be worth about £200 million. Without an alliance, as Branson knew, British Airways would lose millions.

Ayling had good reason to believe that his proposal would, like Lufthansa's bigger alliance, be approved within twelve weeks. Three alliances between American and European airlines had been previously granted immunity from anti-trust laws by the Department of Transportation and Department of Justice in Washington. All had been deemed to be efficient and advantageous for consumers, good for competition, hastening 'open skies' agreements between America and Europe. Ayling's bid for the alliance with American Airlines accepted the inevitability of 'open skies', the removal of all restrictions on airlines landing at Heathrow.

As the self-appointed champion of competition, Branson had always supported 'open skies'. He endlessly opined that allowing any airline to land at every airport was in the consumer's interests. The rigid restraints on airlines flying between Britain and America, he knew, were particularly anti-competitive. But the prospect of their removal terrified Branson.

Under the Anglo-American Bermuda II treaty signed in 1976, access at Heathrow was restricted to two British and two American airlines: British Airways and Virgin, and American Airlines and United Airlines. If Bermuda II was scrapped, every British and every American airline could bid to fly between Heathrow and America. The competition would slash transatlantic ticket prices from London by at least 25 per cent to the same prices enjoyed by continental Europeans. Branson's hard-won duopoly at Heathrow funded his whole Virgin empire. If British Midland, Delta, Continental and any other airline acquired landing slots at Heathrow, the consumer would benefit but Virgin would suffer. His solution was politic. He would continue to support 'open skies' but argue for wholly unrealistic terms.

Until June 1996, as a partner in an alliance, Branson had chosen not to protest to the regulators in Brussels and Washington about the other alliances. While he enjoyed an advantage over British Airways, he remained silent. But Ayling's plea, 'We just want equal treatment to survive', alarmed Branson. Virgin's prosperity depended upon BA not receiving equal treatment. The government, he decided, should be persuaded to prevent BA emulating its competitors. He resolved to throw all his resources into the destruction of BA's proposed alliance, especially through the sympathetic media. His audacious exaggerations usually passed unchallenged by those fearful either of incurring his displeasure or of the threat of a writ. His pose was familiar. 'BA dominates Heathrow,' he told every journalist he could reach. 'It has most of the slots and is very profitable. The government should say, "get on with it and stop coming up with unrealistic ideas".'

The introduction of Virgin's daily flight to Washington would under any circumstances have escalated the squeeze on British Airways. Branson turned a visit to America to launch the new service into a campaign to further hurt his rival.

Robin Renwick, the British ambassador in the US, had agreed to host a party and formal dinner to honour Virgin Atlantic. Dressed in a pullover and surrounded by red-dressed Virgin hostesses, Branson toured the embassy's imposing reception hall, engaging those Americans likely to influence the fate of Britain's airlines. Ignoring the existing European alliances, including his own, the buccaneer set out to persuade the regulators that Virgin's survival was threatened by British Airways' 'monster of the skies'. 'It's not an "alliance",' the master publicist urged. 'It's a whacking great, slow on its feet, uneconomic, self-interested, customer disregarding monopoly launched by the big boys because they can't keep up with Virgin.' That night he was able to reflect about how, once again, he had used his flair to turn arguments upside down.

The following day, full-page advertisements were published in newspapers blaring venomously: 'the world's least favourite monopoly', 'prepare for a rip-off', 'big chief of BA speak with strange tongue' and 'when BA and American Airlines play monopoly twelve million passengers could lose'. He even joked that the new slogan inscribed on Virgin's jets – 'No Way BA/AA' – had been painted by British Airways' contractors. By the end of June 1996, the owner of fifteen planes was threatening to jeopardise the timetable of an alliance combining eight hundred jets. There was a single purpose: accumulating more untaxed profits in his trusts located in the Virgin Islands. Promoting himself had become synonymous with promoting Virgin. In 1996, his year of profits and expansion, the divergence between public and private man became more marked.

Judged by his lieutenants, his transition from relying upon the music-loving Simon Draper and Ken Berry – the pulse beats of Virgin in the 1970s – to his dependence upon the money-driven Trevor Abbott, Will Whitehorn and Stephen Murphy reflected his new preoccupation. Those connected to his airline were among the first to notice the shift.

Dudley Broster, the senior pilot and operations manager of Virgin Atlantic, drew the discrepancy to Branson's attention in October 1996. An advertisement for Virgin Direct used the slogan, 'For years the pension industry has got away with not telling you how much of your money they cream off in charges.' Nine months earlier in Los Angeles, Broster had complained to Branson about the concern of Virgin Atlantic's pilots regarding their pensions. Since then, nothing had happened despite a 'damning' consultants' report. 'You could become very embarrassed,' Broster warned Branson, 'if it was found out that 3,000 of your staff are being screwed by your competitors and so far nothing has been done to rectify the problem.' Broster was also thinking about Ian Frost, a Virgin pilot since 1984, who had contributed over twelve years £46,310 to discover that his particular pension fund in 1997 would be worth just £48,964. 'It's a scandal,' Frost had protested, quite bewildered by his discovery of the size of the commissions taken by Virgin's brokers and insurers which Virgin executives appeared unprepared to adequately explain. Broster ended his letter to Branson, 'I suggest you give personnel a big boot up the arse and get things moving!'

Curiously, the reminder that Branson was occasionally an uncaring employer coincided with his visit to South Africa where he presented himself as an altruist. An earlier warm welcome from Nelson Mandela had roused Branson to promise multimillion-pound Virgin investments in Megastores, cinemas, radio stations, vodka and cola. Nothing had happened. The South Africans also mistakenly believed that Virgin Atlantic's introductory $557 round trip fare to London would be sustained. Some attributed Branson's eagerness to offer the unfulfillable to his new passion for a South African woman. 'I don't know what to do about her,' he confessed to one of his executives. Smitten, his seduction of the woman was arguably different from his manner of accosting Jarvis Astaire, the property developer, at the Miss World competition at the Coronation Ball in Sun City.

'Do you fly Virgin?' Branson asked after their introduction.

'No I prefer flying the flag,' replied Astaire politely, moving to the judges' enclosure.

'You should try our airline,' Branson replied laughing. 'We're starting flights to Jo'burg. They're better than BA.'

Ninety minutes later, Branson reappeared in front of Astaire. His humour had disappeared. Miss Russia had been declared the winner by one point ahead of Miss United Kingdom. Pushing his finger into Astaire's face, Branson was uncouth.

'Are you blind?' he flared at the British judge. 'The British girl was much better.'

'You don't know how I voted,' replied Astaire, startled. Focusing on Branson's finger just inches from his face, he added, 'But now you know why I don't fly your airline.'

Branson did not understand. How could anyone not want to support his battle to defeat British Airways? The regular lunches in Holland Park for travel agents, corporate travel managers and important customers, always essential for Virgin Atlantic's success, were arranged to reinforce his campaign. His celebrity attracted eager guests who, in the afterglow, reconfirmed their affection for Virgin Atlantic. Like his engaging conversations with passengers in Virgin's planes, his showmanship attracted loyalty and earned commercial rewards. The limousines, business class lounge, massage girls, videos and friendly hostesses compensated for the absence of a worldwide air miles programme for businessmen to fly free to their holidays. Even the complaint about Virgin Atlantic's poor punctuality – 'I love flying you Richard,' said a guest, 'but I'm delayed every time' – was brushed aside by a well-rehearsed riposte. 'Sorry,' he laughed, 'but I've ordered an extra plane to prevent that.' The laughter always saved Branson from an embarrassing truth. Bad punctuality had become a serious problem. By contrast, British Airways' alliance with American Airlines would improve its service and profitability beyond Virgin's dreams. The proposed marriage had to be aborted.

Everything depended upon persuading politicians and regulators. His first opportunity was a joint appearance with Bob Ayling before the House of Commons Transport Committee on 10 July 1996. A slight frisson of excitement announced Branson's arrival in the committee room. The power of celebrity gave a certain licence to present himself as the victim of the 'monster monopolist's . . . pure emotional blackmail'. Compared to Ayling's stoic civil servant's delivery, Branson would seek sympathy by uttering laddish denunciations.

British Airways' case is 'ludicrous', the witness fulminated. 'Governments,' he flayed, 'must not be conned by these people into allowing it to happen . . . No industry needs to be protected.' While demanding protection for himself as a significant player in the British economy, BA, he was arguing, should be unprotected. His inconsistency passed without comment, although he appeared to be unaware that several MPs had become less sympathetic after recent reports of his fraught relationships with civil servants.

Branson's relations with Sir George Young, the transport minister, and his departmental civil servants had deteriorated. His regular visits to Young accompanied by a posse of intimidating advisers, demanding that the government should negotiate in Virgin's, not BA's interests, had ended frequently on a sour note. Although Young had never criticised Branson publicly, he had become wary of the frequent visitor.

The tension developed after an invitation to the minister and Anthony Goldman, the senior official responsible for aviation policy, for lunch in Holland Park. Branson had been pressing for some of British Airways' slots and discovered that Young was sympathetic towards BA's survival. 'You're in BA's pockets,' Branson fulminated, ruining his guests' enjoyment of the food. He had previously complained that the government's officials were biased in BA's favour, and even influencing the independent regulators against Virgin.

'You are benefiting from privilege,' countered Young.

'I'm in favour of competition,' replied Branson, reasserting his high moral tone.

The government's sympathy for British Airways' proposed alliance as a strategy for survival outraged Branson. Seeking someone to blame, Branson pinpointed Anthony Goldman, the civil servant. Branson worked up a fury about Goldman. The experienced official had sought in a private conversation to express the government's desire for co-operation between BA and Virgin Atlantic. Branson rejected the suggestion and, in an intemperate letter to Goldman's superiors, he accused the official of 'acting improperly', especially during a meeting at the Office of Fair Trading. Branson's interpretation of their conversation was denied by the civil servant and his superiors. Relations between Branson and the department plummeted.

Sir Patrick Brown, the permanent secretary, and Sir George Young feared that Branson would initiate legal action. Branson, they agreed, would be warned. 'In future,' Young told the tycoon to his face, 'every conversation with you will be minuted by an official and telephone conversations will be recorded.' The politician's anger was undisguised. Branson discovered that Whitehall's sympathy for his position had eroded. But he was undeterred. Even if the incumbents of Whitehall controlled his fate and were unsympathetic, his ambitions and complaints would not be moderated. He expected public sympathy for his cause. 'We have decided, if possible,' he continued at the MPs' public hearing in Westminster, 'to take British Airways on worldwide wherever they fly . . . We are going for broke to try to catch BA, but that is subject to the slots which we cannot get.' Increased competition, he lamented, was impossible because 'Heathrow is full.'

That was, as Branson should have known, inaccurate. Since arriving at Heathrow, Virgin had accumulated five thousand, five hundred slots and, in the wake of Virgin's arrival, forty-six other airlines had started operations at Heathrow. Slots were constantly being traded, allocated and even bought. Twenty-five thousand slots, some at peak hours, remained unallocated and an extra seventy-five thousand slots would become available as technology improved. At that moment, even Branson was secretly negotiating to buy slots from Sabena, the Belgian national airline, to increase Virgin's flights to America. Heathrow, he knew, was only full for British Airways, compelled by the government to expand elsewhere.

The statistics, Branson also ought to have known, were more complicated than he suggested. Fifty-two per cent of Heathrow's passengers to America were transfers by European travellers, changing planes in London, and flying across the Atlantic. Much of that profitable revenue for British Airways, argued Ayling, would diminish if the alliance was not approved. Privately, Branson probably agreed but, in his self-interest, he damned Ayling for 'trying to pull the wool over your eyes'.

Branson left the committee room uncertain about the outcome. The Prime Minister, John Major, had encouraged Ayling to believe that the Eurocrats in Brussels possessed no jurisdiction and that Washington's approval would be successfully negotiated. Branson was set on disillusioning Ayling. His first pincer move to destabilise British Airways was launched in Europe.

Virgin Express had been created in April 1996. Branson had paid £38 million for a 90 per cent stake in a small and barely profitable Belgian registered airline. It operated twelve Boeing 737s from Brussels on charters and scheduled services to Barcelona, Madrid, Milan, Rome, Vienna and Nice. Branson's forecast about his new airline was, as ever, optimistic: 'We plan to make Virgin Express the dominant low cost carrier in Europe. Europe has never had the luxury of low cost airfares. It is going to be massively successful.' Promising 30 per cent price reductions and flights between Europe and

Manchester, Birmingham, Edinburgh and Glasgow, Branson spoke of feeding European passengers on to Virgin Atlantic flights. 'We are going to go into head–to–head competition with [BA] within twelve months,' he asserted. 'We're going to get hundreds of thousands of new passengers.'

As so often, Branson was copying someone else's successful idea – in this case, the model was Southwest Airlines, established in 1973 by Herb Kelleher, an American maverick who undercut the major airlines by offering cheap fares on frill-free 'fun flights' into low cost airports. As with many of Branson's whims, his impulsiveness to strike a deal had overlooked the details. In the case of Virgin Express, the defect had been spotted by Hugh Welburn, the architect of the airline. 'Although the airline will be physically based in Brussels because Brussels airport has ample spare capacity,' Welburn had recommended in his quiet manner, 'Virgin Express's registered headquarters should be in Ireland. That'll avoid Belgium's pernicious taxes and trade union restrictions.' Branson had nodded but had failed to follow his advice. Welburn's entreaty to build a new airline from scratch was ignored by an unsophisticated commercial guerrilla. Nor did Branson listen to David Bonderman of the Texas Pacific Group based in San Francisco. 'Buy Ryanair,' advised Bonderman. Instead, Branson had wanted a deal and a quick start – a black and white fix – rather than the painstaking construction of a new airline.

Once Virgin Express was launched, his bombast was ceaseless. 'We've started a revolution in European air travel,' he recited. 'We'll become the main European carrier within the next two years.' He was forecasting that an airline carrying 2.5 million passengers could overtake in twenty-four months British Airways and Lufthansa who combined carried annually about seventy million passengers. 'We expect $200 million [£128 million] turnover and $10 million profit this year.' Herb Kelleher's airline, after all, had been profitable in its first year and throughout its twenty-three-year existence.

In his rush to emulate Southwest, Branson appointed Jonathan Ornstein, a brash American credited with converting the annual $40 million losses of Continental Express, another no-frills American airline, into a profit. Ornstein, Branson prided himself, was a Best Brain who could be delegated to manage his devolved empire. Under Ornstein's contract, Virgin Express would be floated within two years.

Branson's certainty that Ornstein's self-confidence could build Virgin Express into Europe's major airline was not shared by Hugh Welburn. 'Running a domestic American carrier for two years,' warned Welburn, 'is no qualification for running a European airline operating across six different countries.' Again his hyperactive employer did not seem to be listening. 'The airports are congested and costs are much higher in Europe than America,' continued Welburn to deaf ears. Branson's rush to expand the empire allowed no time for reflection. Branson trusted Ornstein to deliver. The new airline was only part of his frenetic helter-skelter to rank among the Titans.

Branson, the professional David, ached to be hailed as a colossus but an aggressive maverick with a lack of education was handicapped in a new era. Across America, the offspring of the Silicon Valley billionaires were spawning new internet companies whose shares had soared in months from $50 to $4,000 each. Future fortunes depended on technology, communications and the media. Branson's sole acknowledgement of the new dream was Virgin Net, a joint venture with NTL and a deal that had quickly soured. Branson did not appear to understand the difference between ISP (Internet Service Provider) and e-commerce. A succession of Virgin managers, discovering that NTL could not provide e-commerce, were appointed to renegotiate or unravel the deal but Branson seemed unable to grasp either the problems or the opportunities. Having become so dependent for advice upon Will Whitehorn, his publicist, and others in Holland Park he had missed the start of the telecommunications revolution. In consequence, he remained infatuated by the dinosaurs: cosmetics, clothes and shops.

18

Sinking with dinosaurs

In June 1996, Branson approved the creation of the Victory Corporation. A holding company created with Rory McCarthy and to be managed by Virgin's executives, Victory was to produce jeans and cosmetics. Branson's price for allowing McCarthy to be associated with Virgin was steep. Virgin paid just £1,000 for an 11 per cent stake in Victory while McCarthy bought the remaining 89 per cent for £3 million. McCarthy would also be responsible for finding a further £45 million from private investors. 'Can you do that?' Branson asked.

'No problem,' replied McCarthy eagerly.

'I'll be amazed,' smiled Branson mischievously. McCarthy bit at the challenge.

The deal was classic Branson: maximising his opportunity while minimising his risk. 'Protecting the downside,' as he loved to preach, meant that McCarthy risked a heavy price for association with Virgin while Branson only took profits. Understandably, Branson did not warn his new friend that Virgin's record as professional managers was mixed and that many of his retail ventures had ended unhappily. 'The McCarthys are a great find,' Branson told a Virgin director. 'They're putting a lot of money in for nothing.'

By early October 1996, McCarthy reported success. Institutional investors contacted by Société Générale, the brokers, had pledged to fund the entire £45 million. Any association with Virgin was judged to be profitable. Victory would be worth £110 million. Unhappily, overnight, the plan collapsed. 'No one's trusting private investment any more,' McCarthy explained. The exposure of a suspected fraud at Morgan Grenfell had sabotaged private financing. 'SG say a public flotation is the only way. The same institutions will invest, but only in quoted shares.' Public ownership and public disclosure made the buccaneer nervous.

237

Ever since he had bought the Virgin Group back from shareholders in 1989, Branson had preferred not to expose himself to public scrutiny. He disliked the City suits. If they were half-way smart they'd be as rich as himself. Instead, they tutted and carped from their pedestal. Brad Rosser added a further warning: the shares would be floated on AIM, a small exchange. The sale of just ten thousand shares could rock the price. AIM, the Alternative Investment Market, was a poor imitation of New York's secondary share markets. Branson wavered. Rosser and Murphy had finalised a deal giving the impression that Virgin's interest was minuscule and waited for Branson's decision which had to be made on 17 October 1996. Branson trusted McCarthy who was ebullient about the future. At the deadline, Rosser sat in Société Générale's City offices while Branson anguished with Stephen Murphy about the risk. Just after 2 o'clock in the morning, Branson abandoned his caution. It was not his money and Virgin retained management control. 'Let's do it.' His decision suited his strategy to rebuild Virgin's appeal to the rich under-25s. He was bringing Virgin back to the teenagers. Excitedly, he had even returned to the music business.

'Do you want the job, Marc?' asked Branson. They were seated in his Holland Park home. Branson was irritated that Marc Marot, the managing director of Island Records, looked ungrateful. Branson was offering him the directorship of V2, his new music company, with a starting budget of £100 million and the expectation that like Virgin Music it would become another billion-pound company. By any reckoning, the new company was a major trophy but he was sensing no feedback.

'Well?' asked Branson impatiently.

'The problem is Richard, this is all very interesting but my name is not Marc. I'm Nick Rowe.'

Branson's beard twitched. On his original call, the Island Records telephonist had unfortunately connected him to the wrong person. 'Ah well,' he stuttered, searching for a face-saving escape, 'would you like a job anyway? Bit lower down?'

'No thanks,' replied Rowe.

Branson's search for executives was proving difficult. Ever since July 1995, despite his denials, he had contemplated starting a successor to Virgin Music. 'I'm too busy now to be involved in a new one,' he had told inquirers, but he was already looking. He wanted to repeat his glory despite the warnings. 'Lightning doesn't strike twice,' cautioned Brad Rosser, while Al Clark, the wise sage, gently counselled, 'It's impossible to repeat Virgin Music. The spirit has changed.' The warnings goaded Branson to prove his advisers wrong. He had never properly understood that all the successful independent record labels had developed from authentic musical or social roots and he appeared to be piqued that several of his former employees at Virgin Music had proved successful without him.

Steve Lewis and Jeremy Lascelles had built a thriving new label at Chrysalis; Lewis had become the country's most successful independent music publisher; while Ken Berry had considerably improved Virgin Music within EMI. Their success, Branson believed, owed everything to him. He was deaf to those who mentioned his ignorance of music. 'I've made thirty-five millionaires,' he consoled himself, 'and I'll make some more.'

In the four years since Virgin Music was sold, 78 per cent of the world's music industry had been consolidated by six companies. Their market was worth $40.2 billion. Branson wanted just 1 per cent and he would be rich. His relationship with the stars, he believed, would attract the talent. Guided as usual by instinct rather than careful research, he was undaunted by the industry's transformation. Creating one new artist in 1996 required videos, extensive remixes and promotion costing at least £1 million. That was not an obstacle, he believed. He only required, he persuaded himself, an inspirational chief executive. After more rejections because he refused to pay the market rate – $2 million per annum for the best people – he selected Jeremy Pearce, a cerebral, deal-making lawyer and 'ex-Sony A&R legend' who explained how during his twenty-year career he had 'helped discover Oasis'. Pearce was anointed a Best Brain trusted to manage the devolved empire. Not everyone shared Branson's conviction that Pearce possessed the necessary creative vision.

In May 1996, Branson's lawyers registered V2 as his new music company. Inevitably, the parentage was complicated. The registered owner was the Mars Trust, managed by Morgan Grenfell in Guernsey, while the millions to finance V2 appeared from other Branson family trusts, Jupiter, Plough, Cougar, Polestar and Tiger. The independent trustees not unexpectedly favoured investing the trusts' funds in Branson's ventures. Abbott offered the cast-iron guarantee. 'On behalf of Virgin, I agree to this,' he said at board meetings and then, melodramatically twisting in a different direction in his chair, he announced, 'And on behalf of the trusts, I also agree.' Beyond the trusts was an incomprehensible matrix of offshore companies with deliberately complicated share structures to prevent scrutiny and avoid British taxation.

V2's launch, Branson decreed, would be big. Pearce was told to establish offices in America, France, Germany, Holland, Belgium, Sweden, Italy and Australia, and to begin signing the first of sixty artists. Within one or two years, Branson predicted, V2 would rank as a major. Brad Rosser provided the quotation to justify Virgin's risk: 'We're doing it for the same reason we go into any industry – because we believe that the margins are obscene and that we can offer something special.' Virgin's clothing and cosmetics enterprises had been similarly acclaimed but painfully, on the very day of V2's launch, 17 October 1996, those hopes soured.

The news was so bad that grown men shied away from telling Branson. Minutes after Victory Corporation was launched on the AIM exchange at 58 pence, the share price fell to 52 pence. The company's value had dropped £10 million. Superficially, Branson might have been unconcerned. His £1,000 investment was still worth £11 million. But Branson was rightly anxious. The City was obviously cautious. Victory's prospectus had predicted profits by 2000, just two years after the launch of Virgin jeans. But start-up projects, the experts knew, required five years and Branson, besotted by his penny-pinching, had refused to pay the top rates for the best management. Out there, Branson knew, were potentially disgruntled shareholders who would scream if their losses were excessive. 'The brokers,' he grumbled, 'have not looked after us.' Société Générale was his latest target. 'I'm pissed off,' he spat. 'I've spent two years building up a reputation in financial services and it's blown in one day.' For a few seconds there was silence. 'How do we fix it?' he asked, quietly staring at the carpet. To the others in the room it appeared that Branson's anger was fleeting. But they were mistaken. In Branson's opinion, someone eventually would have to bear the blame. His relationship with McCarthy began to suffer.

On 27 November 1996, at a riotous party to celebrate the launch of V2 in a riverside club in Hammersmith, Branson took care to target McCarthy. 'When are we going to do the deal?' he asked emotionally. McCarthy, he had decided, should finance V2 as well.

The company was costing millions more than he possessed. Unfortunately, McCarthy, a shrewd investor, remained uncommitted. V2's prospects, independent experts had told McCarthy, were at best uncertain. Branson's pressure was unremitting. 'I need £7 million fast,' he told McCarthy. 'Short term.' Branson's predicament was curious. A self-proclaimed billionaire was asking for cash from McCarthy whose finances were comparatively minute. But Branson's manner prevented McCarthy asking bluntly: if V2 is so good, why don't you risk more of your own money? Instead, trusting Branson as a friend and unaware of Virgin's predicament, McCarthy transferred £7 million to Branson before signing an agreement.

In reality, Branson's cash mountain had become a molehill, or perhaps had shrunk beyond any value. In the previous months, he had launched new businesses in airlines, clothes, cosmetics, music, television, radio, cola, trains and the financial services. Although the extraordinary publicity about all his enterprises, evidenced by a thick wodge of newspaper articles about himself prepared for reading at breakfast every day, suggested vast wealth, the truth was somewhat different. Other than the airline and Virgin Radio, both of which shared monopoly franchises granted by the government, all of his businesses were performing badly and even losing money. Poor management and no finance had undermined Branson's big ideas. Gradually his 'cash mountain' had disappeared and he was relying on loans secured against his companies. Fortunately, few realised his true predicament, although the fate of Virgin Cola was flaying his image.

By November 1996, on the eve of Virgin Cola's delayed second anniversary ball, Branson was fretting. Virgin's sponsorship of a summer rock festival and the launch of Virgin Cola in Spain had been a failure. Embarrassingly, an overeager Virgin executive, infected by the expectations of reckless hype, had claimed in France that Virgin Cola had outsold Pepsi. 'The rate of sale,' he broadcast, 'is vastly superior to Pepsi's . . . Virgin Cola's 1.5 litre sells 1.5 times more than Pepsi's.' The Americans were outraged, muttering that Virgin had instigated a 'dirty trick' starkly similar to BA's. Virgin Cola in France controlled only 1.8 per cent of market share compared to Pepsi's 80 per cent. Unlike in Britain, where Virgin's inaccuracies were benignly ignored, the offence in France required a public apology. 'Bollocks,' moaned Branson. To deflect the humiliation, Branson self-importantly suggested that Pepsi's £200 million 'blue' campaign was targeted at Virgin rather than Coca-Cola. 'It seemed,' he wrote, 'that we had hit a raw nerve.'

'The Emperor has no clothes,' sighed Gerry Pencer, Cott's chairman. 'We've been seduced by his crap. Especially by his rubbish of looking after the little guy.' Weary of reading Branson's latest exaggeration that his cola was bought by between 8 per cent and 10 per cent of the market, the Cott directors were alarmed by Branson's suggestion that he deploy the 'victim card'.

Over dinner at the Manoir aux Quat'Saisons, a fashionable but somewhat overrated restaurant in Oxfordshire partly owned by Branson, the victim unveiled his wounds. 'Coke,' Branson told everyone 'are out to get us. Just like BA and GTech. They want to keep us out of the market.' Branson could never acknowledge losing any commercial battle. Shops across the world, Branson knew, prominently stocked Coca-Cola to entice shoppers inside. To undermine Coke's success, he would resort to his favourite theme. He would allege foul play and beg government protection against a tyrant. Coca-Cola's phenomenal popularity and its relationship with shops, he would plead, was 'anti-competitive'. Whitehorn had been instructed to spread the news of misdeeds by Coca-Cola, a corporation even larger than British Airways. The honest entrepreneur, said Whitehorn, was the victim of misinformation. Branson's ogreish competitors were issuing false sales figures deliberately deflating Virgin Cola. Coke and Pepsi, suggested Branson's spokesman, were seeking to destroy the dangerous and popular newcomer. This was a public scandal.

Branson's guests, the Cott managers, were perplexed but Nick Kirkbride, Virgin Cola's chief executive, could perfectly encapsulate Branson's thoughts: 'We believe we also have a very good chance of being able to overtake Coke in the UK.'

Branson's gaze had become serious. 'We have statements from people,' he revealed, 'who have said point blank that they dare not stock us otherwise they will lose discounts offered by Coke.' Branson's intimation of secret reports mirrored the surreptitious eavesdropping which he had arranged in his battle against British Airways. In this case, Virgin's salesmen had asked shopkeepers questions drafted by lawyers to produce the convincing evidence. His victory over Coke, he predicted, would be quicker than over BA.

'How can you say that Coke has a monopoly?' challenged Pencer, troubled by a relationship with an argumentative commercial terror-ist. 'Thirty-four per cent of a market is not a monopoly.'

'We'll find statistics to prove it,' he was told. Unlike with Virgin Vodka, another Virgin joint venture which had failed amid familiar rancour, Branson had invested much personal credibility in cola. Researchers had been told to find weapons and, with artistry, they had produced specialised statistics suggesting that Coke controlled 70 per cent of some markets.

Pencer's doubts were brushed aside. Branson's enthusiasm, his fame and the constant reminder about his enviable £1 billion personal fortune suppressed any criticism. He was also a very convincing victim. A Monopolies Commission report had recently ruled that Coke's dominance barred new entries and that was sufficient for Branson to submit a dossier to the European Commission com-plaining that Coke's anti-competitive behaviour was costing Virgin 'several millions of pounds'. Coke, he argued, was 'abusing its market power in the UK and Europe' by giving retailers special agreements and exclusive discounts for meeting targets for sales.

'All he's saying is that it's tough out there,' laughed Coke's spokes-man. 'The trouble with Branson is that he believes sounding off at a press conference is an alternative to a proper marketing strategy.' Condemning Branson as 'naive' was an underestimation of Branson by the multinational. Coke would be asked to give undertakings to the Commission to avoid imposing restrictive and exclusive agree-ments and discount incentives upon retailers, but even Branson realised that the victory was no more than pyrrhic. Coca-Cola's management was marginally destabilised by the nuisance but Virgin Cola was still losing money and its market share remained minimal.

Branson was unwilling to accept personal responsibility for that or any misfortune. Trevor Abbott, he believed, was no longer a vital asset. The 'Black Adder', the ultra-loyal fixer and henchman, had fallen victim to Branson's caprice. He had, Branson decided, become dispensable. Branson, the self-styled 'Great Seducer' proud to spread security among his staff with the assertion, 'I don't think being ruth-less is the way to run a company', occasionally practised the opposite. Abbott became the target for Branson's special brand of dismiss-iveness. 'I'm fed up with Trevor Abbotts,' he complained indiscreetly, even enunciating the name with an extra 's'. The workaholic, one of the few not blessed with the Ralph Lauren look, was damned:

'He makes no contribution. I'm fed up.' Whitehorn, the emperor's loudspeaker, echoed the message for all to hear in the basement canteen in Holland Park: 'Richard's pissed off with Trevor.' Abbott's failure to save Virgin's shops in Europe from financial disaster was another complaint.

'He's fallen off Richard's radar,' the gossip spread among Branson's courtiers. Stephen Murphy, Abbott's deputy, was jostling to be the successor, irritated that Abbott wanted to stay. Did he not realise, Murphy whispered, that his influence had declined? 'You can only say "No" to Richard so many times,' Abbott had told those whom he had dismissed, 'before it becomes time to go.' Abbott, the executioner and the keeper of the secrets, had forgotten his despot's golden rule: 'I believe in benevolent dictatorships . . . providing I am the dictator.' But there was a problem. Dismissals in Virgin had become the exclusive chore of Trevor Abbott. No one could be found to execute the executioner. Everyone knew that Abbott was 'out' but Abbott remained inside, humiliated and gradually isolated. Branson was impervious to Abbott's discomfort. In business, relationships and past loyalties were irrelevant. His only 'awful, recurring dream', he admitted, 'is that I will forget one of my houses'. Murphy, motivated not by money but power, was Abbott's automatic replacement.

By November 1996, when Abbott departed, Branson had still not agreed to the financial terms of their divorce. Unresolved was Abbott's beneficial ownership of shares in Branson's trusts, Abbott's ownership of 5 per cent of Virgin hotels, and the price Branson would pay for Abbott's shares in other Virgin companies, including Virgin Express. To evade tax, Abbott had not disclosed his shares, estimated to be worth over £70 million, but his legal title was irrefutable. Branson could not renegotiate the ownership but, in a mirror of his divorce with Nik Powell, he could dispute the value of the shares and procrastinate about payment.

Around Virgin, Abbott's departure was explained as 'a disagreement with Richard about trains'. Abbott had never agreed with those ambitions. The coincidence of his departure in November 1996 with the fire inside the Channel Tunnel explained the fracture. The restrictions in the tunnel's operations decimated Branson's hope of windfall profits from Eurostar to finance Virgin's inevitable losses during 1997.

By the end of 1996, Eurostar's deficit was £300 million more than anticipated and, despite the insurance payments, was increasing by £26 million every month. Eurostar's accumulated losses were £925 million, double the amount the new owners had anticipated. Branson effectively detached himself from Eurostar. The deal-maker had moved on to a much bigger prize: the franchises for the privatisation of Britain's rail network.

Sir George Young, the Minister of Transport, posed as an admirer. 'Keep Branson enthusiastic,' the minister told Roger Salmon, the first director of OPRAF (Office of Passenger Rail Franchising), 'I'm keen to have him bidding.' Branson provided 'third party validation' to the government's controversial privatisation policy.

Branson and his advisers were guided through the government's prospectus. The certainties built into the proposed contracts removed much of the risk. There were fixed costs payable to other companies for leasing the trains, for using the rail tracks and for stopping at the stations. The bids combined government subsidies and the payment to the government of fixed sums for the right to run the trains. 'It's a licence to print money,' Branson's advisers agreed. 'Can't go wrong.' Not one of them reflected that Branson wanted to profit from the very sin which he had accused Camelot of enjoying.

'Get me someone who can put our bids together,' Branson told Stephen Murphy and Jim Steer, still Branson's adviser despite his misjudgements about Eurostar. Their candidate was Brian Barrett, a bearded fifty-one-year-old marketing expert who had recently retired after establishing Forte's Travelodge hotels. Barrett and Steer had previously co-operated to bid for privatised bus services. Rail privatisation was slightly different. Branson would be bidding for the right to manage the cash flow of a railway without owning any assets. At the end of the franchise, Virgin would own nothing except either the profits or the debts.

As so often, Branson was just following a trend. As a late runner, he had missed the best opportunities. The first franchises awarded to Southwest, First Great Western, LTS Rail and Stagecoach were granted with exceptionally generous subsidies to encourage future bids. Similarly, the new rolling stock companies franchised to lease the trains and wagons, would earn within one year over £900 million profit. The cherries had been picked.

Branson's team identified two franchises offering, they believed, the greatest potential growth: the West Coast line linking twenty-five million Britons between London, Birmingham, Manchester, Liverpool and Glasgow; and the Cross Country franchise, a hybrid of commuter trains travelling through one hundred and thirty stations across Britain from Dundee to Penzance. Both franchises had disadvantages. The Cross Country route depended on seasonal, holiday travel; while the West Coast line, neglected since its modernisation in the 1960s, required new tracks, signals, electric cables and rolling stock. Under the government's prospectus, the successful bidder for the West Coast line was required to introduce high-speed tilting trains and could expect Railtrack to provide modernised tracks and new signalling. With so many certainties promised by the government, Jim Steer created a computer model which calculated that if rail travel just returned to the levels in the 1980s, the franchise holders would earn profits. 'By improving services,' predicted Branson, 'we can get back the lost passengers.'

New facts fed Branson's optimism. In 1996, only 6 per cent of travellers between London and Glasgow used rail, 4 per cent used airlines and the rest travelled by road. Counting on intolerable congestion on the M1 and M6, the saturation of Heathrow and British Rail's failure to sell 35 per cent of all West Coast line seats, Steer predicted that if Virgin doubled the number of passengers, the profits would be huge. Among the new passengers, presumed Steer, were most of the one million passengers who flew between London and Manchester. Steer, it seemed to some, was repeating his Eurostar misjudgement. The Eurostar train had not replaced air travel between London and Paris, nor had France's high-speed trains displaced the fourteen daily flights between Paris and Lyons. Many British Airways passengers, flying from Manchester to one of London's four airports, were not destined for central London or were joining connecting flights. But the minuses did not depress the great salesman.

Virgin would, Branson promised, introduce 'The Concorde of rail', linking London and Manchester in just one hundred and five minutes. As required by the government, Virgin would order tilting express trains to zoom across Britain at 160 m.p.h. Guided by digital signalling on new tracks, they would be similar to Japan's gleaming 'Bullet Train'. Travelling by Virgin trains, Branson promised, would not only be 'fun' but would 'increase quality and bring down prices'.

To win the franchise, Virgin was required to stipulate what subsidies they needed and what payments they would make to the government. The winner was the company offering to pay more money during the licence period than its competitors. On the Cross Country route, Virgin's bid required an initial subsidy of £113 million falling to a payment of £10 million to the government when the franchise ended in 2011.

On the West Coast line, Virgin required £77 million from the government in 1998, declining to nothing in 2003. By then, the new trains would be running and from 2005/6 until the end of the fifteen-year franchise, Virgin offered to pay the government £74.92 million rising to £227 million in 2011. By 2012, the end of the franchise, the Treasury would have received from Virgin £1.24 billion, more than the competing bids by Sea Containers, the successful bidder for the East Coast line, and Stagecoach, managed by Brian Souter.

Virgin proposed to lease forty new tilting trains between June 2001 and 2004, just as the subsidies were replaced by payments to the government. The serious profits would be expected after 2005 when, assuming that the new tracks, signals and trains were installed, the journey time between Glasgow and London fell to less than four hours.

Branson's financial commitment was partly protected. Shares in Virgin Trains, Branson's company, had been offered to four investors – Bankers Trust, J. P. Morgan, Electra Fleming and the Texas Pacific Group. The four had bought 59 per cent of the company for £45 million after Stephen Murphy had outlined how Virgin Trains would earn substantial profits prior to flotation. Branson invested £18 million for the remaining 41 per cent. He did not intend to risk a penny more.

Branson's plan was to extract as much profit as possible, at least £29 million every year, by increasing the company's revenue in 2000 by 30 per cent. Costs were to be cut by dismissing staff, reducing maintenance and closing down buildings; and contrary to his assurances, fares would be increased. To present himself as 'a customer-focused business', he summoned journalists to hear his vision of Virgin Trains in the year 2000. Either by telephone or for the favoured few in his Holland Park headquarters, Branson conjured an image of train passengers enjoying within three years luxuries similar to Virgin Atlantic's. 'We'll have high quality snacks and light meals,' he promised, 'hand-held TV sets, low cost telephone reservations and more staff.' Students and groups would be offered 'deeply discounted fares' and there would be free taxis to stations for first class passengers. All of those benefits, promised Branson, would be provided 'for less' than British Rail's fares. There was only one word of caution. Those improvements, he admitted, 'can't happen overnight, but within two years Virgin customers will notice a visible difference and hopefully will come back for more'. His commitment and the time scale could not be more precise. By 1999, the legacy from British Rail would be effaced. By 2000, the 'Virgin Vision' was a seamless journey at 140 m.p.h. across Britain to catch the Virgin Eurostar train to Paris. His proposal matched precisely the Conservative government's desires.

In November 1996, Virgin was awarded the Cross Country route. 'The final proof,' gushed Sir George Young, 'of the renaissance which is sweeping through Britain's railway industry.' Any man, thought the minister, who can run an airline successfully can similarly manage a railway.

Frantically, Virgin's press machine organised an event for 16 January 1997, the first day of the Cross Country route under Virgin's control. *The Maiden Voyager*, an old train repainted in Virgin's logo, heralded the debut of Branson's rail empire promising the best of Virgin Atlantic's Upper Class service within a smooth, integrated network. Branson was absent in Marrakesh on another attempt to relaunch his bid to fly a hot-air balloon around the world: 'Richard has a maiden voyage of his own to make,' said a spokesman. To mitigate the impression that Branson was ignoring the fate of thousands of passengers for the sake of his publicity, a Virgin spokesman whispered that his ballooning was for the public good – he would be conducting environmental research on pollution.

Branson was not overjoyed by his return to Marrakesh. His relations with Lindstrand were barely civil and he was irritated that Rory McCarthy's good-humoured antics had stolen the limelight at a party in a belly dancers' nightclub. In particular, he had been emotionally distressed by the contributions of both men to a television documentary filmed by Garfield Kennedy during the last launch. Lindstrand had complained about Branson's parsimony and McCarthy had mentioned their lack of preparation. Neither Lindstrand nor McCarthy had displayed the sycophancy Branson expected. Despite his smile, people noticed Branson's silence in the club. A few days later, McCarthy's sudden illness which compelled his withdrawal from the adventure did not appear to disappoint Branson. Alex Ritchie, an outstanding design engineer, was a perfect replacement.

The best distraction as they awaited perfect weather was his mother's enthusiastic friendship with Abel Damoussi, a local business-man, fixer and carpet dealer, who smoothed their relations with the Moroccan government. The arrival by Abel one morning in a new green Jaguar XJS as a replacement for his rusty BMW confirmed that Eve Branson had persuaded her son to buy a local castle for £1.7 million in a deal brokered by the Moroccan.

Those antics and the personal disagreements passed unmentioned thanks to Branson's unspoken understanding with the journalists per-mitted to watch the preparations. In the surge of adulation for his latest attempt, only his heroism was mentioned. A one hundred page black binder lay on his hotel desk – 'My last will,' he choked – to encourage descriptions of 'a man, full of bravado and enthusiasm, ready to die in pursuit of his dream balloon flight around the world'. For the man with 'adventure in my blood', even his wife's disapproval and 'concern' for his children, were ignored. Everything could be sacrificed for his 'ego', commented one observer. 'Nothing will be achieved by us going round the world. We won't push barriers forward, but it will be a magnificent achievement.'

The take-off was perfectly choreographed. Standing near the cap-sule festooned with Virgin Cola cans, with a special link to ITN in London, Branson performed a long, emotional farewell. Just as he had posed endlessly with his wife and children in America and Japan, the man who said, 'I would never involve my family with the press', stood clutching his crying children, gulped back his tears and whis-pered loud enough for the microphones, 'I love you.' After another gulp, he added, 'Just make sure you mow the lawn, ready for a perfect landing when I get back.' His brave children waved. Holly Branson shared her father's bravery since, according to Branson, she had also 'cheated death when she plunged from a cliff' in the Carib-bean, catching herself on shrubs to avoid plunging into the sea. Minutes after the 'brave', 'courageous', 'daredevil', 'intrepid explorer' took off, ranking in the lengthy newspaper reports with those who had 'trekked into the dark and unmapped jungles of Africa', or 'climbed the highest mountains', or 'crossed the Arctic', or 'flew and sailed solo across oceans', Per Lindstrand asked ground control for the whereabouts of the lavatory paper for their round–the–world epic. It had been forgotten. Twenty hours later, the discomfort was abruptly reduced. Over the Atlas Mountains, the balloon was destabilised by draughts. Recovering control of the balloon was impossible. There was no alternative but to land in Algeria. The major impediment was forgetfulness by the ground staff to remove the safety clips holding the fuel tanks. In relative safety, as the balloon began to fall towards the desert, Alex Ritchie climbed on to the gantry of the capsule's protected, flat surface and removed the clips. Soon after, the capsule landed four hundred yards from a desert road.

Lindstrand and Ritchie struggled out of the capsule, dazed by the experience, to witness Branson jabbing the keys of his mobile telephone. Thirty years of practice and wisdom galvanised Branson in his quest for absolutes to utter his immortal sentences to the media: 'I'm so glad to be alive. I truly believe that Alex saved our lives.' In his world of hype, Branson had created a most lucrative crash landing. 'Alex risked his life to save us,' Branson repeated endlessly. No one was more surprised than Lindstrand and Ritchie because there had been barely any risk to Ritchie's life. Marooned in the desert, the incongruity of Branson's performance was startling. There had been no contemplation of escape from a Byronic death, no soulful lament about failure or even a moment of epiphany about survival. While Branson continued giving interviews on his telephone, the local commanders of the Algerian military and air force competed with offers of hospitality. The local governor of the province won the contest. Before he ended the day, Branson knew that his £1 million investment had attracted more attention worldwide than Pepsi's £200 million 'blue' campaign. More importantly, the media was remarkably sympathetic. The 'daredevil tycoon' who 'cheated death', thanks to a 'miracle at 30,000 feet', pledged he would 'have one more try after a family get-together at his luxury London home'. But the note to capture the love of *Sun* readers was his courage: 'I'm already past my ninth life so I realise I'm incredibly fortunate . . . The thing about life is that you have to live it to the full. If someone dies doing something they love, then you can take great comfort from that.' The day ended over a drink with the British ambassador in Algiers.

Branson returned to London in time to bid farewell to Cott. Branson's ambitions to sell Virgin Cola in America had throughout 1996 unsettled the Cott directors who were destabilised by the news that Gerry Pencer was dying of cancer. 'You're off your head going to America,' said Lester. 'You can't even succeed in Britain so you won't in Coke's own territory.' Branson's record in other countries encouraged pessimism. Virgin Cola's sales in France, Japan and Australia had not risen above 2.5 per cent. Guerrilla marketing had failed. The arguments between Cott and Virgin became persistent and ferocious. As each clause, sub-clause and phrase was used by Virgin's lawyers to dispute every decision in the joint venture, Umberto Aquino, Pencer's representative, realised that Branson had turned his guerrilla tactics upon Cott. With glee, Virgin's lawyers quibbled whether a working day started at midnight or 9 a.m., and about the intricacies of every cost. Repeatedly, Cott's directors attempted to discuss solutions, but Branson, with an air of sincerity, pleaded ignorance: 'I don't know anything about these problems.' Pencer's successors struggled to understand why their relations were strained. After all, their chief had enjoyed Branson's hospitality in Necker, Lester had eaten several meals with Branson and they were legally partners. Branson had even pontificated, 'if you strike a fair deal with people they'll come back for more'. But he did not seem to want a fair deal.

'They're on their way,' said Branson, delivering his familiar sentence of execution. The original, complicated contract devised by Abbott had been intended as the prelude to an advantageous divorce. Virgin intended to take over the cola business with minimum payment. There was, Simon Lester discovered, nothing unusual in Branson's technique. Disputing signed contracts, in Branson's opinion, was the privilege of the powerful, a justifiable tactic. That was how Virgin earned money. In Branson's opinion, partners deserved no special mercy.

Like their anonymous predecessors, the Cott directors were troubled by their misjudgement of Branson. On reflection, Lester realised that the tycoon was not particularly interesting. Branson uttered no insight into the world. There was no intellect, no spark which suggested greatness, not even distinctive curiosity. Only polite banalities which concealed a singular purpose of accumulating money and building an empire.

Defeating Cott, through negotiation and renegotiation, creating interminable conflict was 'part of the game'. Usually, the losers did not complain aloud. Public ridicule for being worsted by Branson was professional suicide, so the losers chose silence. Branson benefited from their reticence. The divorce, signed in January 1997, was blamed on 'diverging international strategies', because Virgin wanted to pursue 'more aggressive and radical marketing techniques'. Even the final £505,000 debt owed to Cott was disputed. Branson's self-confidence inured him to any antagonism. He was enraptured by his vision of a new glory, blind to the repercussions to his credibility of his hyperbole. The caravan had moved on.

19

Honesty and integrity

On 7 February 1997, Virgin was awarded the West Coast rail franchise. 'He's got the track record for service and reliability,' smiled Sir George Young, the transport minister. The general election was imminent and the politician eagerly posed with the heroic entrepreneur beside *Mission Impossible*, an ageing locomotive freshly painted in Virgin's colours. Branson offered the minister a glass of champagne. 'He's paid over the odds,' Young told his officials, 'and he's enhanced our credibility.' Smiling beside the minister, Britain's biggest train operator was undergoing a metamorphosis.

As the owner of a monopoly on key routes, Branson expunged any mention of competition and spoke instead about his commitment to public services. 'People in this country,' he said, 'will now witness a remarkable ten years in the history of the railways.' Solemnly, he promised, evoking images of Virgin's charity, to invest £1 billion 'to build the foundations of the revolutionary plans we have for Virgin trains' and double the number of passengers by 2010. Particularly significant, Branson pledged that there would be 'no increase' in fares and that within one year Virgin Trains would hit a magic target of 90 per cent punctuality.

Reality soured the promises on Virgin's first operational day of the West Coast franchise, 10 March 1997. Marshalled at Euston Station, attractive Virgin girls, dressed in red costumes, waited to offer champagne to passengers arriving on the 4.47 a.m. from Holyhead. 'We regret to announce a breakdown on the line,' explained the familiar tannoy voice across the station. By the time weary travellers arrived nearly two hours late, few were keen to sip Virgin's cheap wine or bless Richard Branson for that morning's gimmick, a £17.50 return ticket from London to Manchester.

The brown envelopes enclosing redundancy notices were not Virgin gimmicks. Virgin's business plan depended on annual profits of £29 million. Overnight, the railway's traditional hierarchy was abolished. Without consulting the trade unions, a breed disliked by Branson, the Cross Country and West Coast franchises were merged to save money and 25 per cent of their staff, scathingly damned by Brian Barrett as 'pen pushers', were declared redundant. Annoying British Rail's loyal managers by dismissal or demotion with a wage cut did not appear to trouble Barrett or Virgin Atlantic's financial controllers and engineers who had been seconded as storm troopers for eight weeks to the railway. Reclassifying supervisors as team leaders with a reduction in their annual income from £14,000 to £11,000, was Virgin's priority rather than fulfilling promises of choc ices, mobile telephones and video screens with smiles and serviettes to passengers. Restaurant cars were removed, the telephone inquiry staff in Liverpool were dismissed, experienced production managers at a depot in London were replaced by novices and the budget allocated to GNER in Scotland for servicing Virgin trains was reviewed. Barrett's report about the cuts at the first board meeting was optimistic. Murphy, Whitehorn and their bankers nodded approvingly. No one was surprised that Branson, the president of the company, was absent. Also absent was anyone experienced in directing train operations. Branson's preoccupation was with punctual profits. The trains would have to run themselves as, some evidently imagined, they had for over one hundred years.

In the days before the 1997 general election, Branson's austerity was ignored at the Labour Party's election headquarters. The politicians' preoccupation was to secure Branson's endorsement of Tony Blair. Ever since the Labour Party's research in Essex, after the 1992 election defeat, revealed that Branson was an idol of those working classes who had failed to vote for Labour, Branson had been assiduously wooed. Five years later, the telephone call inviting him to pose in front of a newly painted train at Euston with Tony Blair, four days before the election, surprisingly excited Branson. For good commercial reasons he had never endorsed any political party and denied making any financial contributions. Politics was a superficial concern to a man who was never known to read political biographies. His preoccupation was limited to how the politicians could affect his fortunes. Since so many of his monopoly businesses – airlines, railways, radio and television – depended upon government concessions, it had been sensible over the previous twenty years to woo the Conservatives and the benefits had been mutual.

To guarantee access to his patrons in the anticipated new Labour government, Branson effortlessly abandoned his relations with Malcolm Rifkind, John McGregor and George Young just before their inevitable election defeat. Winners have no loyalty to losers. The Labour leader, Branson knew, was a safe bet and he was anxious for history to record himself standing beside the next Prime Minister, albeit in a venue where Branson posed as a beneficiary of the Conservatives.

As the two smiled for photographers on the platform at Euston Station, speaking perfunctorily about an imminent rugby match, Branson hoped that Labour would confer the same benefits on his fortunes as the Conservatives. Blair's warmth as they travelled towards Milton Keynes encouraged Branson's hopes while dashing Blair's desire. Contrary to expectations, Branson failed to publicly support the Labour Party.

After 9 p.m. on 1 May 1997, as the predictions of a Labour landslide were flashed on television, Branson reassessed his strategy. Labour would govern Britain for at least a decade. He needed to be on the inside; he wanted to share the spotlight. Without any formal invitation, he dashed from Holland Park to the Royal Festival Hall, to enter Labour's celebration party, sought out the television news cameras and gave live interviews indicating his genuine and entrenched support for Blair. As he circulated through the crowds, Branson did not sense their resentment. Many Labour stalwarts watching the interviews had been irritated by his gratuitous appearance after refusing to publicly endorse Blair. 'Mr goody-two-shoes Branson,' as Dennis Skinner smirked. 'There is something about that fellow that I just cannot cling to. He seems to have his finger in every pie.' The distrust was not alleviated by Branson's response to the roars that welcomed the new Prime Minister. 'Not much point in hanging around then,' coughed Branson and departed.

Branson was unconcerned by the snide whispers among Labour insiders. His popularity was rock solid. An opinion poll in 1997 would show that 47 per cent of those questioned favoured Branson, the standard bearer of honesty and integrity, as London's first mayor, far ahead of Ken Livingstone, the second favourite, with 15 per cent of the votes. Momentarily, Branson toyed with the idea of standing. To satisfy his vanity, he consulted a few admirers but cold reason halted his daydream. Throughout his life he had eschewed public scrutiny of his finances and there were a thousand good reasons not to take the risk. He brushed the notion aside. Instead he asked Joan to invite the Blairs to Necker. Unfortunately, Cherie Blair would politely reject the invitation but since there were certain to be invitations to Downing Street, Chequers and Buckingham Palace there would be other opportunities to lobby for his commercial interests. His popularity, he knew, could be more profitably used to secure commercial advantages from politicians both in London and, equally importantly, in Washington.

Like many British tycoons, Branson paid substantial amounts to establish relationships with American politicians. Hiring Ken Levine, a Democrat lawyer, and Jeff Shane, a former official in the Department of Transportation, he had lobbied congressmen, senators and their staff on Capitol Hill who were interested in airlines and could be counted as allies to support Virgin Atlantic and undermine British Airways.

His offensive had started two years earlier, on 4 July 1995. Senator Larry Pressler, the chairman of the aviation sub-committee, was welcomed to Holland Park. The senator for South Dakota was touring Europe to gather support for 'open skies' agreements between America and Europe. Since Branson was a player in America's most important foreign airline market, the senator invited himself for a meeting.

On a hot day, Branson escorted the Oxford-educated politician through his large London garden, enthralling his guest with tales about his ballooning exploits and casually mentioning that a manufacturer in Sioux Falls, Dakota, was a supplier of equipment. 'I love people like you,' gurgled Pressler. 'Risk takers are what we need to crush the big airline corporations. We need people like you to cut fares by half.' Branson smiled. 'I'm sure we can count on your support for open skies,' continued the American. 'I don't support open skies,' mumbled Branson. 'American carriers should not have more slots at Heathrow.' The senator was surprised. 'But you're for deregulation?' he asked. 'Oh, absolutely,' gushed Branson. In the remaining minutes, Branson adroitly camouflaged his contradiction to disguise his self-interest, and regained Pressler as an ally. 'The senator returned,' Branson was told by his lawyers in Washington, 'spreading the word on the Hill that you're good.'

Two years later, in summer 1997, Branson knew that British Airways' alliance with American Airlines had become mired by the aggressive intervention of the European Commission and the self-interested lobbying of United Airlines, Lufthansa and Branson himself. The alliance, Ayling had been told, would only be approved if British Airways accepted crippling reductions on its operations at Heathrow. Alternatively, BA would be compelled by Washington to accept 'open skies' as the price for the alliance.

To protect Virgin's duopoly, Branson had opposed 'open skies', a policy he uncomfortably shared with British Airways. But in June 1997, in his campaign to defeat BA's alliance with American Airlines, he somersaulted and declared his conditional support of 'open skies'. The opportunity was provided by the arrival of ten Congressmen, members of the House of Representatives aviation subcommittee, in London with their wives and staff to investigate why Britain, unlike thirty-one other countries, refused to sign an 'open skies' agreement. Branson and Ayling were invited to meet the politicians for breakfast at the American embassy. Among the group was Representative James Oberstar, a senior Democrat suspicious of big airlines misusing their computers. 'Just the man who understands dirty tricks,' was the message to Branson from Ken Levine in Washington. 'Let's look after them,' Branson told his staff. Their employer's requirements for the group of forty-three were precisely understood.

Wearing electric blue 'Best Dad' socks against a beige suit, Branson arrived for breakfast at the American embassy in Mayfair with an entourage reflecting his importance. Congregated around were Francis Farrow, his British lawyer, Ken Levine, his Washington lawyer and lobbyist, and Barry Humphreys, the former economist at the CAA boasting particular expertise about British Airways. Humphreys's recruitment by Virgin had aroused protests about the conflict of interest which had not displeased Branson. In the background, undermining Ayling's presence, stood Freddie Laker, the symbolic victim of BA's oppression. The whole group nodded in unison as their paymaster spoke with Representative Oberstar, oblivious to his inconsistencies. 'We're a struggling small airline,' he told the politician, 'and we've succeeded despite the worst that BA and the British government have thrown at us.' Oberstar was noticeably impressed, unaware that, on the contrary, Virgin's success owed much to the last Conservative government. Whatever influence Ayling, standing stiffly on the side, might have hoped to score, had disappeared by the end of that night.

'Come and stand by King Richard's throne,' urged Ken Levine. Branson's love of parties and showmanship had combined to offer the forty-three Americans unforgettable hospitality in the Tower of London, hired for the night by Virgin. Before dinner, Branson had joked as his guests gazed at the Crown Jewels and Britain's historic legacy and complimented Branson for arranging unique access. Branson, they agreed, was a superstar and, as Branson himself appreciated, exaggerating his 'success factor' delighted the Americans. Ever since his American publicity machine had negotiated his appearance on countless American television news and talk programmes featuring his wacky smiles alongside Princess Diana and a variety of celebrities, Branson had won a priceless gift for a Briton in America: recognition as 'a fun and friendly guy'. His after-dinner speech reflected the self-confidence of his high ratings.

John Duncan, the chairman of the subcommittee, had flown to London on United Airlines and his baggage had been lost. 'If you'd flown Virgin,' chided Branson, working his theme vigorously, 'you'd have your bags and you'd have experienced a special massage from a Virgin girl.' The spontaneous laughter and the gossip – 'Richard's effective in the subtleties,' they raved – compared favourably with Ayling's omission to invite the group to a meal or even a drink. Branson was guaranteed a warm welcome when he arrived in Washington later that month for a Congressional hearing about the proposed alliance.

Rushing on a tight timetable through the Congressional offices of Senators Mike DeWine, Robert Torricelli and Slade Gorton, Virgin's chief executive was billed by Ken Levine as 'the billionaire and daredevil balloonist who heads Britain's second biggest airline'. Branson did not correct the mistake. Out of the eighty-four million passengers leaving Britain in 1997, 29.6 million were carried by British Airways, 7.6 million by Britannia Airways and just 2.7 million by Virgin Atlantic. The American politicians believed that Virgin Atlantic owned over one hundred big jets, not a mere fifteen. Without the hype, Branson would not have been welcomed into their offices.

Branson had fashioned a plausible argument for Washington. Masking his opposition to 'open skies' – to protect Virgin's shared monopoly at Heathrow – he urged politicians to embrace true 'open skies' by allowing foreign airlines, including Virgin, to fly domestic routes within America. The prospect of Congress changing the laws to allow foreign ownership of American airlines, Branson knew, was zero. No different, in fact, from European governments forbidding Americans from owning airlines in their continent. That similarity was ignored. His stagecraft was brilliantly judged.

Despite his business disappointments in America – music, cola, retail, cinemas and film production – Branson boasted that he could find sales where Herb Kelleher and all the other American airlines had failed. 'We'll invest $250 million in 'Virgin America' to fill the literally thousands of gaps left by Southwest,' he assured his hosts. The notion of Branson filling Kelleher's gaps was derisory, not least because no American had succeeded. However, hype was Branson's oxygen. Even the most powerful politicians, exulted Branson, did not question folk heroes and that gained him access to Senator John McCain, an important player. Branson waited patiently in the domed lobby for McCain to come from the floor of the Senate. 'I support your ideas on deregulation,' said the Vietnam hero, 'but it won't happen early.' Like others on the Hill, McCain overestimated the size of Branson's business and believed that Virgin was a low fare competitor like Laker. After all, Branson claimed the credit for a fall of 40 per cent in transatlantic fares over the previous ten years. Branson naturally never mentioned that some of Virgin's fares were 25 per cent higher than Europe's airlines'. 'He's got deep pockets to withstand the losses,' McCain's aide mentioned to the senator, beguiled that Branson's casual dress authenticated a man of enormous wealth rather than one lurching through a perennial cash crisis. 'So what's your next big adventure?' asked McCain, imagining another global balloon flight. 'We're opening some more Megastores,' replied Branson. McCain looked puzzled.

Branson's next stop was Patrick Murphy, the senior civil servant responsible for aviation in the Department of Transportation. Outside Murphy's tenth-floor window, moored over the Potomac river, Branson had positioned a Zeppelin emblazoned with the Virgin logo. The stunt was successful. Despite twenty-six years in Washington's civil aviation bureaucracy, Murphy's smile was genuine when the tycoon entered his office. As one of the architects of deregulation, Murphy knew every airline boss, remembering especially those who, in the early 1990s, lost $13 billion on failed ventures. 'I welcome all entrepreneurs, Mr Branson,' quipped Murphy benignly, 'but I've had dozens of influential and rich men pass through this office telling me they're going to start an airline. We like them. You only need $200 million to start an airline. But nearly all of them fail. Why are you any different?' Murphy handed his flamboyant visitor a large photo album from his coffee table. Branson flicked through the pictures of the airlines – New York Air, Trump, Air Cal, PSA, Eastern. 'All gone,' laughed Murphy. Eighty-two airlines had disappeared leaving outdated logos as their tombstones.

Branson grimaced. Murphy was the face of reality. Unlike the other recipients of his script, Murphy considered that Branson's offer to start a 'Virgin America' airline was fantasy. Since the crash of a ValuJet in Florida in 1996, not a single new American airline had been established while seven small airlines, still struggling to copy Southwest, feared annihilation by the aggressive big operators. Murphy was, however, polite. 'We'd like you here, Mr Branson, but your government is blocking an "open skies" agreement.' Branson's support for the British veto was well understood by Murphy. The restrictions at Heathrow, Murphy knew, suited Branson. 'You're only demanding access to America's domestic market,' Murphy smiled at the likeable tycoon, 'to stall any open skies agreement.' Branson did not demur. Like all airline operators, Branson only supported deregulation if he could profit and he seemed to have won. Since the British government opposed an 'open skies' agreement, Murphy would recommend that British Airways' alliance be vetoed. With the assurance that the British airline would be crippled, Branson returned to Congress. In the global airline business, Virgin was a flea, but he had assumed the influence of a major player.

During the summer of 1997, Branson was scheduled to testify at three Senate and Congressional committee hearings. Ayling's refusal to attend the first Senate hearing rebounded favourably upon Branson. His aides spread the story that Ayling was unwilling to face the opposition because, they whispered, of dirty tricks. Ayling's non-appearance proves, added Branson thrilled by his rival's maladroitness, the monopolist's arrogance. 'BA's secret plan,' continued Branson, exuding his natural inclination to exaggerate, 'is to cover the globe and stifle competition.'

Entering the imposing committee room for the second Congressional hearing, Branson discarded the last trace of self-restraint. With a flicker of anger, he told America's politicians 'the merger from hell' perpetrated by the 'unrepentant' British Airways was 'one of the most outrageous developments in the history of air transportation'. For good measure, he accused Ayling of lying and predicted that BA would pay a heavy fine in his anti-trust action in New York for its 'illegal methods'. Not one politician appeared to disagree. Ayling, Branson expected, would dig his own grave.

Ayling had not attracted much respect in Washington. The new ethnic art tail designs on the British Airways jets were derided and the Briton's management of BA's previous alliance with US Air had been unsatisfactory. Ayling, however, had offered concessions and support for 'open skies'. The proposed alliance, he told the politicians, would encourage 'market entry not market exit' for the alliance's competitors because BA and American Airlines would reduce their combined transatlantic slots at Heathrow from 62 per cent to 42 per cent over five years. Ayling's offer unsettled Branson. Branson's assertion that BA wanted to keep its 'cosy position' at Heathrow and deny access to other American carriers appeared questionable.

Ayling and Branson were asked to attend a third Congressional hearing a few days later. Soon after their arrival, the hearing was cancelled. Ayling was not pleased to have pointlessly returned across the Atlantic. He was noticeably curt to Mary Walsh, the Transportation Committee's staff member who announced the cancellation. After watching Ayling indignantly leave the chamber, Branson rose. 'Let's all go for a drink,' he chirped. The contrast between the glowering corporate chief executive and the relaxed buccaneer electrified the room. All the committee's staff trooped into the Bull and Feathers for a boisterous session. Embarrassing Ayling gave Branson pleasure. Targeting Mary Walsh, Branson flattered the woman with banter and praise. Soon after, his photograph appeared in her office. British Airways' fate, Branson thought, was sealed.

After his success in Washington Branson was especially fearless in his defence of any threat to Virgin's immaculacy. So many blemishes threatened to erupt by September 1997. On his return to London he resolved to remedy one flaw by engaging the assistance of Rory McCarthy, his ballooning partner. Over the previous six months, their relationship had cooled.

In spring 1997, Virgin's plan to manufacture jeans was terminated after Levi's, the world's biggest jeans manufacturer, announced factory closures. Virgin's researchers had failed to grasp the evidence that sales of jeans across the world had slumped. Branson did not hide his disappointment. As Victory's share price dropped towards 40 pence, the company's executives were dismissed and replacements hired to mastermind Virgin's new strategy: to become a major player in Europe's $5 billion casual wear industry. Virgin was competing to beat Calvin Klein, Tommy Hilfiger, Gap and DKNY. Branson's publicists spoke about 'removing the adversarial nature of the business' and 'doing it better than anyone else'. The new range was to be launched in February 1998.

McCarthy, Branson knew, was still gripped by his association with Branson-the-celebrity and excited that his Victory shares were worth £30 million. Although Branson had decided not to invite McCarthy on another balloon challenge, he snapped at McCarthy's repeated offer 'Is there anything else we can invest in?' He could exploit McCarthy's friendship to finance V2, his languishing music business.

V2's only success, 'Word Gets Around' by the Stereophonics, had cost over £20 million. With no other hits, Jeremy Pearce was compelled to deny 'we're no more than a rich man's play-thing'. During 1996, Robert Devereux, Branson's brother-in-law, had approached Salomons, the bankers, proffering a thick business plan to raise over £50 million but had been rejected as 'unrealistic and too optimistic'. Salvation, Branson decided, lay with McCarthy.

'V2 needs money,' Stephen Murphy told McCarthy, dangling the bait on Branson's orders.

'Is it going to be successful?' asked McCarthy.

'Richard's done it once. He can do it again,' replied the finance director loftily. 'He had the Stones, Janet Jackson, Phil Collins and all the rest. No problem. Stereophonics proves it.'

Branson's personal attempts to lure other stars had failed but Murphy did not feel obliged to reveal that downside, especially to McCarthy. The ambitious accountant resented the socialite's easy access to Branson. 'I don't see why Richard spends so much time with McCarthy,' Murphy had told Trevor Abbott. 'He's no good.' McCarthy ignored the dislike. Trusting Branson as a 'close friend' and 'soul mate', he was a believer, keen to survive in the cabal.

Eight months after Branson had first asked McCarthy to invest, McCarthy signed an agreement on 3 July 1997 to buy a 33 per cent stake in V2 for £55 million. Branson could draw the money over two years. The source of McCarthy's money, Branson knew, was the future sale by the McCarthy Corporation of Q-zar, a computer war game.

McCarthy's money required a reward. 'Come to Necker,' said Branson to McCarthy, soon after banking the first £3 million. He would be invited with the parents of friends of Branson's children. Branson loved playing host on the tiny island's dazzling white beaches, offering every sport, endless food and buckets of champagne. Most visitors were overwhelmed by the Balinese style house, the beautiful bedrooms and Mick Jagger's signature, scrawled like graffiti on a wall. The major blemish that month was the break-up of his sister's marriage. Robert Devereux, the architect of many unsuccessful businesses in Virgin, had abandoned Vanessa for a twenty-eight-year-old accountant employed by Virgin. Abrupt expulsion from the company was not an option. Branson's brother-in-law knew too many secrets. He would remain employed while his severance was carefully negotiated.

McCarthy, as intended, returned to Britain convinced that Branson remained 'somebody special'. Three months later, McCarthy's status deteriorated. His source of the cash for V2 evaporated after his anticipated income from the sale of Q-zar did not materialise. Branson's plan for financing his music business was unravelling just as Victory Vie, his cosmetics brand, was disintegrating.

The launch party for Victory Vie in October 1997 had not featured the Spice Girls and Elton John as Virgin's publicists hoped but Debbie Flett, a reliable model, covered in a towel. Unlike every other cosmetic brand, Virgin had not contracted a glamorous 'face' for sustained advertising. Branson was short of money. Instead, Stuart Higgins, the editor of the *Sun*, had devoted one page to Virgin cosmetics with a photograph of cream being spread over Branson's beard – an original image to seduce young women. Virgin's publicity that 'Vie is already proving what an amazing money-making machine Virgin is' was untrue. Branson's executives at the dreary launch party in Holland Park whispered doom. The projection in Virgin's glossy promotions of one hundred shops dedicated to sell five hundred cosmetic products, they confessed, was unrealisable; as were their predictions that fifteen stores would open before Christmas. Only six shops would be ready. Shortly after, the news worsened. Just four shops opened. 'The original concept,' Branson was told, 'is too bland. No one likes the shops. Folks say they're drab.' Branson nodded, but there were doubts whether he understood. He knew nothing about cosmetics or clothes and his history in retail had been poor. He relied upon others.

'They're screwing up,' Brad Rosser told Stephen Murphy about the Waroms, the architects of the cosmetics idea. 'We need to appoint someone above them.' The accountant froze. 'Fuck it. Let's see how it goes.' Branson, the financial adviser knew, would support his opinion. It was a good moment to squeeze McCarthy whose attempt to float his own company had been abandoned. Their fortunes had been reversed.

'I need money,' McCarthy told Branson.

'I'll think about it,' Branson replied. This was a mess, Branson realised. The Victory Corporation, owning the clothes and cosmetics companies, needed cash and the sponsor of V2, the music company, possessed no money. Virgin's cash-free investment and its reputation were endangered.

Branson pondered a classic package to 'protect his downside'. Four days later, he offered the deal. Virgin would invest £14.5 million in Victory if McCarthy agreed to transfer the company's ownership to Virgin. In effect, McCarthy would be handing over 56 per cent of the shares and his £20 million cash investment to Branson who until then had invested only £1,000. McCarthy would be left with a powerless 25 per cent of the company. Reluctantly, McCarthy agreed. To avoid publicity, the deal would be announced just after Christmas 1997. Nothing should ruffle the impression of success.

Fame and his unblemished reputation for integrity and triumph had become crucial ingredients in the ceaseless search for investors to finance Branson's expansion. 'We're not stretching the brand,' Whitehorn pouted, 'we're building it as a global British brand name' The mood in the stock markets after the first untroubled months of the new Labour government was optimistic, creating the perfect opportunity for Branson to join the stars. The foreboding caused by the flaws – trains, cola, clothes and cosmetics – was temporarily erased by two spectacular deals.

By 1997, Virgin Radio's accumulated losses over four years were £22 million. Despite the transfer to FM, the radio station's managers admitted that its programmes and audience ratings were disappointing. After four years, its audience share had fallen from 3.5 per cent to 2.8 per cent. Branson had again failed to create a media success. That caused him little concern. Virgin's valuable asset was the FM licence. The desire by Apax and J. P. Morgan, the venture capitalists, to recover £16.3 million, their original investment and their loans, compelled Branson to find money. Since he possessed only limited cash, he mentioned in 1996 his usual remedy, flotation of the station for £70 million. Nothing happened and by April 1997, the representatives of Branson's off-shore trusts, apparently acting on Branson's orders, concluded their negotiations with the bankers – the original shareholders – to buy their 25 per cent stake with temporary loans. The agreed value of Virgin Radio was £80 million. Just two weeks after the deal was completed, the bankers were amazed to hear that Branson had welcomed an £87 million bid from Capital Radio for his station. Not only had the original bankers notionally lost £2 million but many were surprised how Branson, the campaigner against monopolies, could encourage Capital to buy its major rival and establish a monopoly in London. But Branson was never minded to explain or even consider the inconsistencies. After Capital's bid was referred to the Monopolies Commission on 31 July 1997, Branson's lawyers argued that the combined companies' domination was in London's interest. To deflect bad publicity, he announced that he was just 'weeks away' from launching two television channels for music and travel to rival Sky by the end of the year. Nothing transpired.

By early October 1997, Branson knew that the Monopolies Commission would recommend that the takeover should be rejected. To extract his profit for the FM licence, his footwork was fast. First, he recruited Chris Evans to introduce the Virgin Radio breakfast show. 'There's no secret about it,' said Branson, 'we plan to give Radio 1 a run for its money.' Secondly, eight weeks later, Evans announced his successful purchase of Virgin Radio for £81 million, financed by loans. Branson and Apax would each retain a 20 per cent interest. The remainder was owned by Evans. Branson's profit, thanks to Lord Chalfont's casting vote three years earlier, was about £40 million, another bonus from a government franchise.

By any reckoning, his coup was impressive. Those who criticised the demise of Victory because of Virgin's poor management were silenced by such an exceptional deal. At critical moments his credibility was always enhanced by unexpected coups. The second was the flotation of Virgin Express, his cut-price European airline, on the American stock market to recover his investment. Supposedly, it was also a launch pad for 'Virgin America'.

The prospectus for Virgin Express, valued at $216 million (£127 million), looked appealing. Branson had bought the company only the previous year for about $65 million. Hugh Welburn's accurate warnings about the old airline based in Brussels had proved perceptive but luck appeared to have cured the airline's plight. Sabena, the loss-making Belgian airline, asked Branson to run its unprofitable route between Brussels and London. The deal enhanced the flotation. Over six months, sales increased 305 per cent and Virgin Express's capacity, using fifteen leased aircraft, doubled. In the prospectus, Branson suggested that the airline's profits had increased by up to 142 per cent. The impression of such success was achieved by the brokers offering confused comparisons of the airline's previous financial performance. The results of six months in 1997 were set alongside three months in 1996.

The airline's admitted deficiencies were considerable. Virgin Express was heavily dependent upon Sabena, it was unknown beyond Brussels and the company would not pay dividends. Buying the shares was a declaration of faith in Branson, especially as he and the trustees planned immediately to bank $50 million of the $87 million raised to cover his purchase price, while retaining 53.4 per cent of the shares to control the company.

The nature of Branson's promises to the shareholders was important, because in the aftermath of his victory against British Airways in 1992, Branson staked his reputation for honesty and straightforwardness on his explicit promises.

Prospective shareholders were told by Branson that his objective was to make Virgin Express 'the leading low-fare scheduled airline in Europe'. Although his solemn promise of overtaking British Airways and Lufthansa within two years had been abandoned, it was only a matter of time, he insisted, before Virgin Express would be serving one hundred destinations at fares up to 75 per cent cheaper than national carriers. 'Virgin Express,' he boasted, 'has £40 million in the bank and Virgin Atlantic is throwing off cash.'

Doubters were urged by Branson to scan Virgin's record which 'is so strong that we can find backers to fund 100 per cent of any expansion while we will be able to keep majority control'. He continued, 'We are now flying on fifteen different routes and fares have come down by 50 per cent. We would love to be able to offer it to the British public . . . if we could ever get the slots to do it.' His lament, 'sadly . . . we have no slots in England', was not quite accurate. He had closed down his operations at Gatwick and, ignoring Hugh Welburn's suggestions, did not want to fly from Luton or Stansted against real competitors, easyJet and Ryanair. 'Too much optimism and not enough realism,' complained Welburn.

For fourteen years, Welburn's quiet, thoughtful reasoning had been accepted by Branson. The publicised plans for Virgin Atlantic's flights to Australia and Las Vegas had been dropped on Welburn's advice as unprofitable. Branson had sided with Welburn in rows with Trevor Abbott. 'You're meddling in a business you don't understand,' Welburn had angrily told the former finance director. 'Controlling costs and pushing up yields is the key in airlines.' But Abbott had been unforgiving and successfully urged Branson to ignore Welburn's caution about Virgin Express. Branson abandoned Welburn's blueprint for a new airline and instead bought a decrepit company based in Brussels, owning old aircraft and burdened by Belgium's draconian legal restrictions on employment and taxation. The final break between the two men was sparked by Branson's endorsement of Jonathan Ornstein's excitable style of management.

Ornstein's orders from Branson were plain: 'Cut costs and offer low fares.' To obey the command, the American fired experienced crews, offered low wages for their replacements and diverted the jets to other countries for servicing. To Ornstein's surprise, the Belgian staff became truculent.

'You fucking Belgians,' Ornstein screamed at meetings, cursing the endless restrictions imposed by the local authorities and trade unions, all spouting different languages. Badly paid and badly treated, even the replacement crews had abandoned Branson. 'We've got to work with them, not fight them,' soothed Branson who relied on Ornstein for a marketing plan and the management of the planes and staff. Quietly, as the costs increased, Welburn resigned.

None of those problems was apparent in the prospectus for investors. Applications for Virgin Express shares were ten times oversubscribed. The $15 shares rose rapidly towards $25. 'We put our toe in the water with Virgin Express,' chortled Branson, 'and investors

– far from living to regret it – have seen a 60 per cent growth on their value of shares.'

Once again, it appeared, Branson had pulled off another coup. He owned a valuable airline at effectively no cost. No outsider could imagine the growing turmoil within his empire.

20

Indelible tarnish

Tuesday, 9 December 1997, was a warning.

In Marrakesh, Branson was in suite 104 on the ground floor of the Sheraton hotel. As usual, there were plates of food and drinks in one of the eight rooms for his guests. Selected journalists and a television crew had been invited to witness the hero signing yet another last will before he was driven to the latest, biggest balloon for another launch to win the global title. Everyone present was aware of his recent argument with Per Lindstrand.

'You can't inflate the balloon during the day,' said Lindstrand, wary of the unpredictable air currents. 'We'll lose it.'

'I'll take full responsibility if we do,' replied Branson.

'Tell that to the crew,' insisted Lindstrand.

Branson drove across to the Moroccan air force base. 'I take full responsibility,' he said.

By midday, the inflation was still not completed. Branson was ready. A mobile telephone rang. The cameraman started filming. Branson's face froze. An unexpected gust of wind, he was told, had struck the partially inflated balloon and, one by one, the sixteen anchor ropes had snapped. The craft had risen and sailed off in the right direction, but unmanned. 'Don't throw my phone at the wall,' begged Whitehorn, fearful of Branson's temper. His usual quest to shift the blame, everyone silently agreed, would be difficult.

In Britain, travellers on that day's Virgin trains knew who to blame for the delays, bad food, locked lavatories and hefty price increases. Branson's denial of responsibility was as usual a topic of his victims' conversation.

On the Moroccan air force base later on the afternoon of the same day, Branson was standing in an aircraft hangar with Per Lindstrand. A telephone rang. The news was worse still.

In a Surrey woodland, Trevor Abbott's corpse had been found

hanging from a tree. The forty-seven-year-old father of five children had committed suicide. His decision to publicly display his torment was revenge. 'Claire,' he said of his estranged wife, 'broke my heart and Richard broke my back.' Between that verbal confession and putting a noose around his neck, Abbott had completed an eight-minute message on his personal video recorder.

Branson, plainly distraught, was silent for some time, staggered by shock. 'Trevor's hanged himself,' he said finally. 'God, he was in my office a week ago. He looked terrible. He even cried. God, I feel awful that I didn't notice anything. We just shook hands and he left. Now it's too late.' He constantly repeated the understandable lament of the survivor: 'God, I just didn't know.'

Critics and admirers alike agreed that the Virgin empire owed an incalculable debt to a sadly desperate man. Even Branson had acknowledged Abbott's indispensability. The Keeper of the Secrets had secured a substantial stake in the offshore trusts. But in the months before his death, Abbott had been unable to persuade Branson to buy his shares for cash. As Abbott's business ventures faltered, Branson continued to reject his pleas for money. Like so many who thrive in the company of a tycoon, Abbott had discovered he lacked five essential qualities to emulate his former employer: ruthless energy, egoism, skill, instinct and, above all, a compelling perform-ance. Over previous months, he had also discovered his lack of leverage against Branson. Abbott might know secrets but he would fear embarrassment, so remained silent. To buccaneers, men without leverage are not entitled to loyalty.

At a memorial service seven weeks later, in the chapel of Cranleigh school in Surrey, Branson was only noticeable by his near invisibility. Seated at the back, he had not contributed to the collection of tributes. Abbott's farewell recorded on a video before his suicide had been discomforting. After a message to his children, he had ended, 'They don't want me at home and they don't want me at Virgin. I must go now.' Branson stayed only briefly at the wake.

Branson had nothing to fear from Abbott's death. On the contrary, cynics speculated that a potential time bomb had been defused. He returned to Holland Park untroubled by any repercussions. Even Abbott's recorded suicide 'note' on the video would remain a secret. Branson's routine was undisturbed, thanks in part to his wife's family.

Joan Templeman's brother John was employed as a driver and

odd-job man; a niece was the nanny; Rose Templeman, a sister, was always available to help; and Dorothy Templeman, another of Joan's sisters, and her partner Simon, cooked in the basement kitchen, serving as a canteen for the staff. Simon's menu, generously called 'family cooking', was unvaried, reflecting the unimportance of food for Branson. Spaghetti, chicken and salad with water, tea or Virgin Cola to drink. Joan's mother was accommodated in a house nearby.

Deftly, his Glaswegian wife's image had been nurtured as part of the performance. To prevent any mishaps, the friendly woman who attracted genuine warmth was never allowed to speak on her own account. Instead, Branson and Whitehorn were her spokesmen. In their crafted description, Joan was described as an 'intensely private person', the 'only person in the world who's totally unimpressed with Richard' and 'a very powerful figure' who in 1990 'put her foot down' and forbade any further risk-taking exploits. The artifice also required a suitable comment about her husband's flirtatiousness which had become aggressive and publicised.

At a recent party in the Roof Gardens, Branson had pushed cubes of ice down the back of a woman's dress and smirked, 'Let me retrieve that for you.' His hand plunged down. 'I cringed as I felt his fingers grappling against my bare skin,' recalled Carole Aye Maung, 'as he shoved his bony hand down the back of my dress.' Inches before he reached his target, Aye Maung pulled away. 'You don't seem to like me very much,' said Branson. 'No. I just don't like people sticking their hands down my back without my approval.' Branson was unconcerned. In business, he was accustomed to rebuffs and it was similar with women. 'Don't tell Joan where I am,' he smiled, taking a cigarette from another guest. 'She's looking for me because she wants to go home. There are some amazing women here, aren't there?'

The adjective most often applied to Joan Branson was 'sassy'. Joan, the public was told, copes with 'the inevitable rumours about his wandering eye. She knows Richard is flirtatious but knows it never leads anywhere. If he wants to have a bit of fun, she won't interfere.' In private she appeared less tolerant. Hearing from a friend about the invention of a chip which could, within one yard, position a person anywhere on the globe, she looked at her husband and jokingly said, 'I'll fix one on to Richard. Then I'll know which bedroom he's in.'

To prove her ordinariness, she even arrived 'by chance' at Self-ridges just as Branson was showing a journalist his 'normal' activity of checking Victory's latest range of clothes. Joan was concerned whether the clothes she had bought for her husband were suitable. In the brief conversation, she explained her late arrival at a formal Buckingham Palace dinner because she insisted on cooking and serving her children's meal before leaving her home. Holly, her daughter, was fifteen years old and Sam was twelve.

Few old friends disputed that celebrity had altered Branson. His use of the royal 'we', first noticed by his friends in the 1980s, reflected his changed personality. But even the excessive self-indulgence had not prepared some for Branson's behaviour after Alex Ritchie's memorial service.

During a practice jump in Marrakesh in January 1998, Ritchie's parachute had become entangled and he crash landed. For eleven weeks, doctors in London had struggled vainly to prevent his death. Branson was naturally upset by the conclusion. One year earlier, Ritchie had been hailed by Branson as 'the man who saved my life'. Ritchie's sons were nevertheless sad that Branson visited their father only three times in hospital before he died and were unsettled why Branson, after the memorial service on 12 April 1998, was hesitating to compensate them as a goodwill gesture, although there was no legal obligation. To their satisfaction, Branson eventually made an ex gratia payment. Some blamed another cultural revolution within Virgin.

Branson's personal relations had in the past been secured by shared financial interests but cloaked by the parties and fun. However, the new recruits to Branson's cabal showed little sense of kinship. Dour money men, intent on maximising Virgin's profits and their personal bonuses – 'gold diggers' was one description – had replaced those early disciples attracted to the Virgin gospel. Overseeing that new breed was Stephen Murphy. The accountant's cold sharpness appealed to Branson. Murphy, feared by Rory McCarthy as 'a shark and a genius', could be relied upon. Murphy enjoyed squeezing.

'We need more money for V2,' Murphy told McCarthy.

'How much?' asked McCarthy.

'£75 million,' replied Murphy without a blink.

Branson's new company was unstuck. The new music industry was more complicated than Branson had anticipated. The boom in compact discs had passed and the high prices were deterring young people. V2's expensive launch of Tin Star, a poor copy of Oasis, had crashed and Virgin's losses on other groups were so far £25.9 million and growing. Contrary to Branson's philosophy of protecting the downside, Jeremy Pearce had hired two hundred and fifty staff and stylishly furnished twelve offices across the world, occasionally with tropical plants, exotic fish and even a staff club. Lavishing money on infrastructure before signing up successful bands contravened Branson's gospel and his money had not bought the authentic roots required to establish a successful music label. Now Rory McCarthy, however short of money, was the only source to fund his £100 million ambition.

Although still besotted by Branson, even McCarthy paused when asked by Murphy for £75 million. His personal fortune, McCarthy painfully acknowledged, had become dependent upon Virgin's success. Sensing McCarthy's caution, Murphy dangled an added enticement, 'Richard's spoken to Ong Beng Seng. He's quite interested.' Ong Beng Seng, the Singaporean owner of London's Metropolitan hotel, ranked among the world's richest men. The mere mention of the name spurred McCarthy's interest. 'We've got a new business plan,' offered Murphy. The document showed how Branson could, with a total investment of £114 million, turn V2 into profit after 2002.

'I'll see if I can put together a package,' suggested McCarthy, reluctantly awed by Branson's ambassador. Finding bankers keen to attach themselves to Branson, he believed, would not be difficult, although the price would be high.

After a game of tennis over the following weekend, McCarthy sought Branson's reassurance. 'Will it work?'

'Sure,' replied Branson.

'I'd be risking everything on you.'

Branson smiled. McCarthy, he thought, was hoping to earn millions by hitching himself to the Virgin money machine. The risk was McCarthy's. For his own part, Branson was proud to have turned risk-avoidance into an art.

The combination of McCarthy and Branson secured the attention of John Wotowicz at Morgan Stanley, the merchant bankers. Anything associated with Branson, Wotowicz believed, was certain to succeed, especially in the music business. The risks, the banker knew, were severe, but the McCarthy corporation had offered a personal guarantee to refund any bond holder if V2 was unsuccessful up to a further £35 million. Such was Branson's magnetism. Wotowicz agreed to raise the money in bonds.

Wotowicz's one-hundred-and-eighty-three-page prospectus offering ten-year bonds worth £75 million was rich with promises. The selling points were Branson's 'twenty-five years' experience in the music industry', his 'intimate relationships with the stars and personalities' and his $1 billion sale of Virgin Music to EMI in 1992. 'V2 intends to become the world's leading independent,' the banker explained, and 'achieve a significant share of the international market and profits'. But the warnings were explicit. Prospective investors were cautioned that the whole business was 'inherently uncertain'. Accumulated losses of over £100 million would have to be repaid after the first profits were earned in 2002. Since investors were guaranteed repayment by McCarthy personally, the money would nevertheless be raised.

'I'm risking more than all my money on you,' McCarthy reminded Branson, who appeared surprised and pleased by McCarthy's success. In turn, McCarthy was relieved by Branson's gratitude. 'This is the deal,' said McCarthy. To maintain his original 33 per cent stake in V2 costing £20 million and to compensate for the losses on Victory, McCarthy would invest a further £25 million cash in V2 and guarantee to pay V2 a further £35 million from his own money if Branson failed to deliver profits. In all, McCarthy was committing £80 million.

Branson nodded. McCarthy, he knew, did not have that money but Virgin's success typically relied upon others to cover the risks. The moment the money was deposited, Branson would transfer £25.9 million, Virgin's entire investment in V2, into the offshore accounts. All the costs of the glittery offices around the world, the tropical fish, the parties and the signing fees for hopeless artists would be recovered. Because McCarthy trusted Branson, he had agreed to bear the burden. 'We're sure it'll work,' Branson reassured him. 'Let's meet for dinner soon.'

The unsentimental attitude towards partners had also infected Branson's relationship with David Bonderman and the Texas Pacific Group. Branson had become disenchanted by the American's conduct as a partner in Virgin cinemas and the coolness was reciprocated. The disillusion had started soon after the purchase of the MGM cinemas in 1995. Despite the rebranding of the cinemas, Branson's forecast of 5 per cent revenue growth and 50 per cent increased profits every year had not materialised. The audiences had barely increased and there were complaints, not least that Coca-Cola was no longer on sale. Virgin Cola was not the first choice of youth.

Branson was remote from those concerns. He rarely attended the board meetings of the Virgin Entertainment Group, relying on Simon Burke, the general manager, and his obedient trustees to care for his financial stake.

The task of the trustees registered in the Channel Islands appeared complicated. Over one hundred separate Virgin companies and twenty trusts were listed as involved in Virgin Entertainment. In a pile of documents fourteen inches thick was the impenetrable history of contracts, loans and tax avoidance structures disguising the single company's share structure which only Stephen Murphy, with the help of Robin Vos, a solicitor at MacFarlanes, was allowed to disentangle. Official board meetings were always held offshore in the Channel Islands, France or America. Unofficially, some were held in Holland Park and Chiswick. Invariably, Murphy represented the trustees.

The labyrinth of the trusts was less irritating to David Bonderman than Branson's failure to deliver the promised profits of the Virgin Entertainment Group which Branson claimed to be worth £500 million, excluding debt. Soon after the Texas Pacific Group (TPG) became involved in August 1997 in a complicated investment in Virgin's Megastores, shops and cinemas across the world, Branson began trying to extract more money from TPG.

Virgin's original valuations of the shops and Megastores had been verified by TPG but subsequently the accumulated losses of European shops were established as nearly £100 million and the annual profits of the shops in Japan, valued at £40 million, were only £250,000. The American Megastores, with the exception of the Megastore in New York, were also revealed to be unprofitable. Considering the huge profits Bonderman's rivals were earning in America's bull market, not least in high-tech shares, TPG's relationship with Branson was a cold shower.

Bonderman offered what he described as a reasonable proposal. Since the true value of Virgin Entertainment was diminishing, he should be entitled to an extra 2 per cent of the joint company.

Branson did not digest his request calmly. 'They're fuckers,' he exploded to a director in London. 'They're not getting it.' In Branson's opinion, the American was a big boy who should have looked after himself. Bonderman's request was rejected.

Branson's outburst was unexceptional. For thirty years, he had camouflaged his ferocious temperament from the public and from nearly all his employees. The public only saw the icon's cool charm, courage and promises of charity. His pursuit of money and power was not equated with the crude ambition of his rivals. Branson's wealth and influence were welcomed because he was an English insider rather than a foreign outsider. All manner of mistakes, misrepresentations and bouts of erratic management had been marginalised or defused by his performance and his genteel background. Excuses had been accepted, goodwill restored and the image repaired. For all his life in the public glare, the raw lucre was discreetly amassed in the shadows. Discretion ruled. But the reality of Virgin's management of the rail franchises ripped apart those careful disguises.

The unexpected rash of newspaper reports damning Virgin Trains shocked Branson. Travellers across the country were complaining that services had sharply deteriorated. More trains than previously were delayed and cancelled, buffet cars had disappeared or were serving worse food at increased prices. Lavatories were increasingly 'out of action', air conditioning in dirty carriages had broken down and distraught passengers were complaining that Virgin's staff were impolite, giving wrong information or shepherding complainants into a herd of taxis. Virgin Rail was generating seven times more complaints than any other operator and the discontent spawned more critical newspaper reports. One train had left Euston without passengers; another train ground to a halt having 'run out of fuel'; one hundred and thirty-three people were counted standing in a single carriage; passengers were routinely travelling in darkness; and often several people discovered they held reservations for the same seat.

Branson was perplexed how to rebut the criticism. His smooth talk about a transport revolution 'in two years' was being derided. The critical headlines were damaging the Virgin brand. 'What the fuck's going on?' he asked Brian Barrett in despair. The chief executive of the Virgin Rail Group was stunned. He had obeyed Virgin's gospel to 'ramp up the revenue fast' and he did not believe the complaints. 'It's just the newspapers, Richard,' he replied. 'Everything's fine. The customers are still coming.'

For Barrett, an individualist who appeared insensitive to Virgin's dependence on good publicity, the continued purchase of tickets by passengers disproved the complaints. 'If they don't like us, they wouldn't travel with us,' he told Branson. 'It's all these anti-privatisation interest groups stirring up trouble.' In the Virgin Trains' office in Birmingham, on the desk of Chris Tibbits, the managing director, lay an unacknowledged letter from a Scottish rail yard explaining that Virgin trains were being dispatched with broken lavatories and unrepaired engine motors because Virgin's service budgets had been reduced. The few remaining British Rail executives within Virgin identified Barrett as the culprit: 'He thinks he can walk on water,' they scorned. Branson's men, though, preferred to blame their inheritance: 'It's all British Rail's fault.'

Unlike his charismatic personal apologies at Gatwick after the late arrival of a Virgin Atlantic jet, Branson could not dash to Euston, Glasgow or Exeter to apologise for late arrivals. 'Give 'em free tickets,' ordered Branson, copying his airline's favoured escape from ignominy. 'Too many have accepted the offer,' reported Barrett, describing how Virgin Trains' booking system had collapsed. Branson issued a new order: 'Sort it.' The offer was withdrawn.

'Sorting it' was delegated to Stephen Murphy and Will Whitehorn, both directors of Virgin Trains. Although Whitehorn was a master of denials, he had never practised his art in the face of such an intense glare of hostile publicity. Yet on 18 July 1997 he offered an unequivocal pledge from Branson. 'Virgin Trains,' Whitehorn/ Branson stated, 'has had serious problems coping with demand since we have taken over . . . We should be on top of things within the next four weeks.' The promise of improvements in just four weeks was praised by Branson. 'Great,' he gushed, 'and let's push the positive for the future.' More promises, often contradictory, flowed from the Virgin machine in Branson's name: 'We are committed to invest £800 million in new rolling stock'; 'by 2000, Virgin trains will be the best in Europe'; and 'we are spending over £2 billion on trains and track on what will be the best railway by the year 2002'. That was all confusing. Virgin Trains would spend nothing on building track and would lease, not buy, the trains.

After the promises, he issued the excuses. 'The British Rail network had had no investment in forty years,' he told one interviewer, which was plainly inaccurate; while another was told, 'Virgin [has] dramatically reduced the number of delays that existed under British Rail.' Train failures had, in fact, risen under Virgin, by arguably 15.5 per cent. 'My tongue's perforated,' Ivor Warbourton, a Virgin Rail executive, complained to a friend, 'just biting it as I listen to Whitehorn's briefings.'

Branson was frustrated. His promises were failing to stem the bad news. Attracting more passengers – the very success which Branson demanded – was even aggravating the problem. There were headlines about Virgin passengers revolting at Crewe railway station, bursting into the station manager's office to complain about cancelled trains. The news junkie's breakfast was ruined by the daily newspaper cuttings. Even the photographs chosen portrayed him as sour. There was, he suspected, a conspiracy to undermine Virgin. Somewhere in London, some Goliath was plotting David's destruction by regurgitating false, unfair news. He slumped into an unfamiliar, introspective gloom, tormented by the criticism. At a dinner in Westminster with the House of Commons Transport Committee, Branson's temper snapped. Brian Donohoe, a Scottish Labour MP, riled Branson about Virgin's failures. 'Your trains are a disaster,' scoffed Donohoe in a thick Glaswegian accent. Intolerant that his status as an unimpeachable icon should be publicly besmirched, Branson stood up, walked across the room, passing the other guests, and poured a glass of water over the politician's head. 'I can't even understand what you're saying,' snarled Branson, forgetting his customary charm. 'Take elocution lessons.'

Desperately, Branson willed Whitehorn to produce a distraction. He was the deceived, not the deceiver. 'What you got?' he urged, anxious for his fixer to invent an escape. After all, in November 1997, Whitehorn would actually transform the crash of a Virgin Airbus at Heathrow with one hundred and fourteen passengers into a success story. Improvising brilliantly, Whitehorn persuaded the media to hail the pilot as a 'Virgin hero' rather than query the defect in the landing mechanism of a Virgin jet. Pure genius, everyone agreed. Whitehorn could transform defeat into victory. If only, Branson wished, Whitehorn could pull a similar trick against the critics of Virgin Trains.

Instead, all Whitehorn offered was 'Branson the Victim'. 'We inherited a mess,' he explained, ignoring the uncomfortable reality that all the new operators had inherited British Rail's trains but, unlike Virgin, others had employed better paid staff with adequate budgets for maintenance.

The odium did not deflect Branson from his single-minded pursuit of maximum profits, although Virgin's strategy was handicapped by an unexpected discovery. British Rail had been more efficient than imagined. Little money, Barrett and Murphy reported to Branson, could be saved except by reducing services. 'We have to spend more than we planned,' he was told. That solution was unpalatable.

Three months after posing by *Mission Impossible*, Branson displayed the Virgin difference. Contrary to his pledge, some fares would increase by 30 per cent during the first two years, more than double the amount charged by most other operators – GNER would increase their fares by 11 per cent – and far higher than the rate of inflation. Under the smokescreen of better value, Virgin Trains introduced twenty-five different tariffs, from £29 to £225, and seven classes of travel, for the identical journey between London and Glasgow. Passengers, after a long queue, often discovered that the best fares were no longer available, or they were occasionally overcharged by 15 per cent because the tariffs were excessively complicated. Cheap fares available on the day of travel and Supersavers except those booked long in advance on specified trains, were abolished. No Virgin executives were perturbed by the protests, nor did anyone detect a hint of embarrassment by the gibberish of Tibbits's explanation that the previous system 'complicated our fare structure and [was] not well differentiated in terms of customer benefit'. In owning a monopoly, practically free from the regulator's powers, Virgin was protected from competition. The rewards for the monopolist, as Branson had repeatedly complained, were the profits – in the first year Virgin would earn £27.7 million – and the power to dictate terms to other operators. 'You're stitching us up,' a smaller train operator accused Whitehorn, irritated by Virgin's negotiations of special deals with Railtrack.

Branson's discomfort was the public's awareness of his profiteering despite the poor service. For the first time, his lifelong preoccupation to increase his fortune was being performed in the spotlight, illuminating an unflattering interpretation of his philosophy: 'We basically look at which businesses we think are taking the consumer for a ride, which are making excess profits. We ask: can we do it differently than they are doing it?' Virgin Trains mirrored precisely what Branson denigrated: earning excessively at the consumer's expense. He could, however, still benefit from the honeymoon. His credit remained supremely high, causing the critics to hesitate. The fund of goodwill fanned the welcome for his new financial services.

The overwhelming publicity welcoming Virgin Direct convinced Branson that Virgin had successfully 'shaken up banking' and would threaten to turn the Big Four banks into the Little Four. 'We will strike at the heart of the big banks' practice of taking advantage of customers,' Rowan Gormley, a South African recruited by Branson, had said. Virgin One, a new joint venture with the Royal Bank of Scotland, copied a formula used in Australia and by First Direct in Britain. Depositors placed all their money in a single account and were obliged to subscribe to a £50,000 mortgage and repay it before retirement. 'Banking is inherently a very straightforward business,' said Branson. 'It astonishes me that it has been allowed to become so complicated.' But his easy confidence was misplaced. His own product was complicated. Depositors were encouraged to raise loans up to the value of their homes but by retirement all loans had to be repaid. Ominously, if the loans remained outstanding, his customers risked homelessness. The British, who raised huge mortgages to buy property, were being encouraged to assume an unusually high risk. Branson's personal appearances in advertisements wearing a red pin-striped suit and bowler, promising to 'turn personal banking on its head' backfired. Depositors could find better fixed-rate mortgages and higher rates of interest for their savings elsewhere.

Branson's realisation that the public was not enamoured with his financial products coincided with the launch by the Prudential of 'egg', a revolutionary banking venture using the internet. Whereas egg had attracted an unexpectedly huge number of new accounts and was forecast within three years to be worth £4 billion, Virgin One languished. Branson was nonplussed. Rowan Gormley, whom he trusted, had assured him that internet banking was a gimmick. Yet the old, traditional Pru, whom he derided, had proved to be correct. There was worse. 'Why are the Amazon people earning billions and I'm not,' raved Branson. 'I want that sort of money too.' Around Holland Park, the courtiers whispered, 'He's angry. He missed a gravy train.' Branson's vision appeared uncertain, even dated.

★   ★   ★

Austerity hung over the celebrations of Virgin Cola's third birthday party. Debbie Flett, Virgin's overused model, jumped with mock excitement out of a huge cake proclaiming the sale of the one billionth can. 'One billion cans is an amazing achievement,' gushed Branson, forgetting that his target had been achieved two years late. Even that claim was doubtful. Cott's reports showed that only one hundred million cans had been produced. It appeared as another fantasy, similar to Branson's latest assertion to the *Sun*: 'We'll outsell Pepsi by 2000. We're well on our way to achieving this.' Although Virgin Cola was sold by some supermarkets, Virgin's annual sales had stuck stubbornly at £28.5m compared to Pepsi's £184.7 million and Coke's £561.1 million. Virgin Cola's stagnancy had become an emotional albatross. Understanding precisely Branson's requirements to bend the facts, James Kydd, his publicist, told inquirers, 'Virgin Cola is making a trading profit.' 'That's not correct,' Nick Kirkbride, Virgin Cola's managing director, intervened. Virgin Cola had lost £2.27 million in 1996/7. The contrast between Branson's ferocious demand for humble apologies from those who made mistakes about Virgin and his curious attitude about his own truth caused no apparent unease.

In his hunt for the elixir of publicity, Branson agreed that lampooning foreigners would sell his cola. In what he hailed as 'Virgin Cola's unmistakable humour', he boasted about his advertisements featuring, in his words, naked Scandinavians, well-rounded Brazilians and fat, naked Finns in a sauna. 'I'm bringing fun back into the cola market,' gushed Branson, introducing 'four dodgy foreign ads'. Reading a waxen script, he continued, 'Cola advertising has been dominated by big-budget American sameness. I believe the British public are bored with this. Forget your "trying to be trendy" American corporate bullshit – you'll see NO supermodels, NO wannabe popstars, NO hidden messages – just good clean British humour.'

Branson seemed to have forgotten his use that same month of semi-naked nurses to launch Virgin Energy and his own recent appearance with Pamela Anderson in *Baywatch*. The supermodel also simultaneously featured on giant poster hoardings in London dressed in black leather with a bursting cleavage to promote Virgin Cola. With Branson's blessing, 'Jimmy the Kydd', Virgin's master of bad taste who threatened 'to throw Coke and Pepsi into turmoil', even commissioned lavatory paper printed with 'Poopsie & Cack' – Pepsi and Coke – for the V97 music festival sponsored by Virgin. 'There is genuine consumer demand for the product,' puffed Kydd, the 'guerrilla marketeer' who spat 'the gloves are off'. Ignoring the reality, he claimed, 'Virgin Cola is doubling its production . . . Coke has been given a jolt by the launch of Virgin Cola.' Sixteen days later, the Iceland chain announced that it was dropping Virgin Cola and reintroducing Pepsi. Virgin Cola had become a manifestation of Branson's entrepreneurship.

Two years earlier, in 1995, Branson had told *Forbes* magazine, 'I'm making £1 million profits a week and the Cola business will be worth £500 million within a year or two.' Branson never admitted defeat despite Kirkbride's admission that Virgin had 'miscalculated'. He cultivated hype at the expense of accuracy. 'Cola sales have more than doubled during 1997,' he said in 1998. The statistics showed, however, that Virgin's share of the market had halved to 2.3 per cent. Even worse, while the demand for cola had grown, only Coke and Pepsi had benefited. His chant, 'We've doubled our market share and will overtake Pepsi in three years', was only substantiated by Virgin's miscalculation of statistics based upon an irrelevant survey. Virgin sales had only increased when its price was dramatically cut and it was sold unprofitably. So far, the Virgin Group had lost £10.5 million, contradicting his assertion, 'We will never lose much money selling Virgin Cola.'

Branson was blind to such prosaic realities. His emphatic denial of any failure was more than business expediency, it was a fundamental gospel. He would never allow himself to be crushed by contradictions. In his constant micromanagement of his self-portrayal as the crusading philanthropist, he even urged Cott to cease handing out copies of *Virgin King*, a sympathetic and semi-authorised biography by Tim Jackson, because he preferred the more sympathetic image conjured in an earlier biography by Mick Brown, a friend. Branson's concern about his image was his strength. His unblemished personality was the foundation of the empire. He prospered thanks to public acclamation of his energy, spirit, hard work, optimism and honesty. Reliant upon his credibility, in early 1998 he took a calculated gamble to allow the public to judge his character. Failure would have been a mortal blow.

The stage, the costumes, the player's supporting cast and the script had been carefully prepared for the gala performance initiated and orchestrated by himself, the plaintiff. A jury had been summoned on 13 January 1998 in London to decide whether Guy Snowden had offered Richard Branson a bribe.

Branson sat self-confidently in the High Court. Slim, tanned, casu- ally dressed in a grey sports jacket, black trousers and an open neck shirt, he smiled constantly at Joan, his wife, and his parents nearby. Other friends and admirers were scattered around the wood-panelled chamber. Busy in front of him stood the diminutive George Carman QC, his sixty-eight-year-old counsel, whose reputation and success in libel trials terrified opponents. The plaintiff passed his hand through his golden hair spotted with highlights. Once again, he was seeking redress as the victim of a gross villainy. 'My integrity is not something that has ever been questioned before,' twinkled Branson, certain that his amnesia would not be challenged by his army of sympathisers. His script, couched delicately in regretful language, mentioned his compelling need to 'get the truth' because it was 'unpleasant and it is hurtful to be publicly accused of lying'. The jurymen among the specially invited audience were fortunately, like himself, not wearing ties. Branson could afford to smile. His opponent's defence, the experienced litigator knew, was crippled by self-inflicted wounds.

Isolated at the other end of the wooden bench, Guy Snowden, looking like a Mafia stereotype compared to Branson, was fiddling with a ball point pen. Snowden was discomforted by several handi- caps, not least his lawyers. He had retained solicitors who were not widely renowned for fighting major defamation cases; he had recently lost his chosen advocate after his appointment as a government minis- ter; and the replacements were two QCs who were proving to be incompatible. Andrew Caldecott QC was a defamation expert but would not be allowed to address the jury; while Richard Ferguson QC was a praised specialist in criminal law lacking proven success in defamation trials. The friction between the two lawyers seemed to be aggravated by Snowden's convoluted defence. As George Carman would crow, 'They do not have the courage to say that Richard Branson has lied.'

Hesitating to call the popular hero a liar, or to allege a conspiracy to lie, or to challenge the veracity of his witnesses, Snowden's defence was that Branson had misunderstood his guest's comments at lunch and subsequently had recklessly misinterpreted those comments to *Panorama*.

Snowden was further handicapped. Branson had collected affidavits from his solicitor, his secretaries, his neighbour and his business associates who all confirmed his shock four years earlier on hearing Snowden's offer of a bribe. Snowden retreated rather than accuse those witnesses of being untruthful.

Unchallenged about his integrity, Branson was handicapped by only one ruling. Sir Michael Morland, the judge, had ordered that Branson was forbidden to mention in front of the jury *Panorama*'s allegations about GTech's corruption, since Branson admitted that he was unaware of those allegations in 1995. Branson found that ruling irksome. His case would be strengthened if the jury knew that GTech had been mired by controversy and investigation. If they heard about GTech's shady history, he knew, Snowden would suffer. As a witness in many trials, Branson understood the advantage of introducing evidence to influence the jury in his favour. On the first day of his cross-examination, Branson ignored the judge's ruling.

At the outset of Richard Ferguson's cross-examination, Branson performed the inarticulate, soft-spoken, inept victim desiring redress for an unfair malignment. Ferguson's punchy challenges were shrewdly deflected. 'You are now trying to distract the jury . . .' Branson accused the lawyer after Ferguson exposed an inconsistency in his replies; or, 'You seem to be questioning my integrity . . .' he wriggled like a centipede after another contradiction was highlighted. But that demure, innocent shroud was cast aside when the opportunity arose resolutely to deliver a stirring speech endorsing *Panorama*'s allegations of GTech's corruption and justifying his desire to prevent similar bribery in Britain.

When the *Panorama* team had arrived, Branson explained, 'I knew that [Snowden's] closest associate in his company had been found guilty . . .' Branson's intervention was damning but incorrect. Snowden's associate had been charged with defrauding GTech itself, not offering a bribe, and was only later found guilty. Moreover, Branson had only learned about GTech's alleged corruption from Killick himself and was uncertain whether the allegations were true. In 1994, when the bids for the lottery were considered, British newspapers had not published articles about GTech's alleged corruption. The judge told the jury to ignore Branson's evidence, but Branson nevertheless continued to recite a further sequence of allegations against GTech which were unproven. 'You are trying, Mr Branson,' snarled Ferguson, 'to inject into this case every piece of dirt which you can rake up.' Branson, Snowden's lawyers would complain, sought to 'expand the prejudice as much as possible'. Branson stared back, apparently mystified. His waspish pucker suggested a hurt innocent.

'I cannot remember,' Branson stuttered repeatedly to sidetrack Ferguson's pressure about his own inconsistencies and to deflect the lawyer's intemperate scolding of himself as a 'crass amateur', a 'bitter man' and a fabricator of 'embellishments' of his notes. 'I'm sorry, my mind has gone a blank,' he replied to one particularly perceptive question.

The humiliation of Branson was short-lived. Ferguson had fallen into Branson's trap, 'rather astonishingly,' as Carman joked. By challenging Branson's integrity rather than his confusion, Snowden's defence was undermined. 'The defendant's case,' summarised Branson's advocate, 'was one of complete intellectual disarray. [Ferguson] seemed to lurch around from opening to closing . . . walking on a tightrope, willing to wound, but afraid to strike.' At the end of his ordeal, Branson smiled briefly, reassured that the jury would trust an unkempt toff rather than a besuited American gorilla.

George Carman matched his client's ruthlessness. In his cross-examination of Snowden, the QC lured the defendant into a disastrous admission that his disputed words to Branson – 'Is there some other business we could do?' – could not have been misinterpreted. 'Mr Snowden,' Carman would accurately summarise about Snowden's suicide, 'has shut the door on room for mistake.'

Branson's credibility rose further as Snowden conceded that his payments to lobbyists in London and their subsequent reports looked 'awkward'; and by Sir Tim Bell's admission that he had 'no reason to doubt [Branson's] honesty and integrity'. Carman's final onslaught was against Peter Davis.

Branson had testified how, on 26 May 1994, the day after Camelot won the licence, he had warned Davis about Snowden's offer of a bribe. Davis had described Branson's recollection as 'untrue', suggesting a lie. Davis's credibility was undermined, however, by a damaging exposure. In reply to Carman, Davis admitted that on the same day as he told Branson that GTech were a 'fit and proper' company to run the lottery, he had secretly confided to Sir Ron

Dearing, the chairman of Camelot, his serious concern about GTech's methods for obtaining contracts in America. Davis's veracity was placed in issue. Destabilised by that exposure, he conceded a mistake. Branson's account of their conversation, he admitted, might be accurate. 'I am afraid you have put doubts in my mind,' he confessed to Carman. Davis's wretched uncertainty mirrored Snowden's plight.

On 2 February 1998, after two and a half hours' discussion, the jury found Branson not guilty of dishonesty and libel and awarded £100,000 in damages. Branson rose and beamed.

Branson had passed a new Rubicon. For the second time he had been vindicated as truthful. Once again he had humiliated corporate Britain. The vanquished foe, an insignificant American businessman, was elevated in the hype as a Titan to endorse the enormity of Branson's achievement.

On the familiar court steps, the victor punched the air to what appeared as a huge crowd of adoring supporters but were mostly journalists and photographers. The nation, Branson believed, would acclaim the toppling of another Goliath. The verdict allowed no other interpretation. His business and his motives were beyond question. 'I don't lie and I can't stand liars,' he told journalists in the Strand. 'My parents always taught me to tell the truth.' Not only had he won, but everyone knew who was the loser. Snowden walked from the court crushed, a lesson to every businessman and banker of the entanglements which could follow an invitation to lunch with Branson.

Celebrating his victory with friends in Holland Park, Branson could reflect that, to his many admirers, he was the honest and courageous champion of the people who smote villainy in its many guises. Regardless of his misleading hype and the poor performance of many Virgin companies, his reputation was pristine. There was intense satisfaction as he daydreamed about the tentacles of an empire built on a unique lifestyle brand. The daydream turned into a nightmare because they still could not play a Virgin lottery.

Before digesting his champagne that evening in Holland Park, Branson capitalised on his victory. Snowden and then Davis had swiftly resigned. Camelot was tottering. He wanted, as he had told *Panorama* in 1995 and Tony Blair subsequently, the lottery managed by a Branson charity. To encourage the government to issue a compulsory order against Camelot, he and Whitehorn hectically telephoned friendly journalists to foster the right atmosphere. A letter, they revealed, had been sent to Tim Holley, Camelot's chief executive, demanding an apology and a payment into charity. The disclosure was accompanied by a quotation in Branson's name: 'GTech has no place in our lottery. The people have lost confidence in the lottery and the lottery belongs to the people, not big business.'

The newly crowned champion of truth presented a selfless version of his original bid to journalists. 'I did not propose to take out any service charges. I would have made nothing,' he said, overlooking the company's unquantified administrative costs. 'All the bids should have been open for public scrutiny,' he repeated, ignoring the independent audit. Branson also alleged corruption. It had been his refusal to respond to 'regular hints' from senior Conservative party officials for donations, he suggested, which had sunk his original lottery bid. He supplied no evidence to prove corruption and his briefings rebounded. Cooler heads agreed that Branson's litigation had aggravated the loss of confidence in the lottery and, without GTech, Branson could not manage the event. By the end of the week, Branson renounced his bid.

Once calm returned, many quiet but influential people in London mentioned their irritation about the demolition of Snowden. The gossips observed that it was Branson who was himself a Goliath, a well-armed warrior who had smitten a foolish American upstart. Those like Branson who aggressively raise the principle of truth, and who demand public accountability from others but fiercely protected the secrecy of their own finances and business, aroused suspicion. Branson's victims also suggested that Virgin's management was chaotic and the empire's finances were weak. The brand, it was said, was a mere house of straw sustained by a bravura performance. Six years earlier, Branson had boasted that Virgin's strength was his management skills and the loyalty he attracted. But that truth was eroding. The losses in cola, Victory, V2, Virgin Direct and his other companies reflected poor management. The dissatisfaction with Virgin Rail confirmed that judgment. Several senior executives were dissatisfied by Branson's style and failure to fulfil his promises. Too often he had hogged the limelight and taken the credit for good decisions, dispiriting the unrecognised managers he needed to retain. Switchboard operators were no longer, in his favourite phrase, 'as important as the managing directors'. Once, Branson had predicted, 'If you have a demoralised staff your company will soon disappear', and the disgruntled were murmuring that his prediction might soon be fulfilled.

21

A slipping halo

The triumphant public vindication in court distracted critics from Branson's embarrassing censure by the transport committee of MPs and peers, members of the All Party West Coast Group. The politicians had met to debate the unusual cynicism expressed across Britain about Virgin's investment in paint to glorify the Virgin brand on trains while reducing the trains' manpower to increase profits.

The thousands of complaints and the raw statistics presented by the regulators confronted Branson and Whitehorn with an unprecedented dilemma. Opraf, the rail regulatory agency, had on 14 September 1997 condemned Virgin's West Coast service as 'disappointing'. Four months later, the criticism was worse. 'West Coast services to Scotland,' reported Opraf, 'have deteriorated over the past year and the recent performance has been particularly bad.' Virgin's average number of trains arriving on schedule was 79.9 per cent, despite Branson's promise to meet the 90 per cent target within the first year.

'Unreliable Virgin Rail heads passenger complaints list' was a newspaper headline on the eve of Branson's journey to Westminster. Some Virgin services were appalling. Only 50 per cent of Virgin trains arrived punctually in Scotland compared to GNER's 80 per cent. 'The service is very poor,' John Swift, the rail regulator, complained. 'Virgin is at the bottom of the league.' The evidence was irrefutable. Virgin Trains' punctuality had deteriorated since the privatisation of British Rail and Virgin was the worst of all Britain's rail operators.

The continuing criticism, an unprecedented experience, exasperated Branson. A man accustomed to the media accepting his own estimation, he was certain that Virgin's publicity machine would smother the cynics. Cushioned by the comforts of Holland Park and Necker island, he persuaded himself that no one would notice his discrepancies: while he preached 'small is beautiful', he had become Britain's biggest train operator; having praised competition, he was exploiting his monopoly to impose huge fare increases; and his declaration that Virgin was serving the customer was sabotaged by his directive to increase the profits. Mishaps in the past had always been forgotten and, Branson hoped, this time his loyal public would also accept that his inheritance from British Rail was to blame. But the halo had slipped. While the mismanagement of his minnow businesses inconvenienced few, Virgin's mismanagement of the railways spotlighted all Branson's weaknesses and illusions: his lust for money; his inaccurate self-publicity; his unwillingness to focus on detail; and Virgin's lacklustre management. To restore confidence, he conducted a charm offensive of Roy Hattersley, the Labour politician, who wrote a lengthy, enthusiastic endorsement for the *Guardian*; and he invited journalists to a visual presentation of Virgin Trains' shining future. But as he stood in the background awaiting images of Virgin trains in 2005 racing at 140 m.p.h. on journeys that would cut the time of travel between London and Manchester to one hundred and five minutes, the slide projector stopped. The screen was black, reflecting, carped the audience, the future. 'Virgin should be renamed Whore,' scoffed Mark Lawson in the *Guardian* about Branson's promiscuous empire the following day. Virgin had become a caricature, reproached as 'incapable of coping'.

Ignoring unpleasant facts was, Branson and Whitehorn had routinely found, Virgin's escape. They relentlessly stressed the positive, asserting the Virgin difference. Mistakes and malfunctions were simply denied. The railway managers who admitted, 'Virgin Trains accepts that the current punctuality performance is not acceptable', were reminded of Virgin's gospel never to admit mistakes. In retaliation, Whitehorn galvanised his publicity machine to produce letters and advertisements for newspapers praising Virgin Trains' achievements. 'There's been a real turnaround on the West Coast line,' repeated the standard letter signed by Branson. 'We are delighted with the quarterly performance results published by Opraf,' Whitehorn had written in Virgin's press release on 15 January 1998. 'Opraf conclude that Virgin Trains . . . are showing one of the biggest punctuality improvements.' Whitehorn's delight about his positive boasts blinded him to the possibility of a backlash.

Branson arrived with Whitehorn in Westminster on 21 January

1998 to face fifty-five MPs and peers, members of the All Party West Coast Group. His complaints about Virgin's inheritance from British Rail had been dismissed before the session started. 'You volunteered to bid for the franchises,' one of Branson's aides was told. 'You made commitments and we expect you to fulfil them.' Branson parried the criticism. Everything was improving, he said, and, once the new trains were introduced, the future would be 'a piece of cake'. Branson beamed. 'Nobody believes a word you're saying,' snapped Eric Maltreat, an official, soon after their introduction. Both Whitehorn and Branson appeared shocked. Virgin was being trashed.

The 'mood music' among Labour ministers disfavoured Branson just as he was once again quietly approaching ministers to seek preferential treatment. Having abandoned his ambition of Virgin as a global entertainment corporation, he proposed himself as Britain's principal transport tycoon. To some it seemed bizarre: running trains and planes required different skills and disciplines to promoting rock bands. To equate the management talents required by the two was absurd but Branson prided himself that he could manage any company. Ignoring the frenzied complaints about Virgin Trains in late 1997, he launched a bid to buy and manage Eurostar.

During summer 1997, Sir Derek Hornby and Adam Mills had forlornly attempted to rescue their consortium. Despite the disastrous tunnel fire, the London and Continental Railways (LCR) group was still paying huge fees to Railtrack, the Channel Tunnel company and French railways. LCR's annual losses rose to £133.5 million on a turnover of £126 million. The flotation had been cancelled but LCR still required £400 million, the first payment of £5.4 billion to build the rail link from Waterloo to the tunnel.

Relations among the members of the consortium were fraught. Branson could not tolerate dislike of himself and twice during 1997 had tried to improve his rapport with Mills. At a party, he had unsteadily walked over to Eurostar's chief executive, thrown his arms around his shoulders and slurred, 'Sorry about everything. Let's get it sorted.' The reconciliation had been as unsuccessful as another attempt in a Notting Hill Gate restaurant. But as much as he sought approval, Branson could not resist pursuing his quarry.

In the midst of his libel trial against Snowden, on 25 January 1998, Hornby and Mills had called on John Prescott, the transport minister. The two executives had expected a routine discussion about the government increasing the £1.8 billion subsidy by a further £1.2 billion. To their surprise, the meeting ended in acrimony. Eurostar, the minister said excitedly, had forecasted carrying nine million passengers during 1997 but only six million had travelled. Virgin's marketing had failed to attract French travellers and many still preferred to use aeroplanes. Prescott refused any further government support and set a thirty-day deadline for LCR to produce a new plan or lose its licence to build the rail link.

In their battle to salve their own financial interests, LCR's directors met at Rathbone Place for a board meeting described later as 'the most devious game of four handed chess'. Each director blamed Virgin's flawed marketing for Eurostar's failure. In response, Stephen Murphy, who was present to represent Virgin's 17 per cent share, had seethed, 'We weren't responsible for marketing. We seconded some people. That's all.' Virgin's denial of responsibility transformed the excited voices into yells. 'It's beyond hate,' growled an engineer contemptuous of Branson's ploys. 'We're going to screw the grin off that weasel.' The meeting ended in disarray. Every player moved to exploit LCR's crisis. Branson had his own game.

'We've gotta get out at a profit,' was the message from Branson's office. 'Or better still, take over the whole company.' Appalling people, cursed Branson, had let him down. His £10 million investment was at risk.

Branson believed he could persuade John Prescott to appoint Virgin, in association with Railtrack, as Eurostar's new owner. Only Virgin, he submitted, could market Eurostar. Since Virgin possessed little cash, Branson proposed a contract without any payment. His ploy, 'protecting the downside' as ever, would succeed if his partners were awed by the Virgin brand. Prescott's reply surprised Branson. 'You've done wonders for the paint industry,' the politician carped, 'but what are you doing for the railways?'

Bewildered, Branson retired rather than risk further confrontation with the government. Days later, he realised that he had been outmanoeuvred. National Express had recruited British Airways to market Eurostar with an extra £140 million government subsidy. Virgin was cast out of Eurostar. The squeeze of Branson had begun.

Opposed to the inclusion of British Airways, Branson voted against the new arrangement using his 17 per cent stake in a company which could not be liquidated. He would profit, he hoped, by obstruction.

'Virgin are sabotaging everything for their own profit,' cursed a director. 'They destabilise and search for tricks for their own advantage.' Branson was sanguine until told that Prescott demanded his departure. Too weak to counter-attack, he held out until Bechtel bought his shares and retreated silently.

The recrimination from the Eurostar partnership, coinciding with Branson's merciless self-congratulation about Guy Snowden's humiliation in court, incited his rival players and their advisers in London to whisper about the dangers of any association with Virgin. Snowden had been destroyed because he accepted Branson's invitation to lunch; Eurostar's shareholders had lost money after Virgin's failure to sell tickets; and Cott was bruised by its ruptured partnership in Virgin Cola. The disenchantment among corporate directors and Westminster politicians that Branson's self-promotion caused an expensive burden for others could not be easily shrugged aside, especially while the public performance of Virgin Trains languished.

Branson's voice during the telephone conversation with Brian Barrett was calm but the anger was unconcealed. 'My friend said that the train was late and dirty and the food was no good.' Barrett listened quietly. The routine never changed. Every time the newspapers carped about the appalling service, he telephoned. Once, he had even called in the middle of the night, disturbing Barrett's family holiday in San Francisco. 'And why is the air conditioning not working?' Branson cajoled. 'And why is Opraf against us?'

'Well, Richard,' replied Barrett. 'The air conditioning never worked. We can't do better till we get new trains.'

'It's so unfair,' groaned Branson, 'all this bad publicity. It's so unfair.'

'Well,' said Barrett, searching for consolation, 'it can't all be bad because we're getting more passengers than ever.'

'That's true,' agreed Branson. The profits were increasing and the four banks, the major shareholders, were not complaining.

Will Whitehorn, the publicist, could not afford to ignore the vilification. To counter the critics and highlight Virgin's success, Whitehorn recommended that Branson should appear on television. The public had always been persuaded by his personal assurances. The best opportunity was an invitation from John Ware, an experienced *Panorama* reporter. Ware's request coincided with an Opraf report that during the last three weeks of December 1997 Virgin Trains had been 90 per cent punctual. That success, Branson decided, could be exploited. 'We've improved the on-time reliability of the Virgin west coast line by 50 per cent over what it was under British Rail,' Branson wrote in the *Daily Express* about his 'miracle'. Like most miracles, the improvement was temporary but it was a good reason to accept *Panorama*'s invitation and promote Virgin's success.

Branson was always cautious about television appearances and expected Whitehorn to extract guarantees to avoid damaging mishaps. *Panorama*, however, was more trusted than others because of the programme's damning documentary about Guy Snowden and GTech. While Branson anticipated offering the usual generalities and promises in the taped interview, he expected Whitehorn, as usual, to carefully organise the filming on the trains. His hopes were not disappointed. In a circular marked 'strictly confidential', Branson's publicists alerted the staff of Virgin Trains that *Panorama*'s programme would be 'our chance to make a good impression so we need to stage manage the event accordingly'. Staff selected to be filmed were to be 'well dressed', show a 'positive attitude and smile', ensure the train was clean and that the buffet was 'well stocked'. Stage-management included receiving in advance the questions Branson would be asked.

On the eve of the interview, Branson was upset. A premature preview of the uncompleted programme, published in Liverpool's *Daily Post*, suggested criticism. 'Branson himself,' reported the *Post*, 'promised privatisation would mean faster, cheaper, better travel [but his failure to deliver] is threatening to devalue the whole of the Virgin empire.'

'That's mischievous and completely untrue,' Branson told *Panorama*'s producers, abruptly cancelling the interview. Hitting hard was a favoured weapon. Especially against an unpleasant truth. 'After ten months of extremely hard work turning around what was the worst railway in Britain,' he continued, 'I am very proud of what our people have achieved . . .' But after negotiations, Branson assured himself that the programme would be favourable and he consented to appear.

His performance started perfectly: 'I think what has been achieved in the last year is, I suspect, better than almost every other train operator in Britain.' The interviewer frowned. The tycoon beamed: 'I am willing to talk hype because I believe we can deliver the hype.'

The 90 per cent target had been hit thanks to 'the best people' and 'fantastic' staff. 'We are now delivering what we believe to be the best punctuality of any operator.'

'But Mr Branson . . .' began John Ware, before unfurling the official statistics that established Virgin's failure to fulfil Branson's promises, especially the 90 per cent target. 'Bollocks,' Branson shouted and stood up. 'It's a trick question. The figures are not worse. The figures are dramatically better.' The atmosphere was chill. Contradictions were intolerable. 'I know where they're coming from,' warned Whitehorn. Branson agreed. Critical questions offended the gospel. Signalling that the interview was over after about ten minutes, the camera stopped. Branson was enraged. His momentary silence was menacing. Ignorant or disingenuous, Branson suggested that identifying an individual train operator's faults was impossible. He appeared to be avoiding personal responsibility. Standing nearby, Brian Barrett knew the unpleasant truth. Railtrack's latest report showed that Virgin's trains were 15.5 per cent less punctual than British Rail's previously. The slender improvement in December was Railtrack's rather than Virgin's achievement. But Barrett said nothing as Branson and Whitehorn attacked John Ware. Both were outraged that Branson's assurances were not unquestioningly accepted. Only enemies criticised Virgin Trains. Ware's use of statistics was offensive. 'It is a silly nit-picking point,' Branson snapped and departed. Vigorous complaints against critics were a favoured weapon in his news management but there was no opportunity on this occasion to prevent the programme's transmission.

Millions watched the consumer's champion on 16 February 1998 abandon an interview rather than explain Virgin Trains' poor service. His ill-temper angered thousands of frustrated Virgin passengers. For his part, Branson professed to be a grievously hurt victim. 'I've given 30 years of interviews to TV companies throughout the world,' he complained to John Birt, the BBC's director general, 'and have never been treated so shoddily before.' He accused John Ware of a 'devious plan' with 'no hint of the trickery [of a] surprise . . . question'. Branson apparently had forgotten that the questions had been provided in advance. Mentioning Virgin Trains' delays, he champed, was 'pointless' and 'thoroughly inaccurate and misleading' since the delays had not increased by 15 per cent but had fallen by 3 per cent. Branson had selected statistics to confuse the indictment. The

0

punctuality of Virgin Trains was sliding towards 70 per cent. Each month, Virgin was receiving seven thousand telephone calls of complaint and, during that year, one hundred and ninety-five thousand letters of protest. In the public's mind, the Virgin brand was for the first time conspicuously tarnished. Branson's operation was under hostile scrutiny. Enemies were insinuating that the unworthy billionaire owned mismanaged, loss-making businesses based in tax havens.

Branson was skiing in Zermatt in Switzerland, when Whitehorn reported the after-shock of *Panorama*. The newspaper headlines faxed to Switzerland were the most damaging in his career: 'Is Branson's honeymoon finally over?'; 'Has the halo finally begun to slip?'; 'Is Branson in a pickle?'; and 'Is Mr Branson paranoid, or are we getting sick of him?' The substance was worse than the headlines. Detailed analysis in *The Economist*, the *Spectator* and later *The Financial Times* suggested that Virgin was financially insecure, struggling with debt. The latest financial accounts registered in Britain substantiated that interpretation. The profits from Virgin Atlantic and the temporary subsidies from Virgin Rail were sustaining the losses on all the other businesses. Branson's boasts about his personal wealth appeared to be exaggerated. The popular but unreliable *Sunday Times* 'Rich List', after marking his fortune up in 1997 from £800 million to £1.7 billion, was about to slash his wealth in 1998 to £1 billion. The impression was of instability.

The irony about Branson's brilliant entrepreneurship was no longer disguised: his two profitable companies – airline and trains – relied on government franchises for protection from competition, while all his businesses exposed to normal market competition were debt-ridden.

The contrast of the brickbats in London with the beauty of the Swiss Alps was unpleasant. Branson's perennial caution about the media had proved justified. Just one glitch on *Panorama* had unleashed abuse, drowning the usual adulation. Some bankers, he feared, would be reluctant to loan the millions he required unless the doubts were suffocated. Fortunately, no one knew the true extent of his debts but his published accounts had revealed losses of £43 million in the previous year. He was paying more to the banks in interest for his loans than he was actually earning from his whole empire. Outsiders were murmuring the unimaginable: that in the long term, if unchanged, the Virgin empire would crumble into oblivion. The accusations were not new, nor was his response.★

Pundits in London, Branson maintained, did not appreciate that his private empire could not be assessed conventionally. Although he could not deny that the airline's latest profits were paying the interest on the loans for all the unprofitable companies, he explained, the credibility of the registered financial accounts was irrelevant because his companies were privately owned. Totally revealing accounts were not required by law. The finances of a private empire, he insisted, concerned only his banks.

But Branson had elevated himself beyond a private businessman. Over thirty years he had assiduously promoted himself as an icon of integrity empowered to limitlessly preach virtue. Branson was not averse to linking his virtue with a new morality, which in turn was the single foundation of the Virgin brand. *Panorama* and the newspaper comments, he feared, imperilled that sacrament.

If the notion developed that the empire was built on sand, the consequences would be dire. 'Almost every new venture we are involved in,' he accurately said, 'has strong outside partners to finance it.' Seducing others to finance his businesses – cola, clothes, cinemas, trains, Virgin Express, Virgin Direct and V2 – depended on maintaining Virgin's pristine image.

Abandoning skiing, Branson began a familiar routine of telephone calls, soliciting journalists and their editors to secure a right of reply: 'Hi, this is Richard calling.' His endearing personal style of addressing everyone on Christian name terms cushioned the unmentioned threat of legal remedies if his request was unjustifiably rejected. Once again he cast himself as the victim of a dirty tricks conspiracy.

'It could all be a coincidence, of course,' he suggested, and mentioned that Virgin's offices had been entered illegally and that he was being followed by private investigators. He did not provide any evidence but said with sincerity, 'One of the things which came out of the [British Airways] court case was just how much money PR companies are being paid to keep an eye on Virgin. We have a lot

---

★ Branson did not dispute the *Economist*'s analysis that travel side earned £67.5 million, the airline earning £45 million, while six other businesses lost £27.8 million. Virgin lost £15.4 million where its ownership of the individual companies was less than 50 per cent.

of competitors and a lot of enemies out there.' To Branson, even an honest critic was an enemy.

Hype and charm were Branson's next defence to extinguish the doubts about his financial stability. 'Our businesses are worth in excess of £3 billion,' he insisted, 'and generating £150 million of cash every year.' Two years earlier, in 1996, he had been content to estimate his wealth at £1.6 billion which was double the previous year's value. To reinforce the success, he had again taken to boasting about his '£250 million cash mountain' and being 'cash rich'. Proving that wealth was difficult.

In response to those who had begun to downgrade the value of his empire, Branson, lapsing into the royal 'we', explained, 'We've been away for a week so we haven't been able to firefight properly.' 'The businesses have never been as strong as they are today,' he told another inquirer. 'We are not broke. We are sitting on a cash pile of around £250 million,' he soothed, without offering any evidence to substantiate that assertion. 'In many ways Virgin is stronger than it ever has been,' he repeated. To bolster the glowing confidence, he reeled off a wish list of successes: 'Virgin Cola will succeed and beat Pepsi,' he predicted; 'Virgin Direct has been an enormous success and our stake is worth £250 million'; and Virgin Atlantic, Virgin Holidays, Virgin Cinemas, V2 and Virgin Trains would all be floated in the near future to reap cash and prove his wealth. 'The airline,' he insisted, 'is worth £1 billion.' Endlessly, he repeated that his empire was undervalued, but the doubters were not persuaded. His optimistic forecasts could not divert attention from the unusual secrecy of his accounts.

The extent of Branson's fortune was more uncertain than ever. Twenty-five years earlier, in the early 1970s, he had transferred the ownership of his British companies to trusts registered in the Channel Islands, but, in 1993, he had established new trusts in the British Virgin Islands as the ultimate owners of his business. To reinforce the secrecy of the ownership of the airline, the equity capital of two companies, Virgin Travel and Voyager Investments, had been converted into bearer shares concealing the shareholders' identity. Branson's intention was to prevent outsiders understanding the ownership of the Virgin empire, the full details of its financial activities and its debts, and to frustrate their identification of the beneficiaries of the trusts. Only Branson, and a small group of lawyers and accountants, understood what lay behind the multi-layered smoke-screen.

The offshore trusts, by 1998, owned at least one hundred and forty-two separate Virgin companies registered in London. 'The decision was tax-led,' Branson admitted. To bewilder investigators and minimise the payment of British taxes, the registered accounts of the principal Virgin companies operating in Britain revealed accumulated losses, interest payments on loans and inter-company debts among a proliferation of constantly renamed companies whose accounting periods were repeatedly altered. Virgin's financial health was obscured. While the crude results of the companies filed by Branson in January 1998 showed sales for the whole group in the previous year of about £1.3 billion plus a further £850 million from those companies partly owned by Branson, there was no evidence of real profits or verifiable values. Many of the companies were loss-making. Virgin Express, V2, Victory, Virgin Cinemas, Our Price shops, Virgin Cola, Virgin Direct and Virgin Retail were all unprofitable. The businesses were kept afloat by loans or by shuffling money from one company to another. There were unexplained trans-actions, such as the sale of a property company by the British parent company to a Virgin offshore company for £50 million, which later reappeared, purged of its losses, as a purchase by a Virgin company based in Britain for £11 million. The debts had been paid either by Branson's partners or by Virgin Atlantic's profits. Even the airline's offshore accounts were uncorroborated by an independent, published audit. Only Branson, Stephen Murphy and selected lawyers under-stood the masterplan of the inter-company contracts among Virgin's offshore companies, and whether the services supplied to Virgin Atlantic by unknown offshore Virgin companies were quoted at genuine values or altered to influence the accounts. Even the know-ledge of a handful of accountants, relocated under Stephen Murphy from London to Geneva to further protect the empire from the Inland Revenue, was compartmentalised to prevent any individual understanding the complete picture. All the public could know was that Virgin Atlantic in 1998 earned net profits of £77 million but paid taxes of only £12.8 million, while Branson's offshore trusts received £30 million in dividends.

Adding further confusion for outsiders, soon after the February crisis, the parent company of Virgin Atlantic was wound up. The company, Virgin Travel Investments Ltd, the parent of Virgin Travel Group Ltd, transferred its investments to Barford Services which in turn issued its shares to Virgin Travel Ltd, the parent company owned by the offshore trusts. Curiously, neither Branson nor Murphy was a director of Barford. To add to the confusion, Branson's accountants declined to explain the latest transactions.★ While the structures and names constantly altered, their fundamental purpose had never varied. But to disguise his purpose, Branson conjured a folksy scenario for public digestion.

The one hundred and forty-two different companies, he professed, reflected Virgin's indulgent paternalism: 'You can then have people running them as if they are their own companies and we can incentivise them as well.' Thanks to his unusual corporate structure, he continued, amplifying his generosity, 'We have created thirty-five millionaires.' To justify the empire's ultimate location in the Virgin Islands, Stephen Murphy asserted, 'It was done to protect Virgin and Richard from investigation and damage by BA.' Evidently, Murphy had forgotten that Virgin was located offshore twenty years before the 'dirty tricks' litigation and ten years before Branson leased his first check-in desk at Gatwick.

The baroque imagery of Branson's publicists – huge profits, cash mountains and the persecuted hero – was limitless. Their efforts might have been in vain had Branson not astonished and silenced his critics by executing once again a spectacular deal, the refinancing of Virgin Trains.

Virgin's bids to win the rail franchises had been financed by four banks – Bankers Trust, J. P. Morgan, Electra Fleming and the Texas Pacific Group – who were contracted to recover their £45 million investment for their 59 per cent stake in Virgin Trains by June 1998. With his usual patter, Branson predicted that the bankers' investment

---

★ Virgin Voyager (VV), the main British company controlling Virgin Atlantic, recorded losses of £4.3m, added to accumulated losses of £13m and interest payments of £8m. Other Virgin companies owed VV £48m, while VV owed to those companies £97m, leaving liabilities of £45m. The VoyGp earned £4.4m but was owed £130m by other companies and in turn owed other Virgin companies £39m. Virgin retail lost £28m on a turnover of £84m. On jointly controlled companies, Branson's losses were £15.4m.

and profits would be repaid by floating Virgin Trains for £250 million on the stock market. The theoretical flotation would leave Branson with a 35 per cent stake. Mentioning flotations was Branson's recycled ruse to attract favourable attention.

Ever since winning the rail franchises, Branson had maximised the profits to entice investors to a honeypot. His success was impressive. In its first eleven months, Virgin Trains had carried 11 per cent more passengers, earned £13.6 million in profits and received £170 million in subsidies. The profits would rise with increased fares. Although Branson could not decide whether Virgin had spent £100 million or £250 million refurbishing the trains, he required considerable profits to cover his future payments to the Treasury. The leasing formula established by the government to finance the acquisition of fifty-three (rather than forty) new trains cost £1.2 billion and relieved Virgin of direct financial responsibility, but Virgin remained obliged to repay the four banks for their original investment. There appeared no alternative but to risk stock market scrutiny. 'This business will be something special very quickly,' puffed Whitehorn, in April 1998, as the prospectus for the flotation was commissioned. 'Something special' had recently entered the publicist's lexicon to promote Virgin.

'Something special' was mentioned, in May 1998, to launch Virgin Cola in America. Adopting a tactic beloved by many British tycoons frustrated by failure or the limitations of Britain, Branson hoped that Americans would be impressed by an eccentric billionaire. Beneath a forty-foot Virgin Cola billboard in Times Square, Branson, dressed in fatigues, stood on an army tank 'flanked by Virgin Cola urban guerrillas'. Ignoring the experts who laughed that 'it would be easier to make a snowman in July in Florida than take on Coke and Pepsi in America', Branson's stunt was to pose as 'the people's capitalist' and proclaim 'the people want him to win'.

In newspaper interviews, Branson knew that he could rely upon David Yelland, recently appointed deputy editor of the *New York Post*. Across a whole page, his admirer reported that young New Yorkers hailed Virgin Cola as better-tasting than Coke and Pepsi. In his interviews, Branson exaggerated his sales in Britain as an 8 per cent market share, while a Virgin circular added the untrue assertion that 'Virgin Cola's volume sales beat Pepsi'. The confusion about sales in Britain was mirrored by Branson's peculiar 'revolutionary advertising campaign' predicting his success in America's $56 billion drinks market. Branson's prose was convoluted. 'Virgin Cola as a brand will be answerable only to its consumers and not, like our competitors, treat them as market share points ... One which believes that the consumer does come first and that their opinions are crucial to the success of the brand – rather than a faceless mass who are there to be dictated to.' The linguistic confusion was a smokescreen.

Branson provided no money. The national advertising campaign did not materialise. Nor did the cola. Virgin's claims that there was 'a strong network of business relationships with some of the most respected distributors and producers in the US' was inaccurate. Branson's only resource was yet another stunt. Standing in front of a wall of Virgin Cola cans, Branson announced a new bid with Steve Fossett, an American stock market trader from Chicago, for the 'dream team' to win the race to fly around the world in a hot air balloon. Once the announcement was made, Branson shuffled away. 'Something special' was a devalued lure until Branson received a telephone call from Brian Souter.

Brian Souter, a self-made tycoon born in Perth, had built Stagecoach into Britain's biggest bus company and was the franchiseholder of South West Trains. Like Branson, Souter had earned quick profits by dismissing experienced staff and cutting costs. Like Virgin, South West Trains was condemned for its service and additionally was threatened with a fine for mismanagement. Unabashed by his notoriety, the trader was content to identify himself with Branson. 'I think we are quite alike,' Souter said. 'We both enjoy taking risks and getting things done [and] we get on socially.' Branson was not offended by the association. On the contrary, unlike the smooth tycoons in London and New York whom he generally shunned, Souter, a maverick who posed no financial or intellectual challenge, was welcomed. Just before Merrill Lynch's prospectus for Virgin Trains was to be published provisionally, Souter had been shown the prospectus and was enticed to pre-empt the flotation and buy a stake. Some believed that Souter's initiative was a surprise, but Branson expected the call. With the detachment accumulated over thirty years to extract the best deal, Branson coolly told Souter, 'I'll let you know.'

Souter's bid confirmed Branson's acumen. Although Sir George Young and the Opraf regulators had chortled about Branson's overpayment for the franchise, Souter was convinced of his own mistake. In his unsuccessful rival bid, Souter believed, he had underestimated the growth of passengers and underestimated how fares could be increased regardless of any criticism. Souter was persuaded that the business was more valuable than envisaged although the success of Virgin Trains after 2002 depended upon a matrix of agreements: Railtrack's £2.1 billion improvement of the track, the delivery of the fifty-three new trains and an increase of passengers from seventeen million to thirty-one million, paying higher fares to fund the payments due to the government after 2003.

Convinced that Virgin Trains could earn profits, Souter agreed to pay £108 million cash and £50 million in Stagecoach shares to the four banks for 49 per cent of Virgin Trains, leaving Branson with the controlling majority. No one was allowed to understand the details of Souter's £158 million risk but, by any measure, Branson had secured an astonishing coup. His original £18 million investment for 35 per cent of the company had become a 51 per cent stake with a value of £140 million in a company valued at £276 million. His four investors had earned a gross profit of £113 million on their original £45 million stake, while Branson had avoided a stock market flotation and had halved his risk. Standing beside Souter on 22 June 1998 after signing the agreement, Branson spoke about 'synergy' and a 'fun investment' to embroider his enhanced monopoly. His unerring ability to get the best deal was once again established, while both Murphy and Whitehorn received over £1 million each for their share options.

The critics were silenced. Souter, whose operations were still unquestionably profitable, had endorsed Virgin's calculations, enhancing Branson's credibility in the City. The advertisement was enviable. Bankers and potential associates were persuaded that Virgin remained a valuable partner. Branson's insistence that his business could not be assessed conventionally appeared justified. 'Over the last couple of years,' he explained, Virgin's management of its investments had created 'around £700 million' in additional value.

To enhance his argument of 'added-value', Stephen Murphy produced the statistics. Virgin had invested nothing in Virgin Express but its 50 per cent stake was worth £60 million on the stock market; Branson's £2.5 million investment for 50 per cent of Virgin Net was worth £30 million; an investment of £24 million in Virgin

Cinemas was worth £60 million; an investment of £7 million in Virgin Direct was worth 'in excess of £50 million'; Virgin had invested £4 million in V2 which after the bond issue was worth £80 million; and his investment of £14 million into Victory was worth £35 million. To Branson's surprise, Murphy's breathless efforts were counterproductive. The unproven new values and Virgin's reliance upon other people's money rekindled uncertainty. Combined with the damage to Virgin Atlantic after the plunge of Japan's economy, Branson's valuation of his empire at £3 billion could not be substantiated.

Among the doubters were some inhabitants of Whitehall. For years Branson had expected official recognition of his achievements. His supporters had often lamented that Britain's most popular businessman had been denied a knighthood or a peerage when so many nonentities were honoured. Representations had been made to William Hague, the leader of the Conservative Party, who agreed to nominate Branson despite his new allegiance to Labour. Tony Blair, however, was irritated by Branson. He had criticised the Dome as 'daft'; he had complained of 'feeling let down' by Blair's uncertain handling of the tobacco industry's sponsorship of sport; and he had derided British Airways' intention to erect a Ferris wheel near Westminster to mark the millennium.

Without Blair's sponsorship, the Honours Committee considering Branson's nomination scrutinised his past more carefully than normal. His purchase tax fraud, his avoidance of British taxes, his failure to dignify UK 2000, the absence of notable charitable bequests and his personal behaviour outweighed his commercial achievements. Any award, the committee always stipulated, was in recognition of public or political services and Branson conspicuously failed to satisfy that requirement. The uncertainty about his finances reinforced their judgement. Their rejection remained unknown until the Downing Street spokesman, to divert attention from a sustained attack on the Labour government's honesty, revealed the decision.

The news hurt. Despite open-necked appearances, the Branson family yearned for recognition and praise by the Establishment. Branson was the victim, suggested his admirers, of enemies who scorned his success and popularity. One solution was to devote more energy nurturing his relationship with Labour politicians, not least through Georgina Graham, appointed as his government affairs liaison to arrange lunches and receptions in the House of Commons. Another solution was to spread even further his social network.

In early summer 1998, Branson was planning his holiday on Necker. Working his way through his telephone book, he issued invitations to share the privilege of frantic activities with himself and his children. To the few who refused his offer, it seemed he was carefree about his guests so long as he was not alone. Branson appeared to be nervous. The hype could not conceal his financial vulnerability. The manifestation was the absence of an invitation to Necker, unlike in the previous year, to Rory McCarthy. Their relationship was dissolving.

Branson was troubled by Victory. While he sat on his Caribbean beach, he sensed his embroilment in another botch. After the abortive launch of Virgin's cosmetics and clothing companies, Victory's share price was sliding. The cosmetics shops had proved disastrous and were being replaced by Tupperware-style 'in-home agents'; and the clothing strategy, after a confusing change to sell designer fashions, had again misfired. Virgin could not finance a multimillion-pound advertising campaign to compete with Calvin Klein, Hugo Boss and Donna Karan and Virgin's styles, as modelled by Branson's daughter Holly for *Cosmopolitan* magazine, were unappealing. Even a bare-backed photograph of Holly, wearing Virgin jeans while lying on a beach on Necker, did not attract buyers. Virgin's wealthier enthusiasts who flew Virgin Atlantic's Upper Class had brusquely avoided Virgin's cola, vodka, music, bridal gowns, holidays and its financial services. Victory clothes, to them, reeked of inferiority. Branson had not understood the sophisticated marketing of fashion. To divert attention, a publicist issued in McCarthy's name some favourable reports about Virgin Vie's 'good initial trading' and hailed Virgin clothing's 'extremely positive response from the leading independent retailers to the autumn 1998 range'. The sticking plaster was crudely fixed.

Unlike Rupert Murdoch and Bill Gates, Branson was lounging during that summer on Necker with sycophants incapable of engaging in an informed debate about Virgin's future. Uncomfortable with those more intelligent than himself, especially the creative polymaths intellectually powered to shape rather than follow the trends, he had always surrounded himself with aspiring traders who satisfied his inexhaustible need for entertainment but failed to provide original ideas. In consequence, Branson watched helplessly that summer while an unprecedented bull market, driven by the new high-tech industries, raged across America and Europe creating thousands of billionaires. His accumulated wealth after thirty years' trade was a pittance compared to the new fortunes. The self-styled entrepreneur was excluded from the bonanza. Entry required ideas and cash and Branson only had excessive debts. He was baffled by his company's deficiencies and infuriatingly his limited exposure on the stock market revealed his imperfection.

The crisis hit on 16 August 1998 while Branson was sunbathing on the beach on Necker. Victory's share price fell to 10 pence, compared to the original 58 pence in October 1996. The share price would certainly fall further after the company's results were released. Branson discussed with Murphy and Whitehorn how to save Virgin from humiliation. Their best ploy, they agreed, was to buy Victory shares to restore the company's value and to reassure shareholders about Virgin's total commitment. Despite Whitehorn's defiant assertion – 'It's definitely not true. Neither Richard nor anyone else in the world has bought any shares' – Branson bought 11 million Victory shares on 20 August 1998 (the next day) for £1.1 million. The share price fell further to 9.5 pence. Branson controlled 78.7 per cent of a company whose losses had increased from £3.7 million to £10.9 million. 'The losses,' admitted Murphy reluctantly, 'will considerably exceed expectations.' Victory was worth nothing more than its cash in the bank, and that was considerably less than the £35 million which Murphy, on Branson's behalf, had asserted in the *Financial Times* just weeks earlier.

Branson's predicament was unpleasant. Victory's demise infected Virgin's hallowed image. The financial institutions who had bought Victory shares blamed Branson and scorned his plea to be 'cash rich' since no one was allowed to count his money. His critics once again gleefully mentioned the weakness of Virgin's brand, the return of his cash crisis and the dangers of involvement with the tycoon. For the second time in 1998, Branson was roused to extinguish doubts. Rather than return to Britain, he spoke by satellite. 'We are taking on a complacent industry with quality products at a good price,' he said to justify Virgin's involvement in clothes and cosmetics. But his apologia was unconvincing. The industry was not complacent. He was failing because the competition was too good and his managers were mediocre.

Beyond the handful of City practitioners monitoring Branson's cavorting, the Victory saga passed unnoticed. The camouflage was reinforced by Branson reminding everyone about his £1 billion airline, his 'conscious decision never to be in a position where I have to sell a company again', and an interview in the admiring *Times* concluding inanely that Branson 'is happy'.

The truth could not be disguised within Holland Park. The atmosphere was infected by drift and crisis. Murphy issued an edict, 'There's no cash in the group. We've got to be careful.' Branson, as always perpetually in motion, appeared lost. Rather than developing the brand, the restless trader was fire-fighting, blind to a new future. His senior executives were clearly inadequate but he knew no alternatives. For the moment, he skated round his dilemma by a favoured escape. He flew to Washington.

22

Fissure

'Oh fuck!' cried Branson. His audience laughed. His frustrated inability to enunciate 'anachronistic' from the notes composed by the speech writer was endearing to listeners at the International Aviation Club in Washington on 24 September 1998. Usually, his special tuition for public speaking by an expert in Oxford overcame such stumbles but on this occasion his amateur performance proved attractive. Of the opportunities to convey his honesty, few were more important than his appearance in Washington to oppose the alliance between British Airways and American Airlines. 'Competition is under threat', was Branson's popular rallying cry.

In his round of meetings with senators John McCain, Herb Kohl and Mike DeWine, and over lunch with senators Robert Torricelli and Howard Metzenbaum, Branson presented himself as the champion of 'unfettered competition'. Senator Robert Torricelli introduced Branson to the conference as the man who 'redefined what the airline industry should be'. None of those politicians knew that their speaker, to protect his cosy duopoly on the North Atlantic, was actively opposing British Midland's application to fly to ten American destinations; or that British Midland did not oppose British Airways' proposed alliance. Skilfully he had concealed his personal fortune's dependence on crippling one of Britain's flagship companies.

Branson's renewed attack against British Airways was synchronised with the addition of six new planes, increasing Virgin's fleet from fourteen to twenty, and the expected delivery of another ten planes over the following eighteen months. All would be deployed on BA's most lucrative routes. Success depended upon weakening BA and especially on blocking its proposed alliance with American Airlines.

But Branson understood the truth about alliances: his new ten-year association with Continental Airlines replaced Virgin's alliance with

Delta on 2 February 1998. 'With these alliances,' said Gordon Bethune, Continental's chairman, 'you're either in there or you ain't . . . and if you're out, ultimately you're dead.' Bethune had honestly admitted that his link-up with Virgin was his tool to delay the inevitable British Airways alliance. 'We've got our Virgin defence in that. This just makes us stronger.' To his audience Branson spoke out of pure self-interest. 'The stranglehold [BA and American Airlines] will achieve over global aviation,' he warned his American audience, 'cannot be overstated . . . Virgin could not withstand the proposed alliance [which] threatens to devastate competition.' His own profitable alliances with British Midland, Sabena and Continental were ignored as was United Airlines' confession that the Star alliance had produced $150 million of extra profits. Instead, Branson speculated about the 'predictable and inevitable' consequences of BA's proposed alliance: 'prices will rise, service will suffer and choices will decrease'. Passengers, Branson lamented, 'face a dwindling number of choices on which airline to travel' because of the alliances. 'That's why I oppose co-operation between airlines. I'm in favour of competition.' He was cheered for preaching competition, but his support was conditional on regulators protecting his advantages.

Seven years earlier, Branson had praised 'deregulation [because it] has actually achieved its main purpose of delivering greater value for the consumer's money'. In Washington in 1998, to protect his financial interests, the king of competition attacked 'twenty years of deregulation' as 'harmful'. A handful of astute American experts in the audience understood his nihilistic agenda: 'He's throwing up red herrings to blow the whole thing up.' Bob Ayling was too modest, too decent, too hapless to engage in warfare and expose Branson. Ayling's reticence and the audience's cheers encouraged Branson to gamble for the jackpot. The smell of blood validated his decision.

Ayling's management of British Airways was frail. The replacement of the successful slogan, 'Fly the Flag', by the unstable advocates of 'Cool Britannia', and an acrimonious strike which cost British Airways over £100 million had devastated the company's morale and profits. BA's share price was halved during 1998. To aggravate Ayling's self-inflicted injuries, Branson revived BA's past disrepute by rekindling memories of its campaign of dirty tricks.

Branson, however, found himself somewhat constrained. Brian Basham had successfully sued Martyn Gregory, the author of *Dirty*

Tricks, for libel in the High Court. Despite the supportive presence of Branson in the courtroom – and he had provided the bulk of the information that Gregory called as evidence – the jury decided that Basham had not 'lied' on behalf of British Airways and awarded substantial damages against Gregory. Nevertheless, on the steps of the New York courthouse, Branson told journalists summoned to hear the progress of his $1 billion anti-trust claim against British Airways, 'We have suffered considerable economic harm because of BA's dirty tricks and monopoly, and I was forced to sell my record company to get through it all.' Flashing his most sincere smile, he continued, 'The public is paying 15 per cent more for airline tickets because of BA's dominance. That must end.'

To his delight, no journalist asked how British Airways could be a monopoly if it sold only 38 per cent of all transatlantic tickets compared to Virgin's 35 per cent. Nor did anyone ask why Virgin Atlantic did not reduce its prices by a further 15 per cent to match European fares. If the question had been asked, Virgin's spokesman had prepared a reply of fluent nonsense: 'Percentages don't matter. Monopoly power is an ability to charge above the competitive level.' Virgin's payment of £184,000 to BA to settle its 'dirty tricks' litigation in London was unknown in New York.

Soon after his performance, Virgin's press office regurgitated another old canard. British Airways was blamed for using Concorde 'in an anti-competitive manner'. To irritate Ayling, Branson's spokesman added, 'it's a great marketing tool and we'd love them. Virgin is negotiating to lease three French Concordes.'

Branson left America convinced that the British Airways alliance was torpedoed. The negotiations between the British and American governments about 'open skies' were paralysed, and Branson's lawyers reported from Brussels equally satisfactory news. Karl van Miert, the European Commissioner who was adjudicating the alliance, was prejudiced against BA. Van Miert had broken his own precedent and ordered a major investigation. While the other airlines had produced thin, single folders to win approval for their alliances, BA and American Airlines had been compelled to produce fifteen boxes of plans, strategies, statistics and business secrets. BA's misfortune was an opportunity too good to miss.

Eleven lawyers and experts were dispatched by Virgin to Brussels to scrutinise British Airways' commercial data. Using that information,

Branson argued that the proposed alliance should be reduced to 50 per cent of the market. To further protect the consumer, he boldly proposed, Virgin should be allowed to control the other 50 per cent. Branson's plea that BA should be compulsorily reduced to enrich himself was benignly received by a Commissioner distrustful of the British government's Euroscepticism.

Karl van Miert was further inclined to sympathise with Branson's complaint that 'Virgin's growth has been delayed and constrained . . . because BA is able unfairly . . . and unlawfully . . . to coerce passengers to fly BA.' In 1998, Virgin would fly a total of 3 million passengers while British Airways flew 35 million worldwide. The Dutchman ordered an investigation of British Airways for 'unlawfully' infringing Europe's competition laws, and approved the alliance subject to British Airways sacrificing two hundred and sixty-seven slots at Heathrow worth $1 billion every year. Branson toasted his success. BA had once again been worsted by Branson helped by its competitors, the major American and European airlines. Virgin's shared monopoly was safe.

With some pleasure, at the end of September 1998, Branson boarded a Virgin jumbo to fly to the Caribbean to launch a new service on another of British Airways' profitable routes. For years, Branson had enjoyed those trips. But the laughter and the airline's success numbed his awareness to reality in London.

The sun had barely risen over the blue sea and white sand when the telephone rang on Sunday, 27 September 1998. The report was that half the Labour cabinet were cursing Virgin. Branson's relentless demand for profits from his mismanaged trains had hit new victims.

Two trains from London to Blackpool, the location of Labour's annual conference, had been delayed for two hours without a buffet car. Virgin was being damned by Labour ministers, suffering the same inconvenience as tens of thousands of daily travellers. For months, Branson had denied the public criticism that his railways were disastrously managed. In evidence at the Snowden libel trial earlier that year, Branson had said about Virgin Trains, 'I would say that we've done a remarkable job.' Throughout the year he had repeatedly denied the fact that 16 per cent of Virgin trains were running late on the West Coast line, double the April figure; he had denied that punctuality between London and Glasgow had fallen to 74.4 per cent, below the regulator's target of 87 per cent; and he

denied that Virgin's Cross Country services were the least punctual
of all the franchises. Virgin had been condemned as the least punctual
rail operator in Britain, yet Branson and his publicity machine
insisted: 'We are still doing much better than British Rail' and claimed
that punctuality was '90 per cent'. Just because Labour ministers were
the latest victims, Branson was not about to change his habits.

Nothing enraged Branson more than bad publicity. For years he
had endured the endless grind across the world of dressing in ridiculous costumes, smiling at thousands of gauche punters and risking
his life for publicity. He loathed those word-sharp journalists in the
Guardian who mocked him with their too-clever prose. 'Many had
suspected,' wrote Mark Lawson, 'the caring People's capitalist of
being, beneath the beard, a vain and greedy twit . . . Now happily
most of us who had to get on a Virgin train can thank Mr Branson
for proving us right about him all along.'

'I despair,' cried Branson, 'about unfair attacks.' All the usual
suspects were blamed – 'teething problems', 'Railtrack', and 'British
Rail' – but not himself. From the Caribbean, Branson swore at his
enemies: 'I do not think I have had quite such a bad week in my
career in business as this week.' There was no remorse. His manager,
Chris Tibbits, told John Prescott, 'There is no other show in town'
and continued planning fare increases between London and Manchester of between 15 per cent and 37 per cent and to Birmingham
of 20 per cent. Some fares increased during that year from £39.50
to £108. 'We are not trying to force passengers to pay more,' said
Branson's spokesman. 'We are trying to give them more choice by
booking earlier.' The doublespeak dissembled the lust for profits.

At the heart of Branson's predicament was a single truth: Branson,
the deal-maker, shied away from the detailed management of four
thousand rail employees. The trains were mismanaged because Barrett, Whitehorn and Murphy appeared unconcerned by the requirement to motivate their staff or to pay salaries to attract the best
managers. Their indifference was not exceptional. The management
of Virgin Atlantic had become similarly blighted.

Repeatedly, the airline staff at Heathrow complained about 'prehis-
toric' conditions and 'low morale' which was blamed on the 'diaboli-
cal' attitudes of Virgin's managers. 'The staff now feel completely
undervalued, demotivated and betrayed,' complained a spokesman,
because of the managers' 'evasive, non-committal and ambivalent

response'. Unknown to Virgin's rail employees, Branson admitted that his airline staff's complaint about 'depression' and 'helplessness' was 'genuine'. While his airline managers could limit bad publicity about their staff's grievances with the promise of free air travel, the unrest in the railways was too widespread for similar containment. The discontent was a sideshow for his major problem, a new cash crisis.

Branson's fortune was sustained on a knife-edge by Virgin Atlantic's success which itself was enhanced by the debilitation of British Airways. The depressing predictions for the airline industry in 1999 threatened that success. The slump in travel to the Far East had increased the number of planes competing across the North Atlantic. Virgin Atlantic's dependence on that route made it more vulnerable than its competitors, especially without substantial reserves of cash.

Although as the owner of a private company Branson was not answerable to shareholders or City institutions, the bankers whose loans sustained Virgin could not be ignored. Their continuing sympathy to advance cash depended upon Branson's persuasiveness. Finding bankers willing to lend money was rarely a problem for the successful rich. Branson had long ago discovered that bankers would snatch his invitations to rock concerts, parties and Necker. Compared to invitations from the usual faceless executives, Branson's glamour was intoxicating and the fun lubricated the flow of loans. To his satisfaction, the bankers' money was secured against shares in Virgin companies valued by other friendly bankers.

Sustaining that construction depended upon keeping the secrets. None of the bankers had been allowed to penetrate the rigid compartmentalisation among all the offshore companies and trusts. They could only guess at the financial problems besetting Branson in autumn 1998. Internally, the directors knew that Branson's boasts of a £1.4 billion cash flow 'throwing off £340 million in cash' was a smokescreen for the Group's absorption of cash to repay debts and interest on loans. Outsiders were referred to Branson's familiar boasts of a '£250 million cash pile', but insiders understood Murphy's warnings of 'belt-tightening' and the rumours that Virgin Holidays might be sold. The status of Branson's six-year-old '£250 million cash mountain' was an enigma.

The symbol of Branson's plight was an Airbus A340, the size of a Boeing 747, languishing underused at Heathrow. Parked in a British

Midland hangar, the jet was towed out in the morning and pushed back at night. Branson's bravado – ordering giant jets when plane prices were low – had misfired. Soon after the delivery of his twenty-fifth jet, he admitted that the dearth of passengers to the Far East and the delayed decisions for new routes had 'sadly' caused 'plenty of flexibility in our fleet'. The consequence was painful: 'We took a risk. We have got more planes than we need at the moment.' Branson's crisis was familiar. His entrepreneurial bellicosity had out-stretched financial reality.

His troubles had been signalled by the collapse of Virgin Express shares from $27.12 in March 1998 to $14 in June. By October 1998, the shares were $8. Within eleven months, the airline's profits had fallen by 77 per cent to £2.45 million. Pilots had defected, a twenty-five-year-old Lockheed Tristar had burnt out and labour relations in Brussels had further deteriorated. Compared to Ryanair and easyJet, both low fare airlines, Virgin Express was at best mediocre.

The airline was notorious for delays. During summer 1998, five Virgin Express planes were grounded in Brussels, unserviced and without crews. 'It's a disaster,' Rohan Alce, Virgin Atlantic's sales director complained to Branson about Ornstein. 'I've never seen anything like it.' In his office, Ornstein's moods swung between jocular concern about press releases, helpless fury about his predica-ment and discussing share prices with American brokers. Beyond his office, outraged passengers were revolting. 'The letters of complaint are mind blowing,' sighed Alce. 'They're all expecting Virgin's ice creams and videos.' Virgin's brand was tarnished. Branson was crest-fallen.

To save his business, Branson announced a partial transfer of Virgin Express's operations to Ireland and a jump in earnings. Once again, like Victory, the losses suffered by Virgin Express's shareholders were only noticed by City practitioners who recalled his optimistic hype one year earlier. But no one had yet focused on the enormous risks he had undertaken, especially to overtake British Airways.

Expansion had become an addiction. His adage that 'small is beautiful' had long ago been forgotten. In autumn 1998, Virgin Atlantic's managers were taking delivery of seventeen new leased aircraft costing £4 billion to serve new routes to Cape Town, Chicago, Las Vegas and other unnamed destinations. To finance his onslaught on British Airways, pay the interest charges on his massive loans and fund the losses in all his other businesses, Branson needed cash. His only source was to float Virgin Atlantic on the New York stock market.

Since the privatisation of Virgin Music in 1988, Branson had floated two companies, Victory and Virgin Express, and benefited from the V2 bond issue. Shareholders in all three new investments, like the former investors in Virgin Music, had lost between 70 per cent and 90 per cent of their money. Business partners also had been bruised and fund managers and bankers had reason to be wary. Branson sought a counterblast, to distract attention and to squash negative opinions. His solution was a volley of unrivalled hype. In September 1998, he published his autobiography, the third book about his life.

Losing My Virginity offered few revelations but gave Branson the excuse for a week-long publicity blitz with unprecedented simultaneous serialisations in *The Times* and the *Sun*. 'If I go out and make a fool of myself,' he admitted, 'I get on the front covers.' Authors usually dress up for the launch, but Branson took everything off. Posing naked for the *Sun*, he promoted a saga of houseboat bonking, wife swapping, sexual diseases, name dropping and confessions of sleaze and crime. To maintain the excitement during that week of self-promotion, he projected his daredevil image by recounting a story of sailing with his first wife in 1974 as passengers on a deep sea fishing expedition in Mexico. A storm erupted and, Branson continued, he and his wife abandoned the boat and swam two miles through the turbulent sea to the shore. In the storm, he recalled, the two fishermen on the boat certainly drowned, which permanently troubled his conscience: 'I had to live with the question of whether the fishermen would have gone out that day if we and the other tourists had not waved a handful of dollars in front of them.' Twenty-four years later in 1998, convincing evidence showed that no fishermen had ever died. When challenged, Branson replied, 'This is wonderful, fantastic, very pleasant news.' Unconcerned by his bad memory, the man whose parents 'always taught me to tell the truth' continued to repeat his 'daredevil' story. In the same vein, to promote his book, he also alleged serious corruption among those awarding the lottery franchise.

His failure to win the lottery still rankled. He had become convinced that the competition was not only unfair but deliberately influenced. Even the subsequent investigation by the influential National Audit Office, he believed, was unreliable. To explain his defeat, he revealed for the first time the mysterious offer of a knighthood and of a 'bizarre' invitation to meet John Major for a dinner in exchange for a donation to the Conservative Party. 'Everything was done by innuendo,' Branson explained. 'It was made clear that if I scratched their back they would scratch mine. I wrote back and said I did not think it was a good idea. I felt it would be invidious at the time.' His failure to make the donation and his rejection of John Major's invitation, he said, cost him the lottery. Branson did not provide any evidence or name his contacts to substantiate his serious accusations. Moreover, the episodes were not included in his book. But he may well have appreciated that a well-timed kick on the eve of the Conservative Party conference would be appreciated by the Labour government and might partially repair the damage which had precluded his award of a knighthood three months earlier. To reaffirm his sympathy for Labour, he also demanded government intervention to 'come down far harder on big companies merging and laying off thousands of people to boost their profits'. Branson's own history of dismissals to earn profits was unmentioned. There were no negative asides during that hectic week of self-promotion. To Branson's delight, Virgin's financial problems disappeared from public attention.

Unlike the obligation of the major airlines to report weakening profits, Branson had no reason to publicly admit any troubles. Virgin Atlantic, a private company, was answerable to no one. Unlike British Airways, it was not obliged to publish every month the numbers of passengers flown, and within the law, it could use a wide variety of accounting practices to present its financial results. With Merrill Lynch preparing a future flotation, Branson offered optimism, predicting that Virgin Atlantic would earn record £100 million profits. The contrast with BA was flattering.

To humble Bob Ayling remained a passion. Anything the British Airways' executive undertook was deemed almost on principle to be opposed or ridiculed by Branson. BA's attempt to resume its traditional and profitable flights to Lagos was opposed by Virgin executives dispatched to Nigeria to snatch the prize; and BA's agreed plan to buy CityFlyer, its own franchise company operating from Gatwick, was damned by Branson as a conspiracy. Virgin, Branson asserted, was entitled to buy BA's company. The deal was referred to the Monopolies Commission.

After fourteen years in the airline business, Branson had become a master of browbeating the regulators to award slots and routes to Virgin. 'Fighting my corner', in Branson's words, was a merciless war for survival. Not only against British Airways but, if necessary, also against British Midland, one of Virgin's code sharing partners. Since Sir Michael Bishop had consistently refused Branson's offer to buy his airline, the relationship with British Midland had become antagonistic. Their 'war' was focused on Branson's search for new destinations, in particular to use the Airbus A340 recently dubbed 'an aircraft in search of a route'. During his campaign, Branson reluctantly exposed some hitherto unpublicised characteristics.

In mid-1998, British Midland and Virgin had applied to the Civil Aviation Authority (CAA) to establish a regular service between Heathrow and Moscow in competition to British Airways'. Branson's airline needed three new destinations every year to sustain his new planes, avoid losses and to fulfil his public pledge to 'overtake BA's profits in two to three years'. Virgin's application was approved by CAA officials who had been persuaded that a Russian airline would share the route in an exclusive partnership with Virgin. Michael Bishop, the chairman of British Midland, was furious. His investigators suggested that Virgin's submission about a Russian partnership was inaccurate. Bishop was allowed to appeal by John Prescott. Appreciating his weakness, Branson had telephoned Bishop to suggest that neither attend the new hearing on Thursday, 26 November 1998. Bishop agreed but subsequently heard that Branson would after all be present. 'Is our agreement still valid?' asked Bishop telephoning from Australia. 'What agreement?' replied Branson. 'I always appear personally.'

Branson arrived at the CAA hearing wearing a new Virgin steward's uniform and a tie. 'I've been at a presentation,' he explained. Everyone nodded. Branson's fondness for dressing up was well known.

Branson's appearance was a distraction from an embarrassment. On his original application, Branson had submitted that Virgin would use either an Airbus A320 or A321 built for medium-haul flights. But only three days before the hearing, Virgin had altered its application, mentioning the possibility of using the giant Airbus A340 languishing at Heathrow. In the strictly regulated airline industry, the CAA would need to be satisfied how Virgin could profitably operate a jumbo jet on a medium-range route, especially since medium-range destinations were British Midland's speciality.

Branson had not always been convincing under cross-examination. Even in the Snowden libel trial, he had been discomforted by the occasional slating of his testimony. In the civil case involving Dave Robinson and the criminal prosecution of Sebastian Clarke, his sworn testimony had not been accepted by the court. Yet before the CAA's regulators, his self-confidence was undaunted. Dangling Virgin's offer of limousines, masseuses, a sixteen-channel entertainment system and more leg room as certain to lure business class passengers away from British Airways, Branson explained, 'We are about to launch Virgin Cola [in Moscow] in six weeks . . . [and] Virgin Megastores.' The jumbo-sized jet would 'spearhead the Virgin name into a new country'. Although neither Virgin Cola nor Megastores would appear in Russia, Branson's pitch was optimistic: 'Russia has got a great future.'

There was no self-doubt in Branson's voice. While he could utter unverifiable exaggerations about Virgin's products and finances, everyone knew the truth about Russia's economy. It was dire and the country did not have as Branson predicted 'a great future'. The number of passengers flying from London to Moscow had nearly halved. Russia's future was in the past and Branson's huge aircraft would fly, at best, half-empty. Losses were inevitable, not least because Virgin's business class frills were expensive. Branson hoped to avoid those details. His personal attendance at the hearing, he expected, would impress the regulators who, like others before, would be swayed by his vision of Virgin Atlantic competing with British Airways on 'ten more routes' across the world, including Tel Aviv, India and Ghana. Irritated by Branson's hype, Bishop authorised his opponent's merciless cross-examination.

'Do you have any A321s available?' Branson was asked, referring to Virgin's written submission that an Airbus A321 would be used. 'We have available both A321s and A320s,' Branson replied. Pushed three times to answer the question, he finally admitted, 'We do not have any A321s at the moment, no,' adding, 'We would hope not to need an A321.' Branson paused. He wanted, he finally admitted, to use the giant A340. The murmurs in the room were discomforting.

His evidence had been inconsistent. 'I wish counsel wouldn't ask questions like this,' he complained. Technical questions, he pleaded, were beyond the remit of the airline's owner. He cursed his poor memory and pleaded ignorance. 'If you are going to do figures,' he told the court to escape further embarrassment about the economics of a large jet, 'I honestly do not know the difference between net and gross . . . I am dyslexic.' The director of more than two hundred companies and a self-proclaimed billionaire who had traded for over thirty years was asserting his ignorance about the most elementary financial detail. Everyone in the court was stunned. The tribunal's chairman threw down his pen. Branson looked sheepish. His appeal was rejected. Branson had reached the beginning of the end.

23

Squeezing friends

A temporary distraction presented itself. The fourth bid to win the race to fly around the world in a hot air balloon was due to start in Marrakesh. Seven others were competing.

Compulsion rather than companionship had brought together Branson's 'dream team', Steve Fossett and Per Lindstrand. Only the Swede could build balloons and his enthusiasm suppressed his commercial sense. He was cheap. Including Fossett as an alternative pilot was necessary while Lindstrand slept.

The take-off from Marrakesh on 18 December 1998 was perfect. Berber tribesmen were thumping on drums and uniformed Virgin girls were waving as Branson, moist-eyed, declared, 'It's all magnificent.' Everyone hoped that twelve days later he would land in Oxfordshire.

'Richard's voyage' was blessed by special coverage in the *Sun*. The newspaper reported with awe, 'Yesterday Richard had piloted the £3 million craft "through the eye of a needle" – avoiding both a massive thunderstorm AND being blown off course over Saddam Hussein's crisis-hit Iraq.' Later, 'Richard had to steer through a passageway' to avoid Russia and Iran. Although Will Whitehorn and Mike Kendrick, the project manager on the ground, spoke about 'Richard flying the balloon', the businessman was a chair-bound passenger chatting on his satellite telephone to pass the time while Lindstrand and Fossett steered the craft sponsored by ICO, the telecommunications company. For seven days, Branson's only minor animosity was towards Fossett's ego. When Lindstrand had answered the telephone and announced, 'CNN want to talk to either of you', Fossett's hand moved even faster than Branson's to grab the receiver.

The mood deteriorated over the Pacific. They had lost valuable fuel meandering off-route on an unauthorised flight over China.

320

The chance of completing the route was less certain and Branson complained about missing Christmas on Necker. His relations with Lindstrand were uneasy. Although the Swede was a genius, pushing back scientific and engineering frontiers to build the world's biggest balloons, he resented Mike Kendrick whom Branson trusted. Lindstrand complained bitterly that Kendrick in London restricted the flight commander on behalf of the paymaster. At least, Lindstrand consoled himself, Kendrick and the other sycophants at ground control were reporting that the media coverage was good. Unlike Branson, Lindstrand was optimistic about their chances.

The commanding pilot was asleep as the balloon sailed towards Hawaii. The weather had worsened. Despite the best efforts of an American coastguard plane and the meteorologists in London, an easy route had not been found into a jet stream across the Pacific. Lindstrand awoke to hear Branson and Fossett arguing about where to land. The decision had been taken by Kendrick in London although there was sufficient fuel to continue flying south around the depression to at least reach the American coast. There was no time even to argue. Branson wanted the journey to end. 'It's a glorious failure,' boasted Mike Kendrick.

The balloon came down on a surfing beach where it was certain to be destroyed. Instead of a hero's welcome, Branson was fined $500 by a disgruntled official for entering the United States in a non-customs area without prior notification. The immigration officer's Christmas Day lunch had been interrupted.

The bureaucrat's churlishness was allayed by the arrival of a white stretch limousine. 'Compliments of Barron Hilton,' announced the bowing black-suited maitre d'hôtel to Branson. 'There's food and drink in the car and the presidential suite is prepared at Waikiki Beach. Fresh clothes have been laid out for you.' Hilton, a balloon fan, had followed Branson's progress from his mansion in Beverly Hills. 'I'm lucky to be alive,' exclaimed Branson about his relatively safe journey. 'The most terrifying ride I've ever had.'

The following morning, Branson flew in a Lear jet, borrowed from a French supplier to Virgin Trains, to Necker. Soon after he arrived in the Caribbean he telephoned Lindstrand. Salvage of the capsule, he heard, had been abandoned but the Virgin crew were still in Hawaii. After three weeks' constant work, through Christmas, they were relaxing. 'Send them home,' said Branson. 'They're costing money. Today.' Branson's care for his own money bred confusion and created victims.

'You're trying to destroy me,' Per Lindstrand spat furiously at Branson shortly after. The balloonist was angry that Branson was querying the costs of the new balloon under construction and refusing to pay the bills.

Three months after his splashdown in Hawaii, the Breitling Orbiter, a hot air balloon piloted by Bertrand Piccard, a Swiss psychiatrist, and Brian Jones, a retired RAF officer, successfully circumnavigated the world. Branson's ambition had been thwarted. Lindstrand's new balloon, ordered by Branson to be completed as fast as possible, had become redundant. After an uninvited appearance in Switzerland to personally congratulate the victors – 'I really wanted to throttle them,' admitted Branson – the loser moved to extricate himself from his own project. Privately, Lindstrand's financial accounts were disputed; publicly a Virgin executive inspired a national newspaper to report Branson's argument about the balloonist's demand for £100,000. 'It's dirty tricks,' scowled Lindstrand to Branson. 'Just what you say BA did to you. I never thought our relationship would come to this.'

In business, there are no friendships, only alliances and, despite Branson's recent recital that 'You don't have to be a bastard to succeed, in fact all bastards fail', only ruthlessness in early 1999 could protect his empire tipping over the edge. The airline's profits of £75 million in 1997/98 had failed to sustain his unsuccessful ventures. Branson's repeated philosophy, 'short-term profits don't matter, we're looking for long-term capital value', was jeopardised by his debts which had accumulated to at least £300 million.

During that financial year, the profits of Virgin Express, the European airline, had fallen from £8.3 million to £783,000; Virgin Management's losses had increased from £7.13 million to £29.2 million; V2 had spent nearly £100 million raised by the bonds and the McCarthys and needed another £45 million despite the planned closure of offices in Australia and elsewhere; Virgin Bride had lost £1.42 million; Virgin Cola had lost £7.24 million; and the trading losses of Virgin Cinemas had increased from £7.6 million to £11.2 million while Virgin Cinemas total debts, as registered in Britain, had increased by £48 million to £190 million.

Temporarily, Will Whitehorn's exhilarated pronouncements of

Virgin Atlantic's £75 million profits concealed the worst of Branson's opaque finances. Enthusiastically, the publicist asserted that Virgin's two hundred and thirteen companies had earned £275 million profit on sales of £3.4 billion. Undoubtedly, Branson approved the publication of those facts although they were difficult to reconcile with those Virgin accounts registered in Britain. Shrewdly, Branson could conceal his plight and avoid an unpleasant observation that all his companies, other than Virgin Atlantic, were loss-makers.

Virgin's financial problems were compounded by a £140 million millstone. In July 1998, Branson had paid £146 million to W. H. Smith in cash to recover the complete ownership of three hundred and five Our Price stores and twenty-four Megastores. Unravelling the disadvantageous ten-year-old deal had been necessary to prevent Smith's buying out Branson's 25 per cent share and trading under the Virgin name in the future.

To fund the deal, Branson borrowed £112.5 million in a high interest bridging loan from Goldman Sachs, Bankers Trust and Bank of Nova Scotia. To repay the loan, he intended to speedily resell two hundred and twenty-nine Our Price shops for £85 million, which was less than his original valuation of £100 million, and keep the Megastores. His ownership of the Megastores, he decided, would be financed by selling high yield bonds worth £300 million to investors. But in September 1998 the bond market crashed and the plan unravelled. His plight was serious. Virgin Entertainment was burdened with debts of about £300 million and he could not find a buyer for Our Price. The best offer was £60 million for shops which were unmodernised and unprofitable. Nothing could be resolved until the Christmas sales had been scrutinised. In public, Branson denied any cash crisis. 'Even if Virgin Atlantic was not making a penny profit,' he said, 'we are sitting on £300 million of cash.'

In San Francisco, David Bonderman knew that Branson could not afford the bank loans. While the American was pleased by his rich return on Virgin Trains and was interested in other profitable deals with Virgin, the cinemas had proved a poor investment. He wanted to sell. Unfortunately, Branson disagreed.

In October 1998, the American refused to invest £20 million in Virgin Entertainment, their joint company, and simultaneously refused to allow Branson to invest the same amount other than as an unsecured loan, a dangerous risk for Virgin. 'Fuck these people,' shouted Branson, 'they're bastards. They'll do what we want.' Lacking the support of his partner, Branson was pressed by the banks for repayment of Virgin Entertainment's loans. Branson recognised the crunch. Despite his hype, he lacked the money to sustain his business. The fate of Virgin Cinemas, a treasured asset, depended on good revenues in the weeks before Christmas 1998. They were dismal. Profits fell by over £1 million. Glancing through the reports at Mill End, his Oxfordshire home, Branson became agitated. Despite his pleasure of being crowned a billionaire by *The Sunday Times*, his fate was being dictated by mere millions of pounds. The momentum was ebbing. 'What should we do with the cinemas?' he asked a director. Selling appeared to be the only solution, but his desperation was well disguised by the optimistic pronouncements broadcast by Whitehorn and himself.

The only glitch in his carefully constructed façade was the Victory Corporation. The clothing and cosmetics company reported losses of £20.7 million which was an embarrassing increase from the previous £9.7 million losses. Victory's shares were stuck at 7 pence, valuing the company at £13 million – the cash in the bank – compared to £110 million at the outset.

As usual, Branson was shy of Virgin bearing the blame. Rory McCarthy appeared to be a convenient scapegoat to obscure Virgin's responsibility for the combined £200 million losses of Victory and V2. The Irishman who had astutely invested in Hemisphere, a telecommunications company, and the Wagamama restaurant chain, was the major casualty. His £80 million investment in the two companies and his guarantee of £35 million to V2 had become worthless. McCarthy, as Branson knew, had invested all his money, the bulk in Branson's businesses and was incapable of providing the new money which both companies required to survive. Branson's solution was harsh.

As the crow flies, Rory McCarthy was about five hundred yards away in his Kensington office as Branson, overlooking his garden in Holland Park, unsentimentally delivered the ultimatum over the telephone to his decidedly ex-buddy.

'The problem,' Branson told McCarthy in his homespun patter, 'is that V2 is not so good. Things haven't gone well.'

'What d'you mean?' McCarthy asked.

'Your holding is worthless. We'll need more money.'

'How much?'

'£25 million,' replied Branson, without a trace of emotion.

'I haven't got it. We've become an empty tin of goodies,' raged McCarthy. The declaration of belligerence incited Branson as he replaced the telephone: 'Well, if he's going to behave like that, then fuck him.'

With Branson's agreement, Stephen Murphy moved to arrange the execution and funeral. McCarthy's shareholding in Victory and V2 was to be diluted into worthlessness. His staff, some employed since 1984, were to be fired. Peter Norris, the discredited chief executive of Baring's Securities, was appointed as Branson's manager of Victory. Relying upon a banker blamed for the collapse of Britain's oldest merchant bank reflected Branson's inability to recruit the best talent in London. 'Peter's my appointed man,' Branson explained to McCarthy. 'If you're rude to him, you're rude to me.'

McCarthy, as intended, was crushed. Virgin's announcement of yet another change in Victory's management and strategy included a carefully approved explanation of the disaster. 'It's all the McCarthys' fault,' said Stephen Murphy. 'We entered into this against our better judgement,' explained Will Whitehorn.

Like Randolph Fields who introduced the idea of Virgin Atlantic and Guy Snowden who accepted an invitation to lunch, Rory McCarthy had discovered the consequences of tangling with the great entrepreneur. 'Our relationship with Virgin has been a disaster,' complained McCarthy. 'He's a smiling assassin,' he added after receiving no response to his detailed letters and telephone calls. 'We're too shell-shocked to protest.'

In Holland Park, Branson could not be very satisfied. Squeezing Rory McCarthy and Per Lindstrand, he understood, had been an irrelevant sideshow to solve his financial predicament. Branson's survival gene sought more drastic remedies.

24

'House of cards'

The worm broke to the surface. Branson's attempt to sell two hundred and twenty-nine Our Price shops collapsed.

In the aftermath of selling Virgin Music in 1992, Branson had often pledged, 'I took a conscious decision that I never wanted to be in a position where I have to sell a company again.' In February 1999, he struggled to maintain his piety. Virgin Cinemas, the Our Price shops and the Megastores were all financial albatrosses but he fought to prevent their disposal.

Like those of the cinemas, the profits of Virgin's record shops over Christmas, despite the economic boom, had been dismal. Branson's weaknesses had undermined his ambitions of an extensive Virgin presence on Britain's streets. Refinancing Virgin's debts on the cinemas and shops by issuing a £300 million high yield bond was no longer realistic. David Bonderman was applying pressure and the banks were demanding the repayment of their loans. Without a new partner willing to invest £110 million, the cinemas would need to be sold. Even that sale would fail to repay all the debts. Only Virgin Atlantic, his single jewel, could provide the necessary funds to sustain the whole empire.

A complete flotation of the airline on the stock exchange was unpalatable to a connoisseur of the shadows. Besides, the record of all three of his publicly financed companies – Virgin Express, the Victory Corporation and V2 – was so disastrous that he could not risk the humiliation of public scrutiny. Victory's shares had fallen from 58 pence to 2¼ pence, Virgin Express's from $15 to $5, and V2's bonds were worthless.

Selling a minority of Virgin Atlantic was the only acceptable strategy. His endurance depended upon successfully enticing partners to finance his private companies in yet another outstanding deal. David Bonderman, a director of Continental Airlines, was asked whether he wanted to buy a 40 per cent stake in Virgin Atlantic. Branson valued the airline at £1.4 billion. Bonderman's estimate was £800 million. By February 1999, their secret negotiations had collapsed. Outsiders suspected nothing. To maintain the smokescreen, the public was offered an exaggeration of Virgin's successes orchestrated by Will Whitehorn.

Will Whitehorn, the former helicopter steward and director of Virgin Trains, presented himself as the leader of the 'extra-terrestrial service development team' masterminding Virgin Galactic Airways, Branson's entry into space tourism. Whitehorn then announced Virgin's purchase of a five hundred thousand acre game reserve in South Africa for £4 million, the company's interest in a South African tourist train and its bid to run South Africa's lottery. (The last two projects failed to materialise.) Finally, he announced new slogans to sell Virgin Cola: 'Open your mouth, I'm coming' and 'You can taste our love every time you swallow'. Sex still failed to sell Branson's sugar water but sex would, he believed, protect Virgin Atlantic's profits which he boasted would rise that year to 'more than £100 million'. That success was the best smokescreen of his financial predicament. To enhance the haze, he reignited his negative campaign against British Airways.

Although Virgin was chosen by two million passengers in 1999, and would not transport ten million as predicted by Whitehorn, Branson believed that his personal and financial survival depended upon mocking the carrier of over thirty-five million people. Vulgarity was his lure for journalists invited on a sex and champagne 'mystery flight' to Amsterdam.

The bait was Virgin's introduction of double beds for passengers buying £6,600 tickets to join the 'Mile High Club'. Unlike British Airways, which had introduced real beds for first class passengers three years earlier, Branson's beds were an artist's impression embellished with the saucy language beloved by Branson's admirers. Lying in pyjamas beside an actress in a mock-up bed, he chortled, 'If you can do it on a cruise ship, at home or in a hotel, I don't see any reason why you can't do it in the air.' Certain that the 'sound of love-making' would be drowned by the aircraft's noise, he laughed 'Why shouldn't we allow couples to explore intimacy in private?' Long ago, he reminded his audience, he had anticipated a 'brothel in the sky'. Subtlety was as alien to Branson as understatement. His purpose was to besmirch BA. 'People,' he scoffed, 'are leaving BA in droves to come to Virgin. That's why BA are panicking and trying to catch up.' His bellicosity was partially justified.

British Airways profits had collapsed by 61 per cent to £225 million, the lowest for six years and real losses were predicted in 1999. BA's imbroglio was magnified by Robert Ayling's abandonment of the 'world images' tail-fin design. Oblivious to the self-humiliation, Ayling sought to rival Branson's 'Mile High' beds by posing for photographers on a British Airways bed, dressed in a white shirt and tie while a fully dressed hostess wearing an absurd hat stood nearby. Only Branson appreciated how his torture of BA deflected attention from a new threat to his own operation.

In May 1999, British Midland was granted a licence to fly across the Atlantic. The only barrier for British Midland's flights was the restriction of the Bermuda II agreement. The pressure from Sir Michael Bishop and the American airlines to realise 'open skies' and destroy the shared monopoly terrified Branson. His rhetoric in Washington two years earlier against the alliance between British Airways and American Airlines and in favour of open skies was forgotten. Disconcertedly, he relied on Robert Ayling to lobby against new competitors. 'Open skies,' Branson predicted in self-interest, 'will not happen in my lifetime.'

That posture encouraged Sir Michael Bishop's dislike and distrust of Branson. In his own search for an investor, Bishop had repeatedly rejected Branson's overtures to combine Virgin's 2 per cent of Heathrow's slots with the 14 per cent controlled by British Midland. The expansion of his airline, Bishop calculated, would be enhanced by embarrassing the self-proclaimed consumer's champion in newspaper advertisements for charging exactly the same high fares as the other three transatlantic airlines. For Branson, who had railed against the 'bad old days when greedy businessmen exploited consumers for their own benefit', it was an unpleasant portent. Bishop was directly endangering Virgin Atlantic's privileges and finances. Branson's concern was masked by launching another aggressive attack against British Airways.

On his initiative, the European Commission had investigated British Airways' commission payments to travel agents although they were similar to every other European airline's including Virgin Atlantic's. To his delight, the Commission imposed a discriminatory fine of £4.5 million against BA. Emboldened by that decision, Branson became reassured that he would obtain a favourable judgement in the New York court for his complaint against BA's dirty tricks. 'My feeling is,' he gurgled, 'that we could really hit the jackpot.' All Virgin's financial problems, he was certain, would be resolved by the anticipated court order that BA should pay Virgin $1 billion damages in punishment. 'The cash would come to us,' he explained. 'Just imagine how much we could have in our war chest to expand the airline.' He praised himself for delivering 'the death-knell of BA's anti-competitive sales incentives' and 'increasing competition'.

The perpetual optimist clung to this hope despite the omen of a mysterious fire on a May Sunday afternoon destroying his offices on the top floor of 11 Holland Park. Branson's reaction was symbolic of his plight. Rushing back to London, he stood outside his damaged home lamenting that 'ten years of files and records' had been destroyed. The ambitious would-be pioneer of the internet seemed to be inhabiting an anachronistic pre-computer age. The promoter of the House of Miracles was only gradually becoming aware that Virgin's reliance upon his personality constantly embracing the new had missed a life-saving opportunity.

Branson was bewildered. Across Silicon Valley, the loss-making new technology ventures justified astronomical values on Wall Street but the stock markets valued his loss-making ventures, despite thirty years' experience, as near worthless. Naturally, he did not recognise the inevitable sclerosis affecting all those approaching fifty, regardless of their youthful and irreverent self-image. No honest *consigliere* in Holland Park warned about the rapid change in the New Economy. No mirror reflected the ageing performer groping to wrest back control of his destiny.

Branson's ignorance about e-commerce and the internet cast a spell of gloom among those puzzled by his resistance to the new technology. 'Richard's angry that others have made fortunes on the net,' Stephen Murphy gossiped over lunch in the basement canteen, 'and he hasn't. He wants to catch up. He's become obsessive about it. He says, "If Amazon is worth billions I want the same."' Murphy's audience collectively shrugged. Since November 1996, Virgin Net had attracted only 160,000 subscribers and lost many others after Branson refused, like his competitors, to abandon subscription fees. He had wasted more than two years. Only after personally using the net at the beginning of 1999 could he begin to appreciate the folly of chasing dinosaurs and overcome his instinctive reluctance to give something away for nothing. Even so, he could not discard his ingrained habit of paying unspectacular wages and strictly limiting his financial investment. To survive in the New Economy, he reasoned, he needed only to stick the Virgin brand on to the latest fashion. During 1999 he decided Virgin's salvation depended upon challenging the young Goliaths of new technology.

For thirty years, challenging Goliaths had become Branson's trademark. Virgin's future, even its existence, he reasoned, depended upon creating the third Big One after the success of Virgin Music and Virgin Atlantic. But in his excited pursuit of success to beget a new empire, he was blind to Virgin's flaws. In technology, much depended upon selecting the best brains and his recent record suggested that his hand-picked executives had damaged Virgin.

By then, successive executives employed to develop Virgin Net had abandoned the company complaining about confusion and parsimony. Bereft of the best, Branson favoured loyalty, especially those who spontaneously asked themselves, 'What would Richard think of that?' Among those trusted was Rowan Gormley, the chief executive of Virgin Direct, who, having failed to produce a profitable finance company within five years, was transferred to revitalise Virgin Net.

Other Virgin executives had not been rewarded for their failure. Jonathan Ornstein, despite the praise two years earlier, had been fired from Virgin Express; Brad Rosser had departed with a £1 million payment; a succession of executives had passed through Virgin Clothes and the Victory Corporation; and Brian Barrett was no longer the manager of Virgin Trains. Of those who remained, Jeremy Pearce at V2 survived, despite limited praise, arguably because no replacement could be found; while Chris Ash, Branson's candidate to manage his new mobile telephone shops, had arrived from Hamleys after the toy store's shares had crashed 45 per cent in the last nineteen months.

Branson was vulnerable to the damage caused by his foot soldiers. The Belgian government had threatened to ground Virgin Express unless the management was reorganised and the airline stopped leasing 'unregulated' planes and crews from Ireland. With the shares trading below $5 compared to a high of $28, the Virgin brand was tarnished.

In the autumn of 1999 Virgin Trains were the least punctual, the most expensive and attracted the most complaints of any operator. Virgin's Cross Country services were 67 per cent worse than 1998 – 'the worst of all Britain's trains', according to the regulator – and there were 145 per cent more cancellations on the West Coast line. Without contrition, the consumer's champion had increased some train fares by seven times the rate of inflation, offering the public the greatest discomfort at the highest prices.

A third casualty was Virgin's finance company. Although its initial success, accumulating £2.1 billion of funds since 1995, was praiseworthy, its rival egg had since 1998 accumulated £6 billion. Virgin's ambitions had cost at least £100 million and profits remained elusive, especially after investors discovered that Virgin's tracker fund charged a 1 per cent fee while some rivals charged ¼ per cent. Other investors were disenchanted that the performance of Virgin's bonds, PEPs and tracker funds was only marginally better than average. The annual growth of Virgin's funds was 4.7 per cent while Legal & General's rose to 6.6 per cent and Fidelity's to 7.5 per cent. The growth of new investors was declining. In 1998, Virgin had sold only 15,000 pensions compared with 129,000 by Scottish Widows.

In public, Branson and Will Whitehorn constantly reaffirmed that the public trusted the Virgin brand. Privately, he was convinced that the new loyalists could best be wooed to any new technology stamped with the Virgin brand.

The most attractive opportunity was offered by Mike Kendrick, the project manager of his balloon races. Engineers in Europe and America, reported Kendrick, had developed software to transform mobile telephones into portable computers. In the first quarter of 1999, Kendrick explained, nearly two million Britons had bought mobiles, three times more than in 1998. Over the following years, billions of pounds would be earned by the providers of mobile telephones and the internet. The apostle of anti-knowledge was mesmerised, less by the revolutionary technology than the prospective fortunes for the winners. 'Virgin Mobiles' had a natural ring. Kendrick had heard of two employees of Cellnet negotiating with another entrepreneur to finance the ground-breaking combination of mobiles and e-commerce. They could, he suggested, be lured to Virgin. For hopefully no financial investment, the Virgin brand would be attached to an existing mobile company and rival

Vodaphone, Cellnet or Orange, all multibillion pound corporations with a decade's experience. Branson was elated. A big new project always galvanised his enthusiasm.

Branson was neither the first nor the smartest. Rather than following, he was chasing the trend. His familiar hype in June 1999 glossed over his weakness: 'We aim to become the biggest provider of mobile phones in Britain within two-and-a-half years.' The outlandish, unrealisable ambition bore a similarity to his pronouncement, 'In two weeks' time, we'll be taking on Amazon on the Internet. But we'll have 400,000 titles, or 50,000 more than Amazon.'

Branson's natural excitement about another new project was depressed by his reliance on the fourth best telephone company. Only One2One, lacking business customers, agreed to a suitable partnership. The telephone company rejected, however, Branson's usual formula of risking their money on his gambles. Rather than allocate Branson 50 per cent of the business for no money in return for the Virgin brand, Virgin was only able to participate in return for an equal investment of £50 million. Compared to venture capitalists eagerly investing huge sums in numerous dot.com fantasies, Virgin's value as a partner, despite Branson's new slogan 'Embracing the New', was plainly less attractive.

Nor could Branson attract dynamic young technogeeks to create his new business. Instead, he relied on James Kydd, the verbose marketing director of Virgin Cola and friend of Will Whitehorn, to market Virgin Mobile. The hype began before selling a single telephone. Whitehorn secured a surprisingly high valuation of £1.36 billion for Virgin Mobile by Investec Henderson Crosthwaite, the City brokers owned by Australian Mutual Provincial (AMP), Branson's partner in Virgin Direct.

The positive publicity encouraged Branson's promotion of his new multibillion pound fortune. 'Up until now,' Branson preened to a chosen audience, 'any venture capital that has gone into financial services or trains or record companies have all made fantastic returns for the long-term holder.' No one openly contradicted that inaccuracy. His only recent profits were £50 million from the sale of Virgin Radio by Chris Evans's Ginger Group despite a loss of five hundred thousand listeners, and from the sale of some hotels. Realists in Holland Park knew that the solitary glow during the summer of 1999 was a front page colour photograph of Holly Branson in the *News of the World* to illustrate an exaggerated report of her friendship with Prince William. The unfortunate reality was impatient telephone calls from his bankers.

The search for a partner to invest £110 million in Virgin Cinemas had failed. Similarly, no buyer had appeared for the two hundred and twenty-nine Our Price shops, the epitome of a dinosaur investment. Buying music in shops was becoming history. The sale was abandoned. Virgin's indigestible debt for the two companies had reached nearly £400 million. Other debts were accumulating. Branson's only source of cash to launch the mobile telephones and e-commerce ventures was Virgin Atlantic and the airline's dividend in 1999 of £50 million had already disappeared. His plight was compounded by an unexpected earthquake: the airline's current profits were steeply declining.

Despite Branson's repeated predictions that, unlike British Airways, Virgin Atlantic was 'increasing its pre-tax earnings' – variously quoting profits of £96 million, £100 million and £120 million in the previous financial year – the circumstances had changed. During the summer of 1999, Branson privately acknowledged, the airline was suffering a 'sudden drop in profits'. Fuel prices had doubled, the competition across the Atlantic was ferocious and the cost of refurbishing his planes was astronomical. A severe cash crisis had struck.

Graham Clempson, his banker at Bankers Trust, recently bought by the Deutsche Bank, and the representatives of the Bank of America, demanded repayment of their loans. While they were prepared to allow Branson time to rearrange the management of his shops, their patience for a sale of the cinemas was extinguished. The banks wanted loans of nearly £200 million repaid. Branson did not possess the money.

Cash crises were not new to Branson but this one threatened to become a meltdown, the final nightmare. The cinemas, Megastores and shops were, with clothes, cola and music, vital for the Virgin brand's relationship with the public. At a single stroke, the edifice was threatened and pertinently, unlike in his last crisis in 1991, he was not the victim of a recession. Virgin was simply the casualty of its own mismanagement. Branson faced an unpleasant reality. His pledge never to have to sell a business was redundant.

In a desperate bid to save the cinemas, Branson asked David

Bonderman, the owner of a 30 per cent stake, to accept some refinancing. The response was frosty. The American was suffering a
new irritation. The Texas Pacific Group had been excluded from
the profits of Branson's new, wholly owned Virgin.com. Branson,
it seemed, had decided that Bonderman was not an ideal partner. In
response, Bonderman demanded that the cinemas should be sold.
On 26 October 1999, Vivendi, a French company, bought Virgin's
thirty-four multiplex cinemas for £215 million. Although Whitehorn
presented the sale as another triumph, the money barely repaid the
company's debts and Bonderman's assured share of the proceeds. The
record shops were the bankers' next target. Only winning 'the jackpot' in the anti-trust case against British Airways in New York could
save his financial plight.

In the weeks before Judge Cederbaum's judgement, the importance of a favourable decision preoccupied Branson. While every
European airline was retrenching, his expansion had gathered pace,
risking huge losses on new routes to India, Chicago and Las Vegas, and
the launch of a new airline in Australia which would cost £200 million.
In public, Branson appeared permanently optimistic, vehemently
denying that he was suffering a cash crisis, but the impediments of aviation regulators and competitors gave good reasons for fear.

The British government had rejected one of his protests and agreed
that British Airways could keep CityFlyer, its franchise airline at
Gatwick; Virgin had been compelled to pay £2 million for slots at
Gatwick; British Airways had defeated Virgin Atlantic and won the
hugely profitable route to Nigeria; and, finally, Sir Michael Bishop
had rejected Branson's overtures and sold a 20 per cent stake of
British Midland to Lufthansa for £91 million. Branson's only amuse-
ment was Virgin Atlantic's latest advertisement featuring two detectives investigating BA's dirty tricks seven years earlier, and the
positioning of an airship over the British Airways Ferris wheel lying
stricken on the River Thames. The slogan on the airship, 'BA can't
get it up', reflected Virgin's intellectual onanism. Pranks which
attracted widespread admiration ten years earlier, now barely raised
a ripple. Branson's self-indulgence was his last laugh before Judge
Cederbaum's judgement.

There was, Branson believed, every reason to expect Judge Cederbaum in New York to imitate the decision of the European Commission and massively penalise British Airways. His certainty of

victory encouraged his merciless rebuke of Robert Ayling as 'an international jewel thief . . . snatching away the precious gem of competition across the Atlantic'.

To his amazement, on 25 October 1999, Cederbaum ruled against Virgin. Despite Branson spending £10 million on legal fees, the judge ruled that Virgin had not produced any convincing evidence. 'Virgin has not raised a genuine issue of disputed fact,' ruled the judge. Branson's entire case against British Airways, continued Cederbaum, relied on a single academic's 'assumptions that have not been supported by market data'. In the judge's opinion, Branson's ten-year campaign alleging BA's monopoly and conspiracy to destroy Virgin was based upon one academic's discredited theory. Judge Cederbaum's decision that Virgin was only subject to normal competition was deeply distressing.

'I'm astonished,' flustered Branson. 'It's not the end of the road.' The litigation, he pledged, would continue. Ayling's appeal to stop the war was rejected by a man sustained by combative relish over the corporation's difficulties. He needed enemies to prove his critics wrong. His defiance camouflaged a major embarrassment.

For years, Branson had basked as the victim of British Airways' dirty tricks. 'Virgin the Victim' and 'Branson, The People's Champion of Truth', had been crafted as an outstanding marketing weapon. In 1993, Branson had rejected Bob Ayling's £9 million offer for a full settlement in the expectation of winning $1 billion. Instead, the final account was Virgin's payment to BA of £184,000.

The humiliation was compounded by the cash crisis. Graham Clempson and other bankers were demanding the repayment of Virgin Retail's debts which, by the end of 1999, were approaching £170 million. Despite the traditional juggling to divert cash from other companies into the Our Price shops, there were unusual difficulties. All of Branson's companies were debt-ridden, the profits from the railways were legally ring-fenced and the airline possessed barely any surplus cash. Will Whitehorn naturally sought to deny the problem. Eight months earlier, the publicist had quoted Virgin's annual profits as £275 million. His assessment of the latest financial year was profits of £330 million. The figures and the increase were inexplicable and unsubstantiated by any published accounts. Wishful thinking did not impress the bankers. At the appropriate times, hyperactive tycoons could be amusing and generate profitable fees but

Branson's glamour was passing. The moment of reckoning was approaching.

The airline was Branson's only source of finance to repay his debts. Flotation was unacceptable. The directors of Air France, after long discussions, were unwilling to buy a minority stake in an airline which Branson valued at 'considerably in excess' of £1.2 billion, a value which was criticised by City analysts as 'starry-eyed'. Casting around for another investor, he approached Singapore Airlines. The same package, rejected by French and American airlines, was offered to Cheong Choong Kong, Singapore's chief executive. For ten years, the state-owned airline had failed to persuade the British government to allow its flights to continue from Heathrow across the Atlantic. Buying a 49 per cent share of Virgin Atlantic offered an opportunity for expansion. History was repeating itself. Just as one decade earlier, Branson had found Japanese investors flush with cash eager to save his business; now the Singaporeans possessed surplus money to secure his survival. Branson's offer, proffering accounts demonstrating the airline's £105 million profits in the previous year, was tempting.

On Saturday, 18 December 1999, at the Four Seasons Hotel overlooking Park Lane, Branson met Cheong Choong Kong, with his mind set on the airline's value at £1.2 billion. The outstanding negotiator calculated that the Singaporean after ten weeks of discussions and a special journey might be reluctant to leave without a deal. He proved right.

'A marriage made in heaven' was Branson's conclusion about yet another spectacular deal which allowed Whitehorn to publicise a headline valuation of £1.2 billion. 'I shall remain chairman and we will have the majority of directors on the board,' said Branson adding a strange pledge at the moment of the sale: 'Virgin Atlantic is not for sale and will never be up for sale.' Even more curious, although understandable, was his emphatic denial that the sale was driven by his debts. 'We haven't got any cash problems,' he insisted in the same voice as his denials eight years earlier before his sale of Virgin Music to EMI. But just as in 1992, the moment of truth was approaching.

To outsiders, Branson still shone as Britain's outstanding entrepreneur. He had been entertained for a weekend at Chequers by Tony Blair, the Prime Minister; he was invited to deliver a Millennium lecture in Oxford; and the sale of one hundred thousand Virgin

Mobile telephones at Christmas encouraged one bank to value his
Internet business at between £3.5 billion and £6.5 billion. To sane
observers, the £3 billion disparity invalidated the valuation but Branson's certainty of attracting one million customers for Virgin Mobiles
by the end of 2000 reinvigorated belief in the brand, even if his new
telephone system had temporarily crashed three weeks after its birth.
The predictions and valuations had seduced major players, including
George Soros, J. P. Morgan, Tesco, EMI, Warren Buffet and Paul
Allen of Microsoft and venture capital funds, to join SpectrumCo,
Branson's consortium, and bid for one of five UMTS bands provided
for the new generation of mobile telephones. None realised their
partner's weak finances. A blitz of announcements in the last days
of December to welcome the arrival of the first tilting train, a Virgin
bid for the Dome in Greenwich, a proposal to open thirty new
Megastores in Asia and new internet services cast a smokescreen over
the demand by Virgin's banks for repayment of loans of £180 million
to the Our Price stores. Hyperactivity, he hoped, would bestow
credibility upon his empire and restore his image as a deal-junkie
rather than a debt-junkie. Unfortunately, his bankers were unper-
suaded.

Just before Christmas Eve, Graham Clempson and other bankers
threatened to march into every Megastore and Our Price shop and
snatch the cash from the tills. Only a desperate telephone call from
Branson, by then on Necker awaiting thirty guests, averted that
danger. 'The Singapore cash will pay off the debts,' he pleaded. 'Just
be patient until the end of January. You'll get your money.' The
bankers relented. Fortunately, his smokescreen was embellished by
Tony Blair who, paradoxically just as a major Virgin business tilted
on the edge of bankruptcy, had finally agreed to award Branson a
knighthood for services to entrepreneurship. The public endorsement
diverted attention from his predicament, helped, he hoped, by a
strange anecdote. 'Two years ago,' he recounted, 'I wrote to Tony
Blair saying I didn't want a knighthood because the bad publicity of
the trains would have made it embarrassing.' But he had not been
offered a knighthood.

The acclamation clearly justified, Branson believed, his second
submission to run the National Lottery. During October, although
he desperately sought that prize, Branson had encouraged doubts in
Whitehall that he would bid. Convinced that he had been cheated

six years earlier, he never ceased to ridicule Camelot's 'dull' lottery which had reduced those regularly playing from 94 per cent of the population to 67 per cent. Yet in recent weeks he had been stung by the Post Office's choice of Camelot rather than himself as a partner for the new franchise and was even surprised by GTech's refusal to co-operate with his bid. Before taking further financial and personal risks, he wanted the Lottery Commission to rewrite the rules to remove what he perceived as Camelot's unfair advantages of possessing an assured consortium of suppliers and a network of terminals in thirty-five thousand shops across Britain. He would only bid, government ministers were told, if there was no requirement for an assured consortium of suppliers, if Camelot was ordered to buy new terminals and if Camelot was requested to divulge the details of crucial commercial relationships.

Branson's position was strong. Government ministers feared embarrassment if Camelot won without a challenge and so, to secure Branson's participation, Camelot was required to spend £100 million on new terminals. The beneficiaries of the waste were the American manufacturers. The losers were the British public and charities. With those concessions, Branson agreed to bid and renounce his demand for a non-profit lottery and espouse 'financial incentives' to maximise revenues.

The atmosphere during his personal announcement on 13 December 1999 that his own private company, The People's Lottery Ltd, would bid for the lottery was modest. The authors of the unsuccessful 1994 bid, Simon Burridge of J. Walter Thompson and John Jackson of Mates, Sketchley and latterly the Victory Corporation, had been resurrected as managers. His company's profits, he explained, would be donated to the good causes. Two other pledges were calculated to secure headlines. He would raise £1 billion more for the 'good causes' than Camelot and his game would award a £1 million jackpot every day of the year. The favourable reaction suggested that Branson would topple Camelot. He was aware of the kudos of victory.

The accolade of the government's unprecedented trust in one individual's ability to raise over £12 billion which had become a vital source of Britain's funding of the arts, charities and tax revenue was immeasurable. But the flaw was equally glaring. Camelot, for all its sins, was a consortium of major British corporations whose regis-.

tered accounts were available for public scrutiny. By contrast, the sole director of The People's Lottery Ltd could no longer conceal in early January 2000 his financial crisis.

Although *The Sunday Times* had been persuaded that Branson was worth £2.4 billion, double the previous year's assessment, Branson was unable to pay £35 million owed to the record companies for supplies to the Our Price shops before Christmas 1999. Bankruptcy loomed and he parried demands for payment with excuses. 'There's money coming,' intimated Branson to pacify the furious complaints, mentioning the sale to Singapore Airlines. Doubters within Holland Park were assured that there was no crisis. 'Richard can always ask his family trustees for £300 million in cash,' Whitehorn and Murphy said, ignoring the legal complications of any such transaction and raising queries about the original source of that money. Exasperated, the producers ceased supplying records. To survive, Branson agreed on 31 January 2000 to the most humiliating terms of trade. Every Monday before noon, a Virgin executive would present each record producer with cash to guarantee that week's record supplies.

To disguise his embarrassment, Branson presented his failure to pay as a protest against the record companies' discrimination in favour of selling music through the internet. The profit margins for shops, complained Branson, were inadequate. Branson was blind to the paradox. Virgin.com, his new Internet company, was encouraging the public to download music through his gateway. The contradiction confirmed Branson's confusion. His plight over a trifling £35 million coincided with the first paragraph of Virgin's obituary.

In mid-January, the flaw in Branson's latest ambition was exposed. America Online (AOL) announced its takeover of the previously mighty Time Warner to create the world's biggest company worth $350 billion. Real value in the internet belonged to those combining a gateway and content. A brand without a mass of subscribers eager to buy its content was an empty vessel. In his rush to embrace the new technology, Branson had espoused a new dinosaur. Too late, he reassessed his plan. Rowan Gormley, the new strategist of Virgin's Internet operations, was relegated to manage a new wine business. The shuffle to save Virgin's fate was ridiculed the following week.

Vodaphone, the mobile telephone company, successfully bid for Mannesman of Germany. Pertinently, Vodaphone had been founded in 1984, the same year as Virgin Atlantic. Sixteen years later, the airline's value was at best £1.2 billion; Vodaphone's new value was £215 billion. That staggering contrast was the drab testament of thirty-three years of juggling by a man praised as Britain's foremost entrepreneur, addicted to his belief that his sparkling ideas, thrown off to a dazzled audience, would profit by his Midas touch.

Branson's battle in early 2000 was not for immediate survival – the money from Singapore Airlines guaranteed that his outstanding debts would be repaid – but for his credibility. A record producer had initiated the first step for a winding-up order. While revising his proposals to raise £15 billion for the lottery and aggressively promoting Virgin Direct by appearing in the nude in an advertisement, he was negotiating with Graham Clempson and his other creditors, to discount their loans of £180 million to £150 million. 'We're not going to act like a load of patsies,' chortled Whitehorn, convinced that Virgin could outface its bankers and reduce the repayment by £30 million by threatening to declare Virgin Retail's bankruptcy.

While Branson sought time until Singapore Airlines paid the publicised £600 million, other debts appeared. V2 required £45 million to continue; Virgin Cola's accumulated debts, after a further loss of £4.4 million, had increased to over £30 million; Virgin clothes (within the Victory Corporation) was closed down after losing another £8.6 million in six months, bequeathing accumulated debts of £60 million; and Virgin Express incurred for the first time debts of £3.4 million. Branson's youth strategy launched four years previously was terminated. The paradox of Branson arriving at that very moment, on Thursday, 30 March 2000, at Buckingham Palace to formally receive his knighthood for 'services to entrepreneurship' from the Prince of Wales passed unnoticed in London. Branson was a hero, not a target for criticism. By a whisker, he had avoided humiliation.

In the early hours of the following morning, Singapore Airlines' money was transferred to Virgin. 'Richard has £600 million in the bank from Singapore Airlines,' sang Whitehorn. That was only possibly accurate for the briefest of moments. Instead of £600 million, Branson had banked only £400 million. One third of the price had evaporated. £100 million, as originally agreed, was invested in the two airlines, and £100 million was discounted after Singapore's due diligence and the payment of share options. Of the remaining money,

£185 million was transferred to Our Price's bankers and suppliers. On Monday morning, Branson possessed only slightly more than £200 million to repay his other accumulating debts. In his familiar denial of a crisis, he asserted, 'We're flush with cash' and claimed to possess '£1 billion in cash'. The succession of payments over that weekend, he insisted, was 'an absolute irrelevancy' to any suggestion of a crisis. The denial was unsustainable. His weaknesses were unresolved. Branson had toppled from his perch on to a slippery, downward path into a self-made trap.

25

Seeking salvation

At 7.30 p.m. on 5 April 2000, Richard Branson stood in the reception room in 10 Downing Street. Cherie Blair, the prime minister's wife, was co-hosting a small reception for representatives of the travel industry. Pointedly, during the course of a conversation, the pregnant QC told Branson with a smile, 'I've been talking to Tony and we agree that we must do something for you.' Branson noticeably returned Mrs Blair's warmth. The prime minister's gifts were valuable. Equally, any politician had good reason to fear that any upset to the popular hero would provoke a ferocious counter-attack. For his part, Branson's wish list was considerable. He desperately wanted the licence for the National Lottery – 'my major ambition in the new millennium,' he had confessed five months earlier – and, equally, he wanted continued protection of the cartel he shared at Heathrow for transatlantic flights. Both were vital for the survival of the Virgin empire, once again heading towards a precipice.

Over the previous thirty years, plucking a profitable reprieve from potential disaster had been the hallmark and foundation of Richard Branson's successive achievements. Any turmoil was concealed by calculated bravado and secrecy. Extremely visible publicity distracted inquisitive onlookers from the smoke and mirrors surrounding his finances. Branson remained a man skilled in the management of his debt.

One clue of Virgin's instability in June 2000 was the unanticipated departure without formal announcement of Stephen Murphy, the finance director who, since Trevor Abbott's ostracism, had masterminded the management of Virgin's principal companies and offshore trusts. Rather than be associated with a conglomerate valued by Branson at £5 billion, Murphy chose to manage a new internet company dependent on a loan of $60 million. The departure of a group finance director without the immediate appointment of a replacement was unusual.

Among Murphy's last chores was negotiating the refinancing of V2, Branson's music company. In the deal brokered by Morgan Stanley with the bondholders, £93 million of debt was expunged and Branson pledged to personally invest £65 million in the beleaguered company. His prize of a revitalised corporation was at the expense of the banks and the McCarthy brothers, who lost their entire fortune, including personal possessions.* Branson did not appear to shed any tears. He shrugged aside the disappointments and ruptured relationships. But Stephen Murphy had reason for concern.

Virgin Cola's losses in the previous year had risen to £4.4 million; Virgin Express's losses in the first quarter of 2000 had risen to £8.6 million; Virgin had lost money in America and was closing some Megastores in Europe; Virgin Trains, according to the new methodology of the Strategic Rail Authority, still suffered the worst punctuality record while its profits relied upon the diminishing subsidy; the future flotation of Virgin Direct, the financial services company, widely promoted in advertisements dominated by Branson, was jeopardised by its continuing losses and the slide in the share price of egg, a rival; and most seriously, Virgin Atlantic's profits were certain to collapse because of rising fuel prices.

Popular attitudes to Virgin were souring as well. The repertoire of flattering reviews in the gossip columns, news reports and financial pages was noticeably diminishing. The printed mention of Branson's name accompanied by photographs was no longer automatically associated with a success story. Will Whitehorn's feverish efforts to encourage friendly journalists and threaten critics were failing to protect his employer's pristine image. Rather than Ricky inheriting the earth, Sir Richard Branson was portrayed as grappling with an unfashionable and indebted conglomerate steeped in the past.

Branson dismissed the harbingers of woe. 'Virgin is in the most successful shape it has ever been in,' he insisted. 'It is one of the few cash rich businesses in Britain. It is the largest private company in Britain and it is the best known British brand name in the world. We have created a number of very, very successful businesses, so

* The banks cancelled £73 million of debt and took a 25 per cent equity stake and the remaining bondholders inherited a 34.5 per cent stake.

where are the problems? There are no major nasties.' While Britain's manufacturing industry was, argued Branson, 'in a state of meltdown' because Britain had not joined the Euro, Virgin's destiny was safe. He justified his confidence by comparing Virgin's businesses to the new dot.com economy. Mesmerised by the magical power of attaching the Virgin brand to computers and e-commerce, he claimed fervently the flawed ideology of the pioneers of dot.com – that vast debts and the ceaseless haemorrhage of cash were the foundation of new empires despite the absence of any saleable assets.

Although since Christmas 1999 Amazon's value had collapsed from £25 billion to £7.5 billion, Branson allied himself to the executives of Amazon and Freeserve who confidently repeated the credo that losses were irrelevant in the creation of real wealth. Their indebtedness was equated by Branson to his own loss-making businesses. That ideology was the foundation of Virgin's new future as Virgin.com. Enshrining it as 'Virgin Home' worth a questionable £5 billion, Branson launched as his salvation an electronic shopping mall to cross-promote endless Virgin services. The risk was considerable.

Just as experienced retailers, driven by fears of the internet, were abandoning the high street, Branson spent £60 million to convert his Our Price shops into 'V.shops' to sell mobile telephones, CDs, and a myriad of new services. The first results were not encouraging. Despite expensive advertising and sharply reduced prices, fewer than 500,000 Virgin mobiles were sold in seven months, compared to Orange attracting 1.2 million new customers in just three months. Worse, many originally contracted to Virgin Mobile were not using their telephones.

Hampered by his limited funds, he nevertheless energetically introduced Virgin Energy to sell the cheapest gas and electricity with the prospect of subsequently offering home removals, decorating, carpentry, plastering and electrical work; he launched Virgin.com/ cars aiming to sell 24,000 cars within the first year at the cheapest prices, although early attempts showed that on occasions some Virgin prices were £2,000 higher than those offered in a local showroom; he created Virgin Money and Virgin Travel as online brokers and travel agents; and promoted Virgin Wine Wizard with the unusual incentive that Branson knew 'nothing' about wine. The only substantive venture was trainline.com, selling rail tickets. Although Branson's prediction of earning £100 million profits by 2003 was optimistic, it was a sound business though jeopardised by an increasingly familiar problem.

Despite Branson's boasts that Virgin was widely regarded as an ideal employer, many of the young staff of Virgin Net had resigned in March 2000 and others followed in April. Their common complaint was Virgin's poor financial incentives. Thirty years earlier, Branson's personality had attracted staff to work for low wages. The new generation was not similarly entranced, especially after those executives expecting to benefit from an early flotation of Virgin Mobile were sharply contradicted, on Branson's behalf, by Will Whitehorn. The boffins wanted a proper share of the wealth they would create and were surprised by Branson's blunt refusal. Their surprise was not shared by a group of Australians.

During Branson's gamble to launch Australian Blue, his new airline, Australians had been introduced to the entrepreneur's character with an unusual revelation. Aggressive lawyers issued threats to all companies registered under the name 'Virgin'. In unexpected letters, the directors were ordered to cease trading under the Virgin name within fourteen days, disconnect their telephones, hand over their stationery for destruction and pay Branson's legal costs. Their protests compelled Branson's retreat and apologies, but the blatant burst of assertiveness revealed his desperation in the bid for aggrandisement.

Branson's new ambitions had been encouraged by endorsements, such as that volunteered by Cherie Blair. While Branson could not be certain whether the prime minister would influence the lottery award, there was no doubt that Virgin Atlantic's fate rested entirely upon the government's preference. In particular, he sensed that John Prescott, the deputy prime minister, was unsympathetic. Recently, Prescott had awarded British Airways an extra daily flight to South Africa rather than Virgin Atlantic, an unexpected blow. Now, it appeared, the minister was inclined to bow to American pressure and amend the Bermuda II agreement and allow rival airlines to fly from Heathrow. If that occurred, Virgin Atlantic's profits could be devastated with dire repercussions on his empire's finances. 'We are very, very worried,' Branson lamented. 'In the last month there has been a shift in government policy. The direction in which the talks are heading leaves us the most depressed we have been in sixteen years.'

The menace was 'open skies', the unfussy phrase which would

destroy the 'legal cartel' which Virgin Atlantic shared with British Airways, United Airlines and American Airlines on all flights from Heathrow to the USA. That cosy arrangement was being uncompromisingly challenged by Rodney Slater, the US Secretary for Transportation, on behalf of all American airline companies and British Midland.

British Midland, which operated 14 per cent of the slots at Heathrow, compared to the 2 per cent allotted to Virgin, had been strengthened by Lufthansa's purchase of a 20 per cent stake in the British airline. As a leading member of the near-unassailable Star alliance, the German airline could, if Bermuda II was amended, launch cut-price services from Heathrow to America, damaging British Airways and Virgin Atlantic.

For years, fearing the competition, Branson had vigorously opposed British Midland's bid to fly from Heathrow to America. In response, Sir Michael Bishop, British Midland's chairman, began to finance an advertising campaign showing how Virgin's maintenance of the Bermuda II cartel had kept the fares of some business class flights from Heathrow over 200 per cent higher than equivalent flights from Europe. Branson resented being labelled anti-competitive but few appeared sympathetic to his self-justifying defences.

To win support, Branson appeared on 7 June before members of the House of Commons Select Committee on Transport to argue against any concessions to the Americans. Unusually, he did not project an insurmountable certainty of victory. 'On a level playing field,' he told the MPs, 'we can beat anybody. We have proved that.' Virgin's airline had 'driven fares down'. Sceptics were visibly unconvinced. Lower fares to Europe owed everything to Ryanair and easyJet, not Virgin Express, and competition by British Midland would reduce transatlantic fares.

That reality was not Branson's only concern. Any amendment of Bermuda II, he knew, would include permission for British Airways to forge a full alliance with American Airlines and possibly merge with KLM. Over the previous four years, Branson had successfully campaigned against every attempt by British Airways to survive the fatal pincer of the three giant alliances which embraced its rival airlines. With flair and persistence, Branson had kept his hostile cards on the deck, face up, while British Airways floundered. BA's weakness empowered Virgin Atlantic. Bob Ayling's plea, 'We just want equal treatment to survive,' had been derided by Branson as pathetic self-interest.

Circumstances had, however, changed. On 10 March, on the eve of British Airways announcing record losses, Bob Ayling had been fired. His replacement, Rod Eddington, an intelligent Australian with a lifetime's experience in the airline industry, had good reason to believe that, in a changed atmosphere, John Prescott would trade 'open skies' for approval of British Airways' alliance to safeguard the airline's survival. That prospect depressed Branson. 'We could be about to see the end of UK aviation as we know it,' he warned, blind to the contradiction that he had just sold practically half his airline to a foreign state without apparently contemplating the effect on British aviation. Protecting Virgin Atlantic's profits was crucial to Virgin's entire commercial survival.

Self-interest had always dictated Branson's ambitions but he drew a distinction between his commercial activities and his bid to run the National Lottery. On the topic of Britain's ritualised gambling habit, Branson presented himself as the crusader, offering to manage the £36 billion business purely for charity.

Branson, the challenger, was certainly disadvantaged. His consortium lacked Camelot's experience to reassure the Lottery Commission that he could efficiently and securely manage a huge operation without mishap. His previous application had failed on several grounds to satisfy the investigators. Over the intervening five years, the controversy surrounding his performance as a business manager raised more questions about his suitability. His failure to fulfil his predicted successes in many different Virgin enterprises, his recurring financial losses and the inscrutability of his offshore trusts were persistent sources of unease. To remove the doubts, Branson established an unnamed holding company without shareholders and seven non-executive directors to supervise the People's Lottery, his new private company, and recruited Don Cruickshank as one of the directors. But that arrangement only aroused further bewilderment.

Offsetting that handicap was Camelot's image and the legacy of the relationship with G-Tech. On the very eve of the Lottery Commission's decision, the management of the American operator had been exposed as unreliable. From July 1998 until May 2000, the American managers had concealed a glitch in the computer software which had marginally affected 113,000 prizes out of the 14 billion tickets sold between 1994 and 1998. Camelot's boast to be irreproachably reliable was flawed. G-Tech's claim to have transformed itself was suspect, reinforcing Branson's original complaint.

In Branson's mind, that revelation should have tilted the balance in his favour. Winning the lottery licence, he knew, would irreversibly confirm him as a pillar of Britain's permanent Establishment. The billions of pounds of lottery money flowing perfectly legitimately through a private company with a single shareholder would place Branson in an unprecedented position of power and influence. Rejection for a second time, however, bore serious implications. Indelibly, he would be cast as an outsider, struggling to save the reputation of a ramshackle empire.

The mid-morning telephone call on Wednesday, 23 August 2000 from Dame Helena Shovelton, the Lottery Commission chairman, to Branson marooned by a hurricane on Necker, appeared initally to deliver bad news. Shovelton's opening words announced that neither Branson nor Camelot had won the franchise.

Despite endless negotiations, Branson had been unable to satisfy the Commission about the financial security of The People's Lottery, his private company. In particular, Shovelton explained, the Commission had identified how the financial claims of lottery players might not be protected if Branson's lottery became insolvent, lost its licence or failed to raise as much money as he predicted. In Shovelton's opinion, Branson's proposals on those crucial financial issues were 'so conditional and so uncertain' that the Commission harboured, 'significant concerns about the financial viability of the People's Lottery if the ticket sales were much lower than expected'. Since the Commission had also concluded that Branson's predictions of increasing sales by 50 per cent were optimistic, Shovelton seemed to be questioning aspects of Branson's bid.

Two months earlier, Shovelton had demanded an 'irrevocable, bankable commitment' that Branson produce £50 million in cash in addition to the £170 million he had already borrowed from his banks. Branson had yet to deliver the last £50 million.

But good news followed. 'We are going to give you one month to satisfy that requirement,' continued Shovelton. Since Branson had recently accepted estimates of his worth as 'in excess of £2 billion', a mere £50 million should not present a problem for Branson. 'We will give them an irrevocable bank guarantee for £50 million,'

Branson would soon after promise, 'so that if sales continue to fall they can call upon it.' Since he did not appear to possess £50 million available in cash in Britain, or even possibly in the Virgin Islands, Branson seemed to hope that within one month he could raise the money from others. The Commission's requirement, an odd stumbling block after six months of negotiations, was easily trivialised by Branson and his executives as an 'error of judgement' on their part. But others interpreted the Commission's stipulation as raising questions not only about Branson's financial stability but also about the Commission's whole process.

After six months and four delays before announcing the unexpected decision Shovelton and her commission of four women and one man had only succeeded in creating confusion. While rejecting Branson but allowing him time to negotiate, Shovelton had rejected Camelot without offering any opportunity of further discussions.

The cause of Camelot's failure was GTech which, according to Shovelton, had failed the 'probity' test. Although only 0.007 per cent of lottery tickets had been affected by the concealed computer glitch in 1998, Shovelton believed that Camelot's relationship with the American corporation undermined the world's most successful lottery operator bidding for a licence renewal. Camelot was particularly angered by the Commission's apparent failure to appear fair. In June 2000, the Commission had asked Camelot to answer its concerns about GTech. The following month, on 28 July, the Commission assured Camelot that GTech would not be declared 'not fit and proper'. Yet three weeks later the Commission had changed its mind and GTech had become the single issue destroying Camelot's bid.

Shovelton's change of heart appeared bizarre. If GTech was a fundamental issue, the Commission might have allowed Camelot the opportunity to resolve the problem, possibly by inserting new security measures or even buying GTech. Or it might at least have begun similar negotiations as those with Branson.

Camelot's protests about the absence of fairness rebounded on Branson. At the outset of his second bid, Branson had himself asked GTech, contracted to 70 per cent of the world's lotteries, to supply his own company. After GTech's rejection, he contracted with Automated Wagering International [AWI], a much smaller American supplier of computer software to lotteries. More than GTech, AWI had in the past been struck by scandal, convictions of its staff for dishonesty and failure to deliver reliable systems in four U.S. states, for which it had been fined by American courts.

Shovelton's easy dismissal of AWI's deliquency as 'historic' while denigrating Camelot and GTech as beyond redemption was endorsed by Branson. Both Camelot and GTech, he commented, lacked 'integrity'. The man who boasted that his lottery would finally allow him to satisfy the 'piles of requests for money from little clubs and charities' he received every day, was already celebrating with champagne. The national mood, he believed, was on his side.

Camelot, Branson urged, should not resort to the courts for a judicial review but 'bow out gracefully'. Challenging the Commission, Branson puffed, jeopardised the lottery's money for good causes. His plea was unsurprisingly self-interested and inaccurate since the lottery would continue uninterrupted. Not surprisingly, he overlooked how in 1994 he had considered a judicial review after losing his first bid for the lottery and only withdrew on his lawyers' advice that any appeal was hopeless. Nine years earlier, however, he had gone to the High Court for that precise remedy after losing his bid for a television franchise.

Camelot rejected Branson's recommendation and, on 29 August, was allowed to return to court on 15 September for a full hearing. Grasping at straws, the operator's maligned directors hoped that by the end of that trial, Branson might have failed to satisfy the Commission's requirements and Shovelton would re-open negotiations with Camelot.

Branson was relaxed about that seemingly forlorn gambit. His most important sponsor, the key ministers of the Labour government, had expressed their support for the Commission's decisions. If Chris Smith was pleased, there was little doubt that Tony and Cherie Blair would also be satisfied.

Four months earlier in Downing Street, Cherie Blair had mentioned her husband's hope 'to do something' for Branson. Winning the lottery had been Branson's desire. Once again, his piggy-backing had proved successful. 'The People's Lottery' was a phrase used in the Labour party's 1997 election manifesto and Branson had revived Labour's title with manifest success. Since Blair was expected to win a second term in the following year's elections, Branson could expect to win more support for his other ambitions from the prime minister and his active spouse.

Branson and Blair, it seemed, epitomised New Britain. Both brand leaders – of Virgin and New Labour – were unrivalled personalities set to dominate Britain in the first years of the new millennium. Their shared mastery of the informal, emotional performance had won unusual popularity. The risks for both to sustain their individual success were considerable. But Branson risked more than the politician and the gambler's moment of truth was approaching.

Fulfilling the Commission's requirement to deliver a further £50 million might be trivial but successfully operating a completely glitch-free lottery like Camelot was, on his past performance, questionable. Failure would shatter his credibility and delight the victims of his ruthlessness. His critics waited to witness their conqueror's demise. Sensing their presence, he remorselessly intensified the search for salvation and permanent adulation. The frenetic pace brought new dangers.

Mired by increasing financial pressures, the public's self-created icon was risking his most important asset to win everlasting fame: his Virginity. The next eighteen months would decide his fate forever.

Acknowledgements

For a man determined to write his own epitaph in his lifetime, an unauthorised, objective biography can be offensive. Sir Richard Branson offered me little constructive help and refused to meet. Fortunately, about two hundred and fifty people who over the years have worked closely with Sir Richard did agree to tell me about their experiences. Most were very generous. They are the principal source of information for this book. Needless to say, I am very grateful for their time, assistance and courage.

In an unusual decision, based upon the advice of the lawyers who vetted this book, it has been agreed that no interview sources will be provided or people individually thanked. Nevertheless, the reader should be assured that every fact stated in this book has been sourced and for obvious reasons has been verified to the satisfaction of the lawyers.

I do, however, want to thank those journalists and others who provided information and advice. Again, many prefer for obvious reasons not to be identified, but of the remainder, I am, firstly, very grateful to Matt Born for his tireless research, involving a great number of frustrating journeys which eventually produced many gems.

I'm very grateful to Robert Barrett for his experience on Branson's genealogy.

Among other journalists whose help was invaluable were Chako Bellamy, Andy Blackman, Robin Denslow, Oliver Figg, Roger Ford, of *Modern Railways*, Martyn Gregory, Sophie Johnston, Robin Katz, Tim Laxton, Chris Lockwood, John Mair, Jonathan Meades, Richard Pendlebury, Lisa Seward, Martin Shelley, Jill Sinclair, Paul Spike and John Ware.

The legal chores were undertaken, with good humour as usual, by David Hooper of Biddle. Michael Shaw of Curtis Brown was steadfast in his support and an inspiration to complete a difficult undertaking. I owe a great debt to them both. Clive Priddle of Fourth Estate was a manifestly good editor.

As always, my principal gratitude is to my family – Veronica, Nicholas, Oliver, Sophie and Alexander – who, with my parents, have endured an arduous year with good humour.

Tom Bower   London, July 2000

Picture Credits

AFP/Corbis UK. AFP/Yoshikazu Tsu. Associated Media. Associated Newspapers. Bryn Colton, Assignments Photographers/Corbis UK. Christopher Cormak/Corbis UK. *Daily Mail*/photo Mike Hollist. Hulton Getty. Hulton Getty/*Express*. The *Independent*/photo Andrew Hassan. PA Photo Library/photos Sean Dempsey. Neil Munns. Tim Ockenden. John Stillwell. Rex Features/photos Etienne Boyer. Simon Brooke-Webb. Brooker. Andre Camara. Brenton Edwards. Nils Jorgensen. Tony Kyriacou. Julian Makey. Sipa Press, Justin Sutcliffe. Richard Young.

Sources

BOOKS

Auto. – Richard Branson, *Loosing My Virginity: The Autobiography*, Virgin, London, 1991

Brown – Mick Brown, *Richard Branson: The Authorised Biography*, Headline, London, 1992

Draper – Derek Draper, *Blair's 100 Days*, Faber 1997

Gregory – Martyn Gregory, *Dirty Tricks: British Airways' Secret War Against Virgin Atlantic*, Little Brown, London, 19??

Jackson – Tim Jackson, *Virgin King: Inside Richard Branson's Business Empire*, HarperCollins, London, 1984

NEWSPAPERS AND JOURNALS

BizWeek – *Business Week*

BrJFP – *British Journal of Family Planning*

DExp – *Daily Express*

DM – *Daily Mail*

DMir – *Daily Mirror*

DTel – *The Daily Telegraph*

Econ – *The Economist*

ESt – *Evening Standard*

FT – *The Financial Times*

Gu – *Guardian*

Ind – *Independent*

IoS – *Independent on Sunday*

ManToday – *Management Today*

ManWeek – *Management Weekly*

MktingEvent – *Marketing Event*

MM – *Melody Maker*

ModRlys – *Modern Railways*

MoS – *Mail on Sunday*

MuWk – *Music Week*

MWk – *Market Week*

NoW – *News of the World*

NS – *New Statesman*

NWk – *Newsweek*

NYMag – *New York Magazine*

NYPost – *New York Post*

NYT – *New York Times*

Obs – *The Observer*

PRWk – *Public Relations Weekly*

SBiz – *Sunday Business*

SExp – *Sunday Express*

SMir – *Sunday Mirror*

ST – *The Sunday Times*

STcolmag – *The Sunday Times* Colour Magazine

STel – *Sunday Telegraph*

T – *The Times*

VF – *Vanity Fair*

WallStJ – *Wall Street Journal*

Television, Transcripts and Other

Bcast – Broadcast

CAA/Moscow – Civil Aviation Authority Public Hearing 26.11.98

HofCTC – House of Commons Transport Committee

HofCTCFR – House of Commons Transport Committee, Future of the Railways, Minutes of Evidence, 25.11.92 HC246

MMCR – Monopolies and Mergers Commission Report Capital Radio and Virgin Radio Holdings, 1.5.99

NAO report – National Audit Office report, 'Evaluating the Applications to Run the National Lottery' 7.7.95 HC569

Panorama IV – *Panorama* Interview 22.9.95

Private Lives IV – *Private Lives* Interview

Tr – Trial Transcript, Branson v. Snowden, January 1998

TTr – Trial Transcript, Virgin Records v. Convoy and others 1985–6

USSCAS – United States Senate and Congressional Aviation Sub-Committee Hearing June 1997

VA/FDCC – Virgin Atlantic Airways Flight Deck Crew Committee Minutes of Meetings

Vcirc – Virgin Circular

Virgin PR – Virgin Press Release

Introduction

xiv 'Pony Canyon's investment' Tim Jackson wrote that Ken Berry started the negotiations in 'early 1989' p. 262. Branson says the relationship was initiated in 1989 by the Japanese; Branson letter to Bower Feb. 2000; xvi 'Three days later' *PRWeek* 9.9.94; 'We intend to' *Gu* 10.9.98.

1 The crime

2 'That's it, gushed' *Private Lives* IV June 94; 'Virgin Records, a' Jackson, p. 31; Auto., p. 98; *DTel* 22.8.98; 3 'Branson's conscience was' Auto., pp. 36, 45, 61, 40; Brown, p. 94 cf. p. 34; *DM* 22.10.91; 4 'At the hearing' *DM* 22.10.91; 9 'In the following' *T* 30.10.86; 10 'His crime was' *Success* Nov. 92 cited *Current Biography* Feb. 95; Auto. p. 90; 'Once Branson had' *DMir* June 84; 'The Millionaires', *Cosmopolitan* May 85; *Sun* 18.6.86; Brown, p. 100ff., *VF* 1992; Auto.,

pp. 85, 91, *Private Lives* IV June 94; 11 'Over Sunday Lunch' Brown, p. 94.

2 The beginning

12 'Sorry, sir, I'll' Auto., p. 41; 'The second ruse' *Ind* 22.2.92; 'The third ruse' Auto., p. 45; Brown, p. 48; *STel* 11.1.98; 13 'Ricky's going to' Jackson, p. 25; *SMir* 9.8.98; 14 'Books, no way' *SMir* 9.8.98; 15 'In an era' *T* 30.10.86; Brown, p. 68; 16 'He plucks, Eve' *VF* May 92; Nicci Gerrard *Obs* IV; 'Profiting from the' *ManWeek* Jul 91; 18 'Mention as a' *Ind* 22.2.92; 'To save *Student*' Brown, p. 72; Auto., p. 51; 19 'At the beginning' *SExp* 3.6.84; *T* 22.11.84; 20 'We're not selling' Auto., p. 63; 'The alchemy of' *ST* 8.6.86; 21 'The compartmentalisation began' *The Face*; 26 'Branson persuaded Newman' *ST* 30.5.93.

3 Honeymoons and divorces

28 'Artistic, purposeful and' Auto., p. 84ff.; 'After the honeymoon' Brown, p. 135; 29 'Taking a standard' Auto., p. 105; 30 'At twenty-three, Branson' Auto., p. 127; 'On the advice' Auto., p. 203; 'Taxes could only' Jackson, p. 59; 31 'For Steve Lewis' Jackson, p. 45; 'Branson's appreciation of' Jackson, p. 47; 33 'Branson flew to' Auto., p. 168; 'By 1976, Branson's' *MuWk* 13.6.94; 'Virgin's costs were' Auto., p. 138; 34 'The Sex Pistols' *Tatler* Mar. 97; Brown, p. 158; 1999 Millennium Speech; 36 'During that period' *Obs* 1.11.87; 'Emboldened by his' *MM* 18.3.78; Warner Brothers writ 24.4.78; *MuWk* 6.5.78; 39 'The marriage reached' Brown, p. 98; *DM* 11.9.98; 40 'But there was' *Today* 23.10.87; *SExp* 28.4.96; 41 'In Branson's mind' *DMir* 8.9.98; 'The following year' Auto., p. 168; 'The windfall from' Auto., pp. 165, 171; 42 'Gossip in the' Jackson, p. 125; Auto., p. 174; 'Rebutting Branson's denials' Jackson, p. 60; 43 'You just spend' Auto., p. 172; 'In Branson's new' Jackson, p. 74; 44 'The unresolved issue' Auto., p. 176.

4 Frustrations

47 'Ignoring her embarrassment' Brown, pp. 227, 237; 51 'The legacy was' *T* 21.4.88; Auto., p. 182; *Gu* 29.4.88 reviewing Brown;

52 'After an inconsequential' TTr p. 28a; 'Branson fully intended' TTr p. 46; 53 'Breezily, in late' TTr p. 18a; 'In the relaxed' TTr pp. 3, 5, 4, 13; 'Branson froze as' TTr pp. 34, 18; 54 'At his recollection' TTr pp. 41, 39, 72; *STcolmag* 30.5.93; 'On the second' TTr, Court of Appeal 15.5.86; 'Something terrible is' *DTel* 22.8.98; *SMir* 9.8.98.

5   Dream thief

56 'Gut instinct rather' Auto., p. 193; *T* 11.12.97; 'You're mad, scowled' Auto., p. 194; 57 'The photographs showed' Jackson, p. 90; 58 'Branson's delay was' Jackson, p. 199ff.; 'Branson was, however' Auto., p. 198; 'In Branson's world' Jackson, p. 91; 60 'In August that' *WallStJ* 20.8.84; 'At the end' *Econ* Oct. 84; 'I'm not on' *WallStJ* 20.8.84; Jackson, p. 205; 61 'His early flights' *Ind* Nov. 91; 63 'In October 1984' Brown, p. 274; 'The complaint was' Brown, p. 274; 'Partners irritated Branson' Jackson, p. 121.

6   The people's champion

65 'The party habit' *Woman* 13.6.87; 66 'Inside Virgin, the' *STcolmag* 30.5.93; 68 'Tod Toleman, a' *Gu* 20.6.98; 'We'll use the' *Daily-NewsNY* 14.7.85; *Ind* 27.5.96; 69 'Stepping from the' Jackson, p. 137; 'His greater bravado' Brown, p. 349; Auto., p. 209; Virgin Placing Document p. 19; 70 'Suddenly free of' Auto., pp. 223–5; Jackson, p. 139; Nicci Gerrard *Obs* IV; 71 'Branson's priority was' Auto., p. 220 Branson claims; 'On 12 August' Auto., p. 214; 'Linked by radio' Jackson, p. 142; 72 'The fans are' Auto., pp. 232, 229; 73 'The television programme' *BizWeek* 30.6.86; 'Hosting parties at' Virgin PR 86.

7   Confusion and salvation

75 'Branson presented himself' *BizWeek* 30.6.86; 76 'Seelig hoped that' *Today* 14.5.87; 'Branson offered no' *BizWeek* 30.6.86; *ST* 19.10.86; 'Those concerned about' *Obs* 2.11.86; 77 'Insiders described a' Auto., p. 255; 'The slick presentation' *STel* 2.11.86; *Obs* 19.10.86; 'The reality, Branson' *DTel* 15.11.86; 79 'Few newspapers and' Brown, p. 379; 'For four weeks' *Campaign* 26.6.87; 80 'On the

transatlantic' *DM* 18.11.87; *ST* 1.2.93; 'Durex, the supplier' *Ind* 11.11.87; 81 'Branson refused to' *Obs* 15.2.87; *STel* 6.12.92; 'Cruick-shank, a critical' Jackson, p. 163; *DExp* 18.8.89; a beneficiary accord-ing to Virgin Express prospectus, p. 55; 82 'Branson's dislike of' Auto., p. 234; 'The tensions at' *Campaign* 3.7.87; *SExp* 22.11.87; 'Branson emphasised, in' *SExp* 22.11.87; 83 'One particular touch' *Today* 13.11.89; 84 'Glancing up from' Auto., p. 245.

8   Returning to the shadows

89 'Branson grinned. His' *Sun* 7.10.94; 'Abbott's genius was' Jackson, p. 232; *T* 10.11.87; 90 'On Monday, 19' Auto., p. 252; 'The City's distrust' *T* 10.11.87; 93 'Although thirty-five' *Ind* 11.11.87; 'Their preference, to' Dr Rosemary Kirkman, Manchester University, *BrJFP* 15 (1990): 107–11; Consumers' Association 89; 94 'We're going to' *Success* Nov. 92 quoted *Current Biography*, Feb. 95; 95 'Sitting on the' Auto., p. 254; 'The public announcement' *SBiz* 20.12.98; 97 'The new debt' Auto., pp. 255, 254; 98 'To an outsider' Auto., pp. 277, 261; Jackson, p. 223; 'Eight months later' Auto., p. 263; 99 'Although Robert Devereux' *SExp* 25.1.97; Auto., p. 177; Brown, pp. 410–11.

9   Finding enemies

101 'Branson's brazen confidence' *Obs* 21.5.89; 102 'Branson con-cealed his' *T* 3.12.87; 'In truth, Branson' Auto., p. 317; 'Although in 1989' *Obs* 21.5.89; 103 'In Japan, Branson' Gregory, pp. 67, 123; 104 'His advertisements were' *ESt* 30.5.90; *T* 20.6.90; *Today* Mar. 89; 106 'The pilots' admiration' *Sun* 25.7.91; *DMir* May 85; 107 'Until Virgin's mercy' *DExp* 30.5.86; 'Burnside's mild gripes' Auto., pp. 280, 291; 'Officials in the' *IoS* 8.1.91; 109 'During the eight-hour' Auto., p. 309; 110 'The opening shots' Gregory, p. 102; *DM* Feb. 91; 111 'Sidney Shaw, Branson's' Auto., p. 313; *Gu* 9.10.91; *FT* 13.8.98; 'Branson's best hope' Auto., p. 331; 112 'Evoking the mythology' *Gu* 30.1.91; *STel* 27.1.91; *SBiz* 20.12.98; Auto., p. 317; 'In the popular' *Sun* 31.1.91, June 92, 7.4.95; 113 'Branson's feigned sur-prise' Auto., pp. 320–1; 'British Airways public' Auto., p. 322; 'I was particularly' Gregory, p. 104; 'Levelling abuse at' Auto., pp. 317, 320; Gregory, p. 139; 'Ever since 1988' Auto., pp. 263, 277, 285, 332; 114 'Laying smokescreens to' *ST* 8.3.92; 'His merchant bankers'

Brown, p. 239; 'Discreetly, Branson invited' Auto., p. 319; 115 'The minister's personal' USSCAS p. 48; 'In March 1991' *Ind* 14.3.91; *Gu* 3.7.93; 'Forty-eight hours later' Auto., p. 326.

10 War and deception

116 'Journalists, Richard Branson' *DMir* 15.8.91; *T* 25.1.92; 'In normal circumstances' *T* 6.4.91; 118 'On board a' *Sun* 6.6.91; *ST* 3.2.91; *VF* May 92; 'Embarrassing British Airways' USSCAS p. 55; 119 'Over the summer' *Today* 29.8.91; 120 'In a letter' Gregory, p. 181; 'Regularly Virgin's accountants' *STel* 27.10.91; 'The partial truth' *Obs* 9.2.92, £33.3m in 1990; 16.2.92; Auto., pp. 353, 334; 121 'In autumn 1991' *Gu* 19.9.91; 122 'His survival required' *Sun* 5.9.98; *Gu* 2.10.91; 'The unexpected appearance' Auto., pp. 357, 332; 'Through charm and' Auto., pp. 355, 357, 332, 340, 341; *Gu* 3.10.91; *Econ* Feb. 98; 123 'In London it' *DMir* 17.10.91; 'In flippant self-congratulation' *STcolmag* 30.5.93; *VF* May 92; 125 'Branson flew to' *Sun* Apr. 92; 'Branson knew Hutchins' Brown, p. 194; 126 'Listening to Hutchins' Auto., p. 316; 127 'He said I'm' Gregory, p. 179; 'Although Branson would' Gregory pp. 277, 328; Auto., pp. 107, 424, 321; 128 'Basham's imagery, however' Gregory, p. 189; 129 'I realised that' Auto., p. 362; 'There had been' Gregory, pp. 205, 206, 202–3; 130 'Branson was hypersensitive' Gregory, p. 174; Auto., p. 415; 'A passenger on' Gregory, pp. 206, 209; 132 'Branson's glee evaporated' Auto., pp. 388, 384; 'Branson was nervous' *DExp* 13.12.91; 'Some of Branson's' *IoS* 21.6.92; Gregory, p. 210; *Ind* 11.1.93; 133 'Frustrated, and under' *DTel* 19.9.98; *ST* 3.11.91; 'The response was' Auto., p. 395; Gregory, pp. 216–17; 'Fire-fighting and spreading' *FT* 21.2.92; Auto., p. 396; 'During Christmas, as' Auto., p. 397; Gregory, p. 11; *ST* 8.3.92, 6.6.93; *VF* May 92; 134 'Basham has been' Gregory trial transcript, p. 859ff., p. 880; 135 'Mike Batt, the' Auto., p. 402; *DM* 7.3.92 Branson: 'There has never been an indep airline that has survived'; 'At that defining' Gregory, p. 269; Auto., p. 402; 136 'The simplicity of' Auto., p. 420; 137 'A Jiffy bag' Auto., p. 414; 138 'The consequences of' Gregory, p. 227; 'Poaching passengers was' Gregory, p. 15.

11   Sour Music

140 'In planning his' *ST* 8.3.92; 141 'As Thornton seduced' Auto., p. 390; 'If the money' *DTel* 2.11.92 admits; 142 'Branson's tears during' Auto., p. 413; *FT* 13.8.98; 143 'Branson stared at' Auto., p. 407; *Anderlust* salon mag. 98; 144 'Since 1967, Branson' Tr 14.1.98, p. 69; 'In denying any' Auto., pp. 413, 321; 145 'Soon after leaving' *ST* 30.5.93; 'Nearly one year' *DTel* 22.8.98; 146 'On his own' *MoS* 9.10.94; 'The truth, Branson' Auto., p. 408; *ST* 8.3.92; *NYT* 3.3.92; *Gu* 7.3.92; *VF* May 92; 147 'In his revised' Auto., pp. 422, 411; Gregory, p. 9; 'Buoyed by the' Auto., p. 433; 148 'There were announcements' *Ind* 25.8.92; 16.7.92; *STel* 6.12.92; 149 'Dan Air's recent' *T* 26.9.92; *Sun* 29.9.92; 'Since British Airways' *Today* 8.12.93; *ST* 29.8.93; 'Branson's proposal was' *Gu* 21.7.93; 150 'Four weeks after' *ST* 3.5.92; 'Eleven weeks later' *T* 22.7.92; 151 'Four months later' HofCTCFR, p. 204; 'Robert Adley, the' HofCTCFR, p. 205; 152 'Adley was scathing' HofCTCFR, p. 206; 'We are talking' HofCTCFR, pp. 204–5; 'I am sorry' HofCTCFR, pp. 204–5.

12   Double vision

153 'Public attention was' *ST* 17.1.93; 'Branson's popularity masked' *T* 25.1.92; *ST* 17.1.93; 'A low-wage policy' Jackson, p. 319; 154 'At the same' Albin to Syd Pennington ltr 22.3.92; Nick Joslin to Albin ltr 27.3.92; 155 'The pilots, Branson' VA/FDCC 10.11.92; VA/FDCC 8.9.92; 'As the libel' Auto., p. 430; *STcolmag* 30.5.93; 156 'British Airways offered' *ST* 7.2.93; 'Surrounded by his' *T* 12.3.93; *ESt* 12.1.93; *Sun* 5.9.98; 157 'Lord King's humiliation' *Today* 21.1.93; 'Carefully reading every' *Gu* 18.1.93; 158 'Each twist of' *Ind* 30.1.93; 'To appreciate resistance' *Gu* 23.2.93, 25.10.93; *DMir* 28.2.95; *FT* 22.1.93; *T* 26.1.93, 18.1.93; *STel* 21.2.93; 'The vulnerability of' Nicci Gerrard *Obs* IV; *Today* 30.4.93; *Sun* 8.9.98; *Gu* 13.2.91; 159 'Securing the support' *T* 19.1.93; 'For years, Branson' *MoS* 30.6.96; *Ind* 22.3.93; 160 'As Marshall stood' *T* 26.1.93; 161 'On the night' *Gu* 23.2.93; *Ind* 23.10.93 citing legal suit; 'Branson's ultimatum was' *Gu* 7.5.93; *DMir* 15.7.99; *DExp* 22.3.93; 'To deepen the' *Gu* 4.3.93; *DTel* 28.4.93; *World in Action* 27.4.93; *DExp* 22.3.93; *DM* 20.1.93; 162 'To further discomfort' *T* 21.3.92.

13   Unfortunate casualties

163 'The telephone call' Tr 14.1.98, p. 48; 164 'Branson's telephone call' Tr 14.1.98, p. 48; 'I'm doing it' Tr 19.1.98, p. 124; *DTel* 22.8.98; 165 'You don't understand' Tr 23.1.98, p. 12; 'Snowden laughed: Look' Tr 23.1.98, p. 37; 'Branson's certainty was' *Obs* 1.6.97; Tr 20.1.98, p. 112; 166 'Snowden arrived at' Tr 23.1.98, p. 158; 167 'Branson was unaware' Tr 21.1.98, p. 42; 'If you read' Tr 23.1.98, p. 37; 168 'After a pause' Tr 23.1.98, pp. 32–3; 'Snowden would later' Tr 27.1.98, p. 89; 'Branson appeared to' Tr 23.1.98, p. 38, Snowden evidence; 169 'Branson's version of' Tr 14.1.98, p. 98; transcript from loo note; 'Snowden either answered' Tr 14.1.98, p. 97; 'Believing that he' Tr 23.1.98, p. 38, Snowden evidence; 'Branson in his' Tr 14.1.98, p. 99; 23.1.98, p. 35; 'The minute the' Tr 20.1.98, p. 145; 21.1.98, p. 76; 'Over the weekend' Tr 21.1.98, p. 167; 170 'By that Monday' Tr 14.1.98, p. 48; Auto., p. 36; 'Four days after' Tr 27.1.98, p. 10; 'In November 1993' Tr 26.1.98, p. 82; 23.1.98, p. 118; 172 'Branson departed with' Auto., p. 332; 173 'In 1992. Hashedate' Jackson, pp. 331, 327–32; *DExp* 25.10.93; 175 'I'm going to' Tr 28.1.98, p. 85; 'On 14 December' Tr 21.1.98, p. 52; *IoS* 19.12.93; *DExp* 15.2.94; *DTel* 27.5.94; 176 'Quietly in January' *T* 29.1.94; 'The brief announcement' *Ind* 8.4.95; *DTel* 13.3.96; *Gu* 31.3.94; 178 'Days later, on' Nicci Gerrard *Obs* IV.

14   The underdog

180 'It's a nasty' *DM* 13.2.98, 26.5.94; *FT* 7.7.95; *PRWk* 9.9.94; 24.5.94 Branson lost FM bid and Sarah Kennedy, *DExp* May 94; 181 'Jackson was then' Tr 28.1.98, p. 91; 30.1.98, p. 44; *T* 11.7.95; NAO report, p. 28; 182 'Predictably, Davis's process' NAO report, p. 27; 'A subsequent independent' NAO report p. *??*; 'At the end' *Panorama* IV, 22.9.95, p. 14; Tr 14.1.98, p. 128; 21.1.98, pp. 146, 152; 28.1.98, p. 96; 'All that remained' *ESt* 1.6.94; 183 'Journalists continued to' *Ind* 1.2.94; *FT* 3.6.94; Branson ltr responding to Lucy Kellaway diary 30.5.94, *MoS* 5.6.94, Branson ltr, explains 'the reason we were upset . . .'; 'One year earlier' *FT* 17.10.94; 184 'Lester was intrigued' *FT* 17.10.94; 'The introduction was' *T* 19.4.95; 185 'The idea was' *ST* 3.2.91; *MWk* 14.10.94; 'The voice on' *Gu* 21.1.95;

'Branson's ambition was' *BizWeek* 26.10.98; Auto., p. 436; 186 'Pencer resolved to' *Gu* 20.6.98; *ST* 13.10.96; 187 'After reflection, no' *MWk* 21.10.94; 'Branson had undertaken' *MWk* 14.10.94; *DTel* 11.10.94; *DExp* 11.10.94; 188 'His launch showed' *SMir* 20.11.94; 189 'Ever since the' *DTel* 20.1.93, 30.4.93, 18.11.93; *Obs* 1.8.93; 'Lord Chalfont, a' *Gu* 21.5.93; *Sun* 4.3.94; *ESt* 25.5.94; 191 'The good news' Tr 21.1.98, p. 17; *Gu* 7.6.95; 'In January 1995' *DTel* 11.10.94; 192 'The venue, Simpsons' *DMir* 28.2.95; *Gu* 21.1.95; 'We're earning £1 million' *Forbes* 95; 'One month later' *Ind* 12.10.94; *MWk* 14.3.95, 24.3.95; 'Branson's response to' *FT* 2.5.95; *Ind* 8.4.95; *MWk* 3.2.95, 1.3% higher than he had claimed a week earlier; *T* 19.4.95; *FT* 2.5.95; *Campaign* 8.9.95; *MWk* 4.5.95; *WallStJ* 22.3.95; *FT* 2.5.95; *T* 19.4.95, Branson admits exaggerations; 'Virgin Cola's first' *Campaign* 5.9.95; *MWk* 30.5.95; 194 'Kydd approved Campbell's' *MWk* 28.9.95, 26.5.95; Vcirc 1.5.95; 'Nielsen's ratings in' *MWk* 16.6.95, between March and May; 30.6.95; *MoS* 9.7.95.

15 Another day, another deal

199 'Offering bottles of' *DMir* 19.5.94; 202 'Money also interested' *SMir* 9.8.98; 203 'Branson knew how' *FT* 13.8.98; 'Branson had been' *Obs* 11.5.97; 204 'At a suitable' *T* 22.6.96; *Time* 8.7.96; *ST* 13.10.96; 'The summer of' *MWk* 21.3.96; *FT* 13.12.96, 23.10.95, 22.11.96; *MoS* 1.10.95; *Today* 24.10.95; *ESt* 9.11.95; *DTel* 5.1.96; 205 'Virgin Direct, launched' *DExp* 9.7.98; *DMir* 28.5.96; 206 'In the first' *DMir* 28.2.95; *MoS* 9.7.95; 'Branson, who revealed' *SBiz* 24.11.96; 207 'It's a profitable' Vcirc Jan. 96; *STel* 31.3.96.

16 Another day, another target

208 'One year after' Tr 26.1.98, p. 44; 'Camelot's defence that' *Obs* 1.6.97; 209 'The businessman's reluctance' *DTel* 22.8.98; *Panorama* IV 11.12.95, p. 15; Tr 12.1.98, p. 95; 13.1.98, p. 44; 15.1.98, p. 36; 'Two months later' *Panorama* prog. 11.12.95, pp. 20–1; 210 'Dressed in a' Tr 19.1.98, p. 21; 'Branson's frequent appearance' Tr 19.1.98, p. 42; Auto., p. 362; 'Normally, he soothed' *Panorama* prog. p. 6; Tr 14.1.98, p. 8; 211 'They weren't particularly' *Panorama* prog. p. 10; Tr 13.1.98, p, 22; 'Mark Killick, the' Tr 14.1.98, p. 123; 19.1.98, p. 149; 30.1.98, p. 49, questioned by Ferguson; 'That soundbite

fitted' Tr 15.1.98, pp. 15, 10–13; 'The climax of' *Panorama* pp. 11, 23; 212 'Picking up the' *Panorama* 11.12.95, p. 12 and pp. 23–4 for slightly different version; Tr 14.1.98, pp. 29, 42, 65, 14, 117; 20.1.98, p. 50; Day 1 of appeal; 'Branson's presentation of' Tr 19.1.98, p. 31; 'Initially, Branson realised' *Panorama* p. 16; 213 'While the video' *Panorama* p. 18; 'But Branson's version' Julia Madonna, his personal secretary, witness statement, accepted by Branson Tr 12.1.98, p. 48; 14.1.98, p. 18; 30.1.98, p. 37 accusation of Branson's 'lies'; 21.1.98, pp. 77–8, 83; 'It's an interview' Tr 16.1.98, p. 100; 214 'Killick also telephoned' Tr 27.1.98, p. 66; 'That morning, Monday' *Gu* 1.5.96; 215 'The transmission of' *ESt* 12.12.95; *T* 16.12.95; *FT* 16.12.95; 'On 15 December' Tr 21.1.98, pp. 144, 146, 152; 16.1.98, p. 54.

17   The cost of terrorism

217 'The two men' VA/FDCC; 221 'No hard feelings' *Gu* 16.5.96; 222 'Special offers, stunts' *MoS* 28.4.96; 223 'A noticeable hint' *European* 2.5.96; *Ind* 27.5.96; 'In the same' *European* 2.5.96; 8.7.96; 224 'The egoism of' *Time* 8.7.96; 'You're not a' *T* 15.10.96; 225 'We'll catch BA' *ST* 10.12.95; 'Virgin's weekly frequencies' American Airlines' submission to EU Com. (IV/36.089) 30.9.98, p. 21; 'Still humiliated and' *USA Today* 12.12.95; *Gu* 11.12.95; HofCTC 10.7.96, p. 64; 226 'To enhance his' *Ind* 13.10.98; 227 'The wheeze was' United Airlines annual report 96, p. 7; 'In 1995, Virgin' *DTel* 24.6.96; 228 'I bet he' *SBiz* 23.6.96; 'The alliances had' American Airlines response 23.6.98; 229 'Under the Anglo-American' *FT* 11.6.96; *DTel* 24.6.96; 'Until June 1996' *T* 22.6.96; 230 'Robert Renwick, the' *T* 27.6.96; 'Dudley Broster, the' Dudley Broster to Branson memo 21.10.96; 233 'Sir Patrick Brown', HoCTC proposed alliance between BA and AA, vol. 2, 24.7.96 p. 64; 234 'That was, as' Sir George Young evidence, HoCTC proposed alliance between BA and AA, vol. 2, 24.7.96 p. 173; 'The statistics, Branson', HoCTC proposed alliance between BA and AA, vol. 2, 24.7.96 p. 34; 'Virgin Express had' *European* 2.5.96; *DTel* 30.4.96; *FT* 11.10.96; *WallStJ* 30.4.96; 235 'Once Virgin Express' *Ind* 10.9.96; *DTel* 2.10.96.

18   Sinking with dinosaurs

238 'Branson's search for' *Sun* 28.7.95; *VF* May 92; 239 'In the four'
NYMag 8.4.96; 240 'V2's launch Branson' *ManToday* Apr. 98; 241
'By November 1996' *MWk* 4.6.96; *Advertising Age* 17.5.99; Auto.,
p. 437; 242 'Over dinner at' *FT* 2.11.96; 'Branson's guests, the'
Cott memo to European Commission, 96; memo Nick Kirkbride
to Branson 16.8.96; 'Branson's gaze had' *SBiz* 24.11.96; 243 'All
he's saying' *FT* 22.11.96; Vcirc 22.1.97; 'Branson was unwilling'
ManWeek Jul. 91; 244 'He's fallen off' *ESt* 10.1.96; 245 'Branson's
team identified' *Panorama* IV 11.12.95; 247 'On the West' *MoS*
22.2.98, in 2002 Virgin has to pay £3.9m, this rises in 2012 to
£220m. Subsidy in 97 was £94.4m falling to £52m by 2002; 'Virgin
proposed to' *ModRlys* Apr. 97; *SBiz* 2.2.97; 'Branson's financial commitment' *FT* 15.8.98; 'Branson's plan was' *Gu* 10.5.97; *DTel*
29.11.96, 30.11.96; *DMir* 30.11.96; 248 'Frantically, Virgin's press'
DM 17.1.97; *IoS* 8.6.97; 249 'Those antics and' *DExp* 19.12.96;
'The take-off was' Auto., p. 229; *DMir* July 97; *DExp* 29.4.91; 251
'Branson returned to' *ManWeek* July 91.

19   Honesty and integrity

253 'As the owner' *Gu* 10.5.97; 'Reality soured the' *T* 11.3.97; 'The
brown envelopes' *ModRlys* Jan. 97; *FT* 6.8.99; 255 'After 9 p.m.'
Draper, pp. 204, 7; 'Branson was unconcerned' *Gu* 17.10.97; *SExp*
19.10.97; 259 'Despite his business' 1997 Branson speech to Congressional Committee investigating American Airlines/BA alliance;
International Aviation Club, Washington, 24.9.98; 260 'During the
summer' USSCAS 4.6.97, 11.6.97, 19.6.97; *ESt* 24.4.97; *DTel*
20.8.97; 'Entering the imposing' USSCAS, pp. 42, 45; 261 'Ayling
had not' *DTel* 20.8.97; 262 'V2's only success' *MuWk* 13.12.97; 263
'McCarthy's money required' *Sun* 12.7.97; 'The launch party' *Sun*
3.10.97; *Obs* 11.5.97; 264 'Branson pondered a' *DTel* 28.12.97;
'Fame and his' *IoS* 10.8.97; 'By 1997, Virgin' Monopolies Commission report Jan. 98, p. 7; *DTel* 12.2.96; *Ind* 7.5.97; *SExp* 15.6.97;
265 'By early October' *MWk* 11.10.97; Bcast 12.12.97; 266
'The prospectus for' *FT* 25.10.96 Prospectus, p. F-34; 'Prospective

shareholders were' Prospectus, p. 5; *DTel* 23.10.97; *IoS* 15.9.96; *FT* 15.8.98 Branson ltr; 267 'None of those' *T* 9.4.98.

20 Indelible tarnish

271 'Deftly, his Glaswegian' *VF* May 92; 'At a recent' *DMir* 24.4.96; 'The adjective most' *SExp* 25.1.97; 272 'Branson's new company' MMCR 1.5.98, p. 59; 274 'I'm risking more' *DT* 1.5.98, p. 59; 276 'The unexpected rash' *DMir* 25.6.97; 277 'Sorting it was' *Gu* 19.7.97; *DTel* 7.8.97 Branson ltr; *IoS* 10.8.97; *Gu* 12.8.97; 'After the promises' *Anderlust* saloon mag. 98; see contra *ModRlys* May 99; *Spectator* 23.2.98; 279 'Three months after' *Gu* 13.3.99, 14.11.98; *NS* 7.11.97; *DM* 29.3.99; *Ind* 5.12.97, 31.10.97; RAIL vol. 347; 'Branson's discomfort was' *Anderlust* saloon mag. 98; 280 'The overwhelming publicity' *ST* 30.6.96; *T* 18.10.97; Pru research/Hall & Partners Brand Tracking Study; 281 'Austerity hung over' *MWk* 30.1.98; *Sun* 30.7.97; *Mkting* 20.2.97; *ST* 3.8.97; 'In his hunt' *Mkting Event* 1.9.97; Vcirc 6.5.97; 'Branson seemed to' *MWk* 22.5.97; *Mkting Event* 1.9.97; *The Grocer* 10.5.97; *MWk* 22.5.97; 282 'Two years earlier' *ST* 3.8.97; *Gu* 18.2.98; *MWk* 30.1.98; *FT* 12.2.98; *ESt* 17.3.99; 283 'Branson sat self-confidently' Tr 16.1.98, pp. 9, 19; 'Isolated at the' Tr 12.1.98, pp. 87–8 Judge excluded that evidence; 12.1.98, p. 92; 13.1.98, p. 47; 'Unwilling to call' Tr 12.1.98, pp. 71, 84; 13.1.98, p. 46; 28.1.98, p. 109; 284 'Snowden was further' Tr 12.1.98, pp. 87–8, 92; 'Unchallenged about his' Tr 12.1.98, pp. 49, 51, 59–60, 66–7ff., 77; 'At the outset' Tr 16.1.98, pp. 67, 121; 14.1.98, pp. 137–8; 15.1.98, p. 4; 'When the *Panorama*' Tr 16.1.98, p. 135; 19.1.98, pp. 1, 8, 140–5, 141; 12.1.98, pp. 51, 58–60, 66–7; 15.1.98, p. 33; Pollock, Appeal Day 1; 285 'I cannot remember' Tr 16.1.98, p. 74; 30.1.98, p. 23; 'The humiliation of' Tr 13.1.98, p. 46; Appeal Days 2, 3; 'George Carman matched' Tr 26.1.98, pp. 56–7; 30.1.98, pp. 68, 73; 28.1.98, p. 113; 'Branson's credibility rose' Tr 27.1.98, p. 42; 'Branson had testified' Tr 27.1.98, pp. 121, 122–4, 134; 28.1.98, pp. 49, 98, 102; 286 'On the familiar' *DMir* 3.2.98; 287 'The newly crowned' *DExp* 10.2.98; *FT* 10.2.98; *Ind* 4.9.98; *Gu* 5.9.98; 'Once calm returned' *ManWeek* July 91.

21 A slipping halo

289 'The thousands of' *Ind* 15.9.97; OPRAF 15.1.98; Booze Allen research for *Panorama 98; 'Unreliable Virgin Rail' ST* 30.11.97; John Swift, rail regulator, 13.12.97; *Scotsman* 16.1.98; 'The continuing criticism' *NS* 7.11.97; *Gu* 6.10.97, 10.12.97; 290 'Ignoring unpleasant facts' Virgin Trains submission to Rail Users Consultative Committee 22.1.98; 'Branson arrived with' *Panorama* IV 16.2.98; 291 'In the midst' *FT* 26.1.98, 30.1.98; *Ind* 30.1.98; 292 'In their battle' *FT* 30.1.98, 20.3.98; 'We've gotta get' *DTel* 21.2.98; 'Branson believed he' *Obs* 8.2.98; *DTel* 12.3.98; *Spectator* 21.2.98; Branson denied hearing that comment, 28.2.98; 'Bewildered, Branson retired' *FT* 13.2.98; *DExp* 14.3.98; 293 'Will Whitehorn, the' *DExp* 10.2.98 Branson ltr; *ESt* 13.2.98; 294 'His performance started' *Panorama* 16.2.98; 295 'Millions watched the' Branson to Birt 3.3.99; *Spectator* 14.3.98; 296 'Branson was skiing' *Ind* 21.2.98; *DMir* 21.2.98; *SBiz* 22.2.98; *ST* Rich List 19.4.98; 'The contrast of' *FT* 15.8.98; 297 'If the notion' *Ind* 21.2.98; 'It could all' *SBiz* 22.2.98; 298 'Hype and charm' *Ind* 21.2.98; *FT* 13.8.98; *ST* 13.10.96; *ESt* 13.2.98; 'In response to' *DTel* 21.2.98; *DMir* 21.2.98; *Gu* 21.2.98; *FT* 1.6.98; 'The extent of' *ST* 5.6.96; 299 'The offshore trusts' *Gu* 20.6.98; 'Adding further confusion' Barford Services accounts 30.4.99 p. 10; 300 'The one hundred' *ESt* 13.2.98; *Econ* 21.2.98; 'Virgin's bids to' *ST* 14.6.98; flotation announced 18.4.98; 301 'Ever since winning' *ESt* 29.4.98; *DMir* article by Branson 30.11.98; 'Something special was' *BizWeek* 26.10.98; *NYPost* 13.5.98; *Fortune* 9.12.98; Vcirc 12.5.98; 302 'Brian Souter, a' *ESt* 22.6.98; 303 'The critics were' *FT* 10.2.99; 'To enhance his' *FT* 25.9.98 ltr from Stephen Murphy; 304 'Among the doubters' *Ind* 13.11.97; *DM* 1.6.98; 306 'The crisis hit' *Ind* 18.8.98; *FT* 25.9.98 ltr from Stephen Murphy; *MoS* 11.10.98; *DTel* 20.3.99; 307 'Beyond the handful' *FT* 13.8.98; *T* 5.9.98.

22 Fissure

308 'Branson's renewed attack' *FT* 13.8.98; 'But Branson understood' *Business Travel News* 23.2.98; US Senate Judiciary Committee on Anti-Trusts 19.3.98; 309 'Seven years earlier' *FT* 13.2.91; 'Branson, however, found' *NYPost* 14.2.98; 310 'To his delight'

NYPost 14.2.98; 'Soon after his' *SMir* 16.10.94; *T* 25.10.98; 'Eleven lawyers and' Virgin submission to EU Com. 1.9.97; Branson ltr to European Commission 9.7.98; American Airlines submission to EU Com.; 311 'Karl van Miert' American Airlines Submission to EU Com. (IV/36.089) 30.9.98, pp. 39–40, based on report by London Economics Jan. 97; 'Two trains from' Tr 16.1.98, p. 79; *FT* 8.10.98; OPRAF's figures; *T* 3.11.98; 312 'Nothing enraged Branson' *Gu* 21.8.98; 'I despair, cried' *Gu* 14.11.98; *T* 5.1.99; *Gu* Oct. 98; 'Repeatedly, the airline' *Skyport* 20.2.98, 4.12.98; 313 'The symbol of' CAA/Moscow 26.11.98, p. 82; 314 'His troubles had' *DTel* 14.11.97; 'To save his' *ESt* 28.10.98; 315 *'Losing My Virginity' Obs* 6.9.98; Auto., p. 129; *DMir* 3.2.98; 'His failure to' *Ind* 4.9.98; 317 'After fourteen years' CAA/Moscow 26.11.98, p. 73; 318 'Do you have' CAA/Moscow 26.11.98, pp. 79, 87, 85.

23   Squeezing friends

321 'The commanding pilot' *T* 26.12.98; 322 'Three months after' *Time* 4.5.99; *MoS* 20.6.99; 'In business, there' *Gu* 20.6.98; *FT* 20.4.99; 'During that financial' *FT* 17.1.00 Branson admits mistakes; 'Temporarily, Will Whitehorn's' *T* 24.4.99; 323 'To fund the' *FT* 22.8.97, 27.11.98, 29.10.98; *Obs* 4.10.98; 324 'The only glitch' *FT* 26.6.99.

24   House of cards

326 'In the aftermath' *FT* 13.8.98; 'Like those of' *FT* 5.2.99; 327 'Will Whitehorn, the' *T* 24.4.99; *Ind* 1.3.99; *Gu* 26.5.99; 'Although Virgin was' *ST* 10.12.95; 'The bait was' *DTel* 8.6.99; *FT* 26.9.93; 328 'In May 1999' *FT* 19.4.99 Branson article urges caution on any open skies agreement with the US govt; USSCAS 4.6.97, p. 53; 'The posture encouraged' USSCAS 4.6.97, p. 35; 'On his initiative' Virgin PR 10.2.99; *T* 15.7.99; *DMir* 15.7.99; *Travel Trade Gazette* 2.8.99; 329 'Branson's ignorance about' *Gu* 24.5.99; 330 'Other Virgin executives' *DM* 5.4.00; 'Branson was vulnerable' *Travel Trade Gazette* 29.11.99; 331 'In the autumn' *DTel* 19.8.99; *Gu* 31.8.99, 22.9.99; *T* 26.8.99; *DM* 19.8.99; 'A third casualty' *DTel* 30.5.99; *FT* 20.2.99, 10.4.99, Mar. 99; 332 'Branson was neither' *ST* 6.6.99; *Los Angeles Times* 23.4.99; 'Nor could Branson' *ST* 1.11.99; 'The positive publicity' *SBiz* 23.8.98; *DTel* 1.4.99, 20.8.99; *NoW* 1.8.99;

333 'Despite Branson's repeated' *Gu* 9.8.99; Reuters 14.10.99; *ST* 17.10.99, 10.10.99; *T* 11.10.99; *Obs* 3.10.99; Ridgeway memo 23.9.99; 'In a desperate' *FT* 13.8.98; 334 'In the weeks' *DMir* 12.10.99; 'The British government' *FT* 5.10.99; 20.10.99; *Ind* 29.9.99; 'There was, Branson' USSCAS 4.6.97, p. 34; 335 'To his amazement' Cederbaum judgement, p. 20; 'I'm astonished, flustered' *ESt* 26.10.99; 'The humiliation was' *T* 24.4.99; *FT* 24.12.99; 336 'The airline was' *FT* 20.4.99; 'To outsiders, Branson' *FT* 24.12.99; *Western Morning News* 21.1.00; 339 'Although *The Sunday*' *Econ* IV 5.4.00; 'In mid-January the' *T* 25.1.00; 340 'Branson's battle in' *Econ* IV 5.4.00; 'In the early' *T* 3.4.00; *Econ* IV 5.4.00.

25   House of cards

343 'Among Murphy's last' *FT* 6.6.00; 'Virgin Cola's losses' *Gu* 27.5.00. 17.6.00; *DTel* 6.6.00; *FT* 17.6.00; 'Branson dismissed the' *ESt* 4.5.00; 344 'Just as experienced' *DM* 17.5.00; *DTel* 4.7.00; 'Hampered by his' *DTel* 3.6.00; *FT* 23.5.00, 24.6.00; 345 'Despite Branson's boasts' *FT* 31.3.00, 26.4.00; *T* 2.3.00; 'Branson's new ambitions' *Econ* IV 5.4.00; *DTel* 6.4.00; *FT* 8.6.00; *T* 347 'Branson, the challenger' 27.3.00; 349 'Branson would soon' *Econ* 26.8.00.

Index

Index

Index

Index

Heath, Sir Edward 15
Heathrow Airport 110, 111, 115, 117, 119, 133, 134, 149, 150, 157, 158, 159, 175, 192, 221, 225, 228, 229, 234, 258, 260, 261, 278, 311, 312, 317, 318, 342, 345, 346
Heaven nightclub, Charing Cross Station 41, 49, 126, 127
Heinko, Liz 210
Hemisphere 324
Heritage Department 175
Higgins, Stuart 207, 263
Hill, Leslie 34
Hilton, Barron 321
Hilton Hotel, Heathrow Airport 186
HMV shop, Oxford Street 77
Holland Park, London (No. 9) xvii, 100, 101, 104, 114, 126, 142, 143, 146, 159, 161, 166, 171, 172, 180, 183, 195, 196, 197, 200, 206, 212, 227, 232, 233, 236, 244, 247, 263, 270, 275, 280, 286, 289, 307, 324, 325, 332, 339
Holland Park, London (No. 11) 196, 329
Holley, Tim 208, 287
Hong Kong 178
Hornby, Sir Derek 219, 220, 223, 224, 291–2
Hotel Esmeralda, Paris 46
House of Commons Select Committee on Transport 151, 232, 278, 346
Howes, Colin 170
Hudson, Keith 36
Hughes, Cherry 80
Human League 43, 47, 60, 73
Humphreys, Barry 257
Huning, Ric 183–4
Hussein, Saddam 111, 320
Hutchins, Chris 125–8, 131, 132

Iceland retail chain 186
ICO 320
Ijichi, Akira xiii, xiv, 94, 95, 98, 99, 142
Independent 183
Independent Television Commission (ITC) 121–2, 135, 190, 210n, 215
India 318, 334
Indursky, Arthur 32
Inland Revenue 3, 30, 31, 44, 144, 299
Institute of Directors 66–7
Intercontinental Hotel, Tokyo xiii
International Air Transport Association (IATA) 123
International Aviation Club, Washington 308
International Time magazine 14
Internet 205, 226, 332, 337, 339, 344

Investec Henderson Crosthwaite 332
Iran 320
Iraq 106, 107
Irvine, Derry, QC 173
Island Records 32, 52, 114, 238
Isle of Wight 63
ITN 156, 189, 249
ITV 49, 112, 134, 136, 162

J. Walter Thompson 338
Jackson, Janet 114, 121, 262
Jackson, John 80, 82, 93, 163, 167, 168, 169, 175, 181, 213, 338
Jackson, Tim 209
  Virgin King 282
Jagger, Mick 7, 263
James, David 149
James, Nicholas 43
Japan
  B in 98–9, 103, 108
  Berry's negotiations xiii, xiv, 92, 94–5
  contract signed 98–9
  railways 151, 152, 246
  Virgin Cola in 193
Jersey 141
Johannesburg 106, 148, 231
Jones, Brian 322
Jones, Tom 6
J. P. Morgan 247, 265, 300, 337
Juliens fish restaurant, Paris 46
Jupiter family trust 239

Kane, Frank 95, 96, 130
Karan, Donna 305
Keith-Roch, Wendy 177
Kelleher, Herb 235, 259
Kendrick, Mike 320, 321, 331
Kennedy, Garfield 76, 84, 108, 248
Kennedy airport, New York 135
Kensington Palace, London 171
Kensington Roof Gardens 41, 66, 91, 92, 99, 107, 271
Kerner, Jacques 33
Killick, Mark 208–9, 211, 213, 214, 284
King, Lord 112, 124, 125, 128, 129, 137, 161, 162, 210, 227
  achievement with BA 109, 110
  the Alka Seltzer incident 123
  announces BA withdrawal of donations to the Conservatives 118
  appointed chairman of BA (1981) 62
  on B 174
  B's ultimatum 138
  and Burnside 106

377

Index

Martin, Michael 153–4
Martin's retail chain 192
Mates condoms 82, 88, 93, 94, 102, 163, 165, 338
Maxims 59
Maxwell, Robert 93
Maxwell Communications 133
MCA 114, 141
Meades, Jonathan 51
Mellor, Tony 1, 2, 19
Melody Maker 2, 23, 37
Mercury 189
Merrill Lynch 302, 316
Metropolitan hotel, London 273
Metzenbaum, Howard 308
Mexico 124, 315
MGM cinema chain 196, 197, 274–5
Miami 74, 148
Microsoft 337
Midland Bank 96
Midwest Express 148
Miert, Karl van 310, 311
Milan 234
'Mile High Club' 327
Mill End, Oxfordshire 48, 73, 324
Mills, Adam 218–24, 291–2
Miss World competition, Sun City 231
Mission Impossible 253, 279
Miyakonojo 108
Monarch Airways 135
Monopolies Commission 162, 243, 265, 317
Monroe, Marilyn 206
Morgan Grenfell 70, 141, 237, 239
Morgan Stanley 273, 343
Morland, Sir Michael 284
Morocco ix, 202, 249
Moscow 317, 318
Moss, Chris 71, 73, 78, 101, 103, 111, 119, 134, 137, 150
Mossiman's 141
Murdoch, Rupert xv, 81, 89, 131, 305
Murphy, Patrick 259–60
Murphy, Stephen 200–1, 224, 230, 238, 244, 245, 247, 264, 272, 273, 275, 277, 292, 299, 300, 303, 304, 306, 313, 325, 329, 339, 342–3
Murray, James 171
Music Box 89
Music Week 125

National Audit Office 316
National Express 198, 199, 292
National Lottery 25, 340, 342

B bids for xi, xv, 163–70, 174–6, 180–3, 191, 315–16, 337–9, 347–8
B charges Camelot with greed 208
Camelot's image 347–8
Necker Island 41, 53, 73, 81–2, 92, 100, 125, 145, 171, 172, 214, 251, 256, 263, 289, 305, 306, 313, 321, 337
New Musical Express 42, 45
New York 41, 106, 116, 162, 176, 177, 195, 225, 238, 261
New York Air 260
New York Post 301
Newark Airport 59, 62, 63
Newman, Tom 31
   advises Oldfield to break from Virgin 44
   and Kristen 28, 29, 40
   leaves Virgin 43
   recording studio 22, 24, 25, 32, 43
   and *Tubular Bells* 29
   wages 26
News of the World 332–3
Newsnight (television programme) 227
Nice 234
Nielsen 194, 204
Nigeria 316, 334
1984 (film) 58, 60, 77
NOP (National Opinion Poll) 201
Norris, Peter 325
Norwich 226–7
Norwich Union 205–6
NTL 205, 236

Oasis 239, 273
Oberstar, Representative 257
The Observer 78
Office of Fair Trading 233
Oflot 175, 181–2
Oldfield, Mike 29, 44–5, 47, 60, 141
'Oliver, Jennifer' 21–2
One2One 332
Ong Beng Seng 273
Ono, Yoko 19
'open skies' agreements 229, 256, 257, 258, 260, 261, 310, 345–6, 347
'Operation Barbara' 127
Opraf (Office of Passenger Rail Franchising) 245, 289, 290, 293, 302–3
Orange 332
Ornstein, Jonathan 235–6, 267, 314, 330
Our Price 98, 299, 323, 326, 333, 335, 337, 339, 341, 344
Oxford University xiv–xvi
Oz magazine 14

379

Index

Seibu-Saison 99, 120, 134, 173
Selfridges department store, London 272
Sex Pistols 34–6, 38, 41, 60, 72, 73, 118
Shamley Green, Surrey 8, 13, 85
Shane, Jeff 256
Shaw, Edward 93
Shaw, Sidney 111
Shell 131
Sheraton hotel, Marrakesh 269
Shipton, near Oxford 24
Short, Alison 32, 40
Silicon Valley 205, 236, 329
Simpsons 27
Simpsons, Strand 192
Singapore Airlines 336, 339, 340
Skadden Arps 98
Sketchley dry cleaning business 163, 338
Skinner, Dennis 255
Sky 265
Skytrain 62
Slater, Rodney 346
Snowden, Guy 163–71, 174, 209–15, 283–7,
    291, 293, 294, 311, 325
Société Générale 237, 238, 240
Sony 239
Soros, George 337
Souter, Brian 247, 302, 303
South Africa 231, 327, 345
South America 145
South West Trains 302
South Wharf Road, London (Virgin Music
    warehouse) 2, 20, 21, 23, 29
Southgate, Colin 141
Southwest Airlines 235, 245, 260
Spain 193, 241
Spark, Ronald 148
Spectator xi, 296
SpectrumCo 337
Stagecoach 245, 247, 302, 303
Stansted Airport 267
Star Alliance 227, 228, 309
Steer, Jim 200, 221, 245, 246
Stenham, Cob 76, 80–1, 82, 89–90, 91, 94
Stereophonics 262
Steward, Sue 16
Stiff Records 37, 51, 52, 53, 135
Sting 47, 108
Stone the Crows 40
Storm 81
Stowe School, Buckingham 5, 12, 14–15, 20,
    40, 43
Strategic Rail Authority 343
Stringfellow's 193

Student magazine 1–2, 12, 14–18, 19, 24, 48,
    183
Student Advisory Centre 21
Stylianou, Chris 5, 43
Sudbury magistrates court, Suffolk 4
Sugarloaf Mountain, near Boston 79, 86
Sun 10, 74, 112, 118, 148, 149, 157, 190,
    207, 250, 263, 281, 315, 320
Sun Alliance 154, 217
Sun and Spendour pub, Portobello Road 26
Sun City 231
Sunday Mirror 188
Sunday Telegraph 78, 95, 130, 134
The Sunday Times 38, 131–2, 133, 144, 296,
    324, 339
Super Channel 89
Swift, John 289

Taffler, Professor Richard 135
Tait, David 66
Taylor, Derek 18–19
Tel Aviv 318
Templeman, Dorothy (B's sister-in-law) 271
Templeman, John (B's brother-in-law) 196,
    270–1
Templeman, Rose (B's sister-in-law) 271
10cc 32
Tesco 186, 337
Texas Pacific Group 196, 235, 247, 274, 275,
    300, 334
Thatcher, Margaret, Baroness 72, 74, 99, 170
Thirkettle, Joan 86, 156, 189
This Is Your Life 73
This Week (television programme) 134–6, 138
Thomas, Ron 135
Thomson Newspapers 70
Thornton, John 138–41
Threshers 186
Tibbits, Chris 277, 279, 312
Tiger family trust 239
Time Out 46, 48–51, 128, 138
Time Warner 339
The Times xi, 104, 149, 219, 223, 224–5,
    307, 315
Tin Star 273
Today newspaper 125, 130, 131, 132
Tokyo xiii, 92, 94, 98, 111, 115, 128, 148,
    174, 214, 215
Toleman, Ted 68, 69, 71, 128
Tomkinson, Martin 51
Tommy Hilfiger 262
'Tomorrow's People' (television programme)
    21–2

Index